Comments on *T.R.M. Howard*

"T.R.M. Howard was a towering freedom fighter. Too often forgotten! The powerful and insightful book, *T.R.M. Howard: Doctor, Entrepreneur, Civil Rights Pioneer*, corrects the historical record and keeps his precious memory fresh for us!"

> —**Cornel R. West**, Professor of the Practice of Public Philosophy, Harvard Divinity School; Class of 1943 University Professor Emeritus, Center for African American Studies, Princeton University

"*T.R.M. Howard: Doctor, Entrepreneur, Civil Rights Pioneer* fills a gap. Too often today we conflate the civil rights movement with the legend of Martin Luther King, Jr. If fact there were countless others who fought for racial justice within an indifferent-and often hostile-society. This is the richly detailed story of one such man. T.R.M. Howard, in both his heroism and his human contradictions, is a human face on America›s greatest freedom movement. And, quite beyond its historical importance, this book is a gripping and moving read."

> —**Shelby Steele**, Robert J. and Marion E. Oster Senior Fellow, Hoover Institution, Stanford University; author, *The Content of Our Character*, *A Dream Deferred*, *White Guilt*, and *Shame*

"*T.R.M. Howard's* wonderfully told story about an important personality sadly unknown to most students of the Civil Rights Movement is a more than welcome corrective. Dr. Howard's life and accomplishments need to be better known!"

> —**Julian Bond**, former Chairman, NAACP

"Dr. Howard was a history maker, and this book brings him to life as a man of courage whose actions and views on civil rights shaped American history."

> —**Juan A. Williams**, Political Analyst, Fox News Channel; author, *Eyes on the Prize: America's Civil Rights Years, 1954-1965*

"If there was a Mount Rushmore of civil rights icons, it would include Frederick Douglass, Martin Luther King, Jr., and T.R.M. Howard. Howard was *that* important to the cause of civil rights. The powerful book, *T.R.M. Howard*, now brings to life this extraordinary figure in African-American history."

> —**Jonathan J. Bean**, Professor of History, Southern Illinois University; editor, *Race & Liberty in America: The Essential Reader*

"The definitive work on the life of T.R.M. Howard. A fascinating narrative that illuminates important aspects of the African American experience in the twentieth century."

> —**Adam Fairclough**, Professor Emeritus of American History,
> Leiden University Institute for History; author, *Better Day*
> *Coming: Blacks and Equality, 1890-2000*

"*T.R.M. Howard* is a necessary biography...Howard played an important part in the Emmett Till story, and in the entire civil-rights era. He deserves to be better known.... One woman in the audience remembered years later Howard's vivid description of the Till killing. Her name was Rosa Parks, and four days after Howard spoke she answered a Montgomery bus driver, 'No.'..."

> —*Wall Street Journal*

"The biography, *T.R.M. Howard*, is an impressive account of the life and contributions of a neglected hero of the black civil-rights movement. As a doctor, entrepreneur, and activist, Howard risked his life for the betterment of others. I highly recommend this excellent book for anyone interested in learning about forgotten and neglected historical figures."

> —**Carol M. Swain**, retired Professor of Political Science and Law,
> Vanderbilt University; author, *Black Faces, Black Interests:*
> *The Representation of African Americans in Congress*

"'While historians have properly acknowledged the contributions of clergymen and grassroots activists' to the civil-rights movement, write David T. Beito and Linda Royster Beito, 'they have too often neglected those made by entrepreneurs and black professionals."

> —*National Review*

"The great and admirable biography, *T.R.M. Howard*, displays the early Civil Rights era in all its messiness and grandeur....To overlook Howard is to miss some important truths about the Civil Rights movement."

> —**Terence J. Pell**, President and CEO, Center for Individual
> Rights; former Deputy Assistant Secretary for Civil Rights,
> U.S. Department of Education

"One of the best biographies I have read in years. It works both as a revisionist project, challenging our understanding of the nature of black leadership in the South, and as a reclamation project, bringing back into the discussion a colorful and important transitional figure who has received little notice from scholars."
　　—**Charles M. Payne, Jr.**, Frank P. Hixon Distinguished Service
　　　Professor of Social Service, University of Chicago; author,
　　　*I've Got the Light of Freedom: The Organizing Tradition in
　　　the Mississippi Civil Rights Movement*

"T.R.M. Howard was not everyone's idea of a civil rights hero, and his accomplishments have been widely neglected. But . . . , he was in fact one of the most effective black civil rights leaders of his generation and a key figure in bringing civil rights to Mississippi and empowering black voters in Chicago."
　　—*Harper's*

"It is my privilege and pleasure to have known and worked with Dr. Howard as he was pursuing the cause of civil rights in Mississippi with the same vim and vigor as it was being pursued in New York, Chicago, and other places. I was also afraid of him. This illuminating biography is a must read for anyone seeking to know more about the civil rights struggle in Mississippi in foregone years. Every acre was a drop of blood and every step was a tear."
　　—**Benjamin L. Hooks**, former Executive Director, NAACP

"The husband and wife team of David and Linda Beito have labored nearly a decade to write a biography, *T.R.M. Howard*, in hopes that they can raise the man's memory from the grave. The book was worth the wait. Well-written and deeply researched, the authors immerse the reader into Dr. Howard's world, one that crossed paths with a litany of American greats such as MLK, Jesse Jackson, Malcolm X, Medgar Evers, and Jesse Owens. Four days after seeing Dr. Howard give an impassioned speech at MLK's Baptist Church, Rosa Parks took her famous stand against Jim Crow. She insisted that it was the thought of Emmett Till, who's lynching was the subject of Dr. Howard's speech, which spurred her to refuse to give up her bus seat. . . . Throughout the book, Mr. and Mrs. Beito do a sparkling job bringing to life Dr. Howard, his energy, his flamboyance, and his personal bravery in battling to establish the rule of law in the South."
　　—*Daily Kos*

T.R.M.
HOWARD

INDEPENDENT INSTITUTE is a non-profit, non-partisan, public-policy research and educational organization that shapes ideas into profound and lasting impact. The mission of Independent is to boldly advance peaceful, prosperous, and free societies grounded in a commitment to human worth and dignity. Applying independent thinking to issues that matter, we create transformational ideas for today's most pressing social and economic challenges. The results of this work are published as books, our quarterly journal, *The Independent Review*, and other publications and form the basis for numerous conference and media programs. By connecting these ideas with organizations and networks, we seek to inspire action that can unleash an era of unparalleled human flourishing at home and around the globe.

100 Swan Way, Oakland, California 94621-1428, U.S.A.
Telephone: 510-632-1366 • Facsimile: 510-568-6040 • Email: info@independent.org • www.independent.org

T.R.M. HOWARD

Doctor, Entrepreneur,
Civil Rights Pioneer

David T. Beito and Linda Royster Beito

Foreword by Jerry W. Mitchell
With an Afterword by the Authors

INDEPENDENT
INSTITUTE

OAKLAND, CALIFORNIA

Independent Institute
100 Swan Way, Oakland, CA 94621-1428
Telephone: 510-632-1366
Fax: 510-568-6040
Email: info@independent.org
Website: www.independent.org

Cover Design: Denise Tsui
Cover Image: Photos for use in the cover uncials T.R.M., include in order, courtesy of *Jet* magazine archives, permission to use from the University of Memphis Press-Scimitar Collection, and courtesy of the Vivian G. Harsh Research Collection at Chicago Public Library.

Every effort was made to locate copyright owners in regards to photos included in this book. When such efforts provided no such information we supplied what information we did have. In the event that a legitimate copyright holder can provide verifiable status of ownership we will be glad to provide the necessary or required credit.

Library of Congress Cataloging-in-Publication Data

Names: Beito, David T., 1956- author. | Beito, Linda Royster, author. | Mitchell, Jerry W., writer of foreword.
Title: *T. R. M. Howard : Doctor, Entrepreneur, Civil Rights Pioneer* / David T. Beito, Linda Royster Beito ; foreword by Jerry W. Mitchell ; afterword by David & Linda Beito.
Other titles: *Black Maverick: T.R.M. Howard's Fight for Civil Rights and Economic Power*
Description: New edition. | Oakland, CA : Independent Institute, [2017] | "Previously published as *Black Maverick: T.R.M. Howard's Fight for Civil Rights and Economic Power* by University of Illinois Press" — ECIP title page.
Identifiers: LCCN 2018009684 (print) | LCCN 2017055815 (ebook) | ISBN 9781598133141 (ePub) | ISBN 9781598133158 (ePDF) | ISBN 9781598133165 (Mobi) | ISBN 9781598133127 (hardback) | ISBN 9781598133134 (paperback)
Subjects: LCSH: Howard, T. R. M. (Theodore Roosevelt Mason), 1908-1976. | African Americans—Biography. | African American civil rights workers—Biography. | African American businesspeople—Biography. | African American surgeons—Biography. | African Americans—Civil rights—Mississippi—History—20th century. | Civil rights movements—Mississippi—History—20th century. | Till, Emmett, 1941-1955—Death and burial. | Mississippi—Race relations—History—20th century. | African Americans—Economic conditions—20th century. | BISAC: BIOGRAPHY & AUTOBIOGRAPHY / Cultural Heritage. | SOCIAL SCIENCE / Discrimination & Race Relations.
Classification: LCC E185.97.H827 (print) | LCC E185.97.H827 B45 2017 (ebook) | DDC 323.092 [B] —dc23
LC record available at https://lccn.loc.gov/2018009684

THIS BOOK IS *dedicated to the citizens of Mound Bayou, Mississippi, a historical beacon of black mutual aid, business enterprise, and civil rights.*

Contents

Foreword

Jerry W. Mitchell

DR. T.R.M. HOWARD never forgot. Even if he has been largely forgotten. The larger-than-life physician and entrepreneur began his campaign to end second-class citizenship for African-Americans long before the U.S. Supreme Court ruled in the *Brown v. Board of Education* case.

In the 1940s, he did his best to improve health care for African-Americans, serving as chief surgeon at a small hospital in Mound Bayou, Mississippi, and also as president of the National Medical Association, formed for black physicians and their patients. By the 1950s, he had attracted more than ten thousand African-Americans to—of all places—the Mississippi Delta to hear such speakers as Congressman Charles Diggs of Michigan.

Howard provided important leadership in the burgeoning Civil Rights Movement, mentoring young African-Americans who became a Who's Who list of civil rights legends, including Medgar Evers and Fannie Lou Hamer. The *Pittsburgh Courier* raved that black Mississippians, "long hungry for a militant leadership, [have] found a forceful and fearless man in Dr. T.R.M. Howard."

When the body of Emmett Till rose again in the Tallahatchie River in the summer of 1955, Howard would be changed forever—and so would the nation. When he saw the casket with Till's body and the face that bore the brutality of the beatings his killers had inflicted, Howard became overwhelmed with anger, vowing that there would be "hell to pay in Mississippi." He turned his Mississippi home into a "safe house" for Till's mother, Mamie Till Bradley, and other witnesses, some of whom he had helped track down.

After the all-white jury let the two killers walk free on September 23, 1955, the jury foreman reassured the press that they wouldn't have deliberated so long (barely beyond an hour) if they hadn't stopped to sip some soft drinks. The casualness of that remark and the killers getting away with the brutal murder of a teenager proved too much for Howard. He barked to reporters that a white man in Mississippi was less likely to suffer punishment for a murder like Till's than for "killing a deer out of season." Some white Mississippians became furious. The segregationist-controlled *Jackson Daily News* called Howard a "big-mouthed...racial agitator," describing him as "Public Enemy No. 1." The next thing the doctor knew, Mississippi was investigating his medical clinic, and he was receiving more death threats than ever before.

Howard lambasted the FBI for refusing to get involved in investigating Till's murder. (The agency maintained that it lacked jurisdiction.) "It's getting to be a strange thing," Howard told a crowd of 2,500 in Baltimore, "that the FBI can never seem to work out who is responsible for killing the Negroes in the South." Word of the speech made its way to FBI headquarters, where Director J. Edgar Hoover publicly criticized Howard for his "intemperate and baseless charges." Hoover opened an FBI investigation into the civil rights leader and secretly enlisted the aid of NAACP lawyer Thurgood Marshall, who disliked Howard.

The crowds kept growing for Howard, Bradley, and others as they talked about Till, and the streets filled with marchers. "100,000 Across Nation Protest Till Lynching," the *Chicago Defender* declared in one headline. On November 27, 1955, Howard spoke about the Till case at the Dexter Avenue Baptist Church in Montgomery, Alabama, pastored by a young preacher named Martin Luther King Jr. A member of the church, Rosa Parks, happened to be there, too. Four days later, she boarded a bus and refused to give up her seat, sparking the modern Civil Rights Movement. She said later the whole time she was thinking about Till.

Howard never lived in Mississippi again. The death threats became too much, and he and his family were forced to move to Chicago. When he finally returned, eight years later, it was to deliver the eulogy for his friend, Medgar Evers, who had been assassinated outside his Jackson home on June 11, 1963. Howard relished his moment on center stage, telling the crowd, "Medgar knew he was hated."

"Yes, yes," they responded.

"For 100 years, we have turned one cheek and then the other, and they've continued to hit on both cheeks."

He cried out, "Now the neck is getting tired now of turning from side to side."

The audience applauded, with some shouting, "Amen."

"Keep on marching!" he told them.

And march they did that day, into the 103-degree heat, more than five thousand of them, including Martin Luther King Jr. and NAACP Executive Director Roy Wilkins—more than anyone could recall for a funeral in Mississippi.

Howard returned to Chicago and faded again from the national headlines.

In this masterful work, David and Linda Royster Beito have returned the sharp-dressing doctor to his rightful place in history.

JERRY W. MITCHELL is an American investigative reporter for *The Clarion-Ledger*, a newspaper in Jackson, Mississippi. He convinced authorities to reopen seemingly cold murder cases from the Civil Rights Era, prompting one colleague to call him "the South's Simon Wiesenthal." In 2009, he received a genius grant from the MacArthur Foundation.

Introduction

THIS IS MORE than the story of a single man. The life of Theodore Roosevelt Mason (T. R. M.) Howard is also a testament to the largely unsung role of the black middle class during the twentieth century—business and professional people who started community self-help organizations, courageously fought compulsory segregation, pioneered the Civil Rights Movement, and helped fund its development.[1]

Few individuals contributed more significantly to these achievements than T. R. M. Howard. He loomed large in such major black newspapers as the *Chicago Defender,* the *Pittsburgh Courier,* and the *Memphis World.* Four years before the Montgomery Bus Boycott, he founded a mass nonviolent movement in the Mississippi Delta. From 1952 to 1955, he organized annual civil rights rallies that sometimes attracted crowds of ten thousand, led a successful statewide boycott, and publicly faced down a segregationist governor. He not only hired Medgar Evers for his first job out of college but was instrumental in introducing him to the Civil Rights Movement. So scathing was his criticism of the FBI's failure to protect civil rights that J. Edgar Hoover took the rare step of denouncing Howard in an open letter. Howard threw himself into the search for evidence to help solve the murder of Emmett Till and gave over his home to serve as a refuge for reporters and witnesses during the trial.[2]

These activities brought Howard national recognition and praise. Paul Robeson, the singer and actor, lauded him as "an energetic and resourceful leader," and the *California Eagle* dubbed him the "most hated, and the best loved, man in Mississippi." In 1956 the *Chicago Defender* gave Howard the top spot on its annual honor roll for "arousing the nation to the criminal conspiracy of white supremacists in the state of Mississippi." Martin Luther King Jr. was not even on the list. Simeon Booker of *Jet* lionized Howard as an "outspoken, fearless, and cunning . . . sectional hero" who had become "part of the Delta's folklore."[3]

Prominent black leaders recognized Howard as a peer and friend. Roy Wilkins of the NAACP thought so highly of his rhetorical skills that he underwrote a national speaking tour in the months after the Till murder. "People call Martin Luther King Jr. the Negro orator of the century," Charles Evers writes. "T. R. M. Howard was as good, or better, and I heard them both in their prime." Howard's speeches also impressed Mamie Till-Mobley, the mother of Emmett Till. She stayed in Howard's home during the trial of her son's accused killers. "The man was dynamic," she recalls. "I just thought he was the greatest in the world." Similarly, A. Philip Randolph, the head of the International Brotherhood of Sleeping Car Porters, saluted Howard's fight against the "racialism and the tribalism of those who would strike down the Constitution."[4]

A wealthy entrepreneur, accomplished surgeon, and fraternal society leader, Howard had a zest for life. He stood out among blacks and whites in the Delta as he sped down the highway in his Cadillac, which was always the latest model. The center of attention in any social setting, Howard was tall, affable, immaculate, and stylishly dressed. Howard's love of having a good time was infectious, and he incorporated it into his civil rights organizing. Crowds flocked to the annual rallies of the Regional Council of Negro Leadership, a grassroots civil rights and self-help organization he founded in 1951, not just to hear speakers such as Thurgood Marshall and Rep. Charles Diggs of Michigan, but also to see such entertainers as Mahalia Jackson, to compete in sporting events, and to sample homemade barbecue.[5]

Unlike many of his better-known peers, Howard thrived as a doctor and entrepreneur before he emerged as a civil rights leader. In 1942 he came to Mississippi to become chief surgeon at the Taborian Hospital in the all-black town of Mound Bayou. The International Order of Twelve Knights and Daughters of Tabor, a fraternal organization of nearly fifty thousand members in Mississippi, used the hospital to give low-cost medical care to thousands of poor people. Within five years, Howard had founded there various business and community enterprises, including a housing construction firm, a credit union, an insurance company, a restaurant with a beer garden, and a thousand-acre farm where he raised cattle, quail, hunting dogs, and cotton. He built a small zoo and park, as well as the first swimming pool for blacks in Mississippi.[6]

Howard left a deep imprint on black social and cultural life in the Delta. Myrlie Evers, who, like her husband Medgar, worked at Howard's insurance company, came closest to capturing the essence of the man: "One look told you that he was a leader: kind, affluent, and intelligent, that rare Negro in Mississippi who had somehow beaten the system." Through his Regional Council of Negro Leadership, Howard championed a message of self-help, mutual aid, thrift, and equal political rights. His business connections came in handy after the Supreme Court's 1954 *Brown v. Board of Education* decision. When the segregationist white citizens' councils imposed a credit freeze on civil rights activists, Howard found creative ways to fight back. At his suggestion, the NAACP organized a national campaign to urge black voluntary associations and businesses to deposit their money in the Tri-State Bank of Memphis. Tri-State, in turn, made this money available to blacks who were victims of the credit freeze.[7]

It is not surprising that Howard became a favorite villain of segregationists. The *Jackson Daily News*, the main newspaper in Mississippi, considered him "Public Enemy No. 1" and a "big-mouthed Negro racial agitator." Howard had a small arsenal in his home, including a Thompson submachine gun, and kept armed guards around the clock. More than once, Howard ran afoul of Mississippi's discriminatory gun-control laws, which denied concealed-weapon permits to blacks.[8]

Howard also had his share of black enemies. Future Supreme Court Justice Thurgood Marshall, who was busily cultivating the goodwill of the FBI, disliked Howard's militant tone and maverick stance. Marshall became so alarmed by Howard's support for a proposed march of a million blacks on Washington, D.C., that he secretly conspired with J. Edgar Hoover to discredit him. According to an FBI report, Marshall had "no use for Howard and nothing would please him more than to see Howard completely crushed."[9]

During this period, Howard reached the height of his national influence, both professionally and in civil rights. In 1955, black doctors from around the country elected him head of the National Medical Association

(NMA), the black counterpart to the American Medical Association. He used this position to promote civil rights as well as to expose second-class treatment in health care. One of the most important accomplishments of his term as NMA president was the Imhotep National Conference on Hospital Integration. Howard was also chair of the board of directors of the National Negro Business League, a black chamber of commerce founded by Booker T. Washington.[10]

In the absence of a predominant local black leader, civil rights activists often turned to activists from other states for inspiration. Few of these were more prominent than Howard. His speeches on the Emmett Till case throughout the country drew thousands and received prominent coverage in the national black press. One of the stops on his speaking tour was at the Dexter Avenue Baptist Church in Montgomery, Alabama, on November 27, 1955. His host was Martin Luther King Jr. Rosa Parks was in the audience. Howard's speech was still headline news in the local black press four days later when Parks refused to give up her seat on a segregated bus. Parks later reported that she was thinking of Emmett Till, a focal point of Howard's speech, when she made her decision to act.[11]

A defining feature of Howard's life was that he remade himself, again, again, and yet again. He was a surgeon, entrepreneur, civil rights leader, and community builder. After his move to Chicago, he became a big-game hunter and party-giver on a grand scale. He dazzled the black social set by staging elaborate and expensive New Year's Eve parties that featured live bands and the best soul food. The guest list often included his friends Jesse Owens, the former Olympic gold medalist, and Robert E. Johnson, publisher of *Jet* and *Ebony*. Howard's unapologetic display of wealth and abundant self-confidence inspired many ordinary blacks in Chicago. They appreciated the fact that he was able to cross boundaries that few other black people could. Dick Gregory, then a struggling young comedian, commented that when Howard's car appeared, "everybody waved . . . it was like Queen Elizabeth driving down the street in London. . . . When Howard walked into a night club, everything stopped. It was like the president walked in." Howard's big-game exploits took him on hunting expeditions to Africa, India, and Alaska. All this added to the mystique of a black man who dared to do the extraordinary.[12]

During the last twenty years of his life, Howard and controversy were always close companions. He worked with individuals in groups dedicated to help women secure abortions, such as the Chicago Clearly Consultation Service and the feminist-oriented Jane. His career culminated in 1972 with the founding of the commodious Friendship Medical Center valued at over $1 million. Blacks on the South Side went there for a broad range of medical services, even podiatry. The center was the largest privately owned black medical facility in Chicago. The comfortable and attractive environment anticipated the patient-friendly health care of later decades. Featured were bubbling fountains; wall posters of Martin Luther King Jr., Isaac Hayes, and Angela Davis; comfortable waiting rooms; a display of Howard's trophies; and soothing music. After *Roe v. Wade* in 1973, many changes occurred at the Friendship Medical Center. A firestorm of criticism ensued when Howard's picture appeared on the cover of *Jet* performing an abortion.[13]

Howard spoke for a civil rights tradition in the South that prevailed before the rise of Martin Luther King Jr. It was a tradition that relied on local talent and preexisting networks of black businesses and voluntary associations. These early activists bore the brunt of initial white opposition to *Brown v. Board of Education* in 1954. In contrast to many of those who came later, Howard used business success as a launching pad into civil rights. In Mississippi, black entrepreneurs, large and small, were more prominent than the clergy as leaders. Business and professional success gave them a degree of independence from white control and pressure that other blacks did not have. In this respect, groups such as the Regional Council of Negro Leadership, the Knights and Daughters of Tabor, and the National Negro Business League represented the fruition of Booker T. Washington's long-term strategy for black improvement. Washington had depicted business, property ownership, the professions, and voluntary associations as the necessary foundation on which to build a movement for political rights.

Howard's life also brings to the surface an older philosophy of civil rights that emphasized the importance of armed self-defense. While he advocated a general stance of nonviolence, he, along with such allies as Medgar Evers, always carried guns "just in case." As one historian put it, these activists combined a strategy of "God, Gandhi, and Guns." Howard anticipated the later campaigns of Robert F. Williams, the head of an NAACP chapter in Monroe, North Carolina, who applied for an NRA charter to form a civil rights–oriented gun club, and the Deacons of Defense in Louisiana, which deployed armed patrols to protect activists during the 1960s.[14]

While historians have properly acknowledged the contributions of clergymen and grassroots activists such as Martin Luther King Jr., Fred Shuttlesworth, Fannie Lou Hamer, and Ella Baker, they have too often neglected those made by entrepreneurs and black professionals. In Mississippi during the 1950s, and probably in other states, they provided the funds and formed the core leadership that kept the movement alive. The story of T. R. M. Howard brings to the forefront the heroic contributions of these men and women to black economic improvement and to the struggle for civil rights.

I

Up from the Black Patch

IT WAS JANUARY 1956. As T. R. M. Howard looked back, he had many reasons to feel a sense of pride. He was one of the wealthiest blacks in Mississippi, had treated thousands of patients as chief surgeon in two of the state's largest black hospitals, and had won election to the presidency of the National Medical Association, the leading black medical society in the United States. His national reputation as a civil rights leader seemed secure. As the founder of the Regional Council of Negro Leadership, he had mentored an emerging generation of activists, including Medgar Evers and Fannie Lou Hamer. In September 1955, Howard had played a pivotal role finding witnesses and evidence in the Emmett Till murder case. At the beginning of 1956, his prospects for a greater future on the national stage looked bright. The *Chicago Defender* had just ranked him first in its annual honor roll.

At age forty-seven, Howard had risen far from his humble origins living in abject rural poverty amid pervasive racial violence. These characteristics set him apart from most of his approximate peers in age and prominence on the national civil rights scene just before the rise of Martin Luther King Jr. They were far more likely to come from middle-class and urban backgrounds. He was born as Theodore Roosevelt Howard on March 2, 1908, in Murray, Calloway County, Kentucky. His parents were Arthur Howard and Mary Chandler Howard. Like their parents before them, they were unskilled tobacco-factory workers. As an article in Howard's college paper later stated, Arthur, inspired by a "spirit of patriotism," had insisted that their first child be named after President Roosevelt. It proved an apt choice, for Theodore's life would often mirror that of his famous namesake.[1]

The Howards had lived for decades in the Black Patch area of western Kentucky and northwestern Tennessee, so named because of the highly prized olive-colored dark-leaf tobacco grown there. They initially labored to grow the crop but later worked in the factories to refine it for chewing purposes. The Black Patch had cast its lot with the Confederacy and segregation was rigid. In the Tennessee portion, blacks almost completely lost the franchise after Reconstruction, but in Kentucky they continued to vote, usually for Republicans, and to serve on juries. But these rights were tenuous and circumscribed by whites, who voted overwhelmingly Democratic.[2]

The Howards originally hailed from Henry County, Tennessee, just south of Calloway County. Theodore's paternal grandfather, Richard Howard, was born a slave in 1863 or 1864. In common with most blacks in the region, he never advanced beyond the economic margins of society. Like his wife, Mary Lassiter Howard, he could neither read nor write. Her father, Andrew Lassiter, was about twenty years old when the Civil War ended. He was Theodore's most direct link to slavery. Theodore may have had Lassiter in mind when he later referred to a story from his "grandfather" who "just before the Civil War . . . had begun to 'feel something.' It was something that works just like religion. He didn't explain what it was, but he said, 'There was something in there that made me feel the war would soon be over and I would soon be free.'"[3]

In 1907 Arthur Howard, then only seventeen, married Mary Chandler, who was a year younger. Like the Howards, the Chandlers had an uninterrupted family history of grim poverty and backbreaking toil. Mary's father, Henry Chandler, was born in May 1865, only a month after Robert E. Lee's surrender to Ulysses S. Grant at the Appomattox Court House in Virginia. He left the farm to be a laborer in a nearby tobacco factory, a typical occupation for blacks in Murray. His wife, Almeda, was a washerwoman in a private home. She was the first of Howard's known ancestors to read and write. Like their parents, Arthur and Mary drifted into semiurban unskilled labor. Arthur secured employment as a twister of chewing tobacco in a factory in Murray, but he may have supplemented the family income through moonshining. Roughly one-third of the town's 2,139 inhabitants were black in 1910, a proportion much higher than the county average.[4]

Mary Howard brought her son Theodore into the world at a time when tensions in Murray were especially high. The year 1908 was probably the most violent in the town's history. As the tobacco wars encroached on Calloway County, locals felt compelled to choose sides. The trouble had started after 1904 when leading Black Patch farmers formed the Planter's Protective Association. The goal was to counter the buying power of the big tobacco companies by pooling their crops in association-owned warehouses. By selling collectively, they hoped to get a higher price than what the tobacco trust usually paid. Within a year, seven out of ten farmers in the Black Patch pledged their crops to the association. But even this level of cooperation did not bring enough market control to determine the price. Independent growers throttled the association's plan by continuing to sell at lower prices directly to the companies. In 1905, frustrated by the failure to establish a cartel to oppose the big companies through voluntary cooperation, some members of the association turned to terror by forming the Night Riders.[5]

Hooded and prowling by night, the Night Riders terrorized all those who did not toe the line for the Planter's Protective Association. Night Riders traveled in mounted patrols that burned crops, warehouses, and factories, destroyed seedbeds, and, in some cases, committed murder. For a brief period, race was not an issue and some black farmers even joined the association. This changed as resentment mounted against the big companies who flaunted "racial etiquette" by purchasing tobacco from blacks at lower prices. The association discovered that blacks might be convenient scapegoats to hide its failure to coerce independent growers. By 1907 many Night Riders in western Kentucky went on a rampage, determined to drive out black farmers. An incidental goal was to make a killing of another sort by snatching up abandoned black property at bargain rates. In desperation, Governor Augustus E. Willson took measures to enforce law and order. He went so far as to take the serious step of announcing his intention to pardon individuals who shot Night Riders.[6]

At the beginning of 1908, the epidemic of violence edged perilously close to Murray. In February and March, whites inspired by the Night Riders attacked blacks in Marshall County (bordering Calloway on the north). Local blacks pleaded in vain for legal protection as they bore the brunt of a sustained campaign to expel them. The *Louisville Courier-Journal* reported: "encouraged by the failure of the Marshall County officials to prosecute whitecaps who have warned and whipped blacks, 100 men rode into Birmingham on March 8, and shot seven men and whipped five others." Blacks fought back—killing three assailants—but this provided only a temporary respite. Overwhelmed by superior numbers, they began to flee. The black population in Marshall County plummeted from 348 in 1900 to 135 in 1910. Less than three weeks after the attacks, the Night Riders lynched a black farmer in Trigg County (just east of Calloway) on the pretext that he packed tobacco for a big company.[7]

One day after Howard was born, the press reported that the first "real night riders have appeared in Calloway county" and were intimidating independent growers and burning barns. A few tried to scare blacks into leaving Murray. The attackers played on white fears that blacks, who had begun to move into white neighborhoods, were "getting out of their place." Violence escalated later in March when more than two hundred masked Night Riders assembled in the eastern part of the county in preparation for a direct assault on Murray. They called it off only after hearing that citizens were carrying guns and determined to resist. On April 2, County Judge A. J. G. Wells of Murray, the nemesis of the Night Riders, warned that he had "direct information from the riders themselves that before the moon changes, they will swoop down on Murray and burn property and beat her citizens and continue to beat and bruise the farmers over the county." Although the announced targets were prominent buyers and bankers, Murray's five hundred or so blacks had every reason to expect an orgy of racial slaughter.[8]

The planned sack of Murray fell apart after the arrival of a detachment of state troops, sent by the governor. This time the Night Riders had gone too far: law-and-order forces in Murray, backed by the governor, rounded up most of the ringleaders. Despite this, a local observer commented that "hardly a farmer comes to town without being heavily armed, and the sale of pistols, rifles and shotguns by local merchants recently has been unprecedented. Many women, also, are armed, practically every housewife has a rifle handy." After a mysterious fire destroyed several stores, the city council passed a law allowing citizens to shoot on sight any suspected Night Riders. The Night Riders were a spent force by the end of 1908. In their wake, they had left a trail of death and destruction, marking these years as the bloodiest in Kentucky since the Civil War.[9]

While the demise of the Night Riders gave some breathing space to the Howards and other blacks, the violence of 1908 left a lasting imprint on Murray's black community. The younger generation, brought up on stories of the Night Riders, embraced armed self-defense. During the 1890s, the famous anti-lynch activist Ida B. Wells had highlighted how blacks in Paducah had successfully used guns to ward off racist attacks. In comments that would have resonated with blacks in Murray, she recommended that "a Winchester rifle should have a place of honor in every black home, and it should be used for that protection which the law refuses to give. . . . The more the Afro American yields and cringes and begs, the more he has to do so, the more he is insulted, outraged and lynched."[10]

For young Theodore, however, the most immediate physical threat was in his own home. Jealousy, fear, and violence had tainted the Howard marriage almost from the beginning. Arthur beat his young wife repeatedly and, on at least one occasion, broke open her lip with his fists. Mary left Arthur for good in December 1910 after he threw a smoothing iron at her that, had it hit with full force, could have killed her. When her father, Henry Chandler, testified at the divorce hearing, he described his son-in-law as a man of "quick and ill temper. Get mad at nothing. He's got a temper like this: He don't want his wife to go nowhere nor say nothing to nobody nor speak to nobody, and do just as he says all the time."[11]

Although Arthur stayed in the community for several more years, he did not show up at the hearing when the judge granted a divorce. Mary and three-year-old Theodore moved in with her parents. Her life took a happy turn when, in 1913, she married Morris Palmer who, like her previous husband, worked in a tobacco factory. They had six children together. Morris was apparently a hard worker and good husband and was respected in the community. The marriage brought her young son some stability.[12]

The poverty of Theodore's childhood was typical of blacks in the area. Almost no middle class existed among them. The vast majority rented their shacks and toiled in unskilled occupations, mostly in the tobacco industry. The family subsisted on a regular diet of biscuits and little else. If any meat was available, the eldest child ate first. Theodore was expected to contribute to the meager family budget and was resourceful in turning up ways to make money. He shined shoes, sold newspapers, and perfected his hunting skills. He later recalled that when he was ten his mother gave him twenty cents each

Sunday to buy four shotgun shells. Her instructions were to return with either two rabbits, two squirrels, or one of each for the family table. She warned him not to waste shells on quail because "there wasn't enough meat on 'em."[13]

Theodore grew up in the close-knit black neighborhood of "Pooltown," derisively nicknamed "Darktown" by local whites. It was also home to his great-grandfather, and four grandparents. He was particularly close to Almeda Chandler, his maternal grandmother, who had helped to raise him after the divorce. She imparted a sense of history and nurtured his prodigious work ethic. In later years, he often referred to her high expectations and encouragement. The annual Emancipation Day festivities in August reinforced the traditions instilled by Theodore's family and community. Blacks throughout the region flocked to the annual celebration in Paducah. There they heard speeches about their history, feasted on picnic lunches, and participated in sporting contests. Reflecting the stereotypes of the period, the *Paducah Evening Sun* reported in 1913, "several thousand dusky celebrators of Emancipation Day invaded Paducah today for their annual joy-making. . . . At least eighty coaches filled with Negroes from Western Kentucky and Tennessee were brought to the city."[14]

Although Emancipation Day was a reminder of liberation and opportunity, whites never let Theodore forget that he was a second-class citizen. Black people had more rights in Murray than in Mississippi or Alabama, but they still were subject to Jim Crow. Theodore attended the Murray Colored School, later called the Douglass School. Despite poor facilities, including weathered, hand-me-down textbooks, the black teachers often boasted a better record in attendance and enrollment than their white counterparts. The fact that blacks in Kentucky continued to vote, occasionally served in Republican conventions, and sometimes tipped the scales in close elections gave some solace. Even so, they took care not to give whites a pretext to use the specter of "Negro domination" against them.[15]

The color line was somewhat more permeable in the tobacco factories where Howard's parents and grandparents worked. His grandfather, Henry Chandler, eventually rose to the job of classer. His duties were to assess the quality of the tobacco product for later sale—a task rarely entrusted to blacks. But Chandler always had to be on guard. In 1910, for example, white workers at the Griffin and Pitts tobacco factory in Murray went on strike after management hired a black classer. The white classers refused to work with him. Their immediate subordinates, four black rousters, in turn, vowed not to perform their duties. In an open letter, six of the striking white classers took special note of the "impudence of these four negro rousters" and angrily reminded their employers "that 95 per cent of the tobacco deliverd [sic] to this firm is raised by the sweat and toil of the Anglo Saxon."[16]

Racial violence was the most terrifying reminder of white supremacy. Whites lynched fifty-four blacks in Kentucky between 1900 and 1919. The *Murray Ledger,* published by Night-Rider sympathizer O. J. Jennings, added fuel to the fire. Its news coverage was racist, even for western Kentucky. The stories ranged from condescending to inflammatory. The double standard was all too evident in its coverage of a twenty-year prison sentence for a white man who killed a "negro wench." With obvious disgust, an article called it one of the "severest sentences ever given by a Calloway county jury" for a white killing a black person. When the *Ledger* reported killings of blacks by other blacks, the general approach was to make light of the circumstances with such headlines as "Another Negro Emancipated" and "Another Murray Coon Is Dead."[17]

In 1916, the *Murray Ledger* reprinted an unusually long story about a nightmarish double lynching that took place in broad daylight in neighboring McCracken County. The events were of more than passing local interest because one of those lynched was Brack Kenley, a native of Murray who had moved to Paducah but occasionally returned to take part in bootlegging. The authorities in Paducah had locked him up on a charge of violent "criminal assault" (which seems to have included alleged rape) of a white woman who lived on a farm. An enraged mob, identified as Illinois Central Railroad employees, broke into the jail with sledgehammers and crowbars and marched Kenley two miles to the alleged victim's house, where she identified him as the culprit.[18]

As they prepared to string him up to a tree, Kenley's cousin drew a pistol and threatened to shoot into the crowd, now numbering as many as ten thousand. The mob proceeded to hang him as well: "Both bodies were riddled with bullets from the pistols of the enraged members of the mob, a fire built under the negroes and their bodies burned to ashes. Then the mob disbursed [*sic*], leaving the charred remains of the two negroes to the solitary buzzard, which slowly circled above the grewsome scene." When the flames died down, spectators picked over the bone fragments and other remains for souvenirs. The *Louisville Courier-Journal* called this "exhibition of bestiality too disgusting to be described adequately. . . . Everyone knew the possibility of it happening in Paducah was great, yet no effort was made to take the prisoner out of danger or to offer real protection. Those features make the degradation of Paducah complete." Blacks in Paducah did not react passively. At least fifty attempted to purchase guns and ammunition from local hardware stores after news reached them about the lynching. Several weeks later, a grand jury adjourned without an indictment when more than one hundred witnesses pled ignorance when asked to name members of the mob.[19]

Many whites in Kentucky condemned the lynching as barbaric, but it seems only to have stoked racist emotions in Murray. Just three months after Kenley's death, a mob of local citizens almost dealt the same fate to Lube Martin. In contrast to Kenley, who had a "bad reputation" and was often on the wrong side of the law, Martin's white and black neighbors held him in high regard. The trouble began when Martin discovered an affair between his wife and Guthrie Diuguid, the white deputy town marshal. Martin filed a sworn statement to the city council complaining that Diuguid was harassing his wife. Diuguid, who lost his job as a result, demanded that Martin retract the statement. Martin did his best to steer clear of possible trouble; he even fled for a time to Henry County, but, in December, he happened on Diuguid on a Murray city street (only a few blocks from Theodore's home). Martin shot and mortally wounded Diuguid, who died the following day. Martin fled the scene but was arrested and charged with murder. Despite compelling evidence of justifiable self-defense, local whites clamored for blood.[20]

Their outrage spiraled out of control when, in January 1917, Judge Charles H. Bush, worried about a repetition of the Kenley lynching, transferred Martin to the jail in Hopkinsville. In retaliation, a mob surrounded the judge, who was staying in the New Murray Hotel, shouting, "We'll hang the nigger or we'll hang the judge." Bush, thoroughly intimidated, ordered the prisoner returned to Murray. Governor Augustus O. Stanley, a committed opponent of lynching, intervened. When the news reached him, he immediately countermanded the order. Then, in a courageous act, he caught the next train to Murray, wiring that he would give the mob a chance "to hang the Governor of the Commonwealth first, and then wreak their vengeance on the negro later."[21]

When the governor arrived, he won over a hostile crowd of four hundred by proclaiming, "I am here without troops, without police protection, practically alone, absolutely unarmed, but I am hedged about by that which is stronger than a cordon of bayonets—the majesty of the law." He ordered state troops to Murray for the duration of the trial. The national office of the National Association for the Advancement of Colored People sent congratulations and funded an article praising Stanley's action. For Martin, the reprieve was only temporary. In February, a jury convicted him of murder and, after several appeals, he died in the electric chair in 1919.[22]

Three months after the governor's showdown with the mob, Murray's blacks cautiously asserted their rights. Showing considerable bravery, a "mass meeting" representing the "colored citizens of Murray" assembled at a local Baptist church. They elected a committee to speak for them that included a teacher at Theodore's school and drafted a carefully worded "law and order" resolution. In language crafted to be as nonthreatening as possible, it expressed "a deep and abiding interest in the welfare of our city" and condemned "all forms of vice and crime." Obviously referring to the recent violence, it pledged to "lend all in our power to aid the officers of the law."[23]

When Theodore was twelve, he experienced a classic life-defining moment during a conversation with Dr. Will Mason, the white head of Murray's main hospital. Mason was no stranger to Theodore's family. He had delivered him and had employed Mary Howard Palmer for several years as a cook. Mason's brother had hired Theodore to look after his two-year-old son as a "white boy's nurse guardian and playmate," a common southern practice. As Theodore was tending his young charge, Mason asked if he wanted to be a doctor. Without hesitation, he answered yes.[24]

Impressed by the boy's ambition and mental quickness, Mason decided to test him. He put him to work in the hospital, first at washing dishes, then, when he was fifteen, as hospital baker. "I used to bake thirty-two loaves," Howard remembered with pride more than two decades later, "sixteen white and sixteen brown, every afternoon between two-thirty and nine o'clock." Later, Mason assigned him such jobs as fireman, head of the laundry, janitor, and orderly. In the meantime, Theodore fixated on the final goal. A decade later, an article in his college newspaper reported that he had honed his medical skills diagnosing and treating the ailments of pets and other animals.

The reporter, probably relying on Howard as his main source, included the nugget that at age sixteen Howard had "removed a dog's appendix, successfully both from his standpoint and the dog's."[25]

Theodore could not have found a better patron and conduit to the outside world than Dr. William Herbert Mason. As a role model, he had a profound and lasting influence. Mason, better known in Murray as "Dr. Will," came from three generations of physicians and had deep roots in Calloway County. His father had achieved a distinguished medical career in nearby Hazel and, like most western Kentucky men of his age, was a Confederate veteran. Soon after graduating from Vanderbilt University, Mason came to Murray to assist during a smallpox epidemic. Although an outsider, he immediately took command. Mason put the infected under quarantine in a pest-house that he had erected on the outskirts of town. The epidemic rapidly waned, and he had a ready-made practice.[26]

In 1910 Mason became a founder of the Murray Surgical Hospital. All the while, he added luster to his professional reputation by speaking at national and international medical conferences and taking classes at the Mayo Clinic. One of his more legendary accomplishments was a successful operation to reattach a man's severed arm. After it was over, the man once again had use of his arm. In 1920, about the time he hired Theodore, Mason opened the seventy-seven-bed William Mason Memorial Hospital, named after his recently deceased father. He recruited his brother, Dr. Robert Mason ("Dr. Rob"), to assist him.[27]

Will Mason also demonstrated unusual accomplishments and creativity aside from medicine. He excelled in the state's favorite aristocratic pastime, horse breeding. His large stable of prize-winning horses included a son of the famous pacer "Dan Patch." He also raised dogs for fox hunting. Adjacent to his hospital, in 1916, Mason anticipated Howard's future behavior by establishing a "zoo" in Calloway County that became a regular attraction for sightseers in western Kentucky. He stocked it with an array of wildlife, including parrots, several kinds of pigeons, peacocks, coyotes, and wolves (constrained by leashes). The most exotic specimens were an alligator in an open cage penned by an iron fence and two buffalos, who occasionally escaped from their corralled pasture to wreak havoc in the neighborhood. He crossed one of the male buffalos with a cow that produced an offspring known as a catalo.[28]

Mason had other qualities, however, that defied the stereotypes of a Kentucky gentleman. Chief among these were his church affiliation (Seventh-day Adventist) and his political loyalties (staunchly Republican). He was chair of the county Republican Party and a delegate to the 1916 national convention. Mason also broke from tradition when he married Ora Kress in 1917, a fellow Seventh-day Adventist, a physician, and the daughter of two medical doctors. She had recently graduated from the Women's Medical College of Philadelphia. Her parents, Dr. Daniel and Dr. Lauretta Kress, had worked alongside the late "prophetess" and Adventist founder, Ellen G. White. The Kresses had served for several years on the staff of the Battle Creek Sanitarium headed by the famous Dr. John Harvey Kellogg. Kellogg's treatment methods, lampooned in the novel and film "Road to Wellville," included hydrotherapy and cornflakes, later marketed for great profit by his entrepreneurial brother. Daniel Kress had achieved renown outside the church as a relentless crusader against the evils of tobacco smoking.[29]

Upon her marriage, Ora had intended to give up medicine and stay home to care for their newborn daughter, but that ended after the onset of a flu epidemic in 1922 when the hospital needed her assistance. She became a permanent member of the medical staff, in charge of both obstetrics and the nursing school. She fully shared her husband's partisan loyalties. She was a delegate to the 1924 Republican National Convention and two years later ran a credible campaign for Congress but lost in the solidly Democratic district.[30]

Theodore had originally attended Murray's AME Church but gravitated closer to Seventh-day Adventism during this period. While Mason had prepared the way for his conversion, Charles M. Kinney, the legendary black evangelist, finished the job. Kinney stood out as a compelling example of how Adventism could be a force for improvement and opportunity for blacks. Born a slave in Virginia in 1855, he was instrumental in building up black membership. The Seventh-day Adventists found a receptive audience among blacks, who liked the emphasis on clean living, health, hard work, and personal regeneration. By 1923 the black contingent in the United States had grown to seven thousand, mostly in segregated churches. Kinney spread the faith in the small communities of western Kentucky by distributing tracts and selling religious books. Because he was very light-skinned, he moved with relative ease between blacks and whites. He made a stop in Murray during one of these forays and, probably through Mason's influence, met, counseled, and baptized Theodore. Converted or not, Theodore's race barred him from the only Adventist church in the area. For the time being, he maintained a membership, along with his mother and stepfather, in Murray's AME church.[31]

When Kinney heard that Mason supported Theodore's dream of a college education, he recommended Oakwood Junior College, an all-black Adventist institution outside Huntsville, Alabama. Mason readily agreed to help with financial aid. In his letter of recommendation in 1924 to the president of the college, Mason praised Theodore as a "splendid boy. . . . You can trust him to do what he says and [he] is a good work[er] a bright smart boy." Mary Howard Palmer also wrote, pledging to do "all I can by the help of the Almighty God to make his years work a success" and asking to be apprised "if he is doing well and if he is not." In his application, Theodore, then only sixteen, promised in words that would have fit as a lifetime motto to "work as much as possible" to help pay expenses. He began classes in the high school portion of the school in September 1924.[32]

In the 1890s Ellen G. White had given her blessing to the establishment of Oakwood for the religious education of blacks. Thirty years later, the whites in the General Conference still held the reins of power. Joseph A. Tucker, who took over as the college's president in 1923, held more liberal views on racial issues than many local whites. He recruited blacks to the faculty and by 1929 they were just shy of a majority. Tucker also broke precedent by visiting the families of students in their homes and entertaining black faculty in his home. This was a difficult balancing act. When local whites warned against seating black professors at his table, Tucker tried to appease them by having the guests eat from trays instead. Even this did not pass muster with suspicious segregationists. When a friend asked Tucker's wife about the couple's social standing in Huntsville, she replied, "We don't have any. We don't even pretend to have any." Geography gave some protection. Huntsville was five miles distant, and the lack of reliable transportation and strict rules kept both its temptations and racial problems at bay.[33]

When Howard arrived in 1924, Oakwood had 146 students and was struggling to define its place. The college catalog restated White's initial hope that the school would "supply the ten million colored people of the country with gospel workers." At times, this goal ran at cross-purposes with an equally strong concentration on "industrial education" based on the Tuskegee model. As did Tuskegee, Oakwood required students to pay for their education through work. According to the college catalog, "Physical labor is conducive to health and study, and of large practical value. All labor assigned should therefore be religiously performed, just the same as if it were a lesson assigned in the class room." Typical jobs for men were in the machine shop and on the farm while women were employed in the print shop, laundry, and tailor shop. In addition to liberal arts courses, Oakwood required church history and Seventh-day Adventist doctrine with a special emphasis on the role of prophecy. Unfortunately for many students, the combination of these courses with industrial training and the liberal arts made it almost impossible to complete the required classes unless they took extra semesters.[34]

It is not surprising that Oakwood students always seemed to be on the go. The day began at 5:30 a.m., with the rising bell, followed by "silent hour" at 6:00 a.m. and breakfast at 6:20 a.m. Classes began at 7:00 a.m. After that was chapel and lunch. Classes or work filled the afternoon, finally ending at 5:30. Then came dinner, evening worship, a two-hour study period, and lights out. A former student commented that a day had barely a wasted moment. Any free time was highly regulated. Institutional rules prohibited students from visiting each other's rooms during study time and required the college president's permission to attend "social gatherings." Other rules proscribed "improper association" between the sexes "such as sentimentalism, flirtation, courtship, and strolling about the campus."[35]

Howard thrived under this Adventist regimen of hard work, discipline, and an exacting moral code. By the end of his first semester, he emerged as the top student leader on campus. At seventeen, he was a founder and the president of the Young Men's Betterment Society. The vice president was his roommate D. J. Dixon, a future black leader in the Adventist Church. The stated purpose of the society was "to inspire young men to love God, respect teachers, and have a greater sense of chivalry." It launched a campaign to raise money for a new administration building. Naturally, this agenda brought the wholehearted cooperation of college officials. One indication of just how much they approved was the appearance of Howard's photo alongside that of President Tucker in a special issue of the *Oakwood Junior College Bulletin* devoted entirely to promoting the society. But Howard never forgot the importance of appealing to students. The society established as adjuncts an oratorical club "to train students in the art of debating and forensic oratory" and a musical club that offered free public concerts. Attracted by these extra services, a majority of all male students soon joined.[36]

As he sought to build up the society, Howard discovered and honed his talents as a public speaker. He laced his speeches with flowery prose and favored such conservative themes as self-improvement, evangelism, and school spirit. Howard's leadership talents and energetic work habits were not the only advantages that gave him a leg up on his classmates. Unlike many, he was comfortable in the presence of powerful whites, as they were with him. In both Murray and Oakwood, Howard had learned to cultivate this ability and put it to good use. He won the confidence of President Tucker, who, according to a classmate, "treated him like a son." Howard helped to look after Tucker's severely handicapped and intellectually disabled young son.[37]

Still intent on a medical career, Howard went to work in Oakwood's small sanitarium. He took courses from the married couple, Drs. M. M. and Stella Martinson, who managed the institution and supervised an attached nursing school. Their methods reflected the Adventist emphasis on diet and water cures instead of conventional drugs and surgery. The class on hydrotherapy featured lessons on sweat baths and radiant heat and the catalog description stated that a "knowledge of [these] simple treatments has been found to be a most excellent means of opening doors for the entrance of the gospel worker."[38]

While at Oakwood, the bonds between Howard and Will Mason only deepened. Howard returned nearly every summer to work in the Mason Hospital. The relationship between this young black man and the older white man was so close that people began to talk. Rumor had it that Howard was Mason's illegitimate or "outside" child. According to a nurse at the Mason Hospital, coworkers told her during his visits that "Dr. Mason's son is here to see him." In the late 1920s, Howard raised eyebrows when he legally changed his name from Theodore Roosevelt Howard to Theodore Roosevelt Mason Howard. Mason's behavior in personal life made the rumors seem even more credible. Although Howard later called his mentor "a saint," nurses in the hospital knew that there was more to the story. Mason's aggressive sexual overtures were notorious.[39]

The rumors that Mason and Howard were father and son made for juicy gossip, but they were probably not true. Howard, for one, apparently never said anything to give them credence. He was not exactly on intimate terms with Arthur Howard after the ugly divorce, but he always acknowledged him as his father. When Arthur moved to Nashville sometime before 1920, Theodore visited periodically and treated the children from Arthur's second marriage as his siblings. Until Arthur's death in 1965, Theodore was a source of extensive financial support in his old age. Perhaps one reason the gossip persisted was that most of those who repeated it had never met Arthur Howard, for he had not lived in Murray for many years.[40]

Relationships like the one between Will Mason and T. R. M. Howard were not unusual. Many successful blacks both in Kentucky and in the South had benefited in similar ways from white patrons. Moreover, Howard did not get a free ride. He worked to earn this trust. He reaffirmed Mason's confidence by passing every test with flying colors and by showing an earnest interest in Seventh-day Adventism. In one respect, the perception of a father-son relationship was accurate. Will Mason's marriage had not produced a son and helping Howard partially compensated for this gap. Ora Mason fully shared her husband's enthusiasm for aiding Howard in his career. Both had good reasons to feel proud. Howard was a highly intelligent and unusually likeable young man.[41]

Howard did not hesitate to fulfill his Seventh-day Adventist obligation to participate in missionary activities. Like hundreds of other college students, black and white, he was a "colporteur" during the summer months. The colporteurs represented the backbone of the church's annual "Harvest Ingathering," which raised money for foreign missions. They traveled throughout the United States hawking books and spreading the gospel. Howard generally worked in the western parts of Tennessee and Kentucky. The colporteurs had personal incentives because they kept a percentage of the book sales. In a typical campaign, about fifty students and teachers met each Sunday morning to pray and receive instructions. Then they broke into "bands" of four or five to canvass their assigned communities.[42]

Howard easily and quickly mastered the arts of colporteuring. Reporting from Tennessee in 1926, he wrote to President Tucker, "Everyone is very proud of the start I have made in life." Two weeks later, after a successful effort in Ridgely, Tennessee, he had greater cause for enthusiasm. After clearing $160 in orders, he exulted "that the Lord is going to wonderfully bless me. . . . for I am out for the purpose of winning souls and I feel that the scholarship will take care of itself." His younger coworkers already looked upon him as a leader. Mason gave his encouragement and loaned the use of his car. During another successful effort in 1928, Tucker was indulgent (perhaps too indulgent) in accommodating Howard's request to start classes late in October so he could stay in the field.[43]

For three summers, Howard continued to perfect his skills as a colporteur. He usually canvassed with four or five Oakwood students and sometimes members of the white faculty. Howard visited all around the Tennessee River Valley, including the small black communities in Alma, Jackson, and Ridgeley. It was a tough sell. The impoverished blacks in the area had little extra money to spend, especially on books sold by representatives of an exotic, and white-dominated, sect like the Seventh-day Adventists. Numbers offer an early indication of Howard's unusual entrepreneurial spirit. In a single summer, he sold hundreds of books and magazines, raising more than $1400. His nearest competitor was not even close. In a report to the *Southern Union Worker,* Howard exclaimed, "I truly believe that some of the seed fell on good ground. . . . The boys are of good courage."[44]

Howard's activities nicely complemented his career plans. Beginning with Ellen G. White, Adventist leaders regarded "medical missionary work" as the "right arm" of evangelism. Calvin Moseley, a classmate at Oakwood who later rose to prominence in the church, described health lessons as the "chief entering wedge" to reach converts. When canvassing for the Seventh-day Adventist Church, Howard and his fellow colporteurs held forth on the moral perils of caffeine, nicotine, alcoholic beverages, and "unclean meats" such as pork. In line with White's message, they touted the physical and spiritual benefits of "nature's" healing methods over drugs for the treatment of disease. They served vegetarian "hygienic" meals to potential converts. White had once written, "Among those who are waiting for the coming of the Lord, meat eating will eventually be done away." The colporteurs combined these lessons with a prophetic message that mankind was living in the "last days" and a time of judgment before Christ's return.[45]

When Howard graduated from Oakwood College in 1929, it was logical that he would continue his undergraduate work at another Adventist school. There was little doubt that he would select Union College in Lincoln, Nebraska. It was the alma mater of his two main white mentors, Will Mason and Joseph Tucker. Just as important, Leo F. Thiel, one of Howard's favorite professors, had recently served as the college's president and could help open doors. As he prepared to leave, Howard anticipated the transition with his typical exuberance and self-confidence. He soon found out, however, that life at Union College was far more complicated than he had expected. While his experiences created opportunities to excel, they also left him with a different view of the world and his place in it.[46]

2

The Education of a "Race Man"

T. R. M. HOWARD's attitudes about religion, politics, and life changed in major ways during the decade after he left Oakwood. He continued to be a leader among his peers, a confidante of powerful whites, and to stand out in the crowd. But by the end of the 1930s, religion was no longer his main priority. His attention turned to more worldly goals such as personal advancement, black economic empowerment, and civil rights. By 1942 virtually all ties to old friends, allies, and patrons had broken or frayed. This evolution was predictable. Howard's intense ambition and restlessness were too overpowering to be confined permanently under the small umbrella of black Seventh-day Adventism.

When Howard arrived in Lincoln, Nebraska, in 1929 to begin classes at Union College, he did not show outward signs of discontent. Still determined to become a doctor, he enrolled in the premedical program. With the help of former college president Leo F. Thiel, he secured a job in the college cafeteria. He must have felt a sense of familiarity as he strolled the grounds. Like Oakwood, Union College had been founded by Ellen G. White in the late nineteenth century to nurture Adventist youth in the faith. Both schools had small student bodies, were located on the edges of larger cities, and had working farms on campus.[1]

From Howard's perspective, the main contrast between Union College and Oakwood was that he was the sole black student. He was only twenty-one, but he was not completely naïve about what this meant. A few weeks after his arrival, he reported to Thiel that as a southerner, he understood the "color line, and I am determined to stay well on my side of the line. . . . I never go in the dining hall and set down at a table where there are others, but I set at a table where there is no one, and other[s] come and eat with me. If 'staying in my place' will cause me to get through Union with friends, I sure mean to do that." For the next two years, Howard did precisely that. A classmate recalls that he consistently, but politely, demurred when asked to dine with her and her friends: "He was not going to disturb the peace. . . . He just very quietly went along his way."[2]

Howard did not face segregation in the classroom, at least overtly. As a part of his premedical training, he examined patients regardless of race. This rarely led to any conflict, but Stanley Hilde, a classmate, witnessed an exception when Howard came to a treatment room to examine a black woman. Says Hilde, "She got on her heel and left! And I saw the whole show. And I said to him, "what about that?" And he said he didn't mind that. He said she's probably pretty much that way, racist and all. And he didn't seem upset about it."[3]

Howard carefully navigated around potential racial trouble, but he had no intention of staying in the background. It was not in his nature to do so. The only question was when and how he would assert himself. He seized the opportunity presented by the annual oratorical contest of the Anti-Saloon League of America at Union College. Normally, Adventist educators discouraged debates as fostering the "strife of competition," but they made an exception for activities that might strike a blow against liquor. Howard's oration, "Ten Years of Prohibition," touted the benefits of the Eighteenth Amendment for blacks. He was in his element on any rostrum. Competing almost entirely against white students, he easily cleared every hurdle. He took the top prize at the college, state, and regional competitions.[4]

Howard's greatest triumph was yet to come. In January 1930, he won the national finals in Detroit speaking before four thousand mostly white spectators as well as a large radio audience. He tried to be modest, but it was hard not to boast. Writing to Thiel, he bragged that applause interrupted his speech eleven times and that at the conclusion, "every one in the room rose to their feet." The league's published proceedings support Howard's version of events. It reported that when he finished "the entire audience rose in a great demonstration which lasted several minutes." Letters of praise flowed in from radio listeners in several states. The *Chicago Defender* ran a story with Howard's photo. He won kudos from Adventist periodicals too. "Like Alexander," one declared, "he has won everything in sight. It is a remarkable achievement and the *Outlook* extends hearty congratulations to Theodore Howard."[5]

The aftermath of his triumph gave a foretaste of life as a national celebrity. Howard loved every minute of it. He later boasted (not implausibly) that he had addressed "more people in the state of Nebraska than any other colored man in the United States." Temperance leaders, hoping to beat back the wet offensive, knew a winner when they saw one. Dr. Ernest H. Cherrington, the secretary of the Anti-Saloon League of America, offered a contract for a ten-state speaking tour for what must have seemed a princely sum of $125 per month plus expenses. But Thiel advised against it, warning that it would sidetrack Howard's medical career and violate his promise to work for Mason in the summer. He counseled Howard not to get the idea "that your life work has been accomplished. . . . Three or four months speaking experience, pleasant though it may be, can not measure up with the four or five years at Medical College."[6]

Although Howard heeded this sensible advice and returned home to Murray for the summer, a discordant tone had crept into his letters to Thiel and Tucker. Howard bristled "that segregation is becoming an administrative policy of the school" and that the faculty showed no interest in him. Finding it harder to turn the other cheek, he confessed "that some of these things are awful hard to drink down." Howard tried to shrug off racial slights but sometimes fell into despair. He feared "for our boys and girls who are to come up here from down there who have not the age and Christian experience to pass through some of the trials that one of color must pass through."[7]

Howard's suspicions that segregation was becoming official school policy were not far wrong. President Paul L. Thompson had a far less tolerant attitude on race than Joseph A. Tucker. Furthermore, Thompson was under pressure from southern white parents ready to pounce on any compromise with the color line. During Howard's second year at Union College, Thompson required that black students sit at a separate table in the dining room. Howard had informally followed this practice, of course, but it was galling to have it imposed officially. Thompson's edict was a slap in the face of Union College's only black student who, despite his accomplishments, had to toe the color line.[8]

While petty discrimination in the college cafeteria was demoralizing, Howard had far more serious brushes with racial injustice during this period. He witnessed the aftermath of two lynchings, experiences he mentioned in an article for the *California Eagle* in 1933. The first was in Emelle, a town in western Alabama in 1930. The catalyst was an argument over payment for a car battery between Clarence Boyd, the son of a white planter, and Tom Robinson, a black man. A gun battle ensued between members of the two families, killing Boyd. A white posse shot one of Robinson's sons when he tried to flee and hanged another son. The posse then killed two other blacks while hunting down surviving members of the family. Howard's recollections were brief but pointed. Traveling through Emelle (misspelled as "Amelia"), he saw "two mutilated bodies of members of my race dangling from the limbs of trees."[9]

More horrific still was a lynching in Maryville, Missouri. In December 1930, the authorities arrested Raymond Gunn on charges of murdering a local schoolteacher. Just before the trial, a crowd of whites, said to have included members of the Ku Klux Klan, abducted the prisoner from jail. The mob, by then increased to more than two thousand, dragged Gunn to the school where the murder had taken place. The sheriff failed to call on a detachment of the National Guard in town, claiming that it would incite more violence. Members of the mob tortured Gunn by attaching pincers to his ears. They chained him to the roof of the school, doused him with gasoline, and set the school on fire. Spectators heard groans as the flames consumed him. After the fire cooled, the crowd picked at the remains of teeth, pieces of bone, and other grisly souvenirs. Howard stated that he had visited the scene one day later: "I went to the spot and with my own hands picked some of the ashes of this man's body with a prayer on my lips to Almighty God as to how long would my people have to be the prey of hooded klansmen."[10]

As Howard approached graduation in 1931, he began to harbor serious doubts about a medical career. He wrote of "being told almost daily" that the ministry, rather than medicine, suited his talents. Lincoln's largest black church offered him its pulpit. He was tempted. Howard confided to Tucker that he had a greater interest in national issues than in "following a reaction in Chemistry." Another reason for the indecision, which he did not mention, was his mediocre grades. In his first year at Union College, he had a B- average, but in the second this slipped to a borderline C-/D+. His best grade during the entire two years, an A in speech, could also be taken as a sign to forsake medicine for a preacher's life. Just as seriously, Mason was in some financial straits and might not be able to extend more assistance.[11]

Howard had some other options, at least for the near term. Tucker offered him a position as dean of men at Oakwood. He prefaced the proposal by emphasizing the dangers of "continually associating with people outside of the Truth." The Methodist Board of Temperance and the Anti-Saloon League of America dangled the possibility of a permanent speaking job. Howard procrastinated but ultimately decided to stay on track with his original plan. He applied to the College of Medical Evangelists of Loma Linda, California, the Adventist Church's main medical college, but went on the protemperance speaking circuit one last time during the summer.[12]

Another issue weighed heavily on Howard. His girlfriend in Murray was pregnant with his child, a child conceived during his summer visit in 1931. Like Howard, the mother, twenty-one-year-old Arzalia Wilson, came from a modest background. Her father worked in a garage and her mother was a laborer in a tobacco factory. Theodore and Arzalia had grown up together. She was quite attractive, and many locals thought marriage was imminent. But Howard did not want to take this step. He left his pregnant girlfriend at the end of summer and arrived in Loma Linda to begin classes in the fall. Their daughter, Verda Wilson, was born in April 1932. Although the truth was well known in Murray, he kept it secret from his white patrons and California friends. The birth of this child was the beginning of a pattern of sexual irresponsibility, selfishness, and deception.[13]

Howard's new school, the College of Medical Evangelists (CME), was the pride and joy of Adventist higher education. Ellen G. White had created it to fill the gap left behind after the church severed ties in 1907 with John Harvey Kellogg's Battle Creek Sanitarium. The CME had initially received a C rating from the American Medical Association (AMA). The AMA was expectably skittish about an institution founded by Ellen G. White and dedicated to training "medical evangelists." It had always distrusted the SDA homeopathic approach to diet and natural healing methods.[14]

As he had at Union College, Howard maintained a cordial, if somewhat distant, relationship with white classmates. More than six decades later, they described him as gregarious, dignified, and hardworking. The CME usually had one or two black students per graduating class. The first was Ruth Temple, who became a respected practitioner in Los Angeles in the 1920s. More blacks would have attended but quotas kept them out. In 1934 Arthur E. Coyne, the dean of the medical school of the Los Angeles campus, defended this policy because of the difficulty of getting work for black students. Under the school's cooperative system, students alternated between a month of study and one of employment (usually in a medical facility of some kind). Because discrimination often prevented black students from obtaining these positions, the CME employed them in the pharmacy of the Ellen G. White Hospital in Los Angeles. Coyne also cited the obstacles to placing black interns. Many northern hospitals had informal rules that barred them. The few available slots in the South and border states were in all-black institutions such as Meharry in Nashville, City Hospital #2 in St. Louis, and the Freedman's Hospital in Washington, D.C.[15]

One other black person was in Howard's class, Louis E. Johnson, and another, Archie Hairston, was in the class just behind him. The three often came as a group to black Adventist weekend social events in nearby communities such as San Bernardino. These alcohol-free gatherings featured musical chairs and other innocent amusements. They allowed Howard to pleasantly reconnect with black peers in the Adventist Church. In Lincoln, by contrast, the black Baptist and Methodist churches were his main social outlets. Yet Howard was not one to confine his activities to social gatherings, religious work, or medical studies. He wanted to change the world.[16]

At the beginning of his second year at the CME, he finally had his chance. Howard enlisted in the remarkable U.S. Senate campaign of white preacher Robert "Fighting Bob" Shuler, the first of many politically incorrect choices. A native of Virginia, Shuler had risen to prominence as a fundamentalist Methodist preacher in Paris, Texas, during the 1910s. His charismatic, witty, and caustic sermons against liquor and other vices made him something of a statewide political kingmaker. In 1920 Shuler had tried to break up an imminent lynching of two blacks held in the county jail. While on his way to the scene, he and the sheriff were "literally trampled down" by the crowd that went on to burn the prisoners at the stake.[17]

Soon thereafter, Shuler accepted the pastorate of the Trinity Methodist Church in Los Angeles. By the end of the 1920s, he had transformed a struggling congregation into a fundamentalist powerhouse of more than three thousand parishioners. Shuler's fame spread because of his jeremiads against vice, liquor, and corrupt machine politics. He was an unrelenting foe of Aimee Semple McPherson, his chief evangelistic rival in Los Angeles, whom he regarded as doctrinally unsound and morally dubious. Politicians courted Shuler's endorsement and feared his barbs. Informed observers credited him with electing John C. Porter as mayor of Los Angeles in 1929.[18]

Readers of a book about a pioneering civil rights leader might be shocked to learn something else: Shuler was a leading defender of the Klan in California during the 1920s. He was not alone. By 1922 the Klan in Los Angeles numbered a thousand members, including the chief of police, the sheriff, and the U.S. attorney. Shuler's support for the Klan was incidental to his political platform, but he never showed misgivings about the Klan's agenda either. Rather, he embraced the Klan primarily because of shared views on Catholicism, Prohibition, and traditional morality. He saw it as a valuable ally in his fight against local machine politicians and vice. The alliance ended in 1924 because of Shuler's perception that the Klan had sold out to Los Angeles's corrupt politicians.[19]

Shuler's most far-reaching accomplishment was his innovative use of radio. In 1926 money from a wealthy benefactor enabled him to start station KGEF. About a hundred thousand listeners tuned in from states as distant as Nebraska (where Howard might have heard it). Shuler's rise to fame as a radio preacher invites comparisons to Father Charles E. Coughlin in Detroit. Both started broadcasting in 1926, projected powerful on-the-air personalities, and reached large national audiences. They shared a populist antipathy to finance capital, bootleggers, modern trends in morality, big business (including such stock villains as William Randolph Hearst), and grafting politicians. But the differences were significant. Though Coughlin's broadcasts had started two months earlier, Shuler was the first to make the leap toward explicitly political topics. Unlike Coughlin, Shuler not only broadcast on his station but owned it.[20]

When Howard came to California in the fall of 1931, Shuler's radio career was in jeopardy and his enemies were drawing blood. Hearst's *Los Angeles Examiner* had petitioned the Federal Radio Commission to take him off the air for alleged factual errors and misrepresentations. In November the commission revoked KGEF's license and found Shuler guilty of inciting "religious strife and antagonism." Shuler appealed on first amendment grounds. Many civil libertarians supported him.[21]

Pending a final court decision, Shuler counterattacked by running for the U.S. Senate in the 1932 election. His main goal was to get back on the radio. The commission would have no power to prevent a candidate from purchasing airtime. Shuler cross-filed in the Republican, Democratic, and Prohibition party primaries. He won only the Prohibition nomination but garnered more total primary votes than any other candidate. While Shuler always defended the dry cause, other issues soon moved to the forefront. He condemned the power of the big banks, the influence of the Hearst interests, and the self-interested behavior of politicians who, in his view, were impeding recovery from the depression. It is not surprising that Shuler relished the role of a champion of free speech and victim of the Federal Radio Commission.[22]

Shuler's record on the Klan makes Howard's support seem surprising. After all, only a year earlier he had complained bitterly about Jim Crow practices at Union College and had witnessed the gruesome consequences of Klan violence. His stand is less of a mystery when put into perspective. Black voters faced few choices. Shuler's opponent, incumbent senator William McAdoo, had also courted the Klan, when he ran for president in 1924. Moreover, by the early 1930s, Shuler scrupulously avoided racist appeals and had developed a reputation for fairness by giving airtime to blacks. The main black newspaper in Los Angeles even took Shuler's side against the Federal Radio Commission. Shuler's station, it editorialized, was the "only one in this section where Negroes can get any place except as buffoons." Howard also had reason to be drawn to Shuler's defense of Prohibition, which complemented his longtime interest in the cause.[23]

Howard's affinity for Shuler had a deeper, more personal, basis. The willingness of a man of such prominence to take an interest in him fed his ego. Edward F. Boyd, Howard's friend and future brother-in-law, had firsthand experience when he saw the two together at Shuler's church. Commenting on the interaction, Boyd explains that Howard "liked to be recognized" and "have a feeling of importance, and boy did he have that feeling." Furthermore, Howard respected Shuler as an individual. Though born and raised in the South, Shuler did not draw the color line in his home or at the dinner table and invited Howard to speak in his church. Howard, as an outsider himself, could relate to a man who had a reputation as a fearless crusader against the status quo. It was a persona that he later adopted for himself.[24]

Shuler, of course, knew full well that cultivating Howard made good political sense. This intelligent and dynamic young man gave an entrée into the black community and helped to counter the stigma associated with his past alliance with the Klan. Howard did not disappoint him. He delivered speeches for Shuler in black churches in several cities. Howard must have been pleased by the relatively tolerant campaign statements on race. Shuler even toned down his anti-Catholicism, pledging to protect the rights of people whether "Catholics, Protestants, Jews, Gentiles, white, black, tan or yellow." The fight to defend Prohibition was a frequent topic in Howard's pro-Shuler speeches. Shortly before the election, he proclaimed that "Prohibition has been a big factor in making the United States the world's wealthiest nation" and "has assisted the buying of homes and made possible the amazing comfort and beauty of American homes."[25]

Although Shuler represented a party that had long ago passed its heyday, Howard had not tied himself to a marginal cause. He had made a calculated and reasonable gamble. An adroit campaigner, Shuler had high name recognition, and many pundits considered him a fair bet to win. He lost in November but polled 25 percent in a three-way race, the best percentage ever for a Prohibition Party candidate seeking such a high office. After the election, Howard maintained a cordial relationship with Shuler and often spoke at his church.[26]

Not long after Shuler's defeat, Howard had what was probably his first encounter with abortion. In February 1933, Howard's classmate Archie Hairston asked Dr. Mathew J. Marmillion, a wealthy black doctor who also owned a 150–room hotel and night club in Los Angeles, to perform an abortion on his girlfriend, Margaret Scott. Like Hairston, Scott was a black Adventist. The abortion went tragically wrong, Scott died, Marmillion stood trial on charges of manslaughter, and the CME expelled Hairston. Under promise of immunity, Hairston testified as a witness for the prosecution. Marmillion loudly protested his innocence and blamed Hairston for the badly botched abortion. He claimed that Scott was already dying when Hairston brought her to his office. Marmillion was not convincing: The testimony overwhelmingly pointed to his guilt.[27]

Black newspapers, however, rose to Marmillion's defense. Rather than directly challenging the facts and testimony, they emphasized his character and accomplishments. In a front-page editorial, "Free Dr. Marmillion," the *Los Angeles Sentinel* depicted him as "a churchman, a giver to charity, a man of integrity." A reporter for that paper even took the opportunity to raise questions about abortion laws. He commented that the trial had "provoked certain comments upon the laws appertaining to birth control, contraception and abortion. . . . This most hushed-up of awkward subjects should no longer be shrouded in silence, evasion, mock modesty and blue stocking." The jury believed Hairston and sent Marmillion, then sixty-two, to prison. Howard probably had no direct involvement, but he was fully aware of what had transpired. An aspiring medical student had every reason to take the plight of the elderly doctor as a cautionary tale of the perils of performing illegal abortions, but, then, Howard was not a typical medical student: His whole life was a story of going against the grain.[28]

For the moment, though, he had other things on his mind. He was trying to win the affections of Helen Nela Boyd, a beautiful socialite from Riverside, California. Helen's brother, Edward, was a high school student when he met Howard in 1932 at a social gathering of Adventists. The two soon became friends. Edward Boyd, who was not a member of the church himself, introduced the charming young man to his sister. The prospects for romance did not look promising. "My sister really wasn't very impressed," Boyd explains, "because he was not a very good-looking man. . . . She was really quite rude to him." Howard was not discouraged. Beautiful, intelligent, prosperous, and refined, Helen was the girl of his dreams. He singlemindedly set out to woo her. Edward Boyd remembers that "he was very kind and very thoughtful . . . and did so many nice things for her." Gradually, he began to win her over with a determined campaign that took nothing for granted.[29]

Aside from the commonality of race, their backgrounds could hardly have been more different. A descendant of black forty-niners, Helen was born in 1909 to Robert J. Boyd (who ran a successful barbershop catering to white customers) and Emma Barrett Boyd (a prosperous real estate broker). She experienced discrimination but to nowhere near the same degree as Howard. Blacks, whites, Mexicans, and Asians lived in close proximity in Riverside, and race relations were better than in many other parts of California. Débutante balls and elite social clubs filled Helen's teenage and early adult years. At the same time, her parents tried to instill a sense of obligation toward the less fortunate. She became the head of a settlement house that served blacks and Mexicans in Riverside. Through the help of Helen and Edward F. Boyd, Howard gained acceptance by the black elite of Riverside and Los Angeles. For the rest of his life, Howard moved almost effortlessly between the black bourgeoisie and the masses.[30]

The Boyds helped to launch Howard's career as a civil rights leader by introducing him to Charlotta A. Bass. She and her husband, Joseph B. Bass, had edited and published the *California Eagle,* the leading black newspaper in Los Angeles since 1912. After her husband's illness in 1932, she assumed full control. Throughout the 1920s, the Basses fought the rising power of the Ku Klux Klan and promoted black business and political advancement. The *Eagle* tried to rebuff attempts to implement segregation by popularizing the slogan, "Don't Spend Your Money Where You Can't Work." Not long after meeting Charlotta A. Bass, Howard won her over. She hired him as "field manager" with assigned duties to build up circulation and write a regular opinion column. On July 7, 1933, the *California Eagle* introduced readers to its new employee: "Mr. Howard is a hard and energetic worker, of loyal and unquestioned integrity, a silver-tongued orator and intensely interested in the growth of development of all people and of the race of which he is identified." The same issue carried the first installment of his column, "The Negro in the Light of History," later changed to "Our Fight."[31]

Howard was never bothered too much about the dangers of overextending himself. Simultaneously with his new job, he took the helm of the California Economic, Commercial, and Political League. Here too, the Boyds were facilitators. Helen's father and other relatives had helped to organize the league in 1930. It was dedicated to advancing black political and economic power but particularly stressed the importance of business ownership and land acquisition. With Howard as president, Helen kept up the family tradition by serving as the league's recording secretary.[32]

In July 1933 Howard settled comfortably into the twin roles of journalist and civil rights leader. For the next year and a half, he covered such varied subjects as international power politics, civil rights, and prostitution. Howard's columns for the *California Eagle* were thoughtful, well-informed, and wide-ranging, especially for someone whose college education had centered on vocational and medical subjects. He closely linked them to the work of the league. He still defended Prohibition but with decreasing fervor. Howard's favorite topics were black self-improvement and civil rights. He regarded himself as one of the "race men" but avoided the antiwhite and Afrocentric rhetoric of more extreme nationalists such as Marcus Garvey.[33]

Howard's columns championed entrepreneurship and a program to teach "thrift and economy" to the young. He was very much a follower of Booker T. Washington, whom he praised as a "towering intellectual genius." Howard recommended a credo of "talking about Negro business, singing Negro business, preaching Negro business, spending our money with Negro business." He urged emulation of Japanese-Americans who had learned the value of "getting together and pulling together," and who, despite intense discrimination, had developed a booming business sector and philanthropic institutions such as hospitals.[34]

Like Washington, he held that many of the problems of black businesses, including unsanitary conditions and the sale of inferior products, were self-inflicted. Characteristically, the workaholic Howard underscored the "value of time." He said that he had stopped using one of the "most fashionable" black-owned barbershops in Los Angeles because the "barber insisted on clipping one minute and talking five minutes. We are living in an age of speed and the Negro barber must realize this fact." Howard called on blacks to make the most of existing conditions and recognize that not every boy was "born to be a preacher, lawyer or doctor." He had no patience for those who discounted menial jobs as demeaning instead of giving them proper due as a means for incremental progress and race pride. As "long as the American people wear shoes," he declared, "somebody is going to have to shine them. . . . the Negro boy who shines shoes should shine them so well that every body in the community would want him to shine their shoes."[35]

History was one of Howard's favorite topics. His analysis of Lincoln was nuanced and, to a great extent, anticipated the views of modern scholars.

He lauded Lincoln's contributions but avoided hagiography. Lincoln was "preeminently the white man's president" who held "the same prejudices of his white fellow countrymen against the Negro." While he hated slavery, it was not primarily because of the harm inflicted on blacks but because it corrupted whites. Lincoln had waged the Civil War to save the Union, not to end slavery. Yet Howard showed empathy for the dilemmas he faced: "Viewed from the genuine abolition ground, Mr. Lincoln seemed tardy, cold, dull and indifferent, but measured by the sentiment of his country. . . . he was swift, zealous and determined." Lincoln's great accomplishment, Howard argued, was to abolish slavery by, in effect, saving the white race from itself.[36]

Howard faulted school textbooks for failure to acknowledge "the Negro as a contributor to western civilization." In his view, they gave a misguided impression that blacks had no other role in history than as slaves. When a white child reads the newspaper and sees "the Negro's name only in connection with some crime: two things are established in his mind for life—the Negro was a slave and he has a criminal mind, on these two facts he establishes his superiority complex." Howard did not want to minimize the contributions of whites, but he supported a balanced treatment. Such a revision, he predicted, was more likely to inspire the youth of both races. As an illustration, he pointed to the lives of two self-made men, Lincoln and Frederick Douglass: "It is a long way from a log cabin in Kentucky to the presidency of the U.S.A., but from the slave pen to the Marshalship of the District of Columbia is farther."[37]

Howard rarely strayed from race-related themes when he commented on the Great Depression, which was at its lowest ebb when he started his column. He praised the New Deal but was skeptical that it would ameliorate second-class citizenship. In some respects, he argued, conditions for blacks had worsened. They were "being gradually reduced to peonage and shut out of the labor unions," and racial hatred was spreading from the southern to northern states. Jim Crow often shaped the distribution of federal funds in projects, such as building the Hoover Dam, and "little of any of it goes to help the sufferings of the Negro."[38]

He backed President Franklin D. Roosevelt but only conditionally. Once the economy improved, the onus was on the president "to say, 'this far and no farther' to mob violence and other injustices which are forced upon the black American." If he failed to do these things, Howard vowed to challenge the "entire new deal program." In the tradition of Booker T. Washington, Howard reiterated the follies of counting on the whims of white politicians and the "profuse diarrhea" of governmental subsidies. Over the long haul, the reliable rule to follow was that the "salvation of the American Negro lies within the American Negro."[39]

Although Howard's economic program was reminiscent of Washington's, his political ideas were immediatist and confrontational. He had no time for the various "bone-headed, pussy-footing, grafting, selfish, dishonest preachers, lawyers, doctors and ratty good-for-nothing politicians and Uncle Toms" who had hoodwinked blacks into voting against their own interests. He advocated creation of a "clearing-house" to enable blacks to unite behind equal-rights candidates. It was essential for blacks to finance their own political campaigns: "Beware of these banquets, cigars and kegs of beer! These may prove to be all that you will ever get for your vote." In a small way, Howard followed this strategy when he chose to help candidates. His tactics were sometimes questionable but were probably typical of other California political campaigns. Howard elaborated on the details to a white classmate. First he spoke in churches to raise money for candidates who promised "the best shake for the colored people." Then, as an inducement, he gave cooperating ministers a portion of the donations.[40]

Howard may have had separatist tendencies but reacted angrily to any attempt to introduce segregation in California. An important flashpoint came in 1934 when a white supervisor at Los Angeles County Hospital offered black nurses a cash bonus to live offsite and eat separately. When they refused, Howard applauded their courage in spurning this bribe. He lamented that in a time of depression segregationists were picking the "taxpayers' pockets" for an expensive plan "to gratify race hatred." Overwhelmed by the general outcry, the county supervisor disavowed the proposal and blamed the superintendent of nurses for usurping her authority. Remarkably, Bob Shuler took the side of the black nurses in this dispute. According to Howard, Shuler recanted his past stands on race and condemned the segregation plan as "un-Christian and un-American." As his association with Shuler revealed, Howard was a bit of a maverick. His dedication to racial uplift did not mean that he automatically lined up behind the candidate endorsed by the black political elite. Howard followed these maverick tendencies by repeatedly denouncing Los Angeles's pro–New Deal mayor Frank Shaw, even though the local NAACP had backed him to the hilt.[41]

This would not be the last time that Howard and the NAACP butted heads. He criticized H. Claude Hudson, the Los Angeles chapter president, for his failure or inability to use the influence he presumably had to get jobs for blacks or to secure greater police protection. Howard charged that Hudson and his allies had not thought "of the Race, but of *self*" when they supported Shaw. In his role as president of the California Economic, Commercial, and Political League, Howard demanded appointment of a black judge and more hiring of blacks in public works. He also assailed Shaw for various misdeeds in office. Many of Howard's criticisms were well founded. In a few years, the once-heralded mayor left office under a cloud of corruption. Not coincidentally, by opposing Shaw Howard aligned once again with Shuler, who had backed Shaw's opponent in the 1933 race.[42]

Howard showed contempt for politics as usual, but his militancy never entailed a defense of communism or other totalitarian schemes. This separated him from many of his contemporaries. During the depression, black and white opinion leaders, shaken by the collapse of the American economy, increasingly embraced the Soviet experiment as the wave of the future. A prominent example was Howard's very good friend and colleague on the *California Eagle*, Loren Miller. But Howard had little time for panaceas.[43]

The influence of Howard's religious background probably mitigated the attraction of leftist politics. The Adventist philosophy on health was proactive but led to profoundly pessimistic conclusions about the future of mankind itself. In her book *The Story of Patriarchs and Prophets* (which Howard had sold as a colporteur during the 1920s), Ellen G. White underscored the indelible stain of original sin. Once fallen man had forsaken the regenerating "tree of life," this curse doomed him to a future of progressive decay. In *The Ministry of Health*, White argued that modern medical experts had failed to understand "the causes underlying the mortality, the disease and degeneracy, that exist to-day even in the most civilized and favored lands. The human race is deteriorating." Because mankind was living in the "last days," the only hope was salvation in Christ. Hence White and the church she led distrusted earthly movements for reform (other than a few exceptions such as Prohibition).[44]

Howard's running debate in the *California Eagle* with "Sonia," a fellow columnist, revealed the continuing influence of Adventist ideas. Sonia, a freethinker and socialist, fired the first shot by lecturing Howard on his inability to realize that social ills such as crime and prostitution were endemic to capitalism. Howard's chief mistake, in her view, was that he did not start from the all-important premise that "men are just what their environment makes them." He was like the doctor who prescribed drugs to deaden the pain of a disease rather than treating the root cause. For Sonia, the permanent solution was to emulate the Soviet Union, "the land which is destined to lead the rest of the world to light and true progress."[45]

Howard took Sonia's bait and counterattacked. Describing himself as a "fundamentalist," he dismissed her "radical" attacks on religion as misguided and dangerous. He said that his "advanced studies in Biology and science have only opened new fields of beauty before me of the greatness of the Creator." Echoing White, Howard concluded that the reality of sin and decay would ultimately frustrate Sonia's grand plans: "The world is sick mentally as well as physically. Nervous diseases are on the increase and it is my opinion that as the world rushes on for what Sonia has pictured as 'higher society' the increase will continue in great proportions." Because humanity was entering into the Final Days, it was doomed to a temporal fate of mounting crime, war, and disease ending with the "complete down fall of civilization."[46]

Howard dismissed Sonia's goal of social perfection as an unattainable "dreamland" based upon a flawed premise about human nature that neglected the determining role of heredity. He used the much-cited example of the Juke family to demonstrate that allowing "feebleminded" couples to procreate burdened future generations. On this issue, Howard admitted to a dilemma between Christian ethics and social realities. Science could extend and save life but at what cost? "Our present system," he cautioned, "helps the unfit to survive and propagate their kind. This is humanitarian and according to Christian principles the right and the only thing to do, but it is ultimate suicide for the human race." In framing the issue in these stark terms of heredity, Howard was pushing the acceptable limits of mainstream Adventist doctrine. Although White had accepted that some mental illness was inherited, she had never gone quite this far. Howard did not claim, as others did, that heredity served as a basis for inferior or superior races. In fact, he never brought race into the discussion at all. He also did not endorse (or explicitly oppose) sterilization and other coercive measures that were favored by many advocates of eugenics.[47]

Ellen G. White would have wholeheartedly approved of one of Howard's political goals: stamping out prostitution on Central Avenue. His columns in the *Eagle* on this subject won him many friends in the black business community and the clergy. The issue allowed him to deploy Adventist moral zeal in the service of economic advancement. Howard framed the matter in terms familiar to a fundamentalist preacher: "Negro business on Central avenue cannot make progress as long as loose, ignorant, filthy women are allowed to sell their ungodly bodies." The peril was particularly great for black youth "who must look upon these vultures who stand watching for prey upon our business street. Our high school boys and girls are not dumb; they know that these women are not weather hens out looking to see when it is going to rain." Despite this often unsympathetic rhetoric, Howard emphasized that desperate economic conditions caused by the Depression had pushed many women into this practice.[48]

The spread of prostitution on Central Avenue, he charged, brought shame to "Negro womanhood" as a whole. As in the South, he emphasized that white men in Los Angeles often played a predatory role. Many came to Central Avenue to seek out prostitutes and, in the process, indiscriminately made insulting advances to all black women. Howard acknowledged that black men in the South were often helpless to protect black women. But their counterparts on Central Avenue had no such excuse. This was symptomatic of a broader problem. Since emancipation, achievements won by ordinary black women were not "because their men protected them" but "in spite of their men." Howard singled out for criticism those black men who likewise crossed the sexual color line. He pitied any who had "felt the urge to leave the Race" to become involved with white women.[49]

Howard combined his fiery moralistic language with surprising recommendations. He matter-of-factly conceded that history showed the impossibility of eliminating prostitution through law and concluded that the realistic solution was an officially restricted district. There, prostitutes could ply their trade under police protection, thus ensuring the freedom of upright black women to patronize legitimate black businesses without harassment: "During the days of the 'redlight' district, no self-respecting man would have dared to move into that district to bring up his family!"

This was heretical thinking. Though a few police officials and politicians had once advocated redlight districts, by World War I a coalition of doctors, clerics (including Adventists), and progressive reformers had largely silenced them. Howard drew his opinions from his religious worldview on the sinful nature of humanity. Any scheme to suppress prostitution was hopelessly utopian. Although Howard had not hesitated to call for prohibition of liquor, his old zeal for a dry America had waned considerably by 1933. Perhaps too, the consequences of his own sexual dalliances in Murray had made him less sanguine about schemes to legislate morality.[50]

Howard's energetic activism was at odds with the Adventist distrust of politics, but the students, faculty, and administrators at the CME did not appear to object. Then again, it is doubtful that many bothered to keep track of happenings in southern California's black political subculture. By all measures, CME officials wished him well in his academic studies and, up to this point, his consistently solid, if not outstanding, performance in the classroom justified their expectations. He maintained a B average for the four years at the CME.[51]

Indeed, Adventist leaders at the CME and elsewhere had big plans for Howard's future. In 1934 they were busily grooming him for a postgraduate career as the first medical director of Riverside Sanitarium and Hospital in Nashville, Tennessee, scheduled to open in a year or so. The hospital represented the culmination of more than a decade of striving by the indefatigable Nellie Druillard. Born in Wisconsin in 1844, she had been a close associate of Ellen G. White. Known affectionately as "Mother D," Druillard (who was white) had spent much of the 1890s as a missionary in Africa, where she befriended Cecil Rhodes, the mining baron and president of the Cape Colony in South Africa. Shrewd investments in Nebraska real estate later made her wealthy. Percy T. Magan, the future president of the CME, and Druillard's nephew Edward A. Sutherland, had founded Madison College in 1907 on a site near Nashville. She managed the college when they left to get their medical degrees at Vanderbilt.[52]

After Druillard nearly died in a severe auto accident in 1924, she took a religious vow to devote the rest of her life to helping blacks. She was eighty at the time. She purchased several hundred acres on the Cumberland River outside Nashville for a small school to train black nurses. When the Seventh-day Adventist Church began to consider raising money for a hospital for black members, she volunteered to donate this land. Sutherland, who headed both Madison College and the Madison Sanitarium, acted as intermediary between his aunt and the Adventist General Conference.[53]

Sometime during this period, Druillard came into contact with Howard, possibly during one of his visits to the Kentucky-Tennessee area. She was quite taken with him and began contributing to his education. By early 1934, Druillard, then ninety, looked forward to the day when he could take the reins at Riverside. In March, at her urging, Sutherland wrote to the president of Meharry Medical College, recommending Howard for an internship upon completion of his fourth year at the CME in 1935. Referring to his aunt, Sutherland explained that "this is probably one of the last things she can do—to prepare this young man to carry responsibility in the little institution she is now conducting."[54]

Arthur E. Coyne, the dean of the CME's School of Medicine, worked closely with Druillard and Sutherland to prepare a place for Howard at Riverside. Within the racial context of the period, he was a valuable, but not uncritical, ally. Writing to Sutherland, Coyne described Howard as "above the average of some of our white boys in his ability to carry on the clinical assignments. At the same time I do not think that you will find Mr. Howard feeling superior in any way, as he has always maintained a very humble attitude." Coyne, Druillard, and Sutherland looked on Howard as much more than a well-deserving black medical student. He was one of their best hopes to spread Seventh-day Adventism among blacks in the South. Hence, they tried to steer him away from considering hospital internships in the North. Because so few such positions were available, convincing him was not hard to do. Perhaps too, they feared that a northern internship would tempt him away from their game plan. Sutherland predicted that Howard "will help us to have a more satisfactory working connection with the colored people in Nashville than we otherwise can get." Coyne shared this enthusiasm, agreeing that he could "build up the colored church in Nashville better than anyone we know of."[55]

Within a few months, much of this goodwill toward Howard had evaporated. At the center of the trouble was a political campaign. Since he had started at the CME, Howard had kept up with his medical studies while dabbling in black activism and journalism. With relative ease, he had moved between the two distinct realms. In 1934, however, everything changed. At first, it was more or less politics as usual. During the summer, the California Economic, Commercial, and Political League launched a sustained campaign to build interest in a grand Memorial Day special event at the Orange Show grounds in San Bernardino. It planned a combination political rally, carnival, band concert, barbecue, and picnic outing. Howard billed it as a nonpartisan showcase of independent black political clout and a counterweight to those black leaders who always kept their eyes on "political power, not realizing that political power without economic power is impossible." He took care to invite the announced, and potential, candidates for statewide office, as well as prominent black leaders such as Charlotta A. Bass, the publisher of the *California Eagle*, and Eugene Taylor, her counterpart at the *California News* of Los Angeles.[56]

Howard's abilities as a showman shined through in his columns advertising the event: "The artistic designs and the soft lights make it look very much like the New York Cotton Club. . . . The beautiful young women of San Bernardino, Riverside and Redlands will serve the food on that day. There is a beautiful fountain shaped like a huge orange where only pure orange juice will be served." It featured a parade led by the Los Angeles Drum Corps, athletic contests, and a carnival with four rides. Howard tried to schedule Duke Ellington as the dance band but ultimately settled for the less prominent Dixie Serenaders.[57]

Upton Sinclair, a candidate for the Democratic nomination for governor, was a featured speaker. This meeting was the beginning of another political alliance. Howard's introductory remarks so impressed Sinclair that he asked him to play an important role in his campaign. Like Shuler, Sinclair was an unlikely politician. He had risen to fame nearly thirty years earlier as the author of the muckraking exposé of Chicago meatpacking, *The Jungle* (1906). Historians have credited the outrage generated by the novel with creating a groundswell for the enactment of the Pure Food and Drug Act. After the success of *The Jungle,* Sinclair wrote numerous, often controversial, works on religion, telepathy, and Prohibition (he was for it). He counted Albert Einstein and Charlie Chaplin among his friends and ideological allies. His correspondence included a heated, but respectful, duel over many years with

H. L. Mencken, a libertarian antisocialist. Sinclair moved to Los Angeles in 1916. He wrote scripts for Hollywood studios but never lost his zeal for left-wing causes.[58]

Sinclair was a self-professed egalitarian and humanitarian but previous references to blacks in his writings were generally intolerant and unsympathetic. In *The Jungle*, they were lazy, "stupid," and vice-ridden scabs who were "savages in Africa; and since then they had been chattel slaves, or had been held down by a community ruled by the traditions of slavery. Now for the first time they were free—free to gratify every passion, free to wreck themselves." In a later work, he matter-of-factly stated that "the average lot of the chattel slave of 1860 was preferable to that of the modern slave of the Beef Trust, the Steel Trust, or the Coal Trust."[59]

In 1933, Sinclair changed his party registration from Socialist to Democrat and laid the groundwork to run for governor. He aspired to overturn the existing capitalist order through a plan to End Poverty in California (EPIC). Under EPIC, taxes, payable in cash, services, or goods, would be raised on big businesses, the state would assume control of idle factories by renting them, and the workers would own the products they produced. The plan included government-owned warehouses for farmers to store their crops in exchange for receipts that could be used to offset taxes. These goods, in turn, were to be exchanged for manufactured goods. Sinclair further proposed "land colonies" for the unemployed to grow their own food on private property rented by the state. Sinclair's ultimate goal was to phase out corporate profit by establishing a society dominated by government-controlled cooperatives relying on a form of barter or "production for use." As unemployment worsened in California, supporters flocked to the EPIC standard.[60]

Just after the Memorial Day event, Howard's columns for the *California Eagle* began aggressive promotion of Sinclair's campaign. He compared EPIC favorably to a plan already put forward by the California Economic, Commercial, and Political League. Sinclair rewarded his young ally by putting him in charge of "the campaign among the negro voters throughout the state." Howard also made regular radio broadcasts for Sinclair.[61]

Howard had made quite a leap in two years from Shuler to Sinclair. The two candidates shared some views, including dry sympathies and a distrust of big business, but their disagreements were equally great. Shuler was an antisocialist fundamentalist minister who, despite denunciations of finance capital, was suspicious of big government and supportive of small business. Sinclair, on the other hand, had little sympathy for organized religion and Christian orthodoxy. As a longtime socialist, he had disdain for the profit motive in any form.[62]

Howard's attraction to both campaigns was more personal than ideological. Shuler and Sinclair had appealed to his vanity by appreciating his talents and putting them to use to reach the black vote. In the case of Sinclair, however, Howard's claim of affinity was not just a cover for his own personal advancement. While Howard did not share Sinclair's taste for panaceas, the league had also embraced elements of the "back-to-the-land" movement that was so popular in the early 1930s. In 1933 Howard counted himself as a "thorough believer in colonization" and recommended that young blacks "be taught that there is more honor in planting a row of beans than running a racket for some political candidate." More broadly, the rhetoric of both the league and EPIC included paeans to economic cooperation. The most important contrast was that the league stressed the need for individuals and voluntary organizations to initiate the program while EPIC relied almost wholly on governmental action.[63]

For a medical student who had lived in California for only three years, Howard had assembled quite a political track record. In two consecutive elections, a prominent statewide white candidate had singled him out as a conduit to black voters. But more was yet to come. In late October Howard was appointed an assistant chair of the state Democratic Party. His main duty was to direct the campaign for all the candidates to win black voters. The *Los Angeles Sentinel,* a new black newspaper, exulted that this was "the first time in the history of the state that such recognition has been given to any member of our race."[64]

As Howard's stock as a political figure soared, it plummeted with the CME and the Seventh-day Adventist Church. By late September, dissemination of Sinclair's past statements on religion had created a stir. With devastating impact, quotations circulated from Sinclair's book, *The Profits of Religion,* published in 1918. The book had castigated modern organized religion as hypocritical, money-hungry, and pandering to superstition. While Catholicism bore the brunt of his assault, Adventism did not escape unscathed.

Sinclair characterized the Seventh-day Adventist Church as a delusional cult and asserted that the Battle Creek Sanitarium peddled overpriced vegetarian food for excessive profits.[65]

Coyne wrote to Sutherland to express his dismay about Howard's involvement in the campaign. He reported that Sinclair had assured Howard a position in his administration and that it would enable him "to finance his medical course without difficulty." He found it astonishing that Howard had aligned himself with a man "who has for so many years openly and actively opposed religion of all sorts and who has blasphemed Christ." Coyne reported that he questioned Howard about a quotation from *The Profits of Religion* that appeared in a pamphlet circulated by Sinclair's enemies. He did not think much of Howard's response that the pamphlet did not reflect the "true meaning" of Sinclair's views because the quotations were taken out of context. Howard was not completely off the mark. The last chapter of *The Profits of Religion* had strongly praised Christ. But Sinclair's version of Christ, as a kind of first-century Eugene V. Debs, bore little resemblance to the Christ of Adventism, or of orthodox Christianity in general.[66]

Coyne related to Sutherland that some students and faculty members had become so infuriated by Howard's campaigning that they were "about ready to ride him out of town on a rail." The content of Sinclair's views was not the sole reason for Coyne's alarm. The election had led to a slide in the quality of Howard's schoolwork, and he was missing classes. Howard was playing with fire, and he must have known it. For someone who had always taken great care to cultivate white patrons, and who had such a bright future laid out for him, his highly visible support for Sinclair took no small amount of courage. He was also lucky. Coyne, for all his outrage, refused to discipline Howard or even to demand that he cease campaigning for Sinclair. He did not want to set a precedent of interfering in the political activities of students and thought it better to let "the matter slide along." Just as important, Coyne persisted in his efforts to secure an internship for Howard at Meharry. Sutherland helped too, but the old enthusiasm had waned for everyone. Coyne had a hunch that "negro politics will lure him away."[67]

Coyne's forgiving attitude toward Howard was unusual given the context of the 1934 election. The contest between Sinclair and his Republican opponent, Governor Frank Merriam, was one of the most polarizing in American history. Sinclair stood accused of atheism and Communism. His supporters, in turn, charged Merriam with a plot to impose fascism in California. The newspapers lined up against Sinclair, including the *California Eagle,* which had stopped carrying Howard's regular columns. The leading educators enlisted as adjuncts in the Merriam campaign. Even while CME administrators resisted the temptation to punish Howard, their counterparts at the University of California at Los Angeles suspended five students for a year because of pro-Sinclair activities.[68]

While Sutherland still hoped that Howard might be "lined up and made to use good sense," his anger, perhaps fueled by thoughts of his aged aunt's emotional investment, boiled over. He reflexively belittled Howard with racial stereotypes: "Howard has shown the weakness that you mention in your letter. However, it is one of the characteristics of the colored people—of losing their heads and getting puffed up." Sutherland's comments indicate that Howard had sound reasons to hedge his bets by considering possible alternatives for his future.[69]

Sinclair's resounding defeat in November left Howard crestfallen. Just after the returns came in, he sheepishly trudged over to Coyne's office to make amends. Coyne, who probably understood Howard better than many other white Adventists, found him to be "much more humble now." Coyne was willing to help, but he was still skeptical. He hoped that Howard would settle down to a medical career in Nashville but thought it likely that sooner or later pursuits "which will put him more in the limelight" would tempt him away. Sutherland, his earlier outburst notwithstanding, exerted his influence to secure an internship. Howard scrambled to put his career back on track. Meharry turned down his application, but at nearly the last minute St. Louis City Hospital #2 offered an internship. Sutherland and Druillard were overjoyed at the news and once again contemplated big plans for Howard's future.[70]

So did Will Mason. Mason had advanced money to Howard during his last year at the CME, and now he needed something in return. In February 1935, a spectacular fire had completely destroyed the Mason Memorial Hospital. Miraculously nobody had died. In all, $150,000 of property, half of it uninsured, went up in smoke. Mason was not deterred. He successfully rallied the community to build a bigger and better hospital. Only two months after the fire, he asked Howard to take charge of a sixteen-bed addition for "colored patients" when he completed his internship in St. Louis. Mason had aided him with this hope—perhaps it was an expectation—in mind. Howard faced pressure from both sides. While nothing was yet in writing, Coyne had the impression that Howard was obligated to take the helm at Riverside Sanitarium in 1936. For a few months at least, it was possible to avoid a final decision.[71]

In June 1935 Howard completed his medical studies on schedule. This was a time of celebration in more ways than one. Howard's persistence with Helen Boyd had finally paid off, and she accepted his marriage proposal. But he kept a carefully guarded secret. He did not tell Helen about Verda Wilson, his three-year-old out-of-wedlock daughter in Murray. The marriage, which took place on the evening of Howard's graduation, was the black social event of the season. Photos of the elegant lawn ceremony dominated the society page of the *California Eagle* under the banner headline "Popular Couple Wed in Riverside Marriage." The bride's parents spared no expense. The article reported that the "large garden was illuminated, flood lights being used at the altar which was erected of white flowers and greenery. Strands of colored lights festooned about the trees and tall candelabras helped light the way." Adventist leaders were not so ready to celebrate. They disapproved of the bride's refusal to convert, despite Howard's repeated pleas. This was serious. The Seventh-day Adventist Church had a strong aversion to mixed-faith unions, especially for someone slated for a leadership role. The marriage reopened wounds that had only partially healed after the Sinclair campaign. Suspicious of Howard's "gentile" wife, other members of the church viewed him with a new level of distrust. They never completely accepted him again.[72]

When Howard began his internship on July 1, 1935, the sixteen-year-old City Hospital #2 in St. Louis was in a state of decay and transition. Few blacks had ever taken pride in it and looked forward to its much-delayed replacement by the Homer G. Phillips Hospital, then under construction. The name itself, City Hospital #2, advertised a second-best and second-class status. The equipment was outdated; the wards were crowded. It was only in 1933 that the city appointed the first black medical director. The overwhelming majority of patients were indigents. Those able to pay used the two black-owned private hospitals.[73]

This was Howard's first sustained experience at a segregated public hospital. He was one of twenty interns, all black. One of his supervisors, William

Sinkler, a resident surgeon, was just beginning a long and distinguished career. Sinkler's reputation was that of an authoritarian and a perfectionist who had the highest standards of patient care. He imparted a lesson to his interns that Howard, if he did not already know it, took to heart. Charity patients, Sinkler cautioned, should never be treated "in any way except with respect, or else you have my word that you will be dismissed." Many years later, he praised Howard as an "ethical" doctor who had shown "promise, with sufficient training, of becoming an outstanding physician."[74]

Uncharacteristically, Howard apparently stayed away from nonmedical activities during his year in St. Louis. Even so, something significant happened that shaped his career. According to Howard's brief account written much later, his experiences at City Hospital #2 convinced him that antiabortion laws were unjust. He said that they had revealed in stark relief the contrast between black women, who would otherwise have terminated their pregnancies, and white women, who could afford to do so. But if Howard responded to these conditions by performing abortions in St. Louis, there is no record of it.[75]

While at City Hospital #2, Howard signed the papers to become medical director of Riverside Sanitarium upon completion of this internship in July 1936. It is doubtful that another decision was possible. In Murray, he would always be in Will Mason's shadow, but in Nashville he could carve out his own niche. The prospects in Murray for a black doctor were not promising—and getting to be less so. The potential patient base there was moving North in unprecedented numbers. For the time being, however, Howard's title as medical director of Riverside meant little. Because of fundraising and construction delays, the Sanitarium had still not opened. The General Conference of the Seventh-day Adventist Church, which owned the facility, provided him an office in Nashville, but his patient demands were minimal. It also gave him a place on the sanitarium's board of directors. As was his lifetime habit, Howard kept more than one iron in the fire. He established a private practice on the side in Nashville and made regular visits to Murray to assist Dr. Mason. As late as February 1937, the same month that Riverside opened, the new Mason Memorial Hospital announced his appointment as head of its "negro unit." Because Nashville was one hundred twenty miles of winding road and river ferries from Murray, this title was pretty much meaningless.[76]

Meanwhile, events in Howard's double life in Murray were spiraling out of control. Somehow, his mother-in-law, Emma Boyd, had uncovered the truth about his out-of-wedlock child and told his wife. The news greatly depressed Helen and cast a shadow over their relationship. Complicating the situation was the death of Arzalia Wilson, the mother of his daughter, in August 1936 from pulmonary tuberculosis. At the time, she was working as a domestic servant. Howard's mother and stepfather, Mary Palmer and Morris Palmer, stepped in to care for his and Arzalia's four-year-old daughter Verda. Helen was physically unable to bear children, but, understandably, took no interest in raising the girl. For the rest of his life, Howard gave Verda financial support. He visited her when he could (which was not often) and always sent a gift on Christmas, but it was a poor substitute for a full-time father. A mitigating factor was that, unlike many men in this situation, he acknowledged paternity and fulfilled some obligations.[77]

During 1935 and 1936, the Riverside Sanitarium moved slowly toward completion. The General Conference and the small black membership shared the cost. The General Conference, which had ultimate authority, entrusted the fundraising to Harry E. Ford, who was slated to share authority with Howard as general manager. Ford had a proven record of success. Few black members had achieved a similar level of prestige and authority in the Seventh-day Adventist Church. He had served for several years on the board of directors of Hinsdale Sanitarium and Hospital, an Adventist institution near Chicago that primarily served white patients. Although not a doctor, he had headed the X-ray and electrotherapy departments. Clearly, the General Conference expected him to keep a watchful eye for them. They were not quite ready to trust Howard with full authority.[78]

When it opened in February 1937, the Riverside Sanitarium rivaled Oakwood College as the greatest black achievement in the Seventh-day Adventist Church. But with a maximum capacity of just twenty-seven patients, it was a modest affair. The services included major surgery and such Adventist treatment methods as hydrotherapy and electrotherapy. An essential part of the mission was to advertise the health philosophy of Adventism. Smoking, of course, was banned. Patients were subject to a highly restricted menu of "grains, vegetables, fruits, milk, and eggs, without meat, tea, coffee, and condiments." Drugs as a form of treatment were discouraged. Also, the rules prohibited visitors from bringing them sugary foods. In promoting Riverside, Ford promised to emphasize "natural procedures rather than resorting to drugs, that nature and natural methods alone can restore the sick."[79]

To outward appearances, Howard had settled down nicely into his job as medical director. Adventist publications carried stories lauding his surgical feats, and he wrote a column on health issues for the newly founded *Message Magazine,* directed toward blacks. Many of his themes were familiar. He warned that the "human race is physically going down hill, and this very condition calls aloud for the Great Physician, and demands His second advent." Howard disagreed with the optimists who pointed to longer lifespans. True, the "feeble and infirm" lived longer than ever before but, when all was said and done, "the average man or woman has more illness in store and fewer years of health today than ever before in the history of the world." Finally, he reiterated that a longer lifespan for "mental defectives" made it easier for them to reproduce and pass down their hereditary flaws. To back up his claim, Howard paraphrased a "noted psychiatrist" who had argued that if insanity continued to increase at current rates, in two hundred years "this world will be one vast insane asylum."[80]

Although Howard seemed on track to becoming a key black leader in the Seventh-day Adventist Church, not all was right at the Riverside Sanitarium. He rebelled against the rules and restrictions imposed by the General Conference. He chafed at the idea of sharing power with Ford, who did not have a medical degree and owed his position in part to his loyalty. Howard was not inclined to play second fiddle in any organization—especially under these circumstances. He had definite opinions on how best to run the sanitarium, many not shared by his superiors. Frederick Crowe, a longtime black member of the Seventh-day Adventist Church, explained that "Howard was very progressive and he wanted more equipment. . . . And of course the General Conference didn't care to give Riverside too much money."[81]

Howard often rubbed administrators and colleagues the wrong way, but most acknowledged his unusually good bedside manner. In contrast to many doctors, Howard took time to speak with patients and ordinary hospital employees, listen to their complaints and recommendations, and express a genuine interest in their lives. Annabelle Simons, a nurse's aide at Riverside, states that he "was very open with his patients" and "would even so much as draw pictures of pathology" to help explain their ailments. Often his approach had amusing consequences, as evidenced by an unorthodox method of caring for postsurgical patients. The general rule, not only at Riverside but at other institutions, restricted patients initially to only drink water once they were able to swallow liquids. Instead, Howard prescribed ginger ale on the second day, a blatant violation of the rule banning sugary foods. When challenged by staff and colleagues, he retorted that he had always ordered ginger ale for his patients. "And if they don't have it," he vowed, "I will bring the ginger ale." The result was general consternation: "Here this little 'up-start' comes along and orders ginger ale on the second day after surgery," Simons comments. "Oh, they couldn't handle that."[82]

The most traumatic event in Howard's life during this period was the death of his mother, Mary Palmer. In July 1937 she had checked into Riverside Sanitarium for a routine hysterectomy. Howard performed the operation himself. Unexpected and shocking complications, however, led to her death. She was only forty-five. Howard had to take charge of the painful task of filling out the death certificate. He attributed her death to the nature of the operation as well as complicating factors such as anemia. Whether or not he blamed himself, the tragedy left him greatly depressed. Annie R. Walls, a friend from Murray, recalls that Mary Palmer's death "tore Theodore up so bad. . . . She was not supposed to have died." Her death created an added dilemma. She had cared for his daughter Verda ever since the death of Arzalia Wilson. Now the girl's future hung in the balance. This was not Howard's shining moment. He did not take her in—but then, Helen would not have allowed it. For a while, Verda went to live with Howard's grandmother, Almeda Chandler, but eventually she ended up with relatives on her mother's side in Detroit.[83]

Howard's life was in transition. A few months after his mother died, he resigned as medical superintendent. It was the climax of nearly continuous conflicts over patient care and other issues. Howard knew that even under the most optimistic scenario, Riverside had little prospect to be anything more than a small-time enterprise. It was hard enough for 150 black members of the Adventist Church in Nashville to maintain a hospital of twenty-seven beds, much less expand it. The four-mile distance from the center of the city was another obstacle to further growth. Quite naturally, many blacks preferred the closer and better-endowed alternatives such as the Hubbard Hospital and the Vanderbilt University Hospital.[84]

Howard's resignation did not yet entail a full break with Riverside. Because of the inability to find a suitable replacement, it continued to rely on his services for the next four years. As before, the church allowed him to use its city office to see his private patients in exchange for making daily visits to Riverside. His relationship with the institution had become almost wholly businesslike and contractual in nature. Howard no longer showed a special loyalty or emotional attraction to Riverside. To those who knew him, it was obvious that his remaining ties with the Seventh-day Adventist Church itself were barely more than nominal.[85]

After Howard resigned as medical superintendent, he finally had freedom to indulge other interests. He spoke frequently before churches and civic groups. After just a short time in Nashville, he was treasurer of the city's National Association for the Advancement of Colored People (NAACP). Joining him in the leadership was Charles S. Johnson, the president of Fisk University. Like his mentor Will Mason, Howard took some time off to visit Rochester, Minnesota, to attend classes at the Mayo Clinic. During this period, Helen Howard also cultivated an independent social life. Although she had no children, she was an official in the "Colored" Parent Teachers Association in Nashville.[86]

Predictably, the strains worsened in Howard's already tenuous relationship with the Riverside Sanitarium. Still unable to find a full-time superintendent, the General Conference relied on him almost by default for patient care. The situation was awkward for everyone. Howard clashed with Ruth Frazier Stafford, the superintendent of nurses. Stafford respected his abilities but resented his unbending attitude. More than sixty years later, she said that "he thought he was the 'whole cheese.' . . . He thought he knew it all." In January 1939 she complained to an Adventist investigator (who shared the general Adventist suspicion of medication as an "unnatural" treatment method) that Howard had typically prescribed "sodium Amytal and Nembutal, and often aspirin three times daily." Similarly, the investigator opined that he "felt it a reflection on his wisdom if sedatives were not given exactly as ordered." Stafford hoped for the day when "a consecrated Seventh-day Adventist Negro doctor could direct the medical work at Riverside."[87]

Another complaint was Howard's looseness in separating his personal interests from those of the institution. An investigator found it difficult to differentiate between the sanitarium's patients and his private patients on any given day. Even with these problems, observers from the General Conference and on the scene spoke highly about his skills. Dr. J. Mark Cox, who occasionally filled in for Howard during these years, praised his "commendable surgical and medical work" at Riverside and stated that the "patients were pleased with his services and his surgery was a complete success."[88]

Besides maintaining a private practice and working at Riverside, Howard was on the staff of Hubbard Hospital at Meharry Medical College. Annabelle Simons, who was also a nurse at the Hubbard Hospital, remembers that the interns "were just awed with his ability to operate and do such a beautiful job. And he operated very fast. And he knew his anatomy so well. I would hear them say, 'Boy, he knows his anatomy.'" During this period, Howard also taught health for a brief time at Tennessee A & I University (later Tennessee State University).[89]

In 1941 Howard's career took a dramatic turn. He accepted an offer from the International Order of Twelve Knights and Daughters of Tabor to be the chief surgeon at a hospital then under construction. It was in the all-black town of Mound Bayou, Mississippi, in the heart of the impoverished rural Delta. Despite past disagreements, he asked Ruth Stafford to come along as the hospital's head nurse. Stafford, ever the Adventist loyalist, declined.[90]

Howard later explained that he had taken the Mound Bayou job because the Mississippi Delta beckoned as an opportune "medical-missionary" field. If so, this would have been a departure from his recent profit-maximizing behavior at Riverside. Some have speculated that he left Nashville because his private practice was not a success. This is possible but also unlikely. Acquaintances in Nashville depict Howard (who never lacked for resourcefulness) as financially prosperous or, at the very least, comfortable during this period. Helen, who already missed the comparative racial tolerance and amenities of southern California, certainly did not want to go. Probably a sense of adventure drove the decision. Nashville, with its three black colleges and large professional class, had limited opportunities to stand out. As chief surgeon of the leading black hospital in the Mississippi Delta, Howard could start anew and carve out his own world.[91]

3

Fraternalist, Entrepreneur, Planter, and Segregation-Era Pragmatist

THE MISSISSIPPI DELTA was close to T. R. M. Howard's heart; so close that many came to believe that he had always lived there. Howard, who developed a habit of referring to "my Mississippi," had reason to feel a special bond. Within a few years, he had mastered his surroundings there and earned his fortune.

The Delta was a flat expanse that encompassed twelve Mississippi counties stretching from Tennessee in the north to Vicksburg in the south. The rich soil enabled farmers to produce more cotton (much of it of the highest quality) than any other place in the United States. In 1940 blacks were more than 70 percent of the Delta's population. Most lived in extreme poverty and worked as tenant laborers or sharecroppers. Despite their majority status, their disenfranchisement was nearly complete. Less than 1 percent of them were registered to vote in 1940. Some black-majority counties did not have a single black voter.[1]

The town of Mound Bayou in Bolivar County, in the heart of the Delta, stood out as an island of black self-rule in a sea of white supremacy. Founded in 1887 by two cousins, Benjamin T. Green and Isaiah T. Montgomery, the community had a fascinating history. Montgomery's father had helped to manage the plantation of Joseph Davis, the brother of Jefferson Davis. Mound Bayou soon earned a reputation as a haven for black entrepreneurship, self-help, and political rights. In 1911 Booker T. Washington praised it as a "place where a Negro may get inspiration by seeing what other members of his race have accomplished." Mound Bayou was one of a handful of towns in the South where blacks had voting rights (though not in the all-white and all-determining Democratic primary) and held office. Benjamin A. Green, a son of Benjamin

T. Green and a Harvard Law School graduate, was mayor from 1919 to 1961. After an early boom era, the town endured two decades of decline when cotton prices collapsed. By 1941 Mound Bayou had hit rock bottom after a fire swept through the business district. Through it all, the town remained a powerful symbol of black pride.[2]

Howard's new employer, the International Order of Twelve Knights and Daughters of Tabor, was probably the largest black voluntary organization in the state. Founded in 1872 by a group of ex-slaves in Independence, Missouri, it was not unlike other fraternal orders, both black and white, such as the Odd Fellows, the Masons, and the Polish National Alliance. It had rituals, colorful drill teams, and a network of lodges. Before the rise of the welfare state, fraternal organizations were leading providers of social welfare. Through a system of cooperative insurance, members and their families secured such services as medical care, employment information, and homes for the elderly. The statement of principles of the Knights and Daughters of Tabor, like that of countless other black and white societies, pledged to advance "Christianity, education, morality and temperance and the art of governing, self reliance and true manhood and womanhood."[3]

Since the 1920s, Perry M. Smith of Mound Bayou, like his father before him, had served as Chief Grand Mentor of the order's Mississippi jurisdiction. Better known as "Sir P. M." to ordinary blacks, he projected the image of a quiet and dignified aristocrat above the fray. Like Howard, Smith was visionary, but he never strayed from the single-minded goal of building and maintaining a hospital. After a decade of persistent lobbying, he persuaded the membership to authorize the project. From 1938 on each member paid an annual assessment into a hospital fund. To drum up support, Smith visited sharecroppers and tenants on plantations throughout Mississippi. One effective fundraising method was to ask individuals to contribute to the cost of a single brick. The hospital plan attracted five thousand new members in four years.[4]

In 1941 Smith, then sixty-three years old, asked Howard to be the chief surgeon for the Taborian Hospital. He was not the first choice. Smith had initially offered the job to Dr. Matthew Walker, a brilliant young surgeon in Nashville. Walker, soon to be appointed chair of the department of surgery at Meharry, had other priorities but recommended his friend, T. R. M. Howard.

In January 1941 Howard signed a contract to be chief surgeon at an annual salary of $4,000.[5]

Before the hospital opened, a key phase in Howard's life drew to a close. His mentor Will Mason died of Hodgkin's disease at age sixty-six. Although their relationship had endured strains in recent years, Howard had continued to speak with reverence about the man who had done so much to rescue him from life as a tobacco twister. In 1945 he confided that Mason had "died four years ago and I still mourn him."[6]

The opening ceremony for the Taborian Hospital in February 1942 attracted as many as ten thousand spectators, the largest gathering in Mound Bayou since Booker T. Washington's visit in 1912. Many black and white local notables gave speeches, but Howard's stood out. An article in the *Taborian Star*, the newspaper of the Knights and Daughters of Tabor, commented that "our Chief Surgeon . . . is also chief in speech-making." Blacks in the Delta had reason to celebrate. Their new hospital was a remarkable achievement. Final construction costs exceeded $100,000; the facilities included two major operating rooms, an X-ray room, a sterilizer, incubators, an electrocardiograph, a blood bank, and a laboratory. Besides Howard, two or three other doctors were on the staff. Annual dues of $8.40 (about $122 in 2018 dollars) entitled an adult to thirty-one days of hospitalization, including major or minor surgery, and a $200 life insurance policy. The annual membership fee for a child was $1.20.[7]

When the Howards came to Mound Bayou, they rented the second floor of the old Isaiah T. Montgomery mansion, then owned by the Knights and Daughters of Tabor. Their next-door neighbor was Mary Booze, who was not only Montgomery's daughter but a member of the Republican National Committee. She and Helen Howard became good friends. The wide gap in age and political attitudes (Helen was a Democrat) was insignificant compared to what they had in common. Both were popular daughters of socially prominent parents in a small black community. Helen gradually added to her circle of friends, mostly from the black upper crust in the area, but adjusting to Mound Bayou was difficult. She later confided that when her husband decided to move, she had "cried her eyes out" at the prospect. Once there, she saw no reason to change her mind. Life in the small town was bleak compared to Nashville's vibrant social scene.[8]

Under Howard's tenure as chief surgeon, the Taborian Hospital met with an enormous response. The Mississippi membership of the Knights and Daughters of Tabor mushroomed to nearly fifty thousand men, women, and children. Most were sharecroppers and farm laborers. Complete rolls of patients for four individual months between 1942 and 1945 are the only data that are available (338 names in all). Of these, 86.6 percent came from the four-county Delta area of Bolivar, Coahoma, Sunflower, and Washington. A few had traveled from as far away as Chicago. Although the members lived in one of the poorest regions of the United States, they were able to provide for their social welfare needs by pooling their resources. It is amazing that Howard had time for his work as chief surgeon. He delivered hundreds, perhaps thousands, of babies and performed about four major operations per day. In addition, he built up a profitable private practice. On Sunday and part of three weekdays, he saw his own patients at the Howard Clinic just across the street.[9]

Howard's medical practice was a springboard for the creation of other enterprises. He did not wait long to start. During his first year in Mound Bayou, he began purchasing land and livestock, including prize Poland China swine. Soon he added more than one thousand hens, three hundred turkeys, and assorted Holstein cattle, sheep, and walking horses. He bred ducks, geese, pheasant, quail, and hunting dogs. He eventually accumulated more than one thousand acres, placing him among the most prosperous black farmers in the state. Howard was faster than most to turn to mechanization. By the late 1940s he had invested extensively in motorized farm equipment, including seven tractors. But the conversion from manual labor was never complete. Even when mechanization reached its full extent, thirty-six families of tenants and sharecroppers still lived and worked on his land. At his clinic, he not only gave medical attention but dispensed vegetable seeds and pointers on the latest farming techniques.[10]

A consistency in Howard's life was his loyalty to family members. He did not hesitate to share his good fortune. He purchased a house for his grandmother, Almeda Chandler, the woman who had done the most to inspire him. His aunt also lived there. Howard hired his uncle, Henry Palmer, to manage his farm. All three apparently lived out their lives in Mound Bayou. His ten-year-old daughter, Verda Wilson, was not so lucky. She continued to live with relatives in Detroit. During the next decade, however, Helen allowed Verda to stay with the Howards for several summers. During these visits, Helen was polite but distant.[11]

Howard did not always have the Midas touch. He had a mixed record in farming, a field in which he had little experience. His tendency to plunge headlong into new endeavors often paid off but also led to some ill-considered decisions. His most spectacular failure was the purchase of a herd of Aberdeen Angus cattle worth $25,000. Edward F. Boyd remembers that the herd "died off like flies because . . . in the Mississippi Delta . . . there's not a blade of grass growing." Despite Howard's attempts at diversification, like most planters in the Delta, cotton continued to be his most important crop.[12]

As Howard rose to greater prominence and wealth, so too did the frequency and intensity of his clashes with the leadership of the Knights and Daughters of Tabor. In retrospect, a conflict between two powerful and determined men like P. M. Smith and T. R. M. Howard was almost inevitable. Howard was not about to take a back seat to anyone. He resented any interference with his discretion to treat patients. His ambitions were not only for himself but for the improvement of Mound Bayou and the Knights and Daughters of Tabor. For his part, Smith had fought hard to become Chief Grand Mentor and intended to retain that position. His ambitions almost exclusively centered on protection and expansion of the fraternal society and hospital he had struggled to create.

Local black power alignments helped to shape the contours of the factional battlefield. Mound Bayou's business and political elite had a predominant voice in the Knights and Daughters of Tabor. Mayor Green, for example, was the attorney of the order. Members of this elite were self-aware, confident, and proud. From their ranks had come the founders of a self-governing black town that had preserved its independence through hard times. They and their children were not about to cede power to an upstart outsider like Howard.[13]

Despite the obstacles that lay ahead, Howard quickly built up a following. He had an important advantage. For thousands of members, he, not Smith, represented the face of the Knights and Daughters of Tabor. When they came to "their hospital," they encountered a charming, prosperous, well-educated, self-confident, and hardworking doctor who treated them with respect and appeared to care about their problems. Howard also began to form alliances with elites both in the community and in the fraternal society. Smith's rise to the top of the Knights and Daughters of Tabor had also given rise to many critics along the way.[14]

Howard made his first move at the Annual Grand Session of the Mississippi Jurisdiction of the Knights and Daughters of Tabor in 1943. He pushed for an amendment to require a vote from the floor, rather than appointment by the Hospital Board, to select the chief surgeon. Of course, this would ensure Howard an independent power base. Just before the vote, a committee of arbitration, controlled by Smith's supporters, headed off the anxiously awaited showdown. It ruled in favor of Smith but gave Howard and his allies a concession by making the chief surgeon an automatic member of the Hospital Board. Both sides made at least an outward show of reconciliation. *The Taborian Star* declared that Smith and Howard "working together in harmony gives Tabor the best obtainable set-up and success will crown their efforts to operate the best hospital in the Mid-South." But an editorial in the same issue implied that this happy state of affairs would end if "the enemies of Tabor continue their efforts to transform a good surgeon into a master politician."[15]

For the present, Howard busied himself with another project: the building of Good Will Park, a recreation center for Mound Bayou and nearby communities. He raised the $40,000 in construction costs from a combination of white and black donors. The formal dedication of the park, located adjacent to the Howard Clinic, was on June 24, 1945. Howard had not lost his knack as a promoter. Featured speakers included Mayor Green and Walter S. Davis, the young and energetic president of A & I State University in Nashville. Howard's attempt to recruit the governor of Mississippi fell through, but none other than P. M. Smith served as master of ceremonies. *The Taborian Star* fulsomely praised Howard for endearing "himself in the hearts of the common-folk. His name is a by-word on their lips. He is indeed a benefactor to mankind. His motto is, 'Others.'" Howard's actions represented far more than blind altruism. Like any good entrepreneur, he showed alertness to the shifting currents of market demand. He realized that the potential patron base for a recreational center had greatly expanded because thousands of friends and family of patients were making overnight stays in Mound Bayou.[16]

The establishment of the park was a revolutionary event for a town that had appeared to be on its last legs just three years earlier. The amenities included an open-air dance pavilion, restaurant (the Green Parrot Inn), hard-surface tennis courts, an Olympic-sized swimming pool (the first ever for blacks in Mississippi), a large sand pile (trucked in by Howard) for children to play in, and a fish pond. Helen Howard did her part as the manager of the Green Parrot Inn, where waitresses clad in uniforms served barbecued chicken and beer to customers. Much of the food came from Howard's farm. The design reflected his philosophy that blacks were ready to patronize a "decent" restaurant that offered more than cornbread and catfish. Repeating the example of his mentor Will Mason, Howard even attached a small zoo to the premises that had monkeys, talking parrots (green, as in the Green Parrot Inn), and an alligator. The park's opening came just in time for Howard to announce completion of an eight-unit rental housing project of modest, but well-designed, concrete block bungalows. They featured such rarities, at least for many blacks in the Delta, as running water, indoor toilets, and electricity.[17]

Howard had not enjoyed this kind of national recognition since his first-prize victory in the Anti-Saloon League of America oratorical contest in 1930. A string of favorable articles appeared in the black press as well as publications such as the *Christian Science Monitor*. Most significant of all was one in the *Saturday Evening Post* by Hodding Carter. Carter, who lionized Howard as a "one-man uplift movement," was a valuable ally. As the publisher of the respected *Delta Democrat Times* in Greenville, he was the most influential white liberal in Mississippi. He supported expanded voting rights and equal treatment, but he kept within certain bounds. A "fair play segregationist," Carter wanted to implement "separate but *equal*."[18]

Howard's comments to the press showed that his philosophy had not greatly changed since his days as a columnist for the *California Eagle*. The main difference was that he modified his tactics to fit Mississippi's realities. As before, he stressed making the most of existing conditions. He admonished black youth to "see the green pastures of opportunity right here in Mississippi. Many things are not as they should be here, but I know of no place in all the world where everything is just as it should be." Howard described himself as a realist who recognized that the "Negro position won't undergo any basic changes in our lifetime."[19]

He suggested that it was "no use for the Negro to kid himself. We know that farming and housework and carpentry and crafts are what lie ahead of most Negro schoolchildren in the South." At the same time, Howard belittled any pretensions by Mississippi's schools to teach these skills as a "mockery." He did not propose a political agenda except in very general terms, recommending "hard work, an improved educational system" and "a practical application of the religion of Jesus Christ." Howard stated that he preferred leading by example "instead of putting all the blame on the white man." He had little use for "speech-making" about racial grievances because he was "too busy trying to do something about them." Howard envisioned Good Will Park as a showcase to illustrate how blacks were ready to spend their money on first-class recreation under conditions of dignity rather than fritter it away on juke joints, "dice games and the dark, filthy rooms in back." On the drawing board (at least in his mind) was a movie theater, a hotel, an auditorium for staging grand opera, and "a national memorial to Negro war veterans." Howard's dream was for Mound Bayou to recapture its past glory as a "progressive little city" and a model of black self-government.[20]

The publicity generated by Good Will Park made it easier for Howard to expand his business interests beyond Mound Bayou. His investments brought him slots on the boards of directors of the Universal Life Insurance Company and Tri-State Bank (both in Memphis). The president of both companies was Dr. Joseph E. Walker. In many ways, he and Howard were cut from the same cloth. Walker had risen from poverty to earn a medical degree from Meharry but chose a career in business instead. He organized the Universal Life Insurance Company in 1923, which eventually had capital of more than $1 million. In 1946 Walker gave Howard the opportunity to join the board of the new Tri-State Bank. From the start, it was one of the leading black banks in the United States. Along with Walker, the best-known board member was Lt. George W. Lee, a Republican Party kingpin in Memphis and author of the pathbreaking *Beale Street: Where the Blues Began.* Howard developed social and business connections with the Martin family, including Dr. W. S. Martin, who owned the Collins Chapel Hospital and the Memphis Red Sox (a team in the Negro Baseball League).[21]

Although fraternal and business matters dominated Howard's energy, he never lost interest in civil rights. In 1946 he sent a personal appeal to Claude Barnett, the head of the Associated Negro Press of Chicago, to publicize the case of Lever Rush. The authorities had executed Rush at 1:00 a.m. in nearby Cleveland, Mississippi, after a hurried and secretive trial that barred black spectators. His true crime, according to Howard, was a consensual sexual relationship with a white woman. Howard appealed to Barnett to ask the NAACP to investigate the case of another man in Indianola scheduled to be executed in the same electric chair for a similar crime.[22]

To top off his community and business accomplishments, Howard worked to bring a two-hundred-bed, all-black veterans' hospital to Mound Bayou. The prospects for getting it looked promising. World War II had created a need for a new hospital, and the Veterans' Administration regarded Mississippi as a logical location. Howard worked closely on this project with Smith and Mayor Benjamin A. Green. Percy Greene, the publisher of the *Jackson Advocate,* the most widely read black newspaper in the state, also gave his support. Greene had already won respect in national civil rights circles for his advocacy of voting rights. But there were complications. The national NAACP was dead set against another segregated hospital in the South, especially under federal sponsorship. In addition, whites in McComb, Mississippi, a city about eighty miles south of Jackson, wanted it in McComb instead. Measured by the raw calculus of votes and power, McComb had the upper hand. It was more prosperous than Mound Bayou and the majority of its citizens could make their voices heard in Democratic primaries.[23]

However, Mound Bayou's apparent disadvantages for segregationists suddenly turned to advantages from their perspective. The interests of an all-black town in Mississippi often coincided with the segregationist goals of white politicians. For many whites, the prospect of thousands of black veterans (some from the North) flocking into racially diverse areas of the state was a mixed blessing. Throughout the country, newspaper reports showed black veterans in the South asserting their rights in a variety of situations. The tripwires for conflict were especially common in larger racially mixed urban areas which had rigid systems of segregation in transportation and other services. If Mississippi was going to get a black veterans' hospital anyway, many segregationists concluded, it was far safer to put it in an all-black, relatively isolated small town. Howard knew this and adapted his arguments to accommodate such fears. He had fought tenaciously against segregation in California ten years earlier but even then pragmatism, rather than strict integrationist ideology, had taken precedence.[24]

In 1945 and 1946 Howard made an all-out push to bring the hospital to Mound Bayou. He advertised his exuberance by displaying a blueprint in the window of the Green Parrot Inn. Along with Smith and Green, Howard visited the office of U.S. Representative Will Whittington, whose district included Mound Bayou, to lobby for the hospital. They also made an appeal to Walter Sillers Jr., the speaker of the Mississippi House of Representatives and a fixture in state politics since the 1920s. Initially, both politicians were receptive to the idea.[25]

Even more fascinating were Howard's efforts to win over Representative John E. Rankin, the chair of the powerful Veterans' Affairs Committee, and Senator Theodore G. "The Man" Bilbo. In 1945 the two were the most notorious race-baiting politicians in the United States. Rankin's main claim to fame was his membership on the House Committee on Un-American Activities. The *Chicago Defender* and other black newspapers often quoted his crude racist and anti-Semitic tirades, which embarrassed even many segregationist colleagues. Nevertheless, in his ability to manipulate the fine points of congressional politics and procedure, Rankin was nobody's fool. On veterans' issues, Howard could not have picked a better person to cultivate.[26]

Bilbo was an even more infamous race baiter than Rankin. A former governor, he had won election to the Senate in 1934, and again in 1940, as a New Dealer. By the late 1930s, he had moved into the front ranks of southern racists. Bilbo championed a bill to use relief funds to promote voluntary migration of American blacks to Africa. His speeches and letters, much like those of Rankin, brimmed over with paeans to white supremacy. He boasted that he was "above the average and therefore better in every respect than the American Negro" and used the salutation "My Dear 'Dago'" in a letter to an Italian-American. His vitriol was notorious. By the end of 1946 he was increasingly on the defensive as Republicans and many liberal Democrats demanded his expulsion from the Senate.[27]

Howard made simultaneous written appeals to Rankin and Bilbo in June 1945, the same month that he presided over the dedication of Good Will Park. Rankin passed on the information to Sillers. Reassured that the staff and patients would all be black, Sillers ventured tentative support, reasoning that it was best for the hospital to be in "a Negro town or a Negro community in order to avoid friction." He did not bother to mention the needs and wishes of black veterans. He acted mainly out of fear that mounting medical demands by blacks were putting an unbearable strain on hospital segregation. Howard's persistence also paid off with Bilbo. Writing to Howard, Bilbo declared, "I think you are right. Mound Bayou is the best place in the world to build just such a hospital. If I can help in any way I will be glad to do it."[28]

But the days had ended when a segregationist imprimatur from the likes of Bilbo and Rankin automatically gave legitimacy to a federal project in the South. A decade earlier, such a hospital would have received nearly universal support from black organizations. By 1945, however, attitudes had shifted because critics of separate-but-equal accommodations had risen to positions of influence in leading civil rights and professional organizations, including the NAACP, the National Medical Association (NMA), and the Negro Newspapers Publishers Association. These opponents viewed a hospital as a dangerous detour from the road to integration. Dr. W. Montague Cobb, a professor of anatomy at Howard University and president of the Medico-Chirurgical Society of the District of Columbia, spoke for many of them. He equated "a new segregated hospital in the home state of Rankin and Bilbo" with "a long stride backward with seven league boots." Voicing similar concerns, an editorial in the *Chicago Defender* questioned the motives of Mound Bayou's leaders (in particular Mayor Green). It dismissed their plan as a parochial "Chamber of Commerce proposition" that would perpetuate "the stain of segregation."[29]

The critics gained momentum in the last months of 1945. They made public and private appeals to members of Congress, including Rep. William L. Dawson, one of two blacks in the House of Representatives. Cobb accompanied a delegation from the NAACP, the NMA, and National Negro Newspapers Association (the main black news wire service) to confer with General Omar Bradley, the head of the Veterans' Administration. Bradley's response did not encourage them. He expressed hope that segregation was slowly passing from the scene but averred that, in the meantime, local hospital managers had the right to enforce "social customs" of racial separation.[30]

As Howard and his allies encountered unanticipated obstacles in the North, resistance emerged at the grassroots from whites. They did not so much object to the idea of an all-black hospital in the state as to putting it in, or near, their communities. A prime fear was that it would foster black assertiveness. This animosity became apparent only weeks after other whites had promoted the idea. Sillers, and to a lesser extent Whittington, backtracked after representatives from the neighboring towns of Merigold and Shelby strenuously objected.

In a letter withdrawing his endorsement, Sillers explained to Rankin that if he had known that "there was any opposition to the negro hospital being located at Mound Bayou" he would have never pressed the idea. He fretted about "the consequences that might flow from the location of this hospital in this county where we have a population of about 75% colored and 25% white." Writing to Howard, Bilbo bluntly admitted that his need for white votes trumped black interests. He apologized but said he had to reverse course "because all my white friends in the immediate neighborhood of Mound Bayou have petitioned me to oppose it."[31]

These were serious setbacks, but the campaign for a Mound Bayou hospital still had a fighting chance. When whites in McComb objected to putting it in their community, the prospects began to improve again. An editorial in Mound Bayou's newspaper accurately observed that whites in McComb and elsewhere were treating black veterans as "'untouchables' or lepers so they must be thoroughly isolated, even from Negroes who would be glad to have them in their midst." Even Bilbo had to marvel at the fickleness and silliness shown by his fellow segregationists. A swaggering letter from J. H. Brent, a white state legislator from McComb, was especially hard to stomach. Brent lectured Bilbo that unless the hospital was kept out of his community, "you fellows will never receive the support you have had heretofore. This is not a threat, just a warning." Bilbo testily responded that originally "nearly all of the governmental and civic entities of the county petitioned me for its location but most of them have changed their minds." Bilbo was angry, but his first priority was to win the 1946 primary. He promised to help keep the hospital out of McComb.[32]

Confronted by opposition from integrationists on one side and hard-core segregationists on the other, Howard showed his mettle. He cleverly tailored his arguments to suit the concerns of both objectors. His letters reveal a subtle mastery of flattery and race sensitivities. Pragmatism was a consistent theme. He depicted a segregated hospital in the state as a *fait accompli*. Once this assumption was granted, he had an opening to both integrationists and segregationists to explain why Mound Bayou was the best location. Howard's approach was consistently audacious but somehow, through it all, he kept his integrity intact. His efforts to influence Bilbo were persistent, self-confident, and direct. He was playing fast and loose with stereotypes. Blacks in Mississippi rarely acted with such boldness toward Bilbo. The senator's voluminous surviving correspondence for this period includes few letters to and from black constituents, although he occasionally interceded on a personal level for employees and other subordinates.[33]

As usual, Howard led off with some ego stroking: "Now, Senator Bilbo as an educated white Mississippian and I an educated Negro Mississippian, we know our separate and mutual problems here in the Mississippi Delta better than people from any other section of our country know them." He cast himself in the role of a realist who understood that the "Mississippi Negro has to accept racial segregation as a basic principle by which both races in our state might make mutual progress." He then laid out the case for Mound Bayou as a model of separate development with its own schools, parks, hotels, and traditions of conservatism and stability. Howard deftly punched the right racial buttons by reassuring Bilbo that the town's leaders "can and will keep out any race friction with an all Negro hospital and all Negro personnel." Any interracial contact would be kept to a minimum, he volunteered, because the veterans and their families were going to stay in an all-black community.[34]

When Bilbo started to back down from his earlier statements in favor of Mound Bayou, Howard's response was to redouble his efforts. He was not a man to take no for an answer, even from Senator Bilbo. He visited the senator's office to make a face-to-face appeal. Bilbo's follow-up letter is a fascinating segregationist artifact from the period. Howard's charm had obviously left its mark. "When you were in my office sometime ago," Bilbo stated, "you impressed me as being a Negro that was on the square." He reassuringly, and predictably, claimed that he had "none of that prejudice that these damn New York Negroes and Jews talk about in my heart. I am really the Negro's friend." But it was more than the usual segregationist boilerplate response. Bilbo related that he had sent Howard's earlier letter to General Bradley, along with Bilbo's own positive letter of introduction. Describing Howard as a "good Negro doctor," it had asked that Bradley read over Howard's proposal "carefully and sympathetically." Bilbo's endorsement was not unambiguous, but it was pretty close. He was careful to cover his tracks, however, cautioning Howard to treat their correspondence with "the strictest confidence because I have been on the square with you and expect you to be on the square with me." He closed half-jokingly: "You and I are going to live in Mississippi a long time unless

I can persuade you that it is in your best interest to hang out your shingle in Monrovia, Africa." Coming from Bilbo that was quite a compliment.[35]

In contrast to Bilbo's reluctance, Rankin continued to champion a black veterans' hospital, although, for unexplained reasons, he shifted his preference from Mound Bayou to McComb. In March 1946 Rankin vowed to fight "the Communist Negroes from other states and a few long-nosed Communists who are from other countries" who were against the hospital. Rankin may have found it easier to take a stand because neither McComb nor Mound Bayou was in his district. Bilbo, by contrast, had to appease white voters throughout the state.[36]

Meanwhile, Howard waged a sustained campaign to win converts in the North. Both he and Mayor Green wrote passionate appeals to Congressman Dawson, a classmate of Green's wife. Howard also sent a letter to Adam Clayton Powell Jr., the only other black member of the U.S. House of Representatives. Powell's reputation was that of a militant integrationist, but he was receptive to Howard's pragmatic approach. Powell wrote to President Harry S. Truman in April 1946 favorably quoting Howard's description of the relative merits of Mound Bayou if Truman decided to go ahead and build the hospital over black protests.[37]

Howard also endeavored to persuade Claude Barnett of the Associated Negro Press. Few men had more extensive contacts with a broader range of black leaders around the country. As before, Howard prefaced his letter to Barnett with the assumption that a new segregated hospital in Mississippi was inevitable. Given General Bradley's statements on the matter, this was not an unreasonable conclusion. The choice, Howard wrote matter-of-factly, had narrowed to a "lesser of the evils" question of location. Unless Barnett took a stand for Mound Bayou, "thousands of Negro soldiers are going to suffer. . . . These soldiers have seen enough hell, why stand by and see them pass through more." He pointed out that McComb subjected blacks to a humiliating 10:00 p.m. curfew. In Mound Bayou they were free of such "petty insults" and had unrivaled freedom in the South to enjoy first-class "educational, health, and recreational facilities." Just as important, the community was on a major thoroughfare, Highway 61, and was a stop on the Illinois Central Railroad.[38]

Barnett did not need persuading. He responded that he supported the hospital because practical and immediate considerations took precedence over "the far off ideal of full integration." In his view, a hospital might actually subvert Jim Crow by standing out as "a shining beacon and lesson to the crackers about the capabilities of Negroes." Barnett prepared the way for Howard's visit to meet President Frederick D. Patterson and doctors at the Tuskegee Veterans' Hospital. After the trip, Howard reported that all had united behind the Mound Bayou location. Moreover, Barnett was able to soften the opposition from the National Medical Association. During a private conversation, E. I. Robinson, the NMA's president, admitted that if a black hospital was inevitable in the state, a Mound Bayou location made sense. Because the NMA had gone on record as "100 percent with the NAACP," however, he was unable to make his views public. Some of Robinson's compatriots were not so reticent. In March 1945 an open letter from C. Herbert Marshall, chair of the NMA's Board of Trustees, to an official of the Veterans' Administration touted the advantages of Mound Bayou over McComb.[39]

Leading Mound Bayouians predicted a great future when President Truman announced in March 1947 that the federal government had decided to build the hospital in their community. It was to be located only sixty feet from the Taborian Hospital and would have five hundred employees. The impact on the small community promised to be dramatic.[40]

By this time, Howard was not in the right frame of mind to share in the jubilation. Other events had turned his life upside down. In January 1947, the Taborian Hospital board voted against renewing his contract as chief surgeon. Howard and his supporters expressed shock. In retrospect, however, it is more surprising that the break did not happen earlier. Trouble between the Smith and Howard factions had been brewing for years. While the exact catalyst for the final rupture is not known, the underlying reasons were familiar enough. From the beginning, Howard had resented the Taborian Hospital board's limits on his authority. He regarded doctors, rather than lay administrators, as the best judges of patient care. There was also some discontent from members who grumbled that the leadership of the Knights and Daughters of Tabor had pressured doctors to show favoritism to relatives and friends.[41]

Howard's critics complained about his thriving private practice, especially his special fee arrangement with the Taborian Hospital. The rules required that patients for possible surgical care be examined first in the Howard Clinic. If they were not hospitalized, Howard collected a one-dollar fee. Because of the constant inflow of patients, the proceeds were highly lucrative. Many complained that it was unfair to members who had paid their dues to be charged yet again. For his part, Howard defended the arrangement as necessary to compensate for his low salary. He pointed out that the board had long been aware of this practice and, at least implicitly, had sanctioned it.[42]

In Howard's view, his long record of contributions to Mound Bayou's revival proved he could do the same for the Knights and Daughters of Tabor if given the chance. He considered the elderly Smith to be the representative of a parochial and cautious elite that lacked sufficient imagination to build on these successes. Howard's critics, on the other hand, feared that he had too much power. Their motivations were not just personal or factional. They saw little justification for abandoning "Sir P. M.," who had completed the Herculean task of financing and building a hospital in one of the poorest regions in the United States. Many complained that Howard's extended interests only detracted from his ability to serve patients properly in the hospital.[43]

Howard was not a man to go quietly in the night. His supporters formed "Your Committee," an informal group that drew heavily from dissidents in the second level of Taborian leadership, including Robert L. Drew, an undertaker in Clarksdale and a former candidate for chief scribe. The most visible member was Walter H. Fisher of Clarksdale, a Deputy Grand Mentor. Your Committee sprang into action by holding rallies and circulating petitions demanding Howard's reinstatement. The members warned that the Hospital Board's decision to hire a white doctor, allegedly for a higher salary, dangerously compromised black control. Their indictment broadened into a critique of Smith's leadership ability and character. They faulted him for dictatorial methods, nepotism, and favoring Mound Bayou's elite at the expense of the "little folk." Your Committee charged that the "Hospital does not belong to any one person, either P. M. Smith or Ben Green, but it is yours and ours." Fisher, in particular, proved a great asset because of his access to a radio station in Clarksdale, where he made regular pro-Howard broadcasts.[44]

The leaders of the Knights and Daughters of Tabor rallied their forces. They portrayed Howard as self-aggrandizing, guilty of "reckless expenditure of hospital money, failure to regard authority," and inattention to his duties because of his outside interests. Another accusation was that he had plotted since at least 1943 to take "over the affairs of the Knights and Daughters of Tabor and make it a one man organization." Smith's defenders depicted Howard as a professional failure whom the hospitals in Nashville had barred because of unethical practices: "Howard had nowhere to operate, hence he became broke and ragged and we found him." As far as can be determined, the latter charge does not hold up. Howard's file with the Mississippi State Board of Medical Examiners includes positive recommendation letters from several respected Nashville physicians. Dr. Edward Turner, the president of Meharry Medical College, stated that he had "good ethical standing" and that his work was "of good quality" while at the Hubbard Hospital. Echoing this assessment were letters from Dr. W. H. Faulkner, the secretary of Nashville's all-black medical society, and Dr. J. E. Sutherland, a classmate at the College of Medical Evangelists and the son of Adventist leader Edward A. Sutherland, who had once groomed Howard to be director of Riverside Sanitarium.[45]

After some brief hesitation, Percy Greene's influential *Jackson Advocate* came down firmly on Smith's side. Citing Edmund Burke's declaration against doctors meddling in politics, Greene questioned Howard's leadership qualifications. He editorialized that "one of the worst opinions and modes of thought among Negroes generally, and often discernable in doctors themselves, is an aura placed around the high earning requirements for the practice of medicine which credits the doctor with knowing more" than anyone else. Greene did not refer to Howard by name, but his meaning was obvious.[46]

Despite this spirited counterattack, Your Committee continued to make headway. It mobilized for the upcoming grand session of the Mississippi Jurisdiction of the Knights and Daughters of Tabor in November 1947 by putting up a full slate of candidates. Howard was not among them (perhaps for strategic reasons). To oppose Smith, Your Committee ran George L. Jefferson, an undertaker in Vicksburg, who was editor of the *Taborian Star*. Young, dynamic, idealistic, and respected, Jefferson was an attractive alternative to the quiet leadership of the elderly Smith. But, as far as everyone was concerned, he was still a stand-in. The *Jackson Advocate* observed that "the Jefferson support was really the support of Dr. Howard."[47]

It is almost impossible today to appreciate the importance of a grand session of the Knights and Daughters of Tabor to blacks in the Delta. Certainly, it was a far more meaningful participatory outlet than any available in the political realm. To put matters in perspective, more blacks usually attended the grand session than were registered to vote in the entire state. The stakes were higher than usual that year. Demonstrations before the meeting led to an unmanageable situation, or so the Smith faction alleged. At this point, the Chief Teller, Fred H. Miller, a powerful ally of Smith, asserted his authority. Miller, who headed the black version of the Mississippi Elks, asked that the white county sheriff count the votes. Miller further ordered participants to give the password to armed law enforcement officers guarding the door. The effect was to incense the insurgents and further reduce any chance that they would accept the results. In the end, Smith's control of the election machinery probably made the difference. The vote was surprisingly close, for he edged out Jefferson by 1,512 to 1,197. Smith's hold on power was never again seriously challenged.[48]

The aftermath dashed any hope for resolution. On the last day of the grand session, the dissidents marched to Good Will Park to proclaim "under the direction of God" their intention to organize a new fraternal society, the United Order of Friendship of America (UOFA) and to build a hospital. George L. Jefferson was Grand Worthy Master but, for undetermined reasons, Robert L. Drew soon took over. Howard was chief surgeon although everyone took it for granted that he was the *de facto* leader of the United Order of Friendship. In 1948 many Americans were turning away from traditional fraternal societies, but in Mississippi their appeal to ordinary blacks remained strong. In recognition of this fact, the founders turned their group into a virtual carbon copy of the Knights and Daughters of Tabor. They created separate lodges for men and women, a children's division, rituals, elaborate regalia, and an elite higher body for members with higher degrees, the Royal House of Media.[49]

Starting an all-black fraternal society and hospital from scratch was a tremendous challenge in the best of circumstances. It was even more of an uphill battle because of the need to rely on an impoverished membership base. The founders of the UOFA, however, wasted no time. They set out to raise $10,000 by Thanksgiving to qualify under the insurance laws and to convert the Howard Clinic and the Green Parrot Inn into a hospital. UOFA officials called on members to donate money for the purchase of equipment as well as to contribute "sheets, towels and pillow slips."[50]

They embarked on the daunting task of persuading enough people to take the risk of paying dues to an organization that, as yet, could not promise any benefits. As a stopgap measure, Howard used a black hospital in Memphis to serve the new members who needed major operations. Howard and his allies hired W. B. Alexander, a prominent white lawyer from Cleveland and a Bilbo supporter, to handle the paperwork and smooth the way. After meeting with Alexander and the organizers, Charles S. Snow, a white attorney from Jackson, urged the head of the Mississippi Department of Insurance to give speedy approval to the application. He advised that many planters wanted to bring order out of chaos and to ensure health care for their tenants. Obviously, a subtext was the fear that they would have to pay these costs. Describing the petitioners as "high-class colored citizens," Snow said it was better that "the element which is not satisfied with the Tabor organization be incorporated therein and leave the Tabor organization with a satisfied membership." Three months later, Sillers, at Smith's request, urged the commissioner to investigate whether the UOFA was violating state insurance laws. But, by that time, it was too late to stop it.[51]

The UOFA's greatest asset, of course, was Howard. A radio speech in 1948 weaved together flowery prose and biblical allusions. He compared the split from the Knights and Daughter of Tabor to "crossing the Red Sea of doubt and despair" and depicted the UOFA as the "promised land." After leaving the "fleshpots of old Egypt," a return to the fold was impossible. But Howard recognized the futility of continuing old factional battles. Noting the opportunities for all fraternal societies, he promised henceforth to "work in peace and harmony" with the Knights and Daughters of Tabor.[52]

Howard and his allies achieved their goals far more rapidly than many had predicted. The new Friendship Clinic opened in May 1948. By the end of the year, the membership had grown to about five thousand in 149 lodges. The UOFA offered essentially the same menu of hospital services as the Taborian Hospital, including major and minor surgery and obstetrics. Howard trained many of the nurses himself and took them to Memphis to pass the necessary tests for higher levels of certification. Many blacks found the Friendship Clinic to be an appealing health-care alternative. Howard had a reputation among his employees for high standards of patient care. Annyce Campbell, a nurse at the clinic, recalled that "if Dr. Howard came along and put his hand in the window, in any patient's room, and it was dust there, or dust on the blinds, then the Director of Nursing Services heard about it."[53]

Conflict between Howard and his opponents did not end after the formation of the United Order of Friendship but, as Howard had promised, it took
a less destructive form. Working as a faction of the Knights and Daughters of
Tabor, Howard's supporters could gain advantage only through electoral jock-
eying, lofty promises, and vilification. The creation of the UOFA, however,
encouraged a more constructive approach of competing in the marketplace to
woo consumers. The end result was that both hospitals had greater incentive
to take into account the needs and wants of patients.[54]

Just as the factional turmoil began to subside, the revival of Mound Bayou
suffered a setback. In January 1949 the federal government cancelled construction of the Veterans' Hospital. It said that it had previously overestimated
the need for beds. The official explanation seems believable, but it is natural
to wonder. A lot had happened in two years. In 1948 Truman had taken a
step away from federal Jim Crow by desegregating the armed forces. Mississippi's voters had solidly backed States' Rights Democratic (Dixiecrat) Party
candidates Governor Strom Thurmond of South Carolina for president and
Mississippi's own governor, Fielding Wright, for vice president. By 1949 Truman had little motivation to back a new segregated hospital in a state that had
spurned him.[55]

With or without the hospital, Howard's stock as a leader continued to
rise, at both the state and the national level. His name was even becoming
a marketable commodity. In 1948 he appeared in the *Chicago Defender* in
an advertisement for Pepsi-Cola, arranged by his brother-in-law Edward F.
Boyd, an executive with the company. A picture showed him in surgical garb
under the headline, "Leader in his Field." The advertisement said that he
had performed "more than five thousand major operations since 1942; Vice
President, Tri-State Bank Memphis; built and operates recreation center and
park for Mississippi Delta youth; cotton planter; breeds and shows prize live
stock." Also in 1948, David Cohn's study of the Mississippi Delta, *Where I
Was Born and Raised*, singled out Howard as a forward-thinking and dynamic
young surgeon who was striving to uplift the rural poor by promoting public
health and self-help.[56]

Much of Howard's success was due to a talent for building business and,
to some extent, social relationships with influential whites. This ability served
him well, especially in Mississippi. It was no small feat to simultaneously

charm the ultra-white-supremacist Bilbo and Hodding Carter, "The Man's" most vocal critic in the state. Howard forged particularly cordial ties with local Jewish businessmen in the Delta. He bought his cars from Ed Kossman, who owned a Buick dealership and headed the Cleveland Industrial Association. The two visited each other's homes socially, and Howard prescribed medicine to help Kossman's wife's headaches.[57]

At the same time, Howard was careful not to cross certain racial boundaries. Boyd remembers two revealing incidents. One time, Howard hustled Boyd out of the way when he saw him conversing with German prisoners of war on a white neighbor's land. Another incident involved a car accident. The driver, a white teenager, admitted guilt and seemed genuinely sorry. He offered to make partial restitution with the small amount of money he had on his person. Boyd demanded full compensation and prodded the boy for the names of his parents. Howard intervened in the conversation and accepted the offer. He advised Boyd that it was inviting trouble to draw in the parents.[58]

On other occasions, Howard was quite bold in his dealings with whites. But he picked his battles. He was more likely to assert himself with the better-educated, wealthy whites with whom he had business relationships of mutual benefit. An example was his encounter with Jere B. Nash, a white planter and farm implements dealer from the Greenville area. Nash had written a letter to a friend (with copies to Carter and Howard) criticizing the wording Howard had used for a mass mailing to promote the Friendship Clinic. Nash was particularly upset that Howard had referred "to an article written by Hodding Carter. Then in his third paragraph from the last, he gives Mr. N. L. Cassibry [the president of the Cleveland State Bank] as reference. I wonder why the discrimination." Many Mississippi whites considered the failure of a black person to use such a courtesy title as a major breach of Jim Crow etiquette. Sending a copy to Carter, Nash scribbled at the bottom: "Hodding looks like they take advantage at all times give them and inch & they always take a mile."[59]

Howard's letter of response to Nash (with a copy to Carter) was cleverly disarming. He composed it to accomplish two goals: first to firmly rebuke Nash and second, and more important, to flatter Carter effusively: "I had to read this letter over several times before I could get the point that you were attempting to make. I take it that you are resenting the fact that I referred to Mr. Hodding Carter, who I consider as one of the most outstanding writers of our age, a man I deeply respect, as a man who has the common decency to write me as Dr. Howard." He underscored the absurdity of Nash's complaint, suggesting that it was "taking a point in race relationship[s] much too far to attempt to prejudice my cause in trying to establish hospitalization for my people."[60]

Especially fascinating was Howard's rationale for omitting the courtesy title for Carter. Instead of taking the easy way out and pleading an oversight, he proudly stated that he had meant to do it all along. Howard explained that "the great writers of America—Upton Sinclair, Sinclair Lewis, Irving Cobbs, Lillian Smith and Hodding Carter—are usually referred to, even by Negro people in Mississippi, by the name that the reading public knows the individual." This rationale was inventive, if almost certainly disingenuous. But it served the purpose of allowing Howard yet again to heap flattery on Carter. Howard pressed his luck a bit farther in the last paragraph. He closed with a not so subtle threat by stating that it would be of "interest" for Nash to know that on his "small farm here at Mound Bayou, I have seven International tractors, and I have, over a period of years, done a very satisfactory (respectful) business with your office at Cleveland." Howard had played his cards well. He could not have hoped for a better reaction. Nash's courteous response seemed to concede his entire case. It was, like Howard's earlier letter, more than a little disingenuous. Beginning with the courtesy title "Dear Dr. Howard," Nash agreed that Howard "meant no disrespect to Mr. Carter." He had only sought to point out the problem, lest other "readers" misunderstand. And then Nash dished out some flattery of his own, commending the "splendid work you are doing at Mound Bayou."[61]

As Howard fought to gain status and respect in the business arena, his private life was less than ideal. He was living the life of a shameless philanderer. He had not always done so. Apparently, Howard had been a loyal husband at the beginning of his marriage. Even then, however, the couple had had difficulties. Helen's discovery that her husband had fathered an out-of-wedlock child, and kept it a secret, was an early sore point. Another was when they learned that Helen was physically unable to bear children. Howard probably did not begin cheating, at least in a major way, until 1945 (ten years after their marriage), when another out-of-wedlock daughter was born. After that, he cast aside nearly all hesitation. He fathered a third daughter in 1948, followed by two other daughters and a son. Remarkably, the last three were all born in a single year: 1951. Of Howard's five children between 1945 and 1951, only two were by the same mother. Even seventy years later, some who knew Howard as a pious and earnest young Christian in Murray and at Oakwood expressed disbelief when informed about his extensive infidelities.[62]

Uncovering the underlying causes of Howard's long march to serial adultery is an almost impossible task. He rarely, if ever, reflected on the reasons for his peccadilloes, much less his apparent aversion to using birth control. Beyond simple male passion, a few things can be said. Most obviously, he was repeating a pattern set by Will Mason, who, though a pillar of the community, had many affairs on the side. As Boyd puts it, Howard's adultery did not really begin in earnest until he was firmly ensconced as "lord of the manor." Clearly, Howard's ego entered into it. He may have looked on his many outside children as further confirmation of his manhood and a guarantee that his legacy would extend to future generations. Unlike many men in this situation, Howard acknowledged his children and tried to provide for them. He was probably the closest to his daughter Sandra, born in 1946, whom he helped send to Catholic school. Sandra's mother, Willie Morgan, was not a girl from the fields but the daughter of a respected grocer and the granddaughter of Mound Bayou's third mayor. She was an intelligent and determined woman. "Daddy . . . used to be down to the house all the time," Morgan remembers, "so I was pretty much familiar with him. . . . Helen, if she was looking for him . . . she would know where to find him."[63]

But there were limits to Helen's patience, and Howard knew it. He took care to maintain outward proprieties. Helen certainly knew what was going on, at least in a rough way, but she was prone to denial. She had grown to love her husband, and she was jealous and more than a little resentful. Nevertheless, she stayed with him. If the truth be told, she liked the lifestyle he gave her. Despite his many affairs, he always remembered anniversaries and never neglected to send flowers at the right time. In a typical gesture, he bought her a new Fleetwood Cadillac as a birthday gift.[64]

Howard had compelling reasons to take Helen's concerns into account. She was a woman of grace and charm who was an asset in any social situation. But their marriage was taking on the character of a business partnership. Howard's eldest child, Verda Wilson, observed the couple on a day-to-day basis during her several summer visits. They were civil with each other, but she came away with the impression that the marriage was based on "mutual understanding, for lack of a better term," and not "a lot of love." Totally left in the cold, of course, were the mothers of his children. Most never married. Though Willie Morgan had success as a businesswoman, she grew resentful. Later, she turned against Howard's daughter as well.[65]

Even as Howard's philandering spun out of control, he and Helen rose to greater prominence in black high society. Black newspapers in Mississippi and Tennessee often reported his, and occasionally her, activities. The couple frequently made the one hundred–mile trip to Memphis for dances and to take part in functions sponsored by Helen's sorority, Alpha Kappa Alpha. For a time, she was the president of the Mississippi State Medical Dental Auxiliary of the State Medical Association. For Helen, what made life in Mound Bayou tolerable was the relative proximity of Memphis. It was a far better social outlet than any to be had in the Delta. Especially after the closing of the Green Parrot Inn, she had little direct involvement in her husband's business and fraternal enterprises.[66]

Howard represented that rare example of a leader who was popular among both the masses and the cream of black society. Of course, it helped that a family friend, Jewel Gentry, was the society page editor of the *Memphis World*. Her columns often had glowing accounts about the memorable dinners and cocktail parties at "Goodwill Farms," the "spacious country estate" of the Howards on the outskirts of Mound Bayou. Prominent blacks both from Nashville and from neighboring Delta communities filled the guest list. Among them were A. Maceo Walker, an official in the Tri-State Bank and the son of Joseph E. Walker, and L. O. Swingler, the editor of the *Memphis World*. Gentry said the following about one of these genteel gatherings: "The yellow jonquils that surrounded the beautiful Howard estate gave some what a country appearance even though the neon signs and strings of bright lights led us right up to the drive, where we were led in by a coachman."[67]

Howard was basking in unprecedented professional and business success at the start of the 1950s. He proudly announced that Dr. John William Brown of Pittsburgh had donated $40,000 to update and expand the Friendship Clinic. Brown gave this money in honor of his sister Dr. Sara Winifred Brown, who had died in 1947. She had belonged to the Board of Trustees of Howard

University and had long advocated improved medical care in the Delta. The circumstances behind the gift are obscure, but it was no small feat. Howard was not far off when he boasted that it was "one of the largest philanthropic gifts ever made by a Negro in America to a Negro charitable cause." Brown's only stipulation was that the name of the Friendship Clinic be changed to the Sara Winifred Brown Memorial Hospital. Howard took the opportunity to score more points with Hodding Carter. He wrote to him that this gift was "the crowning results of the magnificent article which you wrote for the *Post* concerning my efforts at Mound Bayou four years ago."[68]

Once he had finally developed an independent financial base, Howard expanded his realm of influence. He aimed high. In 1950 he set out to overturn the leadership of the General Missionary Baptist State Convention of Mississippi, the leading black religious organization in the state. This seemed like an unlikely enterprise for a man who was still, at least nominally, an Adventist, but Howard had ample motivation to try. The longtime head of the conference, Reverend Harrison Henry Humes Jr. of Greenville, had been Howard's persistent critic through his newspaper, the *Delta Leader*. If any black man qualified as Howard's main nemesis during his remaining years in Mississippi, it was Humes.[69]

The two had crossed swords before. In 1947 Humes had used his position on the Taborian Hospital Board to support Smith's decision to fire Howard. Howard, in turn, had filed a libel suit for $50,000 after the *Delta Leader* had accused him of trying to bribe Humes to support renewal of his contract as surgeon-in-chief of the Taborian Hospital. The biographies of the two rivals actually had much in common. Both had risen far from modest origins. Humes had attended the Arkansas Baptist College and Jackson State College in Jackson. Like Howard, he had imbued a gradualist, self-help philosophy and built up a mass following because of a passionate, down-to-earth speaking style. Both were adept in the fine art of cultivating white support and patronage.[70]

Similarities aside, the two men had significant differences in outlook and style. Humes, who had spent most of his life in the Delta, could not rival Howard's cosmopolitan polish or acceptance in black high society. In his relations with whites, Humes invariably adopted a cautious, even obsequious, tone; any criticism he put forth was ever so gentle and nonthreatening. A case in point was his tenure during the late 1940s as head of the Committee for Better Citizenship. The goal was to ensure greater punishment for black criminals who committed offenses against blacks, a task often neglected by the criminal justice system. It was a worthy cause but ran almost no risk of creating white enemies. Howard entirely agreed with the goal, but it is doubtful that he would have adopted it as an overriding priority. Another reason for the Howard–Humes clash was generational. As Charles M. Payne observes, most blacks "born just before the turn of the century," such as Humes, who was nearly ten years older than Howard, "continued to behave as if they accepted the superiority of whites but seldom really believed it," but those "born in the early years of the century exhibited a great deal more resentment at their station in life." This can be taken too far, of course. In the early stages, the feud had no outward connection to ideology.[71]

In seeking to topple Humes, Howard combined personal ambition and a desire to bring more aggressive leadership to the conference. Asa G. Yancey, the chief surgeon of the Taborian Hospital at the time, described Howard as a hardworking and "energetic" doctor who had "good sound vision." In addition, he "looked ahead and planned things and attempted to make for a better community. But, I'm afraid Howard was number one!" Howard's strategy recalled his Taborian struggle. Rather than run himself, he backed another candidate, Rev. L. S. Sorrell of Clarksdale. Robert L. Drew, the Grand Worthy Master of the UOFA, gave pro-Sorrell radio speeches in Clarksdale. Humes counterattacked with every resource at his command, including articles in the *Delta Leader* and radio speeches. Howard and his allies had overreached. When the members of the General Conference voted in July 1950, Humes won handily. There would be no split this time, and Sorrell pledged to cooperate with the victors.[72]

The defeat must have stung, but in other respects Howard had a firm reason to be optimistic about the coming decade. He was independently wealthy, operated many profitable local enterprises, and sat on the boards of two of the largest black businesses in the United States. He had won national recognition in the black press for his medical abilities, entrepreneurial talents, and community leadership. Yet Howard was never one to sit still and be complacent. In the next few years, he set out to have an even greater impact as a crusader for civil rights.

4

A "Modern 'Moses'"
for Civil Rights in Mississippi

ALTHOUGH HOWARD CONTINUED to thrive as an entrepreneur, planter, doctor, and fraternal leader, his attention turned in the early 1950s toward concerns of racial injustice. It was a logical transition. Howard's core philosophy had not greatly changed since he had led the California Economic, Commercial, and Political League. What had changed was his economic situation. Howard's business and fraternal enterprises were finally on a firm foundation, thus giving him an unusual measure of economic independence. Accordingly, by the end of the 1940s, he not only had the motivation but the means to step up his fight for civil rights.

There were other reasons as well to make the move to civil rights. Economic changes in the state made the prospects for pursuing such a strategy seem brighter. Cotton was still king, but technological innovations, including the introduction of flame cultivators and commercially viable cotton harvesters, had the effect of eroding old habits, loyalties, and constraints. As mechanization spread, more blacks abandoned sharecropping and farm tenancy and left for northern and southern cities. Although a gentleman planter himself, Howard applauded this trend. He predicted that urban life would "make the Negro more resourceful." The decline of sharecropping spurred many black Mississippians to contemplate the injustices under which they suffered and to seek a better life.[1]

As the economic condition of blacks improved, so too did their legal status. White terrorism was receding. Throughout the 1940s, the NAACP recorded seven lynchings in the state, the lowest number since emancipation. Several factors were responsible, including a perception by the emerging middle and commercial classes that Mississippi's continued identification with the rope and torch tarnished the state's reputation and made it less attractive for business investment. The threat of federal antilynching legislation, even through never seriously pressed by Roosevelt or Truman, gave added reinforcement. According to Charles Payne, large southern newspapers by the 1930s "criticized lynchings, at least in principle. By the forties, their criticisms were clearly linked to fear of outside scrutiny."[2]

In 1952 something entirely new happened. The annual survey by the Tuskegee Institute did not record a single lynching in the South. Some softening was similarly apparent in the criminal justice system. For the first time since the nineteenth century, blacks served on juries in Natchez and Greenville and as policemen (albeit confined to black neighborhoods) in Indianola and Biloxi.[3]

Meanwhile, blacks flexed their political muscles, but carefully and cautiously. Between 1940 and 1953, NAACP membership rose from 377 to 1,600. What's more impressive was that black voting registration (never more than 6 percent of the total) soared from 2,000 to 20,000. Overseas service in World War II, greater economic well-being, and time spent in the North nurtured attitudes of political assertiveness. As Howard observed, blacks "who thought they were happy on the plantations of Mississippi have gone North to visit a friend or a relative" and found them "eating better, living in a better house, wearing better clothing, having more spending money, children going to schools and above all having a freedom of mind."[4]

It was the Regional Council of Negro Leadership (RCNL) that came to embody Howard's views on civil rights. He had proposed the group's formation in November 1951 at the annual conference of the United Order of Friendship of America (UOFA). Ironically, the original stated goal was to create a black version of the powerful all-white defender of the established order, the Delta Council, an "oversized chamber of commerce" for the upper crust of business interests and planters. With some success, Howard sought to mollify potential white suspicion by adopting a conciliatory and nonthreatening tone. He pledged to shun demands for "social equality" and to work "hand in hand" with "our Southern white brother." He also proclaimed that "things are getting better all the time for Negroes in Mississippi."[5]

Howard did not explicitly endorse "separate but equal," but his proposals were consistent with that framework. He pushed this framework, however, nearly to the breaking point. At the same time, he took care to reassure whites:

"All I ask is that we be consulted on matters that affect members of our race. We are not organizing to work against our white citizens . . . but to work with them." He called for greater black representation in the leading economic and political agencies such as the Mississippi Farm Bureau. His rhetoric about imitating the Delta Council notwithstanding, the organizational design owed more to Booker T. Washington's uplift philosophy, perhaps combined with a dose of W. E. B. Du Bois's doctrine of the talented tenth, than any white model. Instead of starting from the grassroots, Howard insisted that the mission of his new group was to harness the talents of proven leaders in business, the professions, education, and the church. Put succinctly, his goal was "to reach the masses through the chosen leaders of the masses." In essence, he was suggesting a refined model of the old California Economic, Commercial, and Political League.[6]

The media response to Howard's plan was overwhelmingly positive, particularly in the Memphis newspapers that also served the Delta area. In a rare point of agreement, the black *Tri-State Defender* and the white *Commercial Appeal* showered praise on the RCNL. According to the *Appeal*, Howard had "won international acclaim for his efforts to improve health conditions among Negroes" and "the council's sponsors will meet the challenge and come out triumphant."[7]

Howard cast a wide net in his invitations to the organizational meeting for December 28, 1951. He sent out five hundred letters to blacks in the Delta who represented a broad cross-section of leaders in business, fraternal societies, higher education, farm demonstration programs, churches, and veterans' groups. But his impulsiveness and wishful thinking helped set the stage for trouble. In words that he later regretted, he forcefully implied that the white Delta Council had given its stamp of approval. He may have read too much into earlier conversations with council officials.[8]

Hopes for an "equal partnership" with the white Delta Council unraveled by the end of December. The whole idea was probably doomed from the start. When Howard first made his proposal, white Delta Council officials had reacted with a mixture of suspicion and cold politeness. Contention immediately arose over the original suggestion for a name, the Delta Council of Negro Leadership. In a letter to Howard, council official Maury S. Knowlton stated that lawyers had told him the similarity might create confusion for state chartering agencies and thus undermine the "good will between your new organization and the membership of Delta Council." Eager to appease Knowlton, Howard beat a rapid retreat. He pledged to drop "Delta" from the name, ultimately substituting "Regional," and invited white Council officials to attend the organizational meeting in late December.[9]

The first meeting of the RCNL revealed how much Howard had over-estimated the prospects for white-black cooperation. Both Senator James O. Eastland and journalist Hodding Carter turned down invitations to speak. The most influential white person there was B. F. Smith, the manager of the white Delta Council, and his speech was, at best, lukewarm. While neither endorsing nor opposing the organization, he angered many of those present by stressing that the "Delta Council is not sponsoring this organization and has never authorized the use of its name for that purpose. This announcement is made because of misleading statements which have appeared in the press."[10]

Little did Smith realize what he was doing. Aaron Henry, a cofounder and key figure in the RCNL, later wrote that Howard had not conceived "our council as a civil rights group. . . . But with the strife with the Delta Council, we emerged as an organization opposed to the established system." This was an exaggeration. From the onset, the RCNL had endorsed civil rights causes such as voter registration and a more equitable school system. Moreover, even after the December meeting, Howard did not burn his bridges (such as they were) with the Delta Council, continuing to laud it as "one of the truly great organizations in the state." But while eager to be cordial, Howard was not willing to accept a second-class role. He vowed that if the two groups cooperated, it was going to be as "full partners" and the RCNL was not "going to 'Uncle Tom' and come in the back to the Council table."[11]

Both before and for some time after the falling out with the Delta Council, Howard was fairly consistent in outlook. While he did not directly challenge "separate but equal," he zeroed on the need to guarantee the "equal." Education as a means to end the second-class status of blacks was the top priority. Howard considered inadequate schools to be the primary reason for the northern black exodus. Instead of demanding integration, he called for equal school terms for both races. In Mississippi, the law guaranteed whites eight months while blacks had to settle for less. Howard proposed striking "white" from the state educational law and replacing it with the clause: "Each child, regardless of race, creed, or color, shall be guaranteed eight months of school in each year." He belittled the existing black schools as a "mockery to the word education," pointing out that five thousand white children in Bolivar County had eight well-equipped high schools while ten thousand black students had two substandard ones. At the time, the state spent an average of three dollars for each white child compared to one dollar for a black child.[12]

Howard condemned unequal punishment for crime as a glaring example of "separate but never equal." With a combination of outrage and sarcasm, he underlined the hypocrisy of white men who so readily resorted to mob violence to defend southern white womanhood from black sexual assaults, either real or imagined, but did nothing to stop whites "who pester, bother or rape Negro girls." He said that blacks must never forget "the shame, reproach and disgrace which has been forced upon Negro womanhood in our State," citing three recent examples, including the rape of a twelve-year-old babysitter by a white man that went unpunished. Another facet of unequal treatment was the failure of the courts to punish crimes committed against blacks by other blacks. Agreeing with many conservatives, like Humes, he argued the "greatest danger to Negro life in Mississippi is not what white people do to Negroes but what the courts of Mississippi let Negroes of Mississippi do to each other." He complained that a black killer of a black victim often did not suffer any punishment and rarely went to the electric chair. If he lived on "a big plantation and is a good worker and especially, if he is liked by white people, the chances are that he will come clear of his crime."[13]

Howard's opposition to institutionalized racial supremacy coexisted with, and often complemented, deeply conservative views on fundamental principles. He was not a deep philosophical thinker but rather had no affinity for grand social schemes. While he flirted with black nationalism of a certain type, he never embraced full-blown group consciousness. He invariably expressed admiration for American founding principles, as well as the founders. "There is not a thing wrong with Mississippi today," he flatly declared, "that real Jeffersonian democracy and the religion of Jesus Christ cannot solve." Deep down he was confident about the potential of blacks, when given the opportunity, to overcome prejudice and thrive by practicing the Franklin-esque virtues. He pointed to Jackie Robinson, whom he deeply admired, as an example of a man who "does the job so well that the world forgets that his skin is black. Young people let efficiency and service be your watch word and making money will take care of itself." [14]

Given his longtime belief in self-help, Howard unflaggingly supported black entrepreneurship. Maintaining that the "economic security of the race is tied up in the Negro's support of Negro business," he regarded the other-worldly emphasis of some churches as deeply problematic. He found no encouragement in the fact "that the religious songs that the Negroes like best are, 'Take all this world, but give me Jesus' and 'A tent or a cottage—why should I care, they are building a mansion for me more over there.'" He admonished ministers to start preaching a more practical message of proper diet and "the fabrics of cotton, wool, nylon, rayon, velvet, furs and leather while we are preparing for our golden slippers." They needed to realize that to move forward in this "industrial age, thrift, industry and business efficiency must become an integral part of the Negro's religion." [15]

As war raged in Korea and Senator Joseph McCarthy was at the height of his influence, Howard left little doubt where he stood on the issue of Communism. He wished that "one bomb could be fashioned that would blow every Communist in America right back to Russia where they belong." He pointed with pride to the failure of the Soviet Union to exploit civil rights grievances, stating that blacks were "not interested in any 'Isms' but Americanism." Like many civil rights defenders during the period, he used the specter of Communism as a cautionary lesson. If not dealt with, he predicted, continued mistreatment of blacks could jeopardize victory in the Cold War. Although "America is a Christian nation, a nation that Almighty God has blessed . . . the cause of Democracy is shuddering throughout the world today because of the inequality of Democracy in regards to Negro rights." But as if to reassure whites, he promised that blacks had no interest in "social equality" but added that "we are terribly concerned about equality at the ballot box, equality in education, equality in the courts of the states, equality in the protection of our homes and equality in chances to make our daily bread." [16]

Howard did not entirely discount white claims that many in his race lacked sufficient skills to exercise responsible self-government. In fact, he said that 50 percent of the black population was in that category. But then, he argued, at "least 20% of the white people of our area are not prepared for first class citizenship, yet they enjoy all of the privileges of the ballot box." His recommended solution was not to restrict the franchise but to deploy institutions, such as the Delta Council and the RCNL, "to guide our people in their civic responsibilities regarding education, registration and voting, law enforcement, tax paying, the preservation of property, the value of saving and in all things which will make us stable, qualified conscientious citizens."[17]

Howard thundered about the hypocrisy and other consequences of this racial double standard: "Black soldiers from Mississippi are fighting and dying for a democracy they don't know one single thing about back home." He had no patience with whites who claimed to have special expertise because they had a "mammy" or were raised around blacks. In the first of many quotations reprinted in *Jet* in December 1951, he ventured this suggestion: "You have to be a black man in Mississippi at least 24 hours to understand what it means to be a Negro in Mississippi."[18]

From the moment of its creation, the Regional Council attracted many individuals of ability and prestige. Naturally, the original core drew heavily from the UOFA. They included Robert L. Drew, the Grand Worthy Master of that organization, George L. Jefferson, P. M. Smith's election challenger in 1947, Edward P. Burton, the assistant chief surgeon at the Friendship Clinic, Amzie Moore, a NAACP activist from Cleveland and a gas station owner, and Adam Newsom, the UOFA's Grand Worthy Chaplain. For many, it was their first exposure to civil rights and would serve as a training ground. Moore, Drew, and Burton, for example, became prominent civil-rights activists during the 1960s.[19]

The RCNL also had an interlocking directorate with the Magnolia Mutual Life Insurance Company. Howard had purchased a controlling interest in 1951. During the next two years, the value of the company's insurance, which was written mostly for poor blacks, increased manyfold. Eight of the RCNL's eighty-three officials served on the Magnolia's board of directors. Moreover, of the six top officers of the RCNL, four were directors of the insurance company. Howard was particularly close to Aaron Henry, an NAACP activist, who was secretary of both the RCNL and the Magnolia. Henry's drugstore in Clarksdale often filled prescriptions for patients of the Friendship Clinic.[20]

The Magnolia Mutual Life Insurance Company was also the conduit that brought Medgar Evers both to the RCNL and to the broader Civil Rights Movement. Evers first came to Mound Bayou in July 1952 upon graduating from Alcorn College in Jackson. He was hired by Howard to be one of the company's salesmen. Very shortly thereafter, Evers threw himself into civil rights work by becoming the program director of the RCNL. His brother Charles, the manager of a funeral home in Philadelphia, Mississippi, also joined.[21]

Seven relatively autonomous committees, each headed by a respected black leader in business, education, the church, or the professions, formed the backbone of the RCNL. Howard's close allies chaired the Committee on Race Relations (Burton), the Committee on Voting and Registration (Levye Chapple), and most important, the Committee on Separate but Equal (Henry). The goal of this last committee, according to Henry, was to "get an equal share of every dollar" and to "settle for nothing less than a 'dollar-for-dollar, brick-for-brick distribution of revenues' among Negro and white." The committees reported to an executive board headed by Howard who was also the president. To build mass support and give each leader a greater stake, business meetings took place in different locations each year. The rules stipulated that each town with at least one thousand blacks be entitled to representation.[22]

This organizational design ensured that the RCNL had broad geographical representation. Only eight of its eighty-three officers were from Mound Bayou. The rest came from every section of the Delta. Among them were at least two college presidents, Arenia Mallory of Saints Junior College in Lexington and J. H. White of Mississippi Vocational College in Itta Bena. With the exception of Fred H. Miller, who briefly belonged to the RCNL's Committee on Race Relations, prominent Taborians were conspicuous by their absence. The heads of two key fraternal societies in the state, the Elks and the Afro-American Sons and Daughters, were on the list. The latter group operated Mississippi's largest black hospital in Yazoo City.[23]

A striking pattern of the RCNL's leadership was the low number of clergy. This characteristic set it apart from such groups such as the Montgomery Improvement Association led by Martin Luther King Jr. Only seven of the RCNL's eighty-three officers were ministers and none of these among the top six leaders. Far more important were undertakers, entrepreneurs, professionals, doctors, druggists, and owners of small farms. This was probably not an accident. Although Howard's speeches resembled those of a Baptist preacher both in style and in content, he had always emphasized business and the professions, not the church, as the vanguards of future success. Even if he had felt otherwise, his Adventist affiliation, which had weakened by the 1940s, made it difficult to cultivate close ties with ministers. His history of bad blood with Humes, still president of the state's General Baptist Convention, certainly did not help.[24]

Special conditions in the Delta also served to undermine the participation of the clergy in civil rights. The life of a typical minister did not foster outside involvements. The full-time minister with a large congregation, fairly common in urban areas, was rare. An undertaker, fraternal official, or medical doctor had contact with a larger swath of the masses. Even many successful Delta ministers lacked the independence or the time to take on outside roles. Most either earned their main income from other occupations, such as farming or undertaking, or were leading a hectored, hand-to-mouth existence as pastor of several churches. Especially in rural areas, they heavily depended on whites for money and getting access to plantations. Much like the clergy, black educators, including college presidents and school principals, were highly vulnerable to the dictates of white patrons.[25]

As the experience of the RCNL suggests, historians have not adequately appreciated the importance of businesspeople and professionals as pioneers in early civil rights movements (especially in Mississippi). By affiliating with the RCNL, these men and women were pursuing a practical, though much belated, application of the Washingtonian dictum that the growth of voluntary associations, self-help, business investment, and property ownership was the best precondition for civil rights. On this score, Charles Evers speculates that the self-employed individuals in the RCNL were effective because of a greater ability to draw on independent resources when confronted by outside pressure: "We couldn't afford to work with no white folks. They'd fire us," he remarks.[26]

The role played by the rank and file is difficult to discern. Estimated membership ranged from a low of five hundred to as many as four thousand. The higher figure is plausible, at least for the later period. In 1954, for example, a business meeting of the RCNL attracted two thousand delegates. Even so, the written and oral records show almost no evidence of functioning chapters at the local level. The RCNL's local work appears to have been loosely organized and sporadic. The main contact with ordinary members was either through the committees or at the business and annual meetings. This structure, of course, was consistent, at least in theory, with Howard's vision of creating a leader-centered organization.[27]

The probable scarcity of dues-paying members makes it difficult to assess where, and how, the RCNL obtained its funds. Certainly, it had expenses, for the RCNL did not stint in lavishing free food and entertainment on the many thousands who flocked to its meetings. The ad hoc nature of the local day-to-day activities makes it unlikely that regular dues paid much of the bill. According to Henry, "Money was a problem at first, but then funds came from dues and public appeals and passing the hat at meetings. After the group was well established and publicized, we were able to rely on contributions from all over the country."[28]

The dearth of chapters or a large dues-paying membership did not mean that the RCNL lacked impact at the local level. The best-known members promoted civil rights at the grassroots through an amalgam of organizations. Some overlapped so closely with the RCNL that they were de facto affiliates. In Clarksdale, for example, Aaron Henry (assisted by fellow RCNL stalwarts such as Robert L. Drew) headed the local chapter of the Progressive Voters League since 1946. Henry used this position to press for greater voting rights, better treatment in the courts, and improved facilities at black schools. Other RCNL members worked through the Mississippi Negro Democrats Association. The importance of Howard's United Order of Friendship should not be underestimated. The dozens of lodges in the Delta not only provided meeting places for the RCNL but opportunities for people of like mind to exchange ideas.[29]

On the local level, the RCNL acted as a kind of advance guard for the NAACP. It was a vehicle for such NAACP leaders as William A. Bender, the chaplain at Tougaloo College, Emmett J. Stringer, a dentist in Columbus, and Dr. Clinton C. Battle, a physician in Indianola. During the 1940s, many blacks had avoided identification with the NAACP out of fear of angering whites, many of whom considered it a Communist front. As late as 1949, it had only three branches in the Delta and just one had more than thirty people on the rolls. The advent of the RCNL in 1951, however, emboldened blacks to take the risk of open participation in the NAACP. Henry and Drew took the plunge in 1952 by forming a branch in Clarksdale. During the next three years, RCNL members in Columbus (Emmett J. Stringer), Belzoni (George W. Lee and Gus Courts), and Cleveland (Amzie Moore) followed suit.[30]

The help of RCNL member Percy Greene was critical to building this momentum. Because he published the *Jackson Advocate*, his support carried great weight with proponents of civil rights. Throughout the 1940s, often at considerable risk, Greene had used the *Jackson Advocate* to champion voting rights and equal treatment for blacks. The *Chicago Defender* named him to its honor roll in 1946 for exposing the intimidation of black voters during the Bilbo campaign of that year. Shortly after the election of 1948, Greene had founded the Mississippi Negro Democrats Association to register blacks and encourage participation in the state's Democratic primary.[31]

Greene, a board member of the RCNL himself, devoted a page of small type in the *Jackson Advocate* to reprinting an entire speech by Howard. An article stated that the roster of the RCNL "reads like 'Who's Who' in the state of Mississippi including . . . the great majority of the most widely known, active, forward looking, and successful business and professional men, farmers, educators, and religious leaders of the state." In 1953 the *Advocate* was still praising Howard as "a high type Christian gentleman" who was "dynamic, forceful, courageous, and well informed." The two men had not always seen eye to eye. As a longtime booster of the Taborians during the 1940s, Greene had taken sides against Howard in the factional split. But his views quickly changed after the formation of the RCNL, an organization that espoused causes he had long held dear: voting rights, economic self-help, and equal treatment.[32]

During the 1952 U.S. presidential campaign and later, Howard identified with the Mississippi State Democratic Association. His greatest coup was to persuade U.S. Representative William Dawson of Chicago to be the featured speaker at the first annual conference of the Regional Council of Negro Leadership. No other black congressman had spoken in the state since the nineteenth century. While it was not a campaign appearance as such, Dawson, a member of the National Democratic Committee, probably accepted because it contributed to his longtime goal of expanding national black support for the party. As if this was not enough, Howard arranged for singer Mahalia Jackson to provide the entertainment.[33]

Even Howard's adversaries had no choice but to acknowledge his achievement. Mayor Green, a classmate of Dawson's at Fisk University, accepted the
invitation to ride in the lead car in a parade down Main Street (Highway 61)
that kicked off the festivities. Black schools and colleges contributed three
marching bands. Helen Howard served as official hostess for the crowd, who
ate meals on the lawn of the Friendship Clinic. An estimated seven thousand blacks crowded into a giant circus tent to hear the speakers. Most black
high schools in the state closed and encouraged students to attend. Dawson's
speech was moderate and conciliatory. He cautioned that "we have no right
to expect leaders in politics to commit political suicide by defending us when
we will not support them with our votes." The event put another feather in
Howard's cap. An editorial in the Memphis *Tri-State Defender* lauded him
as "a modern 'Moses' in leadership and inspiration" who had mastered the
art of "translating the truth in terms acceptable to the dominant group." The
"dominant group" did not seem overly concerned. Although a prominent
white lawyer, J. C. Feduccia, who had represented Howard in his dealings
with state insurance officials and in his libel suit against Hume, welcomed
Dawson on "behalf of Mississippi," whites played almost no role and showed
little interest. Despite the great crowds, most newspapers in the state did not
even mention the meeting.[34]

Dawson's speech was the first of several annual grand events that came to
be hallmarks of the RCNL. Each, in the words of Myrlie Evers, was "a huge
all-day camp meeting: a combination of pep rally, old-time revival, and Sunday church picnic." This was the same strategy Howard had pursued with such
vigor during the 1930s. Standard features were a big-name national speaker
from the North, musical performers, and liberal helpings of food and refresh-
ment. To achieve maximum impact, the UOFA held its annual conclave just
before the RCNL event. Attendance was a life-transforming experience for
many younger and future civil rights leaders such as the legendary Fannie
Lou Hamer. "Everyone would gather there," Charles Evers recalls, "and had
something like a festival. And we had music, gospel and blues."[35]

Fortified by his relationship with Dawson, Howard deepened his participation in the Democratic campaign. In August, for example, he and fellow RCNL officials Charles C. Stringer of Clarksdale and Levye Chapple of

Greenville attended the national Democratic Party convention as "observers on behalf of the Mississippi Negro Democrats Association." Although they were not delegates, they anticipated in a small way the attempt to be seated by Hamer and the Mississippi Freedom Democrats at the 1964 national convention. A few weeks before the 1952 election, Howard met with Dawson at a Democratic Party gathering in Washington, D.C. He also showed sensitivity to black Republican concerns by carefully promoting the RCNL as nonpartisan.[36]

Throughout this period, Howard grew closer to his employee and civil rights protégé, Medgar Evers. Evers's wife Myrlie worked as a typist for the company. Later, Howard delivered their first two children. Her vivid description comes as close as any to capturing the essence of the man. He had "a friendly smile, and a hearty handshake, and there was about him an aura of security so lacking among the vast majority of Negroes in the Delta that he stood out as different wherever he went." But she acknowledged that not all blacks shared her assessment. Some "resented Dr. Howard's wealth, but on the whole he was viewed as a brave man, a spokesman for the Delta Negroes, and it was widely believed that he had at least some influence with the white plantation owners."[37]

Although Medgar Evers lived in Mound Bayou, his insurance territory for the Magnolia Mutual was twenty-five miles to the north in Clarksdale. He sold both hospitalization and life policies and collected premiums weekly. He entreated his customers (probably with Howard's encouragement) to join the NAACP and attend RCNL rallies. Most of them lived in extreme poverty. Myrlie Evers says "here, on the edges of the cotton fields, life was being lived on a level that Medgar, for all his acquaintance with the poor of both Mississippi and of Chicago's teeming black ghetto, found hard to believe." Medgar Evers played a key role in one of the RCNL's earliest initiatives in 1952, a boycott of service stations that failed to provide restrooms for blacks. It distributed an estimated fifty thousand bumper stickers with the slogan "Don't Buy Gas Where You Can't Use the Rest Room." A likely influence was the example of the "Don't Spend Your Money Where You Can't Work" slogan first popularized during Howard's days at the *California Eagle*. The demand for gas stations to provide restrooms for blacks, though consistent with the doctrine of separate-but-equal, was risky in the context of Mississippi. In the middle of the campaign, the RCNL discovered that the slogan might violate anti-boycott laws, and so it was revised to "We Don't Buy Gas Where You Can't Use the Restroom."[38]

This campaign galvanized ordinary blacks in the Delta. The RCNL had picked its target well. Blacks were in a position to exert leverage because, as Howard pointed out, they were nearly as likely as whites to own cars. Throughout Mississippi, Henry remembers people pulled in to "service stations and asking in the same breath for gas and to use the washroom. They would drive off when told there were no washrooms available for Negroes." At the height of the boycott, Homer Wheaton, then a college student in Nashville, had a similar experience while on the way to visit Howard. After the attendant began pumping gas, Wheaton asked for directions to the restroom: "He told me they didn't have one. So I told him to take his gas pump out of my car. . . . And I got back in the car and drove off." No small number took their business to the service stations owned by blacks such as that of RCNL official Amzie Moore in Cleveland.[39]

All available accounts testify to the boycott's success. Most white stations began to install extra restrooms. They acted both because of the decline in customers and pressure from national suppliers and chains. Some whites ripped the bumper stickers off the cars, but generally showed no overt hostility inasmuch as the boycott did not entail a direct challenge to segregation. In this respect, the leaders of the RCNL were like the later Montgomery Bus Boycotters who did not initially demand integration but only called for the enforcement of genuinely separate-but-equal accommodation.[40]

Direct comparisons between the two campaigns are difficult, but a case can be made that the RCNL boycotters encountered, and overcame, steeper odds than their later counterparts in the Montgomery Improvement Association. To the casual observer, Montgomery was a better prospect for a civil rights organizer. In the Delta, blacks had a greater chance of being poor, geographically dispersed, and uneducated than in Montgomery, where a number of well-educated, middle-class blacks had access to television and newspaper coverage.

Even as the RCNL's service station boycott was under way, Howard launched an equally high-profile drive against police harassment. For decades, blacks had suffered indignities ranging from petty insults to physical beatings. Howard's timing was excellent. The improving racial climate in the state allowed him to take some risks. The high point of the campaign was a ninety-minute conference with T. B. Birdsong, the commissioner of the state highway patrol. Several RCNL officials accompanied Howard, including Henry, Chapple, Burton, and Drew. To put a human face on the problem, they brought along a minister and a woman from a prominent black family in Marks, Mississippi, who each alleged that highway patrolmen had slapped them. A RCNL news release praised Birdsong's promise to take corrective action but advised that it would be impossible to cooperate with the department's public safety program "if highway patrolmen continue to use their badges of authority as emblems of tyranny."[41]

Meanwhile the RCNL's Committee on Voting launched a sustained, but much less advertised, drive to register and educate voters. Through classes on the state constitution, it helped blacks learn enough to pass muster with local registrars. Fortunately for the RCNL, many members were knowledgeable about the rules because they were from traditional black-and-tan Republican areas, such as Cleveland and Clarksdale, and had always voted. Henry recalls that initially "white opposition to our registration drives was disorganized and generally ineffectual. They did not believe white supremacy was in danger." The RCNL's greatest challenge to the old order was to encourage blacks to participate in the previously all-white, and all-important, Democratic primary. The recent trend was promising. Black voter registration had continued to slowly increase, setting a new twentieth-century record of twenty-two thousand in 1954.[42]

The RCNL attracted many talented and prestigious leaders, but few doubted the pivotal role of Howard's charisma, leadership skills, and financial acumen. His oratory could always attract a crowd. One of the few surviving recordings of a speech from the 1950s indicates why. His style was erudite but down-to-earth, with more than a touch of the theatrical. His stem-winding speeches featured a hard-hitting combination of passion, outrage, grim determination, and biting wit. In delivery and inflection, he was reminiscent of his namesake, Theodore Roosevelt, but he anticipated the populist style of Malcolm X. Howard's effectiveness on a personal level was especially impressive. His life experiences equipped him well to establish a rapport with all classes and social backgrounds. "He made you want to help him," says Wheaton, "he could really charm you. . . . He dreamed not just little dreams but big dreams much beyond the average person." Howard not only took risks but he inspired others to do the same. He was always, as Charles Evers puts it, "pushing young Negroes to buck the old racist system. He built us up, encouraged us, organized us."[43]

Howard's activism had not yet driven him beyond the pale for whites. As before, he maintained civil, sometimes cordial, relationships with white businessmen and planters in the area. Howard's prominence in the RCNL may have aided him on this score, at least for a while. While a number of individuals in the white elite respected and admired Howard, some also recognized the dangers of alienating him. Maurice L. Sisson, an associate of Howard's in both the Magnolia Mutual and the RCNL, concludes that whites "were afraid of Dr. Howard." Other acquaintances and friends from the period, such as Homer Wheaton and Charles Tisdale, have said the same.[44]

Many whites apparently believed that an ill word passed down from Howard would lead their workers to slack off or cause customers to shun their products. Wheaton states that "one of the threats that Howard made was that if certain things didn't improve that black folks would retaliate in every way that they knew how to do it and implied that they'll start in the white folks home." Whether such fears had merit, Howard had clout and did not hesitate to use it. A particular incident stands out. A bank teller in Cleveland had failed to use a courtesy title when addressing the wife of a doctor at the Taborian Hospital. Howard loudly complained and implied that a boycott would follow. Bank officials quickly apologized and fired the employee.[45]

As the RCNL picked up steam, officials in the national office of the pro-integrationist NAACP became worried. Many did not trust Howard. Gloster Current, the director of branches in the national office in New York, informed his boss Walter White that the RCNL's program was "midway of that of the NAACP and the Urban League" and that (contrary to official NAACP policy) it worked "in the separate but allegedly equal framework." Ruby Hurley, director of the regional office in Birmingham, was overt in her hostility. She regarded the RCNL as a "threat to us which I have recognized and have tried to combat." Dismissing Howard as a hopeless case, Hurley declared that all attempts "to bring him around to our way of thinking" had failed completely. She reported that Howard had stated "if the white people wanted to keep segregation they [the council] would just make it very expensive for them." With alarm, and a hint of jealousy, she warned that the RCNL had attracted many NAACP members "who by reasons of formal education or professional status are in natural positions of leadership." Chief among these was state NAACP president Emmett J. Stringer, who also belonged to the RCNL's Committee on Voting and Registration.[46]

As outsiders, Current and Hurley misunderstood the RCNL or, at the very least, did not appreciate the conditions under which it had to operate. Certain black majority Delta counties, such as Tallahatchie, did not have a single registered black voter. Howard, Amzie Moore, and Medgar Evers were anything but timid, naïve, or accommodationist. Inspired by the Mau Mau rebellion in Kenya, Evers had even contemplated waging guerrilla war against the white power structure. Each of these men had repeatedly taken risks in a racial climate that was unusually hostile. By their actions, they had shown themselves ready to confront the status quo. At the same time, they were realists. A direct, or even indirect, assault on the rigid segregation of the Delta was likely to marginalize them completely. Instead, they tried to change the system by concentrating on its weakest points.[47]

Even at its height, too much can be made of the rift between the RCNL and the NAACP, especially in Mississippi itself. Hurley never trusted Howard and rejected his strategy, but, as already mentioned, the two groups were virtually indistinguishable in the Delta. Historian John Dittmer observes that much of the acrimony can be traced to an old-fashioned turf battle and that the differences between the "national NAACP and the RCNL were more territorial than ideological. . . . the NAACP regarded Mississippi as its bailiwick and saw Howard as a potential rival."[48]

The RCNL was increasingly important to Howard but never became all-consuming. Because of his prominence and support for entrepreneurship, the National Negro Business League made him chair of its board of directors. He was also the keynoter for the group's annual convention in 1953. Founded by Booker T. Washington in 1900, the league still had prestige but was struggling to find an identity as mainstream black organizations emphasized integration and political strategies. Howard's Atlanta speech urged the league to establish scholarships and internships for aspiring businesspeople.[49]

He and Helen continued to enjoy the fruits of affluence by taking frequent trips to New York, Chicago, and California. They believed that money was to be enjoyed. Howard indulged in one of his favorite hobbies: playing the horses. *Jet* reported that during one of his forays at the Oak Lawn track in Hot Springs, Arkansas, he hit the daily double "four out of five consecutive days." He won $4,000 on the fifth day, the "second highest winnings in the last 25 years." Less publicized, of course, was the fact that he lost big too. He was always impeccably dressed, habitually changing clothes two or three times a day. According to Wheaton, "Suits and shoes and hats and in the winter time topcoats, just a complete change . . . when Howard walked in everybody in the place knew who Howard was." He made quite an impression driving his brand-new Cadillac or his new air-conditioned Ford Skyliner convertible with leather seats. The organizers of the homecoming parade at Tennessee A & I State University considered his new hardtop Buick Riviera to be so exotic that they asked to use it as the parade car for the college beauty queen. Howard fulfilled the request by personally driving it to Nashville.[50]

Meanwhile, Helen cultivated and broadened her involvement in black society. She was one of the presidents of the Memphis chapter of the Links, Inc., a relatively new organization, which had affiliates throughout the United States. Most members were the wives of professionals, prominent educators, and businessmen. The chapters of the Links sponsored social affairs, including débutante balls, and various philanthropies. This work was not totally unrelated to the concerns of her husband. The Links often held fundraisers for civil rights organizations such as the NAACP.[51]

As he gained recognition for his accomplishments in civil rights, business, and black society, Howard took part in a far more secretive activity: illegal abortions. It was still very much a sideline to his regular medical practice. His motivation seems to have been primarily to help friends rather than to make big profits. He was always discreet. Instead of performing the abortions in a clinic or hospital, he used rented houses. His patients, by most accounts, were often white. In this respect, he was like such black doctors as Joseph Griffin of Georgia. Griffin's biographer, Hugh Pearson, concludes that whites used black doctors for abortions for the same reason they "preferred going to a Negro physician for their VD shots." Even with these practical advantages, it is remarkable, given the prevalent sexual phobias on race, that so many whites tolerated this practice. Apparently, Howard never ran into serious trouble with the law. Abortion was a crime in Mississippi, but enforcement was not particularly energetic. Between 1936 and 1956, the Mississippi Supreme Court considered a handful of abortion cases, and the rulings against doctors were fairly lenient. In performing abortions, Howard, according to his personal doctor and friend Oscar J. Moore Jr., "was an asset to the community. . . . It was not difficult for a black physician to be forgiven for anything."[52]

By the end of 1952, the RCNL's supporters had good cause to be optimistic. Their campaigns against unequal treatment and disenfranchisement seemed to be yielding incremental successes. The most visible harbinger of improvement was Governor Hugh L. White's unprecedented proposal in 1952 to equalize school spending. At the beginning of his term, White had positioned himself as a racial moderate. In November he proposed a 3 percent tax and a bond issue for a crash program to equalize spending for black and white schools. In early 1953 he sold the idea in a speech in Mound Bayou, the first ever there by a sitting governor. The occasion was the eleventh anniversary of the Taborian Hospital. A crowd of six thousand cordially applauded White as well as Walter Sillers, who also spoke. Though Howard was no longer a friend of the Taborians, both the UOFA and the Magnolia Mutual Life published full-page ads welcoming the governor to Mound Bayou.[53]

In a speech during the same month, Howard coyly avoided taking a position on White's plan, stressing the need for "equality in education." But his comments left no doubt that he was skeptical. He portrayed the governor's proposal as a step in the right direction, but he bluntly attributed it to "the drawn lash of the Supreme Court of America." He pointed to the enormous expense for the taxpayers of equalizing the system. Howard did not see how "a poor state like Mississippi" could "support a dual system of public education and maintain the high standards of education today. . . . You and I have fooled ourselves into thinking that there is such a thing as separate but equal." But Howard hesitated to make a radical break. He depicted White's speech as grounds for optimism. When such men, "who have not given Negro education a passing thought, who are worried to death today about Negro education, I say there is bright hope right here in Mississippi."[54]

This uneasy peace endured as the RCNL held its second annual rally in April. The event was a success, although less spectacularly so than when Dawson appeared a year earlier. By scheduling GOP Alderman Archibald J. Carey Jr. of Chicago as the speaker, Howard showed that he would not be constrained by a partisan framework. Carey's well-received speech at the 1952 Republican convention, from which King apparently drew part of his "I Have a Dream" speech in 1963, had made him the most visible up-and-coming black Republican politician in the United States. The rally for Carey was the beginning of a friendship that lasted for the rest of Howard's life. Along with Thurgood Marshall and Adam Clayton Powell Jr., he and Howard were rising stars in a generation of leaders who had reached political maturity during the 1930s and 1940s. All four men were born in 1908.[55]

During the last half of 1953, Howard and the rest of the RCNL gradually moved toward open hostility against segregation as evidence mounted that legislators lacked the political will to implement equalization. Even as the possibility of a pro-integration Supreme Court ruling loomed, they dragged their feet on the necessary funding or new taxes. Although the governor appeared to be sincere, the reluctance of legislators only hardened after estimates that equalization would increase the state's annual school appropriations from $25 to $37 million. A revealing episode during the summer of 1953 fueled this growing leeriness from blacks about equalization. Howard, Moore, and Medgar Evers visited Walter Sillers Jr. to discuss improvements for black schools. During the meeting, Sillers kept his back to them and avoided eye contact. He made vague promises of more buildings. Journalist Adam Nossiter writes that "the deliberate humiliation of the episode left Evers and the others commenting bitterly on the treatment they had received. It was a lesson for the future."[56]

For Howard, the final break with the principle of separate but equal education came in November. A precipitating factor was the failure of school board officials to respond to a complaint by the Coahoma County Citizens Association, led by Robert L. Drew, about a bond issue in Cleveland that had omitted black schools. White officials claimed that had they done otherwise voters would have been alienated because of the added expense. Days later, the annual conference of branches of the state NAACP condemned the governor's equalization plan and demanded an end to segregation. The same conference chose RCNL leader Emmett J. Stringer as head of the state NAACP. In a speech to the UOFA several days later, Howard announced that "every progressive Negro" should support the NAACP's stand. He predicted that trying to create truly separate but equal schools would "wreck the economy of the entire South." He held nothing back. Responding to Governor White's claim that the "good Negroes" of Mississippi rejected the NAACP's resolution, he replied that he "would be very happy if the governor would give me a definition of a 'good Negro.' . . . the thinking Negro in Mississippi knows our state cannot finance a segregated system of education which is equal but separate."[57]

In taking this stand, Howard locked horns with prominent blacks who continued to stand by the governor's equalization plan. He dismissed them as "spineless," and worse, "Uncle Toms" and "Handkerchief Heads." Two of the best-known black defenders of White's plan were John Dewey Boyd, president of the Mississippi Negro Teachers Association, and Howard's old adversary, Harrison Henry Humes Jr. Both had responded to the NAACP resolution by sending telegrams to the governor promising support. Boyd belonged to a subset of black educators who pinned their hopes on equalization to raise the quality of black schools as well as to protect the jobs of administrators and teachers. Acting from similar motivations, Humes predicted that opponents were making a "colossal blunder" and defended black schools as providing more "sympathetic teachers." But Humes had to perform a delicate balancing act. He wanted to preserve his ties with white leaders but could not afford to alienate his Baptist constituency. He repeatedly reminded his white allies about the dangers of delay. Failure to fund and implement the equalization plan on a fast timetable, he advised, "might lead to the replacing of the present conservative Negro leaders by more radical elements." If the situation did not change, he hinted that he would join these "radical elements."[58]

Howard's break with Percy Greene was particularly bitter. Greene's favored strategy was for the RCNL to forgo desegregation in favor of voting rights as a priority. When Howard chastised him for his stand at a RCNL board meeting, Greene "became furious, cursed the Council, and stormed out." Both Howard and the RCNL were objects of Greene's scorn in the *Jackson Advocate*. His editorials charged that leaders like Howard had "adopted one of the worst traits brought up from slavery by the Negroes: that of trying to condemn and belittle everyone else in order to appear 'big' themselves."[59]

Howard's change in course signaled a new spirit of cooperation with the NAACP, now led by his ally Stringer. He took out a lifetime membership and accepted an appointment to the state board on membership. In addition, the RCNL and the NAACP joined forces to support Medgar Evers's application to the law school of the all-white University of Mississippi in January 1954.

Evers made his decision at an NAACP meeting after Stringer opined that the time was ripe to desegregate Ole Miss. For legal advice, he turned to Thurgood Marshall, the special counsel of the NAACP. The Ole Miss administration dragged its feet for nine months before rejecting the application on a technicality. While Evers continued his work with Magnolia Mutual Life and the RCNL, he so impressed the Mississippi NAACP that he won appointment to its state board of directors.[60]

Howard outdid himself when the RCNL held its third annual rally beginning on May 7 in Mound Bayou. The rally featured a powerhouse of speakers representing the cream of black business, political, and fraternal leadership both regionally and nationally. It attracted a crowd of about eight thousand. In addition to Thurgood Marshall for the main address, the lineup included John H. Sengstacke, the editor and publisher of the *Chicago Defender;* Joseph E. Walker, president of Tri-State Bank; and Walter S. Davis, president of Tennessee A & I State University. Especially flattering to Howard were the remarks of James Gilliam, the grand master of the Mississippi grand lodge of the Prince Hall Masons, who dubbed him a "Moses to thy People." The affair was impressive in other ways. Six school bands and a sixty-piece band from Tennessee A & I State University marched in a "Great Freedom Parade" down Main Street while Howard and Marshall waved from a convertible. Local merchants ordered ten tons of meat to feed the crowd of eight thousand. Once again, Howard put the spotlight on models of business and agricultural success. He introduced to the crowd three black men who had risen from "sharecroppers within a short period to that of landowners now possessing land estimated close to $1 million."[61]

Not everyone appreciated Howard's efforts. The most vocal critic was Percy Greene, who walked a tightrope of praising the main speaker, Marshall, while condemning the man who invited him. Greene charged that Howard's motive in staging the event was to achieve the vainglorious goal of becoming the "indisputable, all powerful Super-Leader of the Negroes of the State." To this end, the RCNL had hoodwinked the unsuspecting Marshall to be "the come-on, prop, and color, for its annual meeting; the result being, because of the great crowds . . . is being magnified out of proportion to its actual and potential accomplishments."[62]

Greene had underestimated the achievements of the conference. It was more than a good show. Although the RCNL never had a large dues-paying membership, the forum gave blacks a rare chance to discuss nuts-and-bolts strategies to challenge disenfranchisement and segregation. For example, the RCNL's Committee on Voting and Registration, headed by Levye Chapple, held workshops on registration. The committee's report recounted a litany of informal barriers encountered by RCNL members as they tried to register blacks. In some counties, sheriffs refused to accept poll taxes from blacks while in others clerks turned away those who had already paid. Most memorably, Forrest County registrars "tested" blacks by asking them how many bubbles were on a bar of soap.[63]

An added sense of anticipation filled the air at the 1954 conference. The U.S. Supreme Court's ruling in *Brown v. Board of Education* was just three weeks away. Marshall's remarks reflected a new level of confidence: "Come hell or high water; we'll be free by '63." He and Howard urged the crowd to contribute money for lawsuits against school segregation. Marshall also held a roundtable with Benjamin L. Hooks (the future executive director of the national NAACP, who was then preparing to run for the state legislature in Memphis as a Republican) and other black southern attorneys to formulate possible litigation strategies.[64]

As the conference drew to a close, the participants had every reason to expect a bright future for civil rights in Mississippi. Blacks in the state had a record of consistent progress behind them, and a great Supreme Court victory was just around the corner. For the first time in seventy years, the entrenched system of second-class citizenship in Mississippi was on the defensive.

Events between 1951 and 1954 seemed to justify Howard's approach of weaving together pragmatism and radicalism. He had consistently pushed an agenda of self-help, black business, and political equality whenever opportunities arose. Howard could be fearless in waging war against inequality and disenfranchisement, but he was not a man to tilt at windmills. In the Mississippi Delta before 1953, separate but equal was the only game in town. Howard was prepared to play the game, but under his rules. When separate but equal finally seemed vulnerable in Mississippi, he was equally ready to push his hardest to topple the system. Neither he nor his allies could have anticipated, however, the lengths to which their opponents would go in fighting to defend and expand their state's system of racial supremacy.

5

"The Most Hated, and the Best Loved, Man in Mississippi"

FOR HOWARD, THE Supreme Court's *Brown* decision was the sweetest of victories. It struck down school segregation and thus overturned nearly sixty years of precedent. The ruling appeared to confirm that Howard was right to break cleanly from the separate but equal approach. The immediate aftermath gave him little reason to have second thoughts.

While few whites were happy about the decision, they were generally not itching for a fight either. A random survey in Jackson by the *Clarion-Ledger* showed surprising, if grudging, willingness to comply. After chatting with white customers in his drugstore, Aaron Henry came to the same conclusion. One man flatly admitted that his children would "have to go to school with Negroes and we might as well go along with the law." Similarly, Henry's hometown newspaper in Clarksdale reported that a majority of county school officials were "more optimistic than gloomy," taking the stand "that the final solution will not be as objectionable as it appeared from the court's bare decision."[1]

Urging compliance, Hodding Carter's *Delta Democrat Times* put the blame on the South because of "shocking, calculated and cynical disobedience to its own state constitutions which specify that separate school systems must be equal." Few newspapers went that far, but measured tones were the order of the day. The *Tupelo Daily Journal* urged a moratorium on "high emotion or thoughtless action" while the *Vicksburg Evening Post* advised careful "study" and avoidance of rash behavior. The *Laurel Leader-Call* reminded Mississippians that the "eyes of the world are on us. Whatever we do must be met with even temper, with self control, with a determination to work out what faces us in the spirit of Americanism and true Christianity."[2]

But from the beginning some opinion leaders counseled defiance and resistance. The *Jackson Daily News* was probably the most powerful. Along with the almost equally segregationist *Clarion-Ledger,* it had the highest circulation in the state. Barely days after the decision, editor and publisher Frederick Sullens held out the prospect that "human blood may stain southern soil in many places because of this decision, but the dark red stains of that blood will be on the marble steps of the United States Supreme Court Building. . . . Mississippi cannot and will not try to abide by this decision."[3]

When the dust settled, state political leaders tried to steer a middle course somewhere between compliance and defiance. Governor Hugh L. White, an advocate of a "go slow" approach, convened an early meeting of the Mississippi Legal Education Advisory Committee (LEAC). The legislature had recently established the committee to take all necessary steps to preserve segregation. LEAC favored a carrot-and-stick strategy. The carrot was to offer blacks true separate but equal education through a crash program of spending. The stick was to threaten to abolish the public schools if they turned down the offer. For the time being, the governor and his allies favored persuasion. They had a tough selling job in front of them. Black political attitudes had changed greatly since the previous year. Even Percy Greene now cautiously hailed *Brown.* But segregationists were not without options as they searched for black allies. Humes was one of their best hopes. Even critics who belittled him as an Uncle Tom conceded, at least in private, that he had a popular following. Black educators were especially susceptible to proposals for separate but equal services. Principals and college presidents of black schools had the most to gain from an increase in spending and the most to lose if public schools closed.[4]

The segregationist campaign moved forward on two fronts. Throughout the state, white school boards convened biracial meetings to formulate plans to equalize schools. The Coahoma County school board that had once rebuffed Henry was among them. This time, whites were in a more cooperative frame of mind. Henry noticed that it had finally dawned on them that the Supreme Court decision "would be implemented only if local Negroes agitated for it. If they could placate us, there would be no integration."[5]

Meanwhile, Governor White and LEAC met privately with eight black leaders on July 1. Some of them were Humes; Greene; E. S. Bishop of Corinth, past president of the state Negro Teachers Association; John Dewey Boyd, the president of the Utica Institute; J. R. Otis, the president of Alcorn College; and James H. White, the president of Mississippi Vocational College. James H. White had participated in the early activities of the Regional Council of Negro Leadership but in recent months had distanced himself from Howard. The black attendees issued an upbeat statement that endorsed a "system of schools in Mississippi that will satisfy both its white and Negro citizens without trying to circumvent the decision of the U.S. Supreme Court." Although depicted later as affirming the separate but equal principle, the wording did not bear this out, at least not explicitly. The statement subtly tried to deflate white fears about *Brown* by noting that under a "true program of equalization . . . a school in Mississippi with nothing but Negro students and teachers is no more a segregated school than those schools are in Chicago, New York, Detroit, Los Angeles and other large centers of Negro population outside the South." But few doubted that the eight had assented to the governor's plan. Certainly, politicians and newspapers, black and white, who used the term "voluntary segregation" did not hesitate to make that interpretation.[6]

To broaden support for this agenda, the group of eight recommended that the governor meet a wider cross section of leaders. They realized that blacks were likely to reject any plan unless the process had input from key opponents of equalization such as Howard. Drawing from their suggested list (which incorporated revisions by Howard and others), the governor sent letters inviting ninety black leaders to a meeting on July 30 in Jackson. Humes and James H. White later claimed that Howard had privately assured his backing of the governor's plan before the conference. If true, it was at loggerheads with his public behavior. On July 25 he blasted Governor White's claim that 95 percent of blacks supported segregation as "one of the biggest lies of our day." The eight were confident of dominating a broader meeting, but their opponents had plans of their own. Emmett J. Stringer, Henry, and Howard identified and contacted about seventy on the governor's invitation list. They assembled in a church in Jackson on the night before the governor's conference. Most had probably read that morning's highly intimidating front-page editorial in the *Jackson Daily News*. Menacingly, it suggested that NAACP members "stay away" from the conference.[7]

The events of what came to be called the "meeting the night before" at the church were memorable. Howard and his allies immediately tangled with

Percy Greene, who opposed taking a position either for or against the equalization plan. Greene recommended an emphasis on voting rights instead, a view not so far from the RCNL's original agenda. Boyd, Fred H. Miller, White, and a few others wanted to come out for equalization. Before long, the fence-sitters, like Greene, and supporters of equalization, like Humes, realized that they were outnumbered. The debate became so intense that Howard and Humes almost came to blows. At the end of the meeting, the gathering voted overwhelmingly to endorse *Brown* and selected Howard and E. W. Banks, an undertaker in Jackson, as designated spokesmen. One hour before the scheduled showdown on the next day, Humes, Boyd, and James H. White came by to tell Governor White the bad news. Deeply angered, he almost called off the conference but reluctantly went ahead. He had raised expectations so high that it seemed impossible to cancel now. Earlier that month, the governor had blithely promised that it "is going to be my meeting and I want the press there."[8]

Nearly one hundred blacks, assorted newspaper reporters, and all twenty-five members of LEAC were present. Sillers served as chair. Banks read the prepared statement. It seemed unambiguous: "We can do no other than to endorse and abide by the decision of May 17, 1954, of the Supreme Court." Members of the crowd sprang to their feet and shouted, *"Freedom! Freedom!"* Yet, though few segregationists noticed or appreciated it, the statement showed sensitivity to white concerns. There was no demand for immediate integration, and it pointed out that even after implementation, the vast majority of schools would "be largely white or largely colored" because "the residential areas are largely segregated."[9]

Howard spoke next. If the governor expected any relief from the anti-segregationist onslaught, he did not get it from him. It was vintage Howard, eloquent, passionate, and blunt: "The Negroes who have come here today have not come to help work out any trick or plan to circumvent the decision of the Supreme Court outlawing segregation in the public schools." He portrayed *Brown* as a "just and humane" decision that enabled the United States to champion human rights. Saying that a "chain is no stronger than its weakest link," he concluded that "if Mississippi is a weak link in the chain of American democracy—America is weak." Howard contended that blacks were better able than whites to weather abolition of the public schools because they had such poor schools to begin with. He called for the formation of a biracial committee to iron out the details. His only immediate demand was for admission of blacks to all institutions of higher learning. His main example was the stalled application of a "brilliant young man" (Medgar Evers) to the University of Mississippi law school.[10]

Viewed in hindsight, Howard's speech was neither inflexible nor particularly radical. It contained few surprises for anyone who had followed his career. As he had many times before, Howard reassured skittish whites that no "thinking Negro in Mississippi . . . bothers about social equality." He defended neighborhood schools organized on the "convenience of the children" rather than race. These words, of course, were perfectly within the spirit of *Brown*. He disavowed any intention of getting "in front of the Supreme Court on the 'when and how'" of public school integration. Howard even bent a bit on the hot-button issue of "voluntary segregation" by proposing the alternative of "voluntary integration" pending a final Supreme Court ruling. Under this approach, no "child would be forced to attend any particular school and on the other hand, no child would be denied the right to attend a particular school, solely because of race, creed or color." If Howard and the other speakers were trying to soothe white fears, they were not succeeding. LEAC had reflexively decided, according to Charles C. Bolton, that "if blacks did not support voluntary segregation, they must favor integration and, by extension, social equality."[11]

The rest of the meeting brought more of the same. Speaker after speaker repudiated schemes to circumvent *Brown*. Even the governor's most trusted black allies deserted him. Greene restated his old proposal for partial integration of graduate schools while James H. White avowed "full confidence" in the Supreme Court decision. Both views, of course, were anathema to whites. The only unambiguous backing for the governor's plan was by J. W. Jones, a little-known editor of a black newspaper from Union County. He criticized integrated schools for putting undue competitive pressure on black students and making it difficult for black teachers to discipline white children.[12]

Anxious to turn the tide, Sillers called on the normally reliable Humes. The suspense in the room was almost unbearable as he rose from his chair. Most of those present, white and black, expected him to repeat his defense of the governor's plan from the previous evening. He did not. Continuing the trend of the morning, he announced his refusal to cooperate with any attempt to obstruct the Supreme Court. Much like Howard, he endorsed a biracial implementation committee and reminded LEAC that neighborhood schools (even if officially integrated) would still be largely separate. Humes did not hold back. He issued a blistering indictment of the state's neglect of black education. In black schools, children looked "through the cracks in that floor and see Mother's earth, and through the top—the roof of the house, and study astronomy." Whites had "invited all of this trouble down upon themselves. Negroes were not in the Supreme Court either, it was nine white folks, and they can't be mad with us about that." The prospects for the governor's plan were now utterly hopeless, and Sillers knew it. Only one of the ninety black leaders had come out in favor. Seeing no point in continuing, Sillers fumed, "The meeting is over." He knew, as Henry later put it, "that if he had lost Humes, he had lost us all."[13]

The governor vented his anger in the aftermath. He no longer had any confidence in blacks as possible allies and vowed never to "launch a building program for a group of Negro leaders who will say one thing to me and do another." He cast his lot more openly with hardliners by scheduling a special legislative session to authorize abolition of the public schools. Segregationist rhetoric had undergone a sea change, at least for the time being. In the past, political leaders like Governor White had insisted that a majority of blacks backed them. Now, they seemed to agree with Sillers that "the 95 per cent we thought were in favor of voluntary segregation turned out to be against us." For R. M. Newton of LEAC, the outcome of the conference was proof that blacks wanted nothing less than "to be social equals in every way." He was apparently not listening when Howard and the other speakers denied any interest in social equality.[14]

If the results of the conference angered and depressed the governor and his allies, black delegates were jubilant. Henry left feeling "really proud to be a Mississippi Negro and to have stood with my people." Howard shared in the exuberance of the moment by exclaiming that blacks were "rejoicing all over the state at their leaders' united rejection of the proposed voluntary segregation plan. We will see the schools closed before we accept it." As if to confirm his assessment, the *Clarion-Ledger* reported that blacks had "a gleam in their eyes and a feeling that they have a foot in the door." Even many of the more cautious leaders seemed inclined to agree with the *Memphis World*'s dictum that "a man who goes out and compromises his case after the court has given him a verdict, does so at his own risk."[15]

The optimists did not pay enough attention to what was happening around them. Hard-line segregationists were mustering their forces throughout June and July. A defining moment in the counteroffensive was the "Black Monday" speech delivered in Greenwood in late May by Tom P. Brady, a circuit court judge from Brookhaven. The title characterized the day that the U.S. Supreme Court handed down the *Brown* decision. Buoyed by the favorable response to his speech, Brady hastily turned out a book of the same name that appeared in June. *Black Monday* featured a litany of popular segregationist arguments. As was typical of such fare, a phobia of interracial sex held much of it together. Brady feared that under integration, black and white children would "grow up together and the sensitivity of the white children will be dulled," a condition leading to intermarriage. His most creative proposal was for a "National Federation of Sovereign States" at the grassroots to wage, if necessary, "a cold war and an economic boycott" against defenders of civil rights. While Brady conceded that such measures might be unpleasant, and often unfair to individuals caught in the middle, nothing was off limits if the survival of segregation was on the line.[16]

Responding to Brady's call to arms, six whites met in early July in the Delta community of Indianola (less than forty miles from Mound Bayou) to found the Association of Citizens' Councils. The prime instigator was Robert "Tut" Patterson, a planter and the former captain of the Mississippi State University football team. Ironically, in Clarksdale Patterson had been a boyhood friend of Aaron Henry, the future head of the state NAACP. At first, the Association of Citizens' Councils was a small, semisecret organization.[17]

The Citizens' Council movement and the RCNL were polar opposites in ideology, but they showed similarities in histories, strategies, and organizational structures. The founding of the one was in great part a response to the activities of the other. Percy Greene's *Jackson Advocate* went so far as to claim that Howard's speeches were the main reason "for the rise and growth of the citizens councils in the state." While that statement was an exaggeration, it is not purely coincidental that the first spurt in the membership of the Association of Citizens' Councils was in the summer months as white attitudes stiffened after the RCNL's assertiveness at the governor's conference. In addition, both organizations had initially thrived in the small towns of the Delta and favored strategies of reaching the masses through business, professional, social, and political leaders. Most of the committees of the Citizens' Councils, such as those on politics and elections (to discourage black voting), public relations, and education, had parallels in the RCNL.[18]

After a few weeks, breaches began to appear in the phalanx of black leaders who had briefly united at the governor's conference. Greene was the first to defect. He editorialized that the conference had "failed to reveal the thinking and attitude of the vast majority of responsible Negro leaders." He backed his statement up with the threadbare claim (which had been abandoned by LEAC) that 90 percent of ordinary blacks preferred separate but truly equal schools rather than integration. According to Greene, Howard and Stringer had thwarted the will of this black majority. The duo represented an illustration of "Edmund Burke's saying, that the sides of sick beds and the arms of dentist chairs are not places to train statesmen and leaders."[19]

James H. White, the second major figure to break from the tenuously united black front, singled out Howard for criticism. A long letter to Stringer signified just how much he was now at odds with the RCNL's strategy. He condemned Howard's address at the governor's conference as a terrible blow to racial goodwill and as a foolhardy scheme "to push little Negro children in places where they are not wanted." He dismissed Howard as a reckless "individualist" who had betrayed "the State that has allowed him to pull up by his own bootstraps."[20]

Humes soon joined the defectors. Never again would he stray from his segregationist allies. Like White and Greene, he cast Howard as the villain or the "most outstanding double-crosser of Mississippi," who had "willfully lied" to the governor prior to the conference, falsely assuring support. For Humes, Howard's priorities in life were "Howard and his Cadillac. If it was left up to Howard to make his choice for the development of people, he would prefer to bring some servants from Africa to give him a bath and to serve him as slaves." Greene, White, and Humes protested too much. In part, their counterattack was an attempt to revise the historical record in their favor. Their own words at the conference were so close to Howard's that segregationists had accused Humes, White, and Greene of deception and betrayal, the same charges they now turned against Howard.[21]

This sniping was trivial compared to what came next. When the NAACP petitioned school districts for implementation of integration, the virulence of white resistance caught the organization completely off guard. Walthall County officials, for example, dealt with the NAACP's petitioners by presenting them with grand jury subpoenas. In Amite County, the white sheriff disrupted a NAACP meeting, posed harassing questions to the participants, and seized the records of the chapter. Stringer's experiences were unusually demoralizing. He received threatening phone calls, lost his automobile insurance, and was unable to get loans. His income taxes were audited, probably at the instigation of local whites. In frustration, he resigned as president of the state NAACP. Petition drives in other school districts collapsed even before they began.[22]

It was a similar story throughout the state. A well-known planter in Yazoo County defiantly promised, "We won't gin their cotton; we won't allow them credit, and we'll move them out of their rented houses." More than a few segregationists openly contemplated the merits of violence. One legislator speculated that a "few killings" might "save a lot of bloodshed later on." For the most part, however, segregationists favored economic pressure over physical violence. By the early fall, the membership of the Citizens' Councils had mushroomed to an estimated twenty-five thousand.[23]

Especially in retrospect, it is doubly tragic that many of those whites who fought the hardest against civil rights acknowledged at the time that they were doomed to lose. A Mississippi judge candidly admitted that eventually "schools will be integrated. We all realize that." And yet, Mississippi's whites devoted time, money, and energy to waging a fight that so many thought was ultimately an exercise in futility. Perhaps they acted on the vague hope that delay would somehow make it easier to face the inevitable.[24]

Even as they rebuffed school petitioners, segregationists pushed ahead relentlessly to roll back black gains in voting. Economic pressure, of course, was critical to their strategy. In Indianola, planters denied "strip" (credit for the payment of medical care) to any tenant who was a patient of Dr. Clinton C. Battle of Indianola, a prominent figure in the RCNL and NAACP and supporter of voting registration. Agents of a burial company owned by Charles Evers refused to turn over to him the money they collected from policyholders, allegedly at the suggestion of whites. The lug nuts on the tires of his car were loosened.[25]

Belzoni was a hotbed of intimidation by the Citizens' Councils. The *Delta Democrat Times* found that white merchants had circulated a blacklist of ninety-four registered black voters. If "a man wants credit to buy his groceries, his name better not be on that list. And if he expects to keep working at the mill, he better see he strikes his name from the voters' rolls." A member of the local Citizens' Council demanded that T. V. Johnson, an undertaker, get out of the RCNL and pressured his clients to drop him. Johnson backed down. Throughout most of 1954 and 1955, the local council targeted Gus Courts, a grocer and RCNL activist. The president of the town's bank threatened to cut off his credit unless he resigned as the head of the local NAACP. He complied. But he resisted demands that he stop voting even though he had to move his store because his white landlord raised the rent to prohibitive levels. As yet, Howard's wealth left him relatively insulated, but he too faced trouble. A white insurance man (allegedly connected with the Citizens' Councils) purchased the mortgage on some of his land and demanded immediate payment.[26]

The slow but steady climb in black registration during the previous decade, fostered in part by the RCNL and the NAACP, had ground to a halt. Squeezed by both legal and extralegal measures, the number of registered black voters plummeted from twenty-two thousand in 1954 to eight thousand two years later. In the special election of November 1954, voters overwhelmingly approved a law requiring registrants upon request to write a "reasonable interpretation" of any section of the constitution. In the hands of election officials, of course, this was rigged so that blacks invariably failed and whites invariably passed. Only about five hundred of the state's black voters braved white pressure and turned out.[27]

The emboldened white resistance created fissures in the year-old alliance between the NAACP and the RCNL. Howard came to the conclusion that continued reliance on the national NAACP's strategy of petitioning in school districts was futile. He saw it as akin to hunting a "bear with a cap pistol" and cautioned against getting ahead of the enforcement order of the Supreme Court. This should have not been a complete surprise. He had said much the same thing at the governor's conference. When Howard called a special meeting of the RCNL in Mound Bayou for September 26, all sides anticipated a confrontation. Stringer was so upset by the train of events that he resigned his longtime position as an RCNL officer.[28]

Again, the meeting displayed Howard's finesse in maneuvering through a crisis and turning it into an opportunity. As many as two thousand delegates from forty counties met in a tent after both the AME church and school trustees in Mound Bayou refused them space. They voted, as anticipated, against RCNL participation in any petition drive until a "final and conclusive" decision by the Supreme Court. But, at Howard's insistence, they passed resolutions that ended earlier fears of a formal break with the NAACP. They took the edge off the RCNL's stand by endorsing speedy implementation of *Brown* in Mississippi. Other resolutions demanded full voting rights and immediate admission to graduate and professional schools in higher education. The successful prevention of a rift was a great letdown for Greene. While he praised the original purpose of the meeting, he complained that "Dr. Howard all but covered up the fact that he had led the organization to adopt the statement in regard to integration under a series of bristling generalities, statements and predictions, which aroused continuous applause, while destroying the very purpose for which the meeting was called."[29]

Howard may have retreated on one front but, as was his habit, attacked on another. He boldly announced a counteroffensive against the Citizens' Councils. Howard put forward two strategies to fight the economic pressure, both geared to reducing dependence on white businesses. Instead of buying goods from local white suppliers, he called for getting them from outside by starting "the biggest mail order boom in the history of the South." He also proposed a plan for black businesses, voluntary associations, unions, and churches to deposit their accounts in Tri-State Bank of Nashville. This was a stroke of genius. The extra funds would enable the bank to advance loans to civil rights activists who were otherwise unable to get them. He persuaded his friend, Joseph E. Walker, president of the bank, to give his blessing. As a result, the most memorable legacy of the meeting was the launching of a counterattack against the credit freeze rather than any setback.[30]

The NAACP was receptive to Howard's suggested strategy. By the end of 1954, it had become painfully obvious that the credit freeze posed the main obstacle to the petitioning campaign. Thus, a regional NAACP meeting in Columbus, Mississippi, in early December put Howard's proposal at the top of the agenda. The participants included Howard, Medgar Evers, Charles Evers, and Gloster Current, the NAACP's director of branches. Howard told them a grim story. He estimated that "three-fourths of the white Mississippians would take up arms to preserve segregation." He added that members of the Citizens' Councils had referred specifically to Stringer and himself after suggesting that "a few killings at this time would save much time later."[31]

Howard's main goal, however, was to use the evidence of mounting white pressure to illustrate the advantages of fighting back through the Tri-State Bank plan. He described what had happened after he transferred a large portion of his liquid assets to Tri-State after hearing that members of the councils were snooping into his background. The impact on local bank officials was immediate and salutary. They assured Howard that "although they were under pressure from the citizens council leaders, they in no way intended to succumb to these pressures and hoped he was not starting the threatened Negro boycott by withdrawing his funds from the bank." For Howard, it was an object lesson that the best way to check economic warfare was to answer in kind.[32]

Howard's pitch to the NAACP carried the day. The national office embraced his proposal and made it a major priority. It issued an appeal to businesses and voluntary organizations to transfer their deposits to Tri-State Bank. In the next months, the depositors came to include the North Carolina Mutual Life Insurance Company (one of the largest and oldest black companies), the Brotherhood of Sleeping Car Porters, the Mississippi Prince Hall Masons, the Knights and Daughters of Tabor, the national AME church, and various locals of the United Automobile Workers. Black newspapers kept a running tally. NAACP officials such as Medgar Evers assisted in handling applications.[33]

The NAACP's drive against the credit freeze generated a fair amount of controversy. Howard was naturally in the middle. Some trouble arose because of disagreement and misunderstanding about the purpose of the loans. NAACP and RCNL officials reiterated that sound banking principles would determine eligibility, but something was lost in the translation to prospective applicants. The newspaper coverage fostered the misleading impression that deposits represented a war chest to give aid rather than loans. Similarly, a cartoon in the *Tri-State Defender* depicted a group of "anti-freeze boys" triumphantly passing around buckets of money, each showing an amount and the name of a specific depositor. They poured the contents into a giant barrel labeled "Fund for Credit Freeze Victims."[34]

Howard's announced goal of $1 million in deposits for Tri-State turned into another sore point. The statement sufficiently bothered Wilkins that he wrote a letter of concern in February. He criticized Howard's "fantastic figure" of $1 million as "unfortunate" because it conflicted with the NAACP's stated "modest goal of $250,000, occasionally referring to $500,000." The result was to lead Mississippians to believe "that a huge amount of money was available for them and all they had to do was to step up to the window and ask for it on the claim that they were being persecuted." Wilkins's version of events was not completely accurate. He himself was partly responsible for the misunderstanding. Less than a month earlier, he had projected to Howard "that a minimum of $500,000 will be on hand in a few weeks," a far cry from the total amount raised by the end of 1955 (about $280,000).[35]

Howard's letter of response to Wilkins was audacious even for Howard. He readily conceded that the goal of $1 million "may have been fantastic, so was five hundred thousand but the propaganda value was worth it here in breaking the Citizen's Council's Economic strangle hold." The exaggerated stories of money overflowing in Tri-State's vaults had so awed white creditors that the freeze had "started to thaw from without and from within." He reported that many applicants who had come to him in January or February no longer needed funds because white bankers in Mississippi, who previously had denied credit, had resumed loans—often without the red tape demanded by Tri-State. Howard remarked that "when things are normal here in the Mississippi Delta, it is the easiest place in the world to borrow money on a little security if the banker knows you." Howard elaborated, saying that he had information that banks in the Delta "now loan money to Negroes with less security than at any time since Reconstruction."[36]

Howard was probably right. The credit freeze did begin to thaw during 1955, at least to a degree. Both the NAACP and the RCNL no longer expressed the same sense of urgency about the freeze and the need to promote Tri-State to combat it. In February, for example, Current concluded that the "campaign must have also had a salutary effect because complaints of economic pressures have suddenly ceased to exist." Sylvester Bowens, a farmer from Glendora, told the *Tri-State Defender* that previously recalcitrant white banks had advanced loans to him soon after stories appeared on the anti-freeze fund. "Only Heaven knows," Bowens exuded, "the relief your newspaper and others, the NAACP and Dr. T. R. M. Howard of the Regional Council of Negro Leadership brought to my happy soul." For his part, Howard claimed that Tri-State had met every legitimate demand for loans.[37]

As the crisis seemed to ease, some NAACP officials began to downplay the program, perhaps viewing it as more trouble than it was worth. Ruby Hurley thought that many applicants "who claim economic pressure or are asking for loans are persons who have seen or heard something about the NAACP helping Negroes in Mississippi and some money in a bank in Memphis." Only a relative few, she asserted, suffered genuine pressure because of their beliefs, and most of their credit problems were due to careless debts and ignorance of sound business principles. For these and similar reasons, she asked whether it was "advisable to continue playing up the deposits in Tri-State." Despite misgivings, the NAACP and Tri-State still made loans in special cases during the next year or so.[38]

The campaign against the credit freeze coincided with another public imbroglio over allegations of improper pressure by Howard's draft board. The catalyst was an offhand comment at the NAACP meeting in December 1954 that quickly snowballed. Howard had said that a letter had arrived from his local draft board asking why his status should not "be changed from class 2A, the class I think all doctors are, to class 1A." He speculated that if called up "at the age of 47 . . . with 20 years as a hospital administrator, maybe I could go in as a Lt. Col. and that would satisfy their fancy."[39]

Nothing more happened until a month later, when the national office of the NAACP fired off a news release. Citing Howard's experience, it stated that Clarence Mitchell, the director of the Washington Bureau of the NAACP, had asked the Selective Service System to "investigate pressure of local draft boards on colored advocates of civil rights in Mississippi." The black press picked up on the story. Officials from the national Selective Service promptly denied the charges, claiming that the letter to Howard was purely routine. They assured Mitchell that his age and essential role in the community precluded any possibility of a draft call-up.[40]

The controversy then deepened after news reports that Howard had denied that he was under pressure by his draft board. Wilkins's subsequent letter to Howard was polite, but his irritation was apparent. He recognized that charges of pressure might have merit, reasoning that with "so much smoke there must be some fire," but insisted on the need for solid proof. He warned that "if these complaints do not have a reasonable basis, the NAACP will be rebuked and these incidents, coupled with that involving your draft board, will be used to attempt to show that we are howling falsely." Wilkins noted that the controversy illustrated the necessity of closer coordination between civil rights leaders in Mississippi and the national NAACP.[41]

In his reply, Howard said that the press had misquoted him. He explained that he had merely answered no to a question on whether he had asked for an investigation of his draft board. Furthermore, he insisted that if the NAACP had informed him about the news release he "would have been glad to have cooperated if I could have known what it was all about." Not for the first time, Howard probably had wished that he had kept his mouth shut. In fairness, however, his statements at the NAACP meeting had been somewhat speculative. He had never repeated them to the press, much less asked for an official investigation. If Howard had gone overboard in making the original allegation, the NAACP had also acted precipitously.[42]

White pressure against black assertiveness also took some less obvious forms. One of them was Mississippi's discriminatory gun-control laws. Sheriffs routinely denied blacks permits to carry concealed weapons, including prominent blacks such as Howard. But Howard discovered a way to evade the law. He had a secret compartment in his car where he could stow his gun if the police pulled him over. Several years later, the *Pittsburgh Courier* reported that as Howard "rode the highways, he would take the gun from its secret hiding place and put it in his lap . . . always cocked!"[43]

An incident recorded in a file on Howard compiled by the Sovereignty Commission (a state agency set up to spy on blacks in 1956) is consistent with this description. An officer from the Leland police department stated that he had stopped Howard's car in 1947 for speeding. As he approached, five occupants hurriedly pulled guns from their belts and threw them on the floor. Howard was the only one who did not, perhaps because he stowed his gun just in time. The other men were not so lucky. Each had to pay a fine of $100 on the charge of carrying a concealed weapon without a permit. Because the permit system did not apply to unconcealed weapons, Howard took advantage of his legal right to have them in open view in his car. Like many Mississippians, black and white, he had a long gun prominently displayed in a rack on the window behind the back seat.[44]

As black assertiveness increased, whites came forward with proposals for tougher gun control. The sponsors did not hide the centrality of race in their concerns. White concerns about gun control for blacks was not new. During the late nineteenth and early twentieth centuries, several southern states had enacted gun control laws that restricted access of cheap handguns to blacks. The term "Saturday night special" may have originated during that period as a racial slur. In early 1954 an editorial in the *Clarion-Ledger* had stressed the dangers posed by .22 caliber pistols and rifles. Focusing on the example of an "allegedly 'crazed' Negro" who killed three white men, it lamented that these "weapons are easily obtained and ammunition for them can be bought almost anywhere." If this problem persisted, the editorial continued, laws should be enacted that would ensure the "control of the sale of weapons and ammunition or the keeping of records of all such sales."[45]

In September 1954, a more ambitious proposal "to require registration of all firearms and records on all sales of ammunition" came close to becoming law. The backers explicitly promoted the bill as part of a package of "segregation-supporting" legislation and linked it to the crackdown on civil rights, then just getting steam after the governor's conference. Rep. Edwin White, the main sponsor, declared with alarm that many blacks had purchased guns, making it essential to give law enforcement the power to confiscate guns and ammunition "from those likely to cause us trouble." The Mississippi House approved the bill but it failed to get out of committee in the Senate. In the end, Mississippi's gun culture was too strong an obstacle to legislation of this type. Still, it was a near thing.[46]

Howard's domestic life reflected the turbulence of his civil rights activism. His household had two new additions. One was ten-year-old Ronald Taylor, who was the son of his daughter, Verda. Always mindful of public relations, Howard told everyone that the bright, energetic, and outgoing boy was his adopted son. Previously, Helen had kept her distance from her husband's progeny but it was not so with Ronald. She adored the boy. Her husband felt the same way and came to regard Ronald as a kind of heir apparent. A photo spread in *Our World,* a competitor to *Ebony,* highlighting Howard's daily activities, prominently featured the couple and their "son." Sometime in 1955, the Howards legally adopted a one-year-old boy, Barrett. To complicate matters further, another of Howard's out-of-wedlock children, a son, was born in 1954. Like his older brothers and sisters, he lived with his mother and had minimal contact with the Howard household. Apparently, Howard did not see a contradiction between this extramarital behavior and his public condemnation of our "thrill crazed, jazz–be-bop age, when our youth are willing to do anything or to try anything to experience the psychological reaction of a thrill."[47]

About this time, Howard began a friendship with Arrington High, a Jackson-based publisher and an unforgettable character of the first order. High's place in the historical pantheon of civil rights in Mississippi is not easy to identify. His methods were extraordinarily unorthodox, his personal following was virtually nonexistent, and, unlike Howard, he never distinguished himself in either the public or the private sector. He was born into poverty and obscurity, a state to which he returned at the time of his death. Yet, in his peculiar way, he had a significant impact. He was a one-man revolution. Physically he did not fit the part. He was short, plump, and baby-faced but did his best to compensate through sheer pugnacity. He often kept one eye closed during conversations, giving the appearance, as one acquaintance put it, of a little "tough fellow."[48]

Born in Canton, Mississippi, in 1910, High's early life was shot through with mystery, intrigue, and sordidness. He listed his father as "unknown" on official documents, but people wondered whether he was covering up. Talk spread that his father was "a wealthy white businessman" in Jackson who supported his son's activities but preferred to help from behind the scenes. High seems to have encouraged, and reveled in, these rumors. More than once, he skirted lines of legality and propriety. In the early 1940s, he had already served time in the federal penitentiary in Atlanta, apparently for a confidence scam.[49]

High bounced back by landing a job with the *Mississippi Enterprise,* one of Jackson's two black newspapers. His columns admonished those who would subvert the white power structure: "Let us not listen to outside agitators who tell us that the Southern white man is our enemy." He lost the job after accusing the NAACP of trying to assassinate him. The *Jackson Advocate* dismissed his claim as a desperate ploy to divert attention after a jealous husband almost shot him. In 1944 the police arrested High for soliciting money on false pretenses but later released him.[50]

After two more arrests on charges of false pretenses in shady money-making schemes, High turned over a new leaf by founding the *Eagle Eye,* a primitively mimeographed two-page "newspaper." For the next four decades, he was publisher, editor, reporter, and circulation director. It was originally a gossip rag. None of the pre-1954 copies seem to have survived, but typical stories revealed that "so-and-so was supposed to be in Mound Bayou, but he was in such-and-such place, so the *Eagle Eye* spotted him at such-and-such a place. Oh, he was a trip! . . . It was fun to a lot of people. The ones he didn't ever catch." High's atrocious punctuation, terrible spelling, and inappropriate abbreviations were notorious, but few readers held it against him.[51]

By 1954 High had abandoned apolitical gossip-mongering for civil rights. An article in the *Mississippi Enterprise* praised his instrumental role in promoting voter registration in Jackson. Apparently, High's unpleasant past association with that paper was forgotten or, at least, forgiven. He converted the *Eagle Eye* into a thoroughgoing civil rights publication, billing it as "America's Greatest Newspaper Bombarding Segregation and Discrimination."[52]

The subject matter had changed, but High had not lost his zeal for naming names and spewing invective. His screeds against ignorant "white Miss. hoodlum" politicians made Howard's speeches look tame by comparison. High always went for the jugular, belittling the hypocrisy of segregationists who practiced "bedroom integration." He asked: "If that type of integration is OK, the *Eagle Eye* cannot see why integration in public education wont [sic] work." Howard was High's hero and Humes his nemesis. In early 1955, he proclaimed that "its Howard—*forever* and Humes—*forgotten.* And there is not a single man in the entire state of Miss. who has the respect and good will of 99% of the negro citizens that Dr. T. R. M. Howard has. . . . *WAKE UP,* Humes—the Negro of today will not accept your leadership comprising of the Miss. White hoodlum's ignorance tainted with ounces of thieving silver."[53]

High left no stone unturned in his search for readers. Constantly on the lookout, he made the rounds of black businesses in Jackson, his pockets stuffed with copies of recent issues. His hard work paid off both in Jackson and in the Delta. Jordana Y. Shakoor, who grew up in Greenwood, wrote that her father regularly received copies at his church and then passed them around. He "couldn't get it fast enough. He would often run out of issues long before he reached half the people wanting them." High also had friends in powerful places, including President Walter Davis of Tennessee A & I University. Davis put him up at the presidential mansion during visits to Nashville.[54]

By the end of 1954, northern black newspapers were starting to notice High. A reporter for the *Pittsburgh Courier* came to Mississippi to see him in action: "Passers-by are first asked to purchase the paper for 10 cents but if they are hesitant he'll say, 'Here take it, you need to read it.'" He did not bother himself with turning a profit and devoted only minimal space to advertisements. Local police arrested him several times, usually on charges of distributing the *Eagle Eye* without a permit. But even in Mississippi, the courts saw little legal justification to keep him behind bars. The judge who released High in January 1955 admitted that although articles in the *Eagle Eye* stirred up "racial strife and hatred," they were protected by the first amendment.[55]

High seemed totally oblivious to danger, boasting to police that if they want "to kill me, you know exactly where I live." This brought him admirers, but a few wondered if it was all for show. Charles Evers never really trusted him. He suspected that High was "playing both sides of the road" by publishing his "funny papers." The predominance of evidence does not confirm this. High's methods were offbeat, and he was more than a little odd as a person, but he seems to have been a sincere advocate of civil rights. Certainly Howard thought so. He was well aware of High's oddities and limitations but respected his bravery and zeal. Unlike many of Howard's other civil rights associates, Howard found High to be a consistently reliable and loyal ally during the intense segregationist crackdown of 1955.[56]

Meanwhile, Howard plunged ahead with preparations for an even bigger and better annual meeting of the RCNL in April. As usual, he aimed high in his search for a nationally known speaker by asking Ralph Bunche, the well-known black diplomat. But Bunche, who had once dated Howard's wife in Los Angeles, did not accept because of his duties at the United Nations. This setback was quickly forgotten when Howard scored a coup by lining up Michigan's freshman congressman, Representative Charles Diggs Jr. Only thirty-three, Diggs was one of three blacks in the House of Representatives.

He had personal reasons to accept. His father, Charles Diggs Sr., who accompanied him on the trip, was a native of Mound Bayou. The elder Diggs was better known to ordinary blacks because of his prestigious House of Diggs funeral home in Detroit.[57]

As many as thirteen thousand blacks, some traveling by mule, were in the audience, probably setting an attendance record for any event in Mound Bayou history. If the speeches were any guide, the economic pressure of the previous few months did not have the intended effect. The rhetoric was relentlessly militant. "It's two minutes to midnight, Mississippi," Diggs warned. Howard was more brazen than ever. He predicted that the next governor would be "the candidate who can say 'Nigger' loudest and longest."[58]

Howard further pumped up the crowd with subversive humor. He told them that the late Senator Bilbo, now in hell, had recently "sent a direct message to the capital at Jackson asking to stop treating the Negroes so badly in Mississippi and to give them a break, because they have a Negro fireman down there that keeps the fire mighty hot." Because the joke went over so well, it became a staple of his later speeches. While characterizing economic pressure as "a flop," he counseled against complacency because "the next round will be a well-organized wave of violence." Still, he did not completely abandon hope for racial reconciliation. He stressed that three of the votes for *Brown* came from "noble white southerners: [Stanley F.] Reed of Kentucky, [Hugo L.] Black of Alabama, and [Thomas C.] Clark of Texas."[59]

Howard turned part of the rally into a showcase on the ugliest elements of Jim Crow, including a "parade of victims" of alleged beatings by supporters of the Citizens' Councils. They included Dola Harper, a schoolteacher from Indianola. After she had asked to use a restroom at a bus station, whites beat her so badly that she suffered a burst eardrum. Two of Howard's civil rights allies from Belzoni were on the rostrum. Gus Courts recounted how the Citizens' Councils had deployed economic pressure against the grocery store he owned as he tried to register voters.[60]

Also speaking was Rev. George Lee, an official of the RCNL. The fifty-one-year-old minister and Gus Courts had cofounded the Belzoni NAACP. Between them, they had registered a hundred black voters. Lee had risen far from a childhood of poverty and appeared destined for a better future. He pastored four churches and operated a printing shop and a grocery store.

Later described by Howard as a "close personal friend," he was Howard's kindred soul in family origins, political views, oratorical style, and drive for self-improvement. Simeon Booker, a correspondent for *Jet,* saw how Lee's "down-home dialogue and his sense of political timing" had "electrified" the crowd. "Pray not for your mom and pop," Lee suggested. "They've gone to heaven. Pray you can make it through this hell."[61]

On May 7, Howard's foreboding of economic pressure presaging a wave of violence began to be realized. Just before midnight, a convertible pulled alongside Lee's car while he was on the way to pick up his preaching suit from a tailor-cleaner shop. Two shots fired by an unidentified assailant shattered Lee's jaw and drove him off the road. He never made it to the hospital. The killing followed a written death threat that he drop his name from the voting list. Three friends—Dr. Clinton C. Battle, Dr. Cyril Walwyn, and undertaker T. V. Johnson—performed the autopsy. Battle and Johnson were members of the RCNL, and Walden was chief surgeon of the Afro-American Hospital in Yazoo City. They extracted lead pellets from Lee's face that were consistent with buckshot. The sheriff, who wanted to call it a traffic accident, insisted that they were dental fillings torn loose by the impact of the crash.[62]

A few years earlier, the matter might have ended there, but Lee's wife, Rose, and his friends in Belzoni had other ideas. They sent messages appealing for help to Howard as well as A. H. McCoy, the new state NAACP president. Howard immediately phoned Representative Diggs, who then contacted the national office of the NAACP and the White House. The RCNL and the NAACP each contributed half of a one-thousand-dollar reward for information about the killers. Both groups appealed to Governor White and the FBI to launch investigations. White spurned them, stating that he did not answer letters from the NAACP. The sheriff finally admitted that bullet wounds were the cause of death but speculated that Lee was a "lady's man" and that the assailant was an angry husband.[63]

Howard's first important encounter with the FBI was two days after Lee's murder, when agents came to Mound Bayou to question him. The FBI had opened an investigation to determine whether Howard was a victim of extortion. It appears that the impetus came from Diggs, who had heard about death threats against him. The FBI report stated that Howard denied receiving "a letter, note, or any type of threat prior to 8:00 p.m., May 9, 1955." The absence of threats is surprising, given his high-profile opposition to segregation. Howard did state that he "had heard through sources not identified that a fund of $1,000 was being solicited" to hire someone to kill him.[64]

If the agents needed a reason to believe that Howard had legitimate fears for his safety, they got it during the middle of the interview, when he received a threatening phone call from an anonymous caller. The conversation lasted about five minutes. After Howard explained his views on integration, the caller threatened: "You better go slow if you want to live long." This did not seem to greatly alarm the FBI agents, who responded to Howard's request for protection by referring him to the local authorities. They did follow up, at least in a perfunctory way, by questioning individuals who allegedly had information about Lee's killers.[65]

Lee's funeral in Belzoni kept the case in the news. A key factor in building interest was Rose Lee's decision to make it an open-coffin ceremony. As a result, readers of the *Chicago Defender* and other newspapers could share her outrage by viewing a photo of her husband's mutilated corpse. Howard spoke. Booker was impressed less by the anger of the mourners than by their obsequious deference to white authority: "A white detective walked through the crowd without touching a soul. A pathway opened automatically as if the Negroes, even with their backs turned, could feel the presence of an approaching white man." A subsequent NAACP-organized memorial service in Belzoni drew more than one thousand. Wilkins shared the speakers' platform. Howard said that some blacks "would sell their grandmas for half a dollar, but Reverend Lee was not one of them."[66]

The NAACP and the RCNL combed the Delta looking for evidence. It was later said that Medgar Evers "cut his teeth" on the Lee case. He continually fed information to the press. The RCNL and the NAACP did their best to keep the story in the news, but interest soon started to wane. Also, cracks were appearing in the RCNL's leadership. Arenia Mallory, an early RCNL official, was the first of many to have second thoughts. She publicly denied news stories that she had attended the Mound Bayou meeting in April and promised never to "disrupt the good relationship we have in Mississippi among the races." The FBI investigation continued in a formal way under the civil rights division. It gradually ran out of steam, although it had identified credible white suspects, and agents had opined that potential witnesses were afraid to talk. No charges were ever brought.[67]

The United States Supreme Court's long-awaited enforcement order on May 31 further overshadowed the Lee case. In deliberately vague language, it directed that school integration proceed with "all deliberate speed." In Mississippi the response was as it had been in 1954. The NAACP doggedly decided to resume petitioning in local school districts, concentrating on the major population centers of Vicksburg, Clarksdale, Natchez, Yazoo City, and Jackson.[68]

As in the previous year, the RCNL struggled to find a middle ground. At a special meeting in Mound Bayou, two hundred of its officials simultaneously voted to reject formal participation in petitioning while endorsing the NAACP effort. In a letter to McCoy, Howard explained that he wanted to avoid needless duplication. He stressed that "you are our leader and we are with you. Let us know your program and we will follow, with our money, with our voice and with our information." There were unstated reasons too for Howard's reticence. Most obviously, he had every reason to anticipate a repetition of the 1954 disasters. Moreover, deep down he seems to have regarded voting rights, not desegregation, as the priority. Hence, the RCNL meeting set a goal of raising $100,000 for court suits to protect voting rights. On a related matter, *Jet* reported that the RCNL had a "hush-hush" long-term plan to elect a black congressman (Howard perhaps?) in the Delta. Finally, the RCNL proposed that the governor call a biracial conference "to work out race problems."[69]

Howard's critics, black and white, dismissed proposals for another conference or, for that matter, any negotiations. Percy Greene in the *Jackson Advocate* belittled him as comparable to "the Pied Piper, whose loud and intemperate speech and predictions . . . is leading a group of unthinking and unrealistic Negroes over the precipice to be drowned and destroyed in the whirlpool of frustration and hate." The *Jackson Daily News* was less lyrical but equally dismissive. An editorial praised Governor White for brushing aside the request for such a notorious "racial agitator and strife-breeder." The governor, it added, had "one experience with Howard's impudence, arrogance and insolence and is not in a mood to hear any more of it."[70]

On their side, NAACP officials were not inclined to pick fights with the RCNL. The bitter experience of 1954 was still fresh in their minds, and they realized that it was foolhardy to risk an open break. Better to calm the waters instead. After he heard rumors of a possible falling out with Howard, A. M. Mackel, the new president of the state NAACP, wrote to Wilkins to express his concerns. He defended Howard as an invaluable ally. Howard, Mackel stressed, had "many contacts with the masses and they believe in him. . . . Howard has the common touch. He takes time out to contact the 'little fellow.'" Mackel cautioned Wilkins not to underestimate Howard's value as a counterweight to Humes. They were "the best known men in the state, they have the largest followings of any two individuals." Wilkins wrote back reassuringly. He declared that the RCNL "may not be able to go all the way with us on every project but if they are willing to assist, to give us moral support, and above all not to give aid and comfort to our common opponents, we welcome him and them."[71]

Wilkins's portrayal of a happy division of labor was not entirely accurate. Several top NAACP officials persisted in their dislike and distrust of Howard, most notably Ruby Hurley. As recently as April, she had recommended against calling on him "any more than absolutely necessary. He is not, nor do I believe he ever will be, a friend of the NAACP." Wilkins did not follow this advice. His relationship with Howard, although never completely free of tension, was generally positive.[72]

As it turned out, the NAACP did not have the luxury of leaving anything to chance. It met unified, determined, and ruthless resistance in every location. The Yazoo City NAACP, for example, submitted a petition signed by fifty-three black parents to desegregate the schools. The local newspaper, in close cooperation with the Citizens' Councils, published all the names. Firings, boycotts, and threats soon followed. Many petitioners dropped their names, and by the end of the year fourteen fled the community. George L. Jefferson, Howard's friend who had run for Chief Grand Mentor against P. M. Smith in 1947, endured the full force of white resistance in Vicksburg. During the height of the school petitioning, someone burned a cross on his lawn. Although his funeral home survived, many said that the worry drove him to an early grave.[73]

The petitioners in Clarksdale held up better under the onslaught, but they too went down to defeat. On August 2, Aaron Henry proudly announced that the local NAACP chapter had submitted upward of three hundred signatures, more than twice the number elsewhere. A look at the names on the petition underscores the close *de facto* relationship between the RCNL and NAACP. Among the signers were Henry, the secretary of the RCNL, and three of the vice presidents and committee chairmen, John C. Melchor, Drew, and Burton.[74]

Segregationist opposition mobilized with devastating efficiency. Two days after Henry's announcement, a local chapter of the Citizens' Councils was formed. Before this time, Coahoma was the only Delta county that did not have representation in the movement. Later that month, Judge Brady spoke to a thousand whites at the first official meeting. The *Clarksdale Press Register* sent a not-so-subtle message to the NAACP by publishing the names of the petitioners. By the beginning of September, eighty-five of the signers had dropped their names because of pressure. The debacles of 1955 were so complete that the NAACP did not try again for many years to file school desegregation petitions in Mississippi.[75]

The voting rights of blacks throughout the state were equally in peril during that year. All candidates in the primary for governor in August disdained to solicit or accept black support. Howard, of course, was beyond the pale. Mary Cain, a relative racial moderate among the candidates, blamed him for "destroying racial barriers and mongrelizing the Negro and the white race." On election day, local officials, especially in smaller towns and rural areas, diligently followed the advice of the executive committee of the state Democratic Party to challenge the qualifications of black voters. In Cleveland and Belzoni, election officials separated out their ballots and put them in envelopes. Only about five hundred of the state's black voters braved white pressure and turned out. Everywhere the loss of the franchise was precipitous. Thomas Tubb, chair of the Democratic Party, expressed the prevailing view: "I don't believe that the Negro ought to be allowed to vote in Democratic primaries. . . . The white man founded Mississippi and it ought to remain that way."[76]

When Mound Bayou's city fathers opened the ballot box sent to them by white election officials, inside were notes from the county candidates promising not to accept any votes from the town. Mayor Green, in one of his ever-so-occasional open displays of assertiveness, sent the completed ballots to the county election committee as required by law and promised "to keep on putting them in the ballot box. Some day we're going to elect somebody and then they won't throw them out."[77]

Election-related violence led to the murder of yet another black leader. On August 13 Lamar Smith was gunned down in broad daylight on the courthouse lawn in Brookhaven, the hometown of Judge Brady. Smith, age sixty-three, was a farmer and, according to the *Jackson Advocate*, "widely known in state Elks and Masonic circles." During the primary election campaign, he had helped black voters fill out absentee ballots. Howard later described Smith as a "close personal friend," but no evidence exists of a direct connection between Smith and the RCNL or NAACP. The murder seemed like a throwback to the open violence of a previous generation. It happened in front of many witnesses but failed to go to trial because nobody was willing to testify. Strangely, it did not generate nearly the same amount of outrage as the Lee case and dropped quickly from the pages of the black press. The Eisenhower administration showed little interest. Arthur Caldwell, the chief of the Civil Rights Division, refused to take jurisdiction because the killing involved a state and not a federal election.[78]

The segregationist crackdown did not faze Howard a bit, if outward appearances are any guide. He was getting noticed more than ever outside the South. The *California Eagle,* for example, called him the "most hated, and the best loved, man in Mississippi." He was the focal point of an article in *Ebony* on "The New Fighting South." Accompanying photos showed thousands under a tent at the RCNL rally in April and the indefatigable Arrington High as he hawked copies of the *Eagle Eye.* The article emphasized the physical dangers faced by civil rights leaders. Under the heading "Death List" were pictures of Howard, Clinton C. Battle, Medgar Evers, Gus Courts, Emmett J. Stringer, A. H. McCoy, and T. V. Johnson. *Jet* covered Howard almost weekly. Booker visited Mississippi several times to see him. Booker's remembrances later appeared in his book, *Black Man's America.* Booker played up Howard's common touch and ability to inspire ordinary people. Several years later, he could still picture the "tall, broad-shouldered physician with his arm around a Delta mother. 'Sis Lou, you're a mighty healthy woman to raise some eight kids.'" According to Booker, Howard liked to tell "the joke about a dark-skinned foreigner walking into a Jackson, Mississippi, cafeteria and being told by a waitress that they didn't serve Negroes. Said he, 'I don't eat Negroes.'"[79]

In terms of achieving credibility from black leaders, Howard's biggest personal triumph was his selection as president-elect of the National Medical Association. Under the association's rules, he did not take office until August 1956 to serve out a single one-year term ending in August 1957. The election was quite a step up for a man who had left his first two important hospital positions under a cloud. Howard had finally won the acceptance in the black medical community that had long eluded him. The sixty-year-old organization had five thousand members and represented the cream of the black medical establishment. Timing was crucial, of course. Electing Howard was the perfect way for the NMA to send a clear pro–civil rights message.[80]

Howard's life in August 1955 was an unsettling combination of accomplishment, adulation, and life-threatening danger. The single constant was uncertainty. Howard seemed well on his way to becoming a significant national black leader. At the same time, his future place in Mississippi was in serious doubt. Whites, who had earlier respected him, now reviled him. Howard's embrace of the *Brown* decision had destroyed most of his once-considerable ties with the white establishment. This was no small loss in a state where personal relationships counted so heavily. The RCNL was still formidable, but it faced a segregationist offensive that never seemed to lessen in intensity. If Howard lost this civil rights fight, his economic and social achievements, possibly his life, would be imperiled. Even while he celebrated his election to the NMA, critically important events were unfolding in the small Delta town of Money that would forever change the course of Howard's life.

Howard and his mother, Mary Palmer, in front of the African Methodist Episcopal Church in Murray, Ky. (ca.1932), Courtesy of the late Verda Harris, a gift to the Beitos.

Gospel singer Mahalia Jackson and Rep. William L. Dawson of Illinois pose (front row) at the Howard estate during the first annual conference of the Regional Council of Negro Leadership, Mound Bayou, Miss. 1952. Original photo by the late John Gunn, photographer for the *Chicago Defender* newspaper, from the author's collection.

The Howards entertain guests at their Mound Bayou home. Seated are Esther Burton, Dr. Edward Burton, and Helen Howard. From the archives of the now defunct *Our World* magazine.

T.R.M. Howard chairs a meeting of top officers of the Regional Council of Negro Leadership, Mound Bayou, 1955. From the archives of the now defunct *Our World* magazine.

The crowd, numbering more than ten thousand, gets excited as RCNL officers hand out voting registration information at its annual conference in May 1955. at RCNL annual conference, May 1955. The conference met under a circus tent in Mound Bayou. From the archives of *Jet* magazine, a division of Johnson Publishing, which is now defunct.

T.R.M. Howard checks barbecued chicken at the same conference. The crowd ate three tons. RCNL leaders were well armed. Note the rifle on top of the box. From the archives of *Jet* magazine, a division of Johnson Publishing, which is now defunct.

In a speech at the RCNL conference, T.R.M. Howard angrily recounts for the crowd how Nathanial Bell (to his right) was beaten by police. From the archives of *Jet* Magazine, a division of Johnson Publishing, which is now defunct.

In September 1955, witnesses and guests pose in the courtroom in Sumner, Miss., during the trial of the accused killers of Emmett Till. Left to right: Add Reed, unidentified witness, Mamie Till Bradley (later Mamie Till-Mobley), T.R.M. Howard, Rep. Charles Diggs of Michigan, Mary Amanda Bradley. Permission for use granted by the University of Memphis Library, Memphis Press-Scimitar Collection.

Shame Of Mississippi

Chicago Defender cartoon on the recent killings of George W. Lee, Lamar Smith, and Emmett Till. T.R.M. Howard is coming to the rescue, followed by national NAACP leader Roy Wilkens. (September 10, 1955)

Wrong Foe, Wrong Place, Wrong Time

A cartoon from the *Baltimore Afro-American* newspaper during Howard's public feud with J. Edgar Hoover, director of the F.B.I. over the bureau's failure to find the killers of Emmett Till and other African Americans. (February 4, 1956) Permission to use from *Baltimore Afro-American*.

Republican candidate T.R.M. Howard meets President Dwight D. Eisenhower in Chicago on the eve of the 1958 election for the House of Representatives. From the archives of the William McBride Papers, and the Vivian G. Harsh Research Collection of Afro-American History and Literature, at the Chicago Public Library. No copyright owner available.

T.R.M. Howard poses in the Safari Room of his Chicago mansion as "America's greatest black hunter," about 1971. Courtesy of the late Stephen Gardner Birmingham, photographer and novelist.

T.R.M. Howard moved easily between the worlds of the masses and the wealthy. Members of the Afro American (and sometimes white) elite flocked to his ostentatious parties on New Year's Eve in Chicago. In this photo, Jesse Owens, the famous Olympian, "crowns" Howard as king of the party for 1972. Also pictured is Owen's wife Ruth. From the archives of the *Chicago Defender.*

T.R.M. Howard at his desk at the Friendship Medical Center, about 1975. In 1972, Howard founded the multimillion-dollar Friendship Medical Center on the South Side, the largest privately owned Afro-American clinic in Chicago. Courtesy of the late Sandra Morgan.

6

"Hell to Pay in Mississippi"
The Murder of Emmett Till

AUGUST OF 1955 was shaping up to be one of the happiest months of Howard's life, and he was determined to get some enjoyment. He headed off to Los Angeles for an extended visit with the Boyds and to accept the presidency of the National Medical Association (NMA). Despite the honor, he had more than enough cause to be discouraged and anxious. The initial indignation over Lamar Smith's murder was already fading. The killing of George W. Lee seemed a distant memory. He must have wondered who would be next. He did not have to wait long to find out. As Howard arrived in Los Angeles to accept the presidency of the NMA, the opening act of a tragedy was under way in Mississippi. The final outcome helped to reshape not only Howard's life but the entire course of black history in the United States.[1]

On August 20, 1955, a fourteen-year-old boy from Chicago, Emmett Louis Till, took the Illinois Central Railroad to Mississippi to spend time with his cousins Maurice and Simeon Wright, Wheeler Parker (also from Chicago), his great-uncle Mose Wright, and Wright's child Robert. His mother, Mamie Bradley (she later changed her name to Till-Mobley), had not relished the thought of letting him visit the state that she had left as a child. Her son had little direct experience with Mississippi's strict and intricate codes of segregation and white supremacy. But he was determined to go. As an extra precaution, Bradley carefully reminded him to show deference to whites in any encounter.[2]

Till's destination was Leflore County. Located on the eastern edge of the Delta, it was uncomfortably close to the recent violence. Humphreys County, the scene of the Lee murder, was next door. Leflore County was rural and isolated, even by the standards of the Delta. Nearly two-thirds of the residents were black, but almost none of them had the right to vote. Poverty was pervasive. Blacks earned a median family income of $1,400 compared to a $5,200 for whites. Mose Wright was better off than most. He was a tenant farmer but had improved his situation through hard work, thrift, steady habits, and proficiency in the backbreaking art of cotton picking. Over the years, he had acquired a four-bedroom house, a vegetable garden, and some livestock. He had served as a Christian minister and was well regarded for his quiet dignity and sincerity.[3]

Till had been in Mississippi for only four days when he had the encounter that led to his death. He joined Maurice and Simeon Wright, Wheeler Parker, Ruthie Mae Crawford, and three local boys in taking the car to buy treats at Bryant's Grocery and Meat Market, a little general store in Money. Money, despite its name, was a sleepy, small, poor hamlet, not far from Greenwood and about three miles from the Wright farm. Behind the counter that day was twenty-one-year-old Carolyn Bryant, an attractive white woman. Roy Bryant, Carolyn's husband, who was the owner of the store, was out of town.[4]

The controversy about what happened next has taken on almost Rashomonesque proportions over the decades. The initial newspaper accounts, which drew heavily on the statements of the cousins who were at the scene, generally agreed that it all began when an older boy dared Till to go into the store to "look at the pretty lady." Never one to shrink from a challenge, he walked in and bought bubblegum. One of the boys started to worry about what might be happening, went in, and dragged Till outside. As Till was leaving, he said "goodbye" (not "goodbye, ma'am"). He followed up with a loud "wolf whistle," apparently directed toward Carolyn Bryant. Later, it was said that he uttered "ugly remarks" but, if he did, nobody except Bryant was close enough to hear.[5]

In 2017, Carolyn Bryant admitted parts of her story were false to historian and author Timothy Tyson.[6] Even in the earliest reports, the story was not as simple as it seemed. Till's friends and family members pointed out, for example, that a stutter caused by a childhood bout with infantile paralysis often made him hard to understand. According to Mose Wright, he "had a habit of whistling and hollering at girls, but he only did it for fun. He didn't mean any harm." Till and his cousins scurried for the car after it appeared that Carolyn Bryant was running to get a gun. The car sped off toward Mose Wright's farm. Hoping it would all blow over, everyone in the group promised not to repeat the story. For a while, it looked as if they had made the right choice. Two days passed without incident.[7]

Nothing could have prepared the cousins for the traumatic events of August 28, 1955. Around 2:00 a.m., two men knocked furiously on Mose Wright's front door. They were Roy Bryant and John William Milam (also called "Big Milam") of Glendora. The half-brothers presented a sharp contrast. Bryant was thin, tall, passive, and indecisive—the type to blend into a crowd. Milam was impossible to ignore. At 235 pounds and six foot two inches tall, he was a bear of a man. He was bald, brawny, and used to getting his way.[8]

When Mose Wright answered the door, Milam demanded to see "the boy that done the talking down at Money." Mose and Elizabeth Wright futilely tried to appease them through profuse apologies, promises to discipline the boy, and offers of money. Milam cut them off. He asked Mose Wright for his age. When Mose said he was sixty-four, Milam responded that he better not interfere or "you will never live to get to be sixty-five." Mose Wright spotted a person who he said had a voice lighter than a man's waiting in the car. In addition, he saw a third man outside on the porch. Nobody could get a clear view because of the darkness. Wright guessed that the man was black. Milam and Bryant searched the house until they found Till. As they prepared to leave, Milam instructed Elizabeth Wright "to get back in that bed, and I mean, I want to hear the springs." They took Till outside. The person in the car said Till was the boy they were looking for. They ordered him to get in, and drove into the darkness toward Money.[9]

The Wrights nervously waited until the afternoon of the next day. Finally, Elizabeth Wright's brother Crosby Smith volunteered to drive into Greenwood to tell Sheriff George Smith about the kidnapping. The sheriff questioned, and then arrested, the half-brothers. They admitted to abducting Till but said that they had dropped him off in front of the store after Carolyn Bryant told them that he was not "the right one." Smith did not find the mysterious third kidnapper who had waited on the porch. Although he had named Carolyn Bryant in the first warrants, he decided not to make an arrest because "she's got two small boys to take care of."[10]

Almost overnight, the kidnapping captured the attention of black news outlets, such as *Jet* and the *Chicago Defender*, and civil rights leaders, including Howard. His comments were strident. He predicted that if the "slaughtering of

Negroes is allowed to continue, Mississippi will have a civil war. Negroes are going to take only so much." He also conferred with Mamie Bradley by phone. While this was happening, the Civil Rights Division of the Department of Justice and the FBI briefly considered whether they had jurisdiction but just as quickly demurred because the kidnappers had not crossed state lines. On the morning of August 31, an accidental discovery confirmed the worst possible news about Till's fate. A fisherman spotted two human knees bobbing on the surface of the Tallahatchie River. They belonged to Till. The murderers had taken great care to cover up their crime. Using barbed wire, they had tied the body to a heavy cotton-gin fan-wheel. Through a quirk, it tangled in branches and failed to sink to the bottom. The corpse was badly mutilated.[11]

Howard, who was in Chicago for a previously scheduled speech when Till's body was found, expressed outrage. Vowing that there would "be hell to pay in Mississippi," he demanded a federal investigation. Roy Wilkins, the head of the NAACP, was usually circumspect in his public statements, but this was different. Caught by the emotion of the moment, he suggested that "Mississippi has decided to maintain white supremacy by murdering children." No lynching or murder had ever so completely galvanized black Americans. Mamie Bradley's insistence that the body be put on public display in Chicago made the difference. She wanted the world to see "what they did to my boy." In May, Rose Lee had allowed an open-coffin ceremony for George W. Lee, but the impact was not nearly as profound. The combined effects of a gunshot to the head, a severe beating, and exposure to the elements had horribly disfigured his body. The top of the skull was missing, the head had a one-inch bullet hole, the tongue protruded grotesquely, the skin was badly decayed, and an ear, an eye, and a tooth were missing. As many as a hundred thousand mourners filed past Till's casket during the four days of public viewing. The line stretched around the block.[12]

For a while, white Mississippians appeared to share the outrage. Newspapers and political leaders vociferously condemned the murder and demanded swift punishment of the guilty. To the *Clarksdale Press Register*, it was "a savage and senseless crime. . . . If conviction with the maximum penalty of the law cannot be secured in this heinous crime, then Mississippi may as well burn all its law books and close its courts." Hodding Carter's *Delta Democrat Times* of Greenville warned that if the state was unable to "accomplish justice in this matter . . . we will deserve the criticism we get." The *Greenwood Commonwealth* featured a front-page editorial stating that the "citizens of this area are determined that the guilty parties shall be punished to the full extent of the law." Governor Hugh White sent a telegram to the NAACP promising a vigorous prosecution. In taking this action, he broke from a previous self-imposed ban on communications with that organization.[13]

This interlude of righteous indignation did not last long. Within a few days, a full-scale backlash had set in. Whites showed increasing anger about the drumbeat of criticism of Mississippi from the northern newspapers and civil rights leaders, particularly Roy Wilkins. Another bad portent for any hope of conviction was the change of jurisdiction from Leflore County (where the kidnapping occurred) to Tallahatchie County (where the body was found). Prominent blacks, including Simeon Booker, a reporter from *Jet,* and Ruby Hurley, the southeastern director of the NAACP, had consistently praised Sheriff George Smith of Leflore County. To Howard, who was usually unrelenting in his criticism of Mississippi's white leaders, he was the "most courageous and the fairest sheriff in the entire State of Mississippi." Nobody would say that about Sheriff Henry Clarence Strider of Tallahatchie County. His actions, more than those of any other individual, undercut the chances of a serious and thorough investigation.[14]

Strider's most devastating legal bombshell exploded on September 3, when he voiced doubts that the body pulled from the river belonged to Till. Abandoning even the pretense of objectivity, he speculated that it was an NAACP "trick" and that Till was still alive. This was too much for George Smith's deputy, Ed Cothran. He pointed out that he had been present when Mose Wright identified the body after seeing a ring that had belonged to Till's father and bore the initials "L. T." (Louis Till). When confronted by this evidence, Strider and his defenders upped the ante. They retorted that the NAACP had planted the ring on an unidentified corpse. According to one theory, Howard had aided the conspiracy by donating a cadaver from Howard's Sara W. Brown Hospital. Even whites who believed that the defendants were guilty recoiled at the prospect of convicting two white men for such a crime. If Milam and Bryant had killed the young man, after all, it was for the lofty goal of protecting the purity of white southern womanhood. Even if most whites disapproved of the murder, they did not necessarily regard the offense as serious enough to justify a prison sentence, much less the death penalty.[15]

Despite these ominous signs, a Tallahatchie County grand jury surprised observers by approving murder and kidnapping indictments of Milam and Bryant on September 7. The upcoming trial, scheduled to begin on September 19, had the makings of a major legal showdown. The jury was all-white, although Tallahatchie County was two-thirds black. Because the county did not have a single registered black voter, under the law for the selection of jurors, it could not have been otherwise. Courtesy of money raised by local citizens, Milam and Bryant hired a dream team of five lawyers led by Jesse J. Breland, a graduate of Princeton. Assisting him was John W. Whitten Jr., a cousin of Jamie Whitten, a member of the U.S. House of Representatives.[16]

At the helm of the prosecution was District Attorney Gerald Chatham, a seasoned professional. Although he was an elected official, he had little to fear from racist popular pressure, at least in political terms. After a long career, he was approaching retirement. In addition, Governor White delegated Robert B. Smith III, a former FBI agent and highly regarded attorney from Ripley, to assist the prosecution. The prosecution's chief liability, of course, was the outright obstruction of its principal law enforcement officer and investigator, Sheriff Strider. More worrisome still was the readiness of whites to embrace Strider's claim of an NAACP hoax, or at least give it lip service.[17]

Even before the trial, the Howard home in Mound Bayou had taken on the character of a "black command center" and haven for journalists, witnesses, and prominent visitors. Mamie Bradley stayed there. She came away with pleasant memories of playing with T. R. M. and Helen's adopted baby, Barrett. The tight security in and around the house left a deep impression on guests. It was so impregnable that journalists and politicians from a later era might have used the word "compound" rather than "home" to describe it. Simeon Booker characterized Howard's security arrangements as "a model of dispatch and efficiency." Strangers passed through a checkpoint, and guards were on duty around the clock. Bradley particularly remembered "an old man with a long shotgun" who she was told "really knew how to use it." Firearms were ubiquitous, including a pistol strapped to Howard's waist. When Cloyte Murdock of *Ebony* had difficulty getting her luggage through the front door, she looked around the corner and saw a cache of weapons on the other side. Another visitor spied a magnum pistol and a .45 at the head of Howard's bed, a Thompson submachine gun at the foot, and "a long gun, a shotgun or rifle, in every corner of every room."[18]

The Howard home also had an uninvited guest. He was Frank Young, an ordinary plantation worker who had traveled some distance. Arriving around midnight on Sunday the day before the trial, he insisted on talking with Howard. He had a remarkable story to tell. Young reported that he had direct evidence linking Milam and Bryant to the crime. About six o'clock on the morning of the kidnapping, black witnesses had seen a 1955 green and white Chevrolet pickup truck pull onto a plantation three miles west of the small town of Drew in Sunflower County. The manager of the plantation was Leslie Milam, a brother of J. W. Milam and Roy Bryant. The truck had four white men in the cab and three black males in the back. The one in the middle was Emmett Till. After it parked, the entire group walked into an equipment shed (often described as a "red barn") on the property. Young and other witnesses began to hear what sounded like a beating. Slowly the cries died down and were heard no more. Two blacks, including Young, walked in closer to get a better look. They saw J. W. Milam come outside to get a drink of water from a well. Sometime later the truck pulled into the shed. When it drove away, a tarpaulin covered the back, and the boy in the middle was missing. Witnesses placed two of J. W. Milam's black employees, Henry Lee Loggins and Levi "Too Tight" Collins, or both, in the kidnapping party.[19]

These revelations were earthshaking. They could provide eyewitness evidence of the kidnapping and possibly murder and shift the trial venue to Sunflower County. Throughout the first day of the trial, Howard and others did their best to confirm the story before going to the authorities. Meanwhile, the proceedings went forward as scheduled.[20]

The residents of the modestly sized, and predominantly black, town of Sumner were suddenly thrust into the middle of a spectacle. A thousand or more journalists and curiosity seekers filled the streets, hotels, and restaurants. Reporters had flocked to Sumner from all over the country, including Chicago, New York City, Dallas, and Atlanta. They represented such diverse publications as the *New York Post, Ebony, Jet,* the *Chicago Defender,* the *Memphis Press-Scimitar,* the *St. Louis Post-Dispatch, Life, Time,* and the *Nation.* Among the reporters were David Halberstam, Murray Kempton, John Herbers of the United Press, and James Kilgallen, the father of Dorothy of "What's My Line," and best known for his coverage of the Lindbergh baby kidnapping trial. Even the Communist *Daily Worker* sent a correspondent: Rob Hall, the white son of a banker from Pascagoula, Mississippi. Local residents did not show fear or anger at this homegrown Red in their midst but reacted with a mixture of cautious cordiality and confused curiosity: imagine a white Communist who talked and acted just like them! Hall reciprocated to some extent. His stories were generally dispassionate and balanced. In a rare investment of resources for an age when television news was in its infancy, NBC assigned a film crew. Newspapers from as far away as Moscow, Paris, and London took a keen interest in the trial as a critical test of American justice and race relations.[21]

By some measures, Sumner had already flunked that test. Although the courtroom was able to accommodate two hundred people, Jim Crow rules forced black spectators to squeeze into an allotted twenty-three seats in the very back on the right. They were a majority of the crowd outside. The white reporters had seats at long mahogany tables near the judge's bench, but the black press had to make do with a small card table. They had to endure Sheriff Strider's cheerful greeting of "Hello, Niggers" as they filed in from lunch. "Oh God, if that man had been an actor," Mamie Bradley later wrote, "he would have played the part of a racist Southern sheriff. He looked the part. He lived the part. . . . He was malicious, he was hostile, he was in charge."[22]

The first day of the trial had many fascinating aspects, but it was a sideshow compared to what was happening in Mound Bayou. Howard, various NAACP members, and others were trying to round up witnesses to confirm Frank Young's midnight account. Howard's impulsiveness again clouded his judgment. He told several black reporters about Young's visit, including Booker, James Hicks of the *Afro-American* of Baltimore, and Robert M. Ratcliffe of the *Pittsburgh Courier*. Although he asked them to keep it quiet until the witnesses were in safekeeping, he was taking great risks. Confronted by the possible scoop of a lifetime, Hicks reluctantly resisted the temptation to file a story. In fairness, Howard may have hoped to deploy the reporters in the search for evidence. If so, he had some basis for this hope. Hicks had been able through independent sources to uncover rumors that Sheriff Strider had checked Loggins and Collins into a jail in Charleston, Mississippi, to keep them from testifying.[23]

Much later that evening Howard participated in a strategy meeting, at the the office of the Magnolia Mutual Life Insurance Company, in Mound Bayou to decide how to move forward on the new evidence. Those attending included Booker, Hicks, Hurley, and L. Alex Wilson of the *Chicago Defender.* They agreed to contact trusted white reporters who would, in turn, act as intermediaries with law enforcement officials. They promised to keep the story secret until Tuesday night, when the witnesses to the events in Drew would be gathered together to talk with reporters and law enforcement officers. Participants at the Mound Bayou meeting selected John Popham of the *New York Times* and, upon Howard's recommendation, Clark Porteous of the *Memphis Press-Scimitar.* Porteous was a good choice. He was thoroughly familiar with local conditions and was well regarded by blacks.[24]

Howard miscalculated badly in his subsequent phone conversation with Porteous. He failed to secure his pledge to bring Popham and no one else. When Porteous arrived in Mound Bayou, Popham was not with him. More seriously, he brought along (probably for company) two reporters, W. C. Shoemaker and Jim Featherstone, from the arch-segregationist *Jackson Daily News.* When Howard met with them, he compounded his earlier mistake by blurting out the entire story before extracting a promise of secrecy. He only remembered to ask for such an assurance after he had finished. After much frantic back-and-forth discussion, the three agreed to hold the story when the others promised that they would be the only white reporters at the meeting. Now chagrined by his mistake, Howard offered to provide protection for the new witnesses.[25]

As the second day of the trial moved forward, few reporters had any inkling of these maneuvers. The proceedings began routinely, at least under the circumstances. The sensation of the morning was the first courtroom appearance of Mamie Bradley and Rep. Charles Diggs, who stayed for the second time that year in the already crowded Howard home. Each day, Howard escorted Bradley and Diggs from Mound Bayou to Sumner in an armed car caravan. Bradley asked to ride in Howard's air-conditioned Cadillac, but Howard refused her because it would have made a more inviting target for snipers.[26]

As Bradley entered the courtroom, a throng of reporters peppered her with questions. Did she have any new evidence to offer? What did she hope to accomplish by testifying? How had she been treated? The atmosphere was menacing. White children fired cap pistols at her as their fathers slapped their knees and laughed loudly. Nobody had bothered to arrange seating for Diggs in the crowded Jim Crow courtroom, but he avoided an awkward situation by pulling up a chair at the black press table. Law enforcement officials hurriedly continued to gather evidence about the incident in Drew.[27]

By noon, prosecutors decided that the time had come to act. Citing a "startling development," they asked Judge Curtis M. Swango for more time to track down witnesses and pursue leads. Despite objections from the defense, he granted a half-day recess until the next morning. The sheriffs of Sunflower and Leflore counties and special state investigators examined the alleged site of Till's beating at the Shurden plantation near Drew. They apparently did not invite Sheriff Strider, now working as a de facto witness for the defense. The hurried investigation did not include scientific tests. No bloodstains were apparent from a purely visual search of the equipment shed's floor, which was covered with corn and soybeans. Howard claimed that someone had tipped off the criminals, enabling them to clean up the site in the preceding hours. The investigators had greater success in their search of an abandoned cotton gin near Itta Bena, where they discovered that a gin fan-wheel (possibly the same one tied around Till's neck) was missing.[28]

Meanwhile, Howard, black and white reporters, and assorted civil rights activists were scrambling to find, protect, and assemble all the witnesses at 8:00 p.m. in Mound Bayou. Hurley, donning a red bandana, went undercover as a sharecropper. None of the witnesses showed up at the scheduled meeting. Advance news about the search may have scared them. The whole investigation appeared on the verge of collapse. Sheriff Smith, who said he had been trying to find other guilty parties since the beginning of the investigation, urged them on: "These witnesses have a story to tell. We've got to find them if it takes all night." Thus, what Booker called "Mississippi's first major interracial manhunt" was under way.[29]

Working together, law enforcement officials and blacks divided into several racially mixed groups and rushed at high speeds in their cars to find and bring the witnesses to Drew for safekeeping. Howard promised to help relocate them to Chicago after the trial. The searchers found Frank Young about 1:00 a.m., but he insisted that he would talk only with Howard. Because Howard was delayed, Young eventually left but promised to appear the next day. They had better luck with the other witnesses. The most valuable of these was Willie Reed, eighteen, who had seen the incident at the equipment shed. He stayed for the rest of the trial in Howard's Mound Bayou home, which was probably the one place in Mississippi he could feel safe. Reed later said it was so secure that it was just "like trying to get into the White House." Unfortunately, Loggins and Collins were nowhere to be found.[30]

Although the prosecution kept the witnesses to the beating in reserve, the third day of the trial was still eventful. Especially dramatic was Mose Wright's description of Till's early morning abduction. The method of questioning carefully followed the Delta's rigid etiquette of white racial supremacy. Not even lawyers for the prosecution used courtesy titles. They addressed him as "Uncle Mose" or "Old Man Mose." Wright testified in depth about how Milam and Bryant had barged in, searched the rooms, and threatened him and his wife. The testimony was consistent with the theory that others took part in the abduction. Wright reiterated that two people waited outside. One was a man shrouded in the darkness on the porch who was peering down as if hiding his face. When asked whether the man was black or white, he answered that he did not know but that he "acted like a colored man" because "he stayed outside." The crowd laughed. They knew what he meant. Wright was unable to give many details about the other person in the car but said that the voice "seemed like it was a little lighter voice than a man's." Wright was confident, direct, and held firm despite a withering cross-examination from the defense. The testimony reached a climax when Chatham asked him to identify who had abducted his grand nephew. In an act of considerable bravery, he stood up, pointed to Milam, and said, "There he is."[31]

The high drama continued on Thursday. In the morning, the prosecution called Mamie Bradley, who had been observing the trial from the black press table. The lawyers called her "Mamie," rather than Mrs. Bradley. In moving testimony, she painstakingly told how she had confirmed through close inspection that the mangled body was her son. The defense lawyer's cross-examination implied something sinister about her $400 burial policy on Emmett. She handled his full cross-examination with composure. Bradley seemed, in the words of Murray Kempton, to be trying mightily to "bridge the gap" between herself and the jury.[32]

After a delay of a day, the prosecution finally produced its lineup of "mystery witnesses." The linchpin of the state's case, Willie Reed, was an unsung hero of the Till trial. His explosive testimony confirmed key facts in Young's earlier account to Howard. Reed lived next door to the plantation managed by Leslie Milam near Drew. While walking to a country store at six o'clock on Sunday morning, the day after the kidnapping, he saw a green and white 1955 Chevrolet pickup truck pull into the equipment shed on the plantation managed by Leslie Milam. Four whites were in the cab and four blacks in the back. One of them was Till. Reed had been able to identify him after the fact from a picture in the newspaper. He continued: "I came on by the barn. . . . I heard some licks like somebody was whipping somebody. . . . A whole lot of them. . . . It sounded like a human being." When Reed edged in closer to hear, he saw a big bald man come out to drink water from the well. The man carried a pistol in a holster. When asked by the prosecutor to identify the man, Reed stood up and pointed to J. W. Milam. Reed was visibly nervous, but despite the best efforts of the defense to challenge his testimony, he held firm. Reporters described him as one of the prosecution's strongest witness.[33]

The others who followed Reed on the stand gave further corroboration. One was Mary Amanda Bradley (no relation to Mamie Bradley), fifty years of age and a sharecropper in the Milam-managed plantation. She lived just adjacent to the equipment shed. Reed came by her house to tell her about the strange cries. From her window, she saw a truck with four men outside. One of them looked like J. W. Milam. Another witness was Add Reed, Willie Reed's grandfather. He claimed to have walked past Leslie Milam and another white man that morning. Because the witnesses did not hear gunshots (and thus evidence of murder), prosecutors decided not to suggest a change of venue to Sunflower County. They were operating under a plausible theory that Milam, Bryant, and company had roughed up Till in the shed but had not killed him there.[34]

The statements of the witnesses left many unanswered questions. Reed said that the he did not know the other blacks on the truck other than Till. Although on the prosecution's witness list, for example, Frank Young never testified. It is not clear why, although a newspaper report indicated that he was outside the courtroom but left, perhaps unaware that he was supposed to enter and identify himself.[35]

The final two witnesses were for the defense, Carolyn Bryant and Sheriff Strider. The prosecution objected that Bryant's testimony was not relevant to the case. Swango ruled that it was inadmissible, but he still let her undergo questioning though not in the presence of the jury. This was probably his most bizarre decision. Despite Swango's admonition, the substance of her testimony probably leaked to the jury, thus almost certainly prejudicing the prosecution's case. Her depiction of Till diverged sharply from that of Mamie Bradley. She said that a "nigger man" had come into the store, put his hands around her waist, and asked, "How about a date, baby?" He taunted her with "unprintable" words when she resisted, boasting that he had been "with white women before." In answer to a defense lawyer's question about whether the "man" had a speech defect, she said that he did not.[36]

Strider reiterated his earlier accusations and added the claim that the corpse fished from the river was of a man who was "as white as I am." The defense tried to plant further seeds of doubt by calling Dr. L. B. Otken, a physician in Greenwood. Otken asserted that the corpse was so decayed that it must have been in the river eight or more days and that it was impossible to determine the race.[37]

That evening, reporters explored hot tips on tantalizing rumors about Loggins and Collins. An unidentified source told L. Alex Wilson that Sheriff Strider had locked the pair in jail under false names ten days before the trial. Supposedly, the arrest came after someone saw Collins washing blood from a truck. When questioned by a black man, he said it was from a deer hunt, though deer were out of season. The implication, of course, was that Strider was trying to suppress evidence during the trial. Wilson, Booker, and an assistant to Diggs tracked down someone able to identify the two men. Wilson and his colleagues had wanted to make a surprise inspection of the jail. Porteous brought the proposal to District Attorney Chatham and Sheriff Smith. They turned him down, stating that they had already checked the jail for Collins and Loggins but found nothing. The trial was speeding toward conclusion and was not going to be delayed by a second round of "startling" new evidence.[38]

The last day was anticlimactic. Defense attorney Whitten's closing argument hammered hard on the themes of race and conspiracy: "There are people in the United States who want to defy the customs of the South . . . and would commit perhaps any crime known to man. . . . They include doctors and undertakers and they have ready access to a corpse which could meet their purpose." Chatham's summation for the prosecution was passionate, deeply moving, and compelling. He shouted that the defendants "were dripping with the blood of Emmett Till" and belittled the defense's conspiracy theory. If Strider now thought that the corpse was white, then why had he said on August 31 that it was the body of a black boy? (Chatham could have also asked, but apparently did not, why Strider had called on the services of a black undertaker.) As to Dr. Otken, "if he can't tell black from white, I don't want him to be writing any prescriptions for me." He singled out Willie Reed for praise, emphasizing that defense attorneys had failed to "break him down although they tried in the worst way." Robert B. Smith III went even farther and said that Reed's courage in coming forward showed that he had "more nerve than I have." Chatham made his own appeal to local traditions, warning that "unless you judge this case on its merits it will endanger the precepts and examples which we hold dear in the South." Just as Chatham closed, Mamie Bradley whispered to a reporter, "He could not have done any better."[39]

In the end, none of it mattered. On September 23, the jury deliberated for an hour and eight minutes before rendering a verdict of not guilty. According to one juror, if they "hadn't stopped to drink pop, it wouldn't have taken that long." Sensing the coming bad news, Mamie Bradley, Mose Wright, and Diggs had not bothered to wait for the verdict or the inevitable celebration. Howard drove the group, which came to include Mose Wright, Reed, and Mary Amanda Bradley, to Mound Bayou, where he arranged their transportation to the airport in Memphis. Milam and Bryant were not out of the woods yet. They still faced charges of kidnapping in Leflore County.[40]

With Howard's help, Willie Reed settled permanently in Chicago. Mary Amanda Bradley and Mose Wright joined them there. Howard remained in contact with Reed and Mamie Bradley for quite some time. He was later her doctor, and he was the featured speaker at a benefit to raise money for Reed. In later years, both expressed considerable admiration for Howard and gratitude for his guidance and protection during the trial.[41]

It was probably not within the realm of possibility to secure a murder conviction against Milam and Bryant. The most obvious problem was the composition of the jury. The prosecution had stumbled badly in the selection process by allowing them to come primarily from the deeply prejudiced hill country section of the county. Another mistake was the decision to screen out anyone who knew Milam and Bryant. This backfired because, by all indications, people who had dealings with the brothers were more likely to dislike them.[42]

Members of the jury had apparently made up their minds before any witness appeared. A few years after the trial, Hugh Stephen Whitaker asked each of them about their reasoning. They all confirmed that they believed that Milam and Bryant were guilty; only one gave any credence to Strider's claims of a planted corpse. They denied that their verdict was a response to criticism of Mississippi or perceived interference by northern agitators. Quite simply, they regarded killing a black male for insulting a white woman as not serious enough to merit the prescribed punishment. According to Whitaker, all "parties concerned—the judge, prosecuting attorneys, defense attorneys, the jury, and the accused—knew that a verdict of not guilty was certain."[43]

This raises a closely related problem of how fair and thorough the conduct of the judge and prosecutors was. At the time, most outside observers, black or white, commented positively on their performance. They singled out Judge Swango for praise, but Robert B. Smith III and Gerald Chatham were not far behind. A few days after the verdict the *Tri-State Defender* reported that it was the "unanimous opinion of Negro press correspondents at the Till trial that Judge Curtis M. Swango was impartial and fair and further that he would have been a satisfactory representative if on the supreme court bench." Other kind words for the prosecutors and judge came from Mamie Bradley, Diggs, Hurley, and Dan Wakefield of the *Nation*, although Hurley privately expressed "grave reservations about the amount of effort that went into preparation for the case by the state." Similarly, Booker wrote that he was "proud of the law enforcers" and "personally knew they had done what they could."[44]

Howard, by contrast, was always pessimistic about the likelihood of a fair trial or thorough investigation. A few days before it started, he estimated the odds against the defendants getting more than ten years in prison at fifty-to-one, and his hopes dimmed after that. Just before the acquittal, he suggested that a white man was less likely to suffer a penalty for such a crime than for "killing deer out of season." Once the verdict was in, Howard expanded on this critique. He put forward a compelling case. Investigators and prosecutors had never scientifically tested the equipment shed or Milam's truck for bloodstains, fingerprints, or related physical evidence. They failed to call expert witnesses to refute claims that the body was not Till's or to order an autopsy. They did not conduct ballistics tests matching the make or model of Milam's gun to the bullet wound in the body. The search for Loggins and Collins, in no way a sustained one, lasted only a half day, hardly enough for such critically important witnesses.[45]

Other shortcomings add weight to Howard's indictment. Many were traceable to the hastiness of a five-day trial. Even under the best of circumstances, there simply was not enough time to track down leads such as any possible connection between Collins and Loggins and the alleged "third man" in Mose Wright's testimony. Just as seriously, the prosecution did not call Leslie Milam as a witness.[46]

It would be a mistake to dismiss the trial as a total sham. The outright obstruction of the county sheriff was more than enough to thwart any fair-minded prosecutor or investigator. Still, when taken as a whole, the trial too often seemed like a matter of going through the motions. As one northern observer put it, "It is only *formal* justice that we get in such a situation as this. A casual effort is made at correctness in the forms of a trial under Mississippi law, but what of the effective substance of justice?" Revealingly, both Howard and Porteous agreed that prosecutors Chatham and Smith seemed annoyed when they learned about Willie Reed and the new evidence.[47]

The mechanics of the trial itself also left much to be desired. The prosecution did not offer adequate guidance to several witnesses, most especially Willie Reed. Young, terrified, and bewildered by the strange environment, he was left on his own as he tried to navigate his way through the predominantly white crowd in the courtroom. Some of the mistreatment of the black witnesses resulted from the normal, but highly unequal, Jim Crow conditions of Tallahatchie County. While the judge allowed Milam and Bryant to use the "white" restroom in his chambers, for example, the black witnesses had to walk three blocks to a black restaurant. Fortunately for them, the predominantly black crowd outside gave them an escort and protection.[48]

The Till case propelled Howard into the national black media and civil rights spotlight as never before. His picture and his comments appeared frequently in *Jet*, the *Chicago Defender*, the *Pittsburgh Courier*, the *Afro-American*, and the *California Eagle*. No other civil rights leader was so closely identified with the case in the black media. Shortly after the murder, for example, the

Chicago Defender featured Howard as a central figure in an editorial cartoon. Titled "Shame of Mississippi," it showed two bodies, Till and Lee, dangling from a tree. A determined T. R. M. Howard marched to the rescue followed by Roy Wilkins in the rear.[49]

As blacks saluted Howard, whites in Mississippi reviled him. His high-profile role made him more notorious than ever in the Delta. In a letter to one of the defense attorneys, Henry J. Davis, an elderly segregationist from Clarksdale, deplored "the contemptible act of Clark Porteous going down-at-night to hob-nob with the most, most offensive 'Dr. Howard' and set themselves up as detectives to further mess things up." For Davis, the emerging local white solidarity for Milam and Bryant evoked inspiring memories of his youth in Greenwood during the 1880s when he had seen firsthand how the redeemers had violently crushed black political power. Coming from a diametrically opposed perspective, John H. Telfer, a union leader who attended the trial, noted the widespread revulsion against Howard. Sumner's white storeowners told him that they never "had any trouble until the northern (Negroes) came down. Dr. Howard of Mound Bayou is the biggest agitator around." These complaints were heard far beyond the Delta, however. In a joint editorial published on the day after the trial, the *Jackson Daily News* and the *Clarion-Ledger* singled out "Dr. T. R. M. Howard, arrogant leader of the NAACP in Mississippi," for condemnation.[50]

The editorial reflected a hope that the acquittal of Milam and Bryant would allow the whole affair to fade into the past. It recommended that it "is best for all concerned that the Bryant-Milam case be forgotten as quickly as possible." No doubt, most whites in Mississippi heartily agreed. The next few months convincingly proved, however, that this expectation was wishful thinking. The murder was not likely to be shelved as had so many senseless racial killings in the history of the state. Instead of putting the story of Emmett Till's murder to rest, the verdict resulted in fallout that gave the case a renewed lease on life.[51]

More than a few considered the killing of Emmett Till to be the catalyst for the modern Civil Rights Movement. According to Louis E. Lomax, it signaled the beginning of the "Negro revolt," and Clenora Hudson-Weems regards Till as "the sacrificial lamb of the Civil Rights Movement." For Amzie Moore, it "was the beginning of the Civil Rights Movement in Mississippi." This may be an exaggeration, but it is not a great one. The least that can be said is that the Till case significantly spurred the momentum of an existing movement.[52]

The whole affair certainly spurred Howard. The verdict added to his determination to confront white racial supremacy and helped his popularity to soar. Before the Till case, most of Howard's speeches were to gatherings of the relatively small, interlocking network of black professional, philanthropic, social, and business organizations. With the notable exception of the annual RCNL rallies, the crowds rarely numbered more than a few hundred. After September 1955, his typical audience was in the thousands, and his sponsors included labor unions, political organizations, and especially local NAACP branches.

Howard's usual subject matter was the recent violence in Mississippi, focusing on the murders of Lee, Smith, and especially Emmett Till. He emphasized the failure of law enforcement to track down such crucial leads as the role played by Collins and Loggins. Now he also blamed the northern leaders who had failed to challenge Jim Crow and the system of violence that surrounded it. In keeping with Howard's habit of doing everything in a big way, he turned his guns on a formidable target: the Federal Bureau of Investigation.

Criticizing the FBI, at least in a sustained way, was a perilous enterprise in 1955. Celebrated in movies, novels, and television, the agency had a reputation for efficiency and incorruptibility. Most Americans still subscribed to the ideal of the heroic and methodical G-men who had brought down John Dillinger and smashed the plots of Nazi saboteurs and Communist atomic spies. J. Edgar Hoover reached the apex of his power during the 1950s, and Eisenhower's Department of Justice gave him free rein. In his nearly thirty years as director, Hoover simultaneously inspired emotions of respect and fear from political leaders and journalists, both black and white.[53]

Howard's first shot across the FBI's bow was in a speech to the Baltimore NAACP on September 25. This was two days after the acquittal of Milam and Bryant. Why, Howard asked, had federal investigators failed to find Lee's killers five months later? It was "getting to be a strange thing that the FBI can never seem to work out who is responsible for killings of Negroes in the South." The main culprits, in Howard's view, were southern-born FBI agents. It made no sense to believe that "a man that's trained a certain way from birth; lived under a certain code of ethics that fails to recognize a Negro's rights" could transform "his whole nature by pinning an FBI badge on him." He called for the president, the attorney general, and "J. Edgar Hoover, himself" to have a conference on the problem.[54]

Howard's speech generated a flurry of memos between FBI officials the day after an account of it appeared in the *Baltimore Morning Sun.* No one was more upset than Louis B. Nichols, head of the FBI Crime Records Division. For nearly twenty years, Nichols had jealously guarded the FBI's public image. A biographer of Hoover credited him with "almost single-handedly creating the FBI's vast public relations empire." Nichols had a knack for managing controversies even while covering the bureau's tracks. He favored an indirect approach. Noting that the offending speech was at an NAACP forum, Nichols recommended that the FBI turn to its friends in that organization. He had a basis for this strategy. A quick search of FBI records revealed that Howard had important critics in the NAACP national leadership. During the Lee investigation, an unidentified "NAACP representative in Washington, D.C." had given the bureau a copy of Ruby Hurley's damning memo to Roy Wilkins. Written in April 1955, it stated that Howard "is not, nor do I believe he ever will be, a friend of the NAACP." At the suggestion of Nichols, Hoover wrote a letter to Thurgood Marshall, the special counsel of the NAACP, asking that he "set the record straight" and thus neutralize the effect of Howard's speech.[55]

Nichols' choice of Marshall was not a coincidence. It was the culmination of an increasingly cordial relationship between the two men. It had not always been so. During the 1940s Marshall had condemned agents in terms no less strident than those used by Howard in his Baltimore speech. Recently he had become more conciliatory. He began to view the FBI as a potential ally in the NAACP's sustained campaign to identify and purge Communists who had made alarming inroads in the organization. Nichols started to share confidential information about suspected black subversives, and Marshall reciprocated by pulling his punches when commenting on the FBI.[56]

Marshall's response to Nichols's request was positive, far more so than either Hoover or Nichols had any reason to anticipate. As asked, he wrote an open letter to Hoover accusing Howard of "misstatements of facts" in his Baltimore speech. But this was only a prelude to what came next. In his letter, Marshall volunteered fulsome praise of the FBI's "full and complete" investigative job "as far as the Mississippi situations are concerned." Echoing a rationale long used by Hoover to justify inaction, he asserted that the FBI was unable to do more because of a lack of authority under federal laws. This declaration was quite a break from Marshall's previous, or for that matter later, utterances, and it is improbable that it was entirely sincere.[57]

Marshall's opposition to Howard cannot be explained by his desire to root out Communists in the NAACP. He never claimed that Howard was a Communist, nor, for that matter, did the FBI. The Memphis office of the bureau reported that it had no derogatory information on Howard in its files, at least prior to his Baltimore speech. Neither Marshall nor the FBI would have had a strong case had they tried to make such a charge. Howard was a radical in certain ways, but he had impeccable anti-Communist credentials dating back to his *California Eagle* debates with "Sonia" in the 1930s. Later, he had barred Communists from RCNL membership and zealously condemned the Soviet Union and its apologists.[58]

Juan Williams's revealing expression "Machiavellian Marshall" offers the best clue to understanding the controversy. According to Williams, Marshall was "a pure political player. His idealism had shrunk as he took steps to protect his turf and power within the NAACP as well as to nurture relationships that offered him entrée into mainstream power and politics." Marshall knew that establishing a record of cooperation better positioned him to call on the FBI to intercede favorably in civil rights investigations. Still, his specific animus toward Howard is hard to fathom. By outward appearances, their dealings had always been friendly. Marshall had appeared at the RCNL's annual conference in 1954, and the event was a stunning success. Perhaps in the interim he had come to agree with Hurley and other critics that Howard was a loose cannon and, just as seriously, a potential rival to the NAACP.[59]

Black newspapers showed little interest in Marshall's letter to Hoover. They were still fixated on the Till case. Potential civil rights turf battles were of secondary concern, especially since breaking news kept them busy. Shortly after the acquittal of Milam and Bryant, L. Alex Wilson of the *Chicago Defender* and Medgar Evers tracked down the whereabouts of Collins. Loggins continued to be elusive. Possibly Collins had privately indicated to his black protectors that he had knowledge of the crime. With Howard's assistance, Medgar Evers and other civil rights activists hid Collins at several locations (including the Howard home for a short time). Subsequently, they smuggled him to Chicago for questioning by Euclid L. Taylor, the general counsel of the *Chicago Defender*. Wilson appeared to be on the verge of a journalistic coup. A source quoted by *Jet* predicted that Collins would "tell an amazing story of how he was deliberately held a prisoner until the trial was completed."[60]

Taylor's questioning was intense, but the whole affair did not live up to expectations. Collins denied that he had ever met Till or had knowledge of the kidnapping or murder. He said that he was at home asleep in Glendora at the time of the abduction. Collins claimed that he did not see Milam again until Monday morning, a day after the murder. He stated that during the trial both he and Loggins were hauling gravel in Minter City on instructions by Milam's brother-in-law. Collins said that Loggins had left for St. Louis on the advice of relatives. He denied that he was in jail either during the trial or at any time. He said that nobody had ever questioned him about the case. When asked whether he thought Milam was capable of the crime, Collins answered in the negative because "he was too nice a man to do it. He treat too many colored people nice. . . . He was mean to white people, though."[61]

Taylor and Wilson were skeptical of Collins's truthfulness. They cited several discrepancies. For example, although Collins stated that he did not know Mary Amanda Bradley, he admitted that he knew her when she showed up during the questioning. Still, they were not able to shake his overall story. As hopes for a break in the case dimmed, the grand jury in Leflore County considered whether to try Milam and Bryant for kidnapping.[62]

Howard held out little hope for a guilty verdict. Speaking in Baltimore, he cautioned the audience not to "get all worked up about this kidnapping trial. It will surprise me if the kidnapping part of it ever goes on trial." Howard may have respected Sheriff George Smith of Leflore County, but he had lost all shreds of confidence in Mississippi's courts. He said that Mississippians "want the rest of America and the world to know that the colored Mississippian has no rights that the Mississippi white man must respect."[63]

In early November, a Leflore County grand jury questioned witnesses, including Willie Reed and Mose Wright, who had returned to the state one last time to testify. They need not have bothered. Although Milam and Bryant had admitted to abducting Till, the grand jury did not issue an indictment. The defendants were released; they were never again called to answer for their crime. Hodding Carter's *Delta Democrat-Times* despaired that a "grand jury has told the world that white men in Mississippi may remove Negroes from their homes against their will to punish them or worse, without fear of punishment for themselves. . . . It will be a long time before Mississippi recovers from the injury the Leflore County grand jury has done to our state and to humanity."[64]

Marshall's letter to Hoover did not lead the NAACP national office to break with Howard. In fact, there is no evidence that it even considered doing so. The national NAACP continued to draw extensively on Howard's services as a speaker throughout 1956. It is easy to understand why. Everywhere that Howard went, he drew crowds and raised money that poured into NAACP coffers. His controversial speech in Baltimore netted more than $3,000. He also raised $4,000 in Gary, Indiana, $8,000 in Los Angeles, and about $1,000 each in Newark and New York City.[65]

While Wilkins did not comment publicly—or, as far as can be determined, privately—on the Marshall–Howard row, he doggedly defended Howard in other contexts. Shortly after the appearance of Marshall's public letter to Hoover, Wilkins assured an NAACP branch official in Texas that Howard had "cooperated very actively, closely and enthusiastically with the NAACP." Four days later, he emphasized to the president of the Gary branch that he had "no quarrel with . . . Dr. Howard. He has done many fine things for the NAACP and has spoken for meetings of some of our branches where the entire net proceeds have gone to the NAACP. His organization is doing a good work in Mississippi and cooperates with our program there." Wilkins, ever the pragmatist and realist, did not begrudge Howard's pursuit of separate fundraising opportunities. He pointed out that although he "makes a good appeal for support for NAACP work . . . he pushes Howard also and that is all right with me. In several places he has raised money for his Regional Council, but has never horned in on our meetings to do it. So far, he has played square with us." Wilkins was right. Despite Howard's understandably parochial interest in the RCNL, he had conscientiously promoted the NAACP. His speeches repeatedly stressed the importance of contributing to its success. The NAACP was, he argued, the "only organization that the Mississippi white man is afraid of."[66]

Howard's main theme in his speeches, of course, was the violence in Mississippi, especially the Till murder. He urged reporters to challenge the "old lie" of southerners that "is getting so old that it ought to stink, even to them! Every time they get ready to lynch a colored person in the South, it's got to be about some white woman." His retelling of the "red barn" story was particularly moving and included details, and perhaps embellishments, that had not appeared in Reed's testimony. At the trial, for example, Reed reported hearing "licks and hollers" but in Howard's account he also heard Till beg, "Mama, Lord Have Mercy, Lord Have Mercy" while his tormentors taunted, "Get down, get down, you black bastard." In early October, for the first time, Howard implicated a third black man, "Hubbard," in the murder.[67]

Howard would not let the matter rest. He repeatedly pressed for a federal investigation of allegations that Strider had prevented crucial witnesses from testifying. He tried a direct approach, and more than once. In October Howard sent telegrams to Vice President Richard M. Nixon, Attorney General Herbert Brownell, and Sherman Adams, the assistant of the president, asking that they meet black leaders from Mississippi. The purpose would be to take action against "the dastardly dangerous situation in Mississippi today" including the systematic denial of "life, liberty and the pursuit of happiness." He ran into a dead end. Howard was not able to get any further than Maxwell Rabb, the secretary to the cabinet and the president's chief adviser on minority affairs. Nixon's secretary Rosemary Woods reported to her boss that Rabb was not answering Howard's letter and "feels V.P. should stay out of this if possible." Nixon took this advice. Howard had no better luck with Brownell, though he made a creative attempt. When Brownell met with publishers from the National Negro Press Association, Howard came as a guest of a participant. One of Brownell's aides turned him away when he discovered that he was not a publisher.[68]

Howard's most vocal ally in his campaign to spur federal intervention was James Hicks of the *Afro-American.* Hicks had participated in the frantic search for witnesses during the trial. In November he sent an open letter to the Department of Justice suggesting specific leads that could verify that Loggins was on the murder truck and that Collins and Loggins were in jail during the trial. To all this, Hicks added a bloodcurdling detail. He said he knew people in Glendora who could verify that Collins had boasted "that the hole in the Till boy's head was not a bullet hole, but a hole drilled in his head with a brace and bit by one of the white men." Unlike Howard, Hicks never mentioned Hubbard's possible role.[69]

In his speeches, Howard subjected his audiences to an emotional roller coaster of anger, sorrow, and righteous indignation. His rendition of the Till murder invariably moved crowds to "open weeping" and occasional "screams." But Howard did his best to make sure that nobody went home feeling dejected or helpless. He punctuated his prose with caustic, but ultimately uplifting, doses of humor. He took obvious delight in taunting white supremacists by exposing the absurdities of all they held dear.[70]

One of his favorite stories was about his friend George L. Jefferson, the head of the Vicksburg NAACP. After Jefferson filed petitions calling for local school integration, the Ku Klux Klan burned a cross in front of his funeral home. In Howard's retelling, Jefferson then telephoned the county sheriff and said that "they have burned a cross in front of my funeral home. I'm sure that you and everybody in Vicksburg knows where my wife and my family lives. I understand that they are going out there to burn a cross. And, Mr. Sheriff, I just want to tell you that Mississippi laws requires [sic] separate ambulances for transportation of colored and white persons and inasmuch as the white hearse can't carry a colored man or a colored hearse can't carry a white man, I'm telling you that when that group comes out my home to burn a cross, I have already got my colored ambulance standing by. I want you to send a white hearse along because somebody's going to be hauled away." To loud applause, Howard closed with a punch line: "Needless for me to tell you that the cross in front of George Jefferson's home had not been burned up until last night."[71]

The editors of the *Jackson Daily News* were not amused. On October 15, a special editorial, "An Enemy of His Race," criticized Howard at length. It quoted his version of the Jefferson cross-burning incident as well his old standby joke about Senator Bilbo's message from hell. "Talk of this sort," the editorial icily concluded, "can serve no purpose whatever except to widen the breach between the white and colored races. Howard is an enemy of both races and should be regarded as such." Five days later, the *Jackson Daily News* weighed in again by deploring more of Howard's "incendiary" speeches. It suggested that it was time to find "a good padlock for his mouth." As if this was not enough, a third editorial on October 25 was entitled "Howard's Poison Tongue." Disputing Howard's recent declarations about the prevalence of lynching in Mississippi, it called him "Public Enemy No. 1 of the Negro race in Mississippi."[72]

In the North, by contrast, Howard was getting praise and winning recognition in the top ranks of celebrities and social leaders, both black and white. Black journalists showered him with such accolades as "Mr. America" and the "fighting 'Man of God.'" While he and Helen were guests in October of Jessie Vann, the publisher of the *Pittsburgh Courier,* she met with singer Marian Anderson. Howard had lunch with Jonas Salk, the discoverer of the polio vaccine, who provided him a guided tour of the Pittsburgh Medical Center. In November the liberal American Veterans Committee gave him a special award. The presenter, Bill Mauldin, the chairman of the committee and the legendary cartoonist for *Stars and Stripes,* praised Howard's "magnificent work" in civil rights. Later that month, he met in Chicago with actor Sammy Davis Jr., who promised "to headline a show of stars" to raise money to aid civil rights in Mississippi.[73]

A year-end burst of violence in Mississippi cast a pall over these events. It started soon after Howard and Marshall put aside their differences long enough to share the speakers' platform at the NAACP state conference of branches in Jackson. The first victim was Gus Courts, a sixty-five-year-old black grocer who headed the Belzoni NAACP. Courts had been a close associate of Rev. George Lee and, like him, had spoken at the RCNL rally in Mound Bayou in April. On November 25, as he was checking receipts at the cash register in his store, he was struck by a shotgun blast from a passing car. Despite serious wounds, including one in the abdomen, Courts refused to go to the local hospital. A friend drove him to Indianola to be treated by Dr. Clinton C. Battle, an activist in both the RCNL and NAACP, and then to Mound Bayou for surgery in the Taborian Hospital. After a long stay, he recovered.[74]

A witness said that the fleeing assassin was white but was unable to make a positive identification. Courts later stated that he was almost certain that it was the head of the local Citizens' Council. Members had threatened him repeatedly during the last year for registering voters. They had also organized an economic boycott against his store, cutting deeply into his business. Shortly before the shooting, a filling station operator had warned Courts that "they are figuring on getting rid of you. I don't know how and I don't want to know."[75]

Howard could barely contain his anger when he heard about the shooting. Predicting, accurately, that nobody would be arrested, he sent another telegram to the U.S. attorney general, demanding that the federal government step in. He asked, "Are you going to sit there and see us all killed, one by one, and not use the power of your office to do one thing about it?" Howard used the message to throw his support behind calls for a march on Washington in January. He said that he was "asking 1,000,000 red-blooded Americans to march on Washington in protest to the deaf ear that you and the Administration have turned to the violence in Mississippi."[76]

He was trying to breathe life into a moribund strategy. The first proposal for a march on Washington had been made in 1941 by A. Philip Randolph of the Brotherhood of Sleeping Car Porters. Randolph had postponed the protest after a fearful Franklin D. Roosevelt, then trying to mobilize support for the war, backed down by issuing an executive order banning racial discrimination in defense industries. During the war, Randolph and his allies, who continued to be leery about the sincerity and effectiveness of the order, periodically discussed holding the march. After a lull of more than a decade, the Till murder prompted black leaders, notably Adam Clayton Powell Jr., to broach the proposal again. The *Daily Worker*, the official publication of the Communist Party, lent its support, but the NAACP kept its distance. Howard's endorsement gave momentum to these calls.[77]

Howard used his first scheduled speech after the shooting to publicize the proposed "Freedom March to Washington." He drew an overflow crowd on November 27 in Montgomery, Alabama, at the Dexter Avenue Baptist Church. His sponsor was the Omega Psi Phi Fraternity. Although the event made the front page in local black newspapers, including the *Alabama Tribune* in Montgomery and the *Birmingham World*, his comments received almost no national coverage. Montgomery, after all, was a relatively obscure stop on an itinerary that included Baltimore, New York City, Washington, D.C., Pittsburgh, and Los Angeles.[78]

The official host was the church's new twenty-six-year-old pastor, the Reverend Martin Luther King Jr., who gave the invocation and benediction. King was just emerging as a force in Montgomery but was almost completely unknown nationally. The special invited guests for the event were Autherine Lucy and Polly Myers. Both had recently applied to the University of Alabama in the hope of becoming its first black students. Lucy briefly attended in February 1956 but was expelled after a hostile crowd intimidated the university administration.[79]

While Howard's Montgomery speech promoted the Freedom March and gave an update on the shooting of Gus Courts, he also covered some familiar ground. He reviewed the arrangement with Tri-State Bank and how it had been used to fight the economic freeze. He commented at length on the Lee, Smith, and Till murders and deplored the federal government's failure to intercede. The admonishments of Hoover and Marshall had not muted his critique of the FBI's failings in civil rights. "It seems strange," he observed, "that the FBI which could solve the explosion of an airliner in mid air in less than a week could not solve the slaying of a Negro in Mississippi." Howard was referring to the FBI's successful use of technical and scientific analysis to reveal the perpetrator of a plane bombing in Colorado on November 1. The incident served as the opening scene of the bestselling book *The FBI Story* in 1957, as well as the subsequent movie of the same name starring James Stewart.[80]

Sitting in the audience was Rosa Parks, a seamstress and NAACP official in Montgomery. Many years later, she singled out Howard's appearance as the "first mass meeting that we had in Montgomery" after Till's death. She particularly remembered his detailed description of the crime. Only four days after his speech, Parks made history by refusing to give her seat on a city bus to a white man in violation of a segregation ordinance. She later emphasized that Till's murder was central to her thinking at the time of her arrest. Soon, a group of black ministers and civil rights activists organized a boycott of city buses. The new Montgomery Improvement Association, under King's leadership, quickly emerged to head this movement.[81]

Howard's presence in Montgomery on the eve of the boycott is intriguing, and it is natural to wonder what impact it had on King's thinking. Unfortunately, King's correspondence during the months before the boycott is sparse, and none of it mentions Howard. It would have been surprising, however, if his example, including his highly visible role as a civil rights leader, did not have an impact, if only an indirect one. Of course, King and Parks were well aware of the Till case, which was highly visible in Alabama's black press. In his first book, *Stride toward Freedom,* King wrote, "Today it is Emmett Till, tomorrow it is Martin Luther King. Then in another tomorrow it will be somebody else."[82]

Meanwhile, the campaign of Howard and others to arrange a conference with the Eisenhower administration was having some effect. As the crisis of Mississippi heated up after the shooting of Courts, E. Frederic Morrow, the highest-ranking black on Eisenhower's presidential staff, tried to communicate the urgency of the situation. On November 29 he wrote to Maxwell Rabb that blacks in Mississippi "have formed an underground and are determined to protect themselves by methods that, if used, can only lead to further terror and bloodshed." He suggested that Nixon or Adams sit down with a dozen prominent black leaders "to exchange views on this very dangerous problem." Rabb's response was to call Morrow in for a dressing-down a few days later. He may have already read Howard's missive to Brownell. Rabb complained to Morrow that black civil rights leaders "were being too aggressive in their demands and that ugliness and surliness were showing through." If Howard hoped to get relief for Mississippi, he would not get it from the president or his advisers.[83]

Just as the Montgomery Boycott started to build up steam, the Mississippi Delta was the scene of more racial bloodshed, this time in Glendora. It developed out of an altercation between Elmer Kimbell, a white cotton-gin manager and a friend of J. W. Milam, and Clinton Melton, a black gas station attendant. Melton was "highly respected" by local whites and had no involvement in civil rights. Kimbell was driving Milam's car when he pulled into a local gas station on December 3 and told Melton to put in two dollars' worth of gas. Angered when he found out that Melton had filled up the tank instead, he drove away promising to get even. True to his word, Kimbell returned with a shotgun and fired three times at Melton, killing him. He drove to Milam's home, where he was later arrested.[84]

In the days after the murder, Howard, acting on behalf of the NAACP, advanced fifty dollars of short-term help to Melton's widow and small children. As he prepared to go to trial in Sumner, Kimbell claimed self-defense, but few whites seemed to believe him. Judge Curtis Swango denied bail, and the Glendora Lions Club passed a resolution that expressed "repentance" for the crime and promised to contribute financially to help the family. As in an earlier trial in Sumner, the initial white outrage did not have enough strength or staying power to produce a conviction. Four months after the shooting, a jury found Kimbell not guilty of murder. Even more tragic was the mysterious death of Melton's wife during the trial. After an apparent heart attack, her car overturned into a bayou. Her two children were rescued from drowning just in time. Soon after the Melton murder, Hodding Carter bleakly reported that "things aren't good here at all and they seem to be getting worse. Sometimes I think our state is trying to commit suicide."[85]

The pressures on T. R. M. and Helen left them increasingly isolated and under siege. The litany of bad news so alarmed Howard's daughter Verda, then living in Detroit, that she insisted on the return of her son Ronald. With much regret, they complied. They had closely bonded with the boy. Meanwhile, Howard's depiction of conditions in his home state was becoming markedly apocalyptic. He predicted "terror and bloodshed in Mississippi more violent than anything that has happened in North Africa, if something isn't done."[86]

One by one, Howard's allies and friends in the white elite dropped away, most notably Hodding Carter. For nearly a decade, Carter had praised Howard as practical, forward-looking, and dynamic, but by early 1955 Howard's militant rhetoric and attacks on segregation had alienated him. In response, Howard, who had once lauded Carter as one of the greatest American authors, dismissed him as a double-talking "pseudo-liberal." The break with Ed Kossman probably hurt the most. For years, Howard had bought many of his cars and farm equipment from Kossman's automobile dealership in Cleveland. The business relationship had mushroomed into friendship. Howard trusted Kossman to look beyond race. Thus, it was extremely hurtful to him when he heard the news that Kossman, although a Jew, was an officer in the local white Citizens' Council. The chairman of the council's legal committee was W. B. Alexander, a lawyer from Cleveland, Mississippi, who had handled the paperwork when Howard had created the United Order of Friendship.[87]

To top it off, Howard became embroiled in legal troubles. In October, Jim Winters, a former farmhand on the Howard plantation, filed a damage suit for $25,000. He charged that Howard had pulled a gun on him, cursed him, and confiscated his pickup truck for a debt. Winters alleged that Howard had hired him at a rate of five dollars per day but had paid him three. The suit still had not come to trial in December but was looming.[88]

Pressure or not, most observers took it for granted that Howard would stay in Mississippi. He had never said anything to indicate otherwise. In October, he declared that "Mississippi is my home, and progress is being made there. This is the first time Negroes testified against white men in a murder trial." At another point, he insisted, "I just cannot leave. Too many people believe in me. . . . What would happen to their faith if I ran away?" Although he was then on the road more often than not, he said that he felt "so uncomfortable out of Mississippi." A few days after the murder of Melton, he reiterated his determination to stay "and fight until we win. If I leave before that time, they will take me out in a wooden box."[89]

For this reason, both his allies and enemies could hardly believe it when they read otherwise. On December 14 newspapers widely reported that Howard's family had left Mississippi for Los Angeles and that he had sold eight hundred acres, including his house and main plantation, valued at nearly $200,000. The purchasers of most of the land were black. He still retained property in the area valued at $100,000.[90]

Despite this, Howard continued to stay in Mound Bayou, at least for a while. He slept in the Sara W. Brown Hospital, where he conducted his business affairs and civil rights activities. He was increasingly driving less conspicuous cars on the highways that he borrowed from others. His statements to the press in the weeks after the sale of the property were those of a conflicted man. He talked of maintaining his permanent residency but then spending half the year in Los Angeles. He did not think "that's unusual because we visit California ever so often." At the same time, he indicated that he had sent his family out of the state because of fear for their safety. He reported that none of the people who threatened him had left their names, but he had "given them credit for having too much sense to burn crosses in Mound Bayou." But he was beginning to hedge. He said he had several offers on the table including a job at Riverside Sanitarium: "Something could happen today that would make it necessary for me to leave Mississippi permanently, so if I were standing before the judgment seat I could not tell you whether I will move from Mississippi in ten days or ten years."[91]

By the end of December, it was apparent to almost everyone that he was going to leave. He did his best to put a good face on the situation, arguing that he could "do more for Mississippi Negroes outside of the state. It's better to be alive outside than to be underneath six feet of soil in Mississippi." Soon, he resigned as president of the Magnolia Mutual and as chief surgeon of the Sara W. Brown Hospital.[92]

A small corpus of oral folklore emerged in the decades after Howard's departure from Mississippi. Especially intriguing was the story that he escaped in a casket. Hardly anyone who had known Howard in Mississippi believed it, but more than a few of his acquaintances in Chicago took it seriously, including his son Barrett. The details vary and are either secondhand or thirdhand. One version is that the sequence of events began when Howard heard that white racists had issued a secret order to kill him. As a diversionary tactic, his supporters announced that he was dead and that they were preparing for the funeral. He was then put in a casket and loaded on a train for Memphis. Oscar J. Moore Jr., Howard's personal doctor for many years in Chicago, said that he heard the story firsthand from Howard, who explained that "some of the radical elements around there had a death threat against him. . . . And it was a real death threat and he had only time, he had only moments to spare."[93]

The chief problem with the credibility of the casket story is a lack of eyewitnesses. Matthew Havard, a friend and business associate, heard about it from others "but I knew better so I didn't ever think about it. . . . No, I didn't see him when he left. But I know when he took things. I know his chauffeur went up there a couple of times and took things and come back and got him and went out. He ain't smuggled out of nowhere. He ain't had no reason to be smuggled out." The accounts of James Hicks and Homer Wheaton offer directly different versions of Howard's flight. Hicks writes that "Howard saw that it was time for him to go. They had threatened him. So I said, 'I'll drive you.' He had a lot of money and he put it in a pillow slip, in cash, with his valuables. We put it in the back of this you-drive-it car and I drove him to Memphis." Wheaton states that he drove Howard out of town and that Hicks was not in the car. According to Wheaton, Howard had decided to leave after talking on the phone with his friend, Walter S. Davis, the president of Tennessee State University. On instructions from Davis, Wheaton made the trip to Mound Bayou. After a home-cooked late-night dinner, he drove Howard to Nashville in the early morning hours. Both Hicks and Wheaton are reliable sources, and their versions can probably be reconciled. Howard left and returned to Mississippi several times during this period, and thus Wheaton and Hicks might have taken him out on separate occasions.[94]

To sum up Howard's exit as a single dramatic incident would be a mistake. The process of moving was gradual rather than sudden. The level of tension may have varied on one or more of these trips, but it did not seem to deter him from coming back afterward. He had certain advantages that other civil rights activists in the state lacked. The nearly all-black surroundings ensured a certain level of security. Any white stranger in Mound Bayou or its environs would have stuck out like a sore thumb. As in most small towns, news of untoward happenings spread rapidly. But it is equally hard to believe that he made up the casket story out of whole cloth, especially since so many people who knew better could have contradicted him. Howard was capable of exaggeration and wishful thinking but, if the historical record is any guide, he was generally truthful when describing his past.[95]

Actually, the casket story has a plausible basis, although not in the context of a final escape from Mississippi. Audley M. Mackel Jr., the son of the head of the state NAACP, recalls that his father had once used this method to smuggle Howard out of Vicksburg. It was at the time of the Till trial, and race relations were at a low ebb. Howard and Mackel had often conferred in Vicksburg, but this time both men decided that it was unsafe for Howard to drive back to Mound Bayou in his own car. They feared for his life because his license number was public knowledge. Also, his expensive car (especially for a black man) was conspicuous on the open highway. To avoid detection, Mackel arranged to have Howard smuggled out in one of the hearses of his family's funeral home. The front of the hearse had only a single seat, and secrecy was essential. Thus, for a brief time, Howard hid in a casket until it was out of town. The driver took Howard to Greenville to change cars for the final leg of the trip to Mound Bayou. Audley M. Mackel Jr., who was in Vicksburg at the time, was not a witness to each stage of the process, but his father kept him apprised of the situation. His story is believable.[96]

Howard told some sort of casket story to family members and friends. Of that, there can be no doubt. It is possible that his listeners confused the timing with his flight from Mississippi. In interviews, many of them seemed unsure about the specifics. Naturally, the likelihood that they would forget the details has increased over the decades. As will be discussed later, they may have confused what they heard with another colorful casket story involving Arrington High's escape from Mississippi.

Personal security was the most frequently cited reason for Howard's departure from Mississippi. He said that he had been told that the white Citizens' Councils had put a price of $1,000 on his head and issued orders that he be killed by the first of the year. He elaborated that the "men who are supposed to liquidate me have already been appointed." According to a rumor, whites had planned to bomb a church in Cleveland, Mississippi, where Howard was speaking.[97]

A few dismissed the seriousness of these dangers. "He ain't left because of threats," insists his former associate Matthew Havard. "I don't know who was threatening him. He might have had some, but he didn't act like to me he had none, and I saw him every day." Havard represents a distinct minority. Howard had compelling reasons to be concerned. Helen, who, he said, was "cracking up" under the strain, certainly took these fears seriously. The eight-man death list first reported by *Ebony* in its article on the RCNL conference was the most obvious indicator of the mounting danger. In addition to Howard, the names were George W. Lee, Gus Courts, Clinton C. Battle, Emmett Stringer, A. H. McCoy, T. V. Johnson, and Medgar Evers. By the end of the year, Lee was dead, white economic pressure had successfully intimidated Johnson, shots fired into McCoy's living room had barely missed his child, and Gus Courts, who was still recovering from his wounds, would soon move to Chicago. In a few months, Battle also fled. Even before the list had appeared, white pressure had led Stringer not to run for reelection as NAACP president.[98]

While the fact that Howard lived in an all-black town helped his level of safety, it was no guarantee. As Charles Evers says, "It was risky anywhere you were. Mound Bayou was just a small little particle in a whole big wide plantation of whites. Mean whites!" Bill Stout of CBS News was uncomfortably close to the truth when he called Howard "the man with the shortest life expectancy in the United States." Arguably, the white violence showed the effectiveness of Howard's fight against economic pressure. As Charles Payne points out, civil rights activists had "forced whites to use violence by refusing to yield to anything less [than their due]. Thus, the level of white violence is an ironic index of the forcefulness of Black activism." It was Howard, after all, who had described white pressure as "a flop" at the RCNL annual conference and predicted, presciently, that "the next round will be a well-organized wave of violence."[99]

Violence was undoubtedly a factor in Howard's decision to leave, but not the only one. Aaron Henry was one of several persons to hint that he had other motivations. In an interview several years later, he said that Howard "was a longtime fighter in the struggle. . . . the pressures finally got to him; I won't say he had to leave, but he left." Observers suggested several additional reasons, including personal finances and political ambition. The zealously anti-Howard *Jackson Advocate* pointed to business difficulties as the precipitating factor. A lengthy article reported that the Magnolia Mutual and the UOFA had fallen into disarray. One allegation was that donations received from white planters had enabled Howard to live in a "home modeled after the estate of an English squire." The author of the article considered it almost certain that "the departure of Dr. Howard will end all of his organizations and activities here."[100]

Howard could be loose in financial matters, and not always scrupulous about promptly repaying debt, but his holdings were not teetering on the edge of collapse. The business in force of the Magnolia Mutual under his leadership had grown from under $7,000 to more than $900,000 in December 1955. In Howard's defense, the director of the company, W. A. Zuber of Tupelo, responded to the *Jackson Advocate* article in an open letter. He said that instead "of taking money from the company, Dr. Howard with a group of his friends, contributed to the clearing of indebtedness and refinancing of the company, which put it on a sound base for the best interest of its policyholders. . . . there are no outstanding or unpaid claims in our office due our policyholders." The UOFA continued to operate the Sara W. Brown Hospital for another decade and survived as an organization until the late 1970s. The Magnolia Mutual did not suddenly collapse either but, for reasons that are unclear, it gradually wound down operations over the next four years.[101]

Howard was not on the verge of a financial debacle, but this does not mean that economic self-interest played no role in prompting him to leave. Howard was an intensely ambitious man. Especially as economic pressure bore down, he might have seen the prospects for future business successes as limited and dwindling. As more blacks migrated north, after all, the potential customer and membership base for his organizations and enterprises promised to shrink further. He could continue, but he was not a man to be content in a world of limits. In the short term, white pressure accelerated the process. Charles Evers suggests that constant harassment served to frighten away many of Howard's regular customers.[102]

Also, the chances for any future political outlet for Howard were rapidly diminishing. While all offices were, of course, closed to him, he may have indulged in wishful thinking about the future in the heady period after the *Brown* decision. By the end of the year, the wave of white violence and the crackdown on black voting made that dream, far-fetched to begin with, even more impractical.[103]

Segregationists were overjoyed at Howard's impending departure. An editorial in the *Clarion-Ledger* said that Mississippi was lucky to be free of such a "dangerous agitator" who was "hell-bent on stirring up strife between the races." The *Jackson Daily News* could barely contain its glee. In "Good Riddance," it editorialized that, by leaving, Howard had "rendered the greatest service he has yet performed for the state. Dr. Howard is not a desirable citizen. He is a radical agitator who devotes much of his time to stirring up ill feeling between the races. . . . Howard's room is much preferred to his company. All possible speed should accompany his going."[104]

Despite these caustic farewells, Howard was not quite ready to make a complete break from Mississippi. Vowing "to continue our fight," he boldly announced that the RCNL would help coordinate the NAACP's national campaign, "Operation Mississippi Airlift." The goal was to collect clothes, food, toys, and other supplies to help victims of the credit freeze. In December and January, Howard visited several cities to solicit funds and in-kind aid. The support was generous. Contributors in New York City gave two hundred baskets. After a speech by Howard, the Los Angeles NAACP sent two thirty-five-foot trailer trucks of gifts. With Mound Bayou serving as the central distribution point during the Christmas holidays, the organizers stated that five thousand people in the Delta had received aid. Howard's old rival, the Knights and Daughters of Tabor, helped to distribute the goods.[105]

As he planned future civil rights activities, Howard was no longer able to take for granted the cooperation of Mound Bayou's town fathers. Mayor

Benjamin A. Green had never been Howard's ally, but he had not obstructed him. I. E. Edwards, who had just become acting mayor during Green's illness, took a more aggressive approach. He told a reporter that town officials "look forward to banning wholesale meetings" of organizations that used "radical methods that tends to stir up strife." When asked if he was referring to RCNL, he replied, "No comment!" Aaron Henry charged that Edwards was "attempting to hoodwink white plantation owners by presenting himself as opposed to Negro progress." Howard condemned the ban as a violation of freedom of assembly and promised to hold the annual meeting of the RCNL in Mound Bayou again.[106]

Even with the unrelenting tensions in Mississippi, Howard had reason to celebrate as the new year began. On January 7, the *Chicago Defender* gave him the top spot in its annual honor roll. In bestowing the award, it praised him for "arousing the nation to the criminal conspiracy of white supremacists in the state of Mississippi." The *Jackson Daily News* responded with an editorial condemning the award to "the big-mouthed Negro racial agitator who was told by people in his hometown, Mound Bayou, that his room was preferred to his company."[107]

Howard had other good news during this difficult period, though it came somewhat too late to be of great help. After disappearing mysteriously in late December, Jim Winters signed an affidavit stating that he was dropping his damage suit. Smelling blood, pro-segregationist newspapers had publicized the case, but Howard had the last laugh. During an appearance in Memphis in early January, he triumphantly displayed the affidavit for reporters. Winters stated that Howard's enemies had offered to pay him $15,000 in cash to file the charges and had threatened that he would be "thrown in the Tallahatchie River" if he balked. Howard could not have asked for a better conclusion to the case. "Other people are responsible," Winters told the press, "for me bringing this false charge against Dr. Howard. Threats were made against my life. . . . I must be able to live with myself and I cannot be a traitor to my race by entering into a false charge." This was an important victory for Howard, but he did not have long to savor it. Only three days after Winters signed his affidavit, the Till case rocketed back into the headlines.[108]

7

"Time Bomb"

Howard, J. Edgar Hoover,
and the Emmett Till Mystery

DESPITE HIS SLOW, reluctant, and phased departure from Mississippi during the first half of 1956, Howard's public identification with the state where he had lived for more than a decade was stronger than ever. A startling development reignited the Emmett Till controversy, always smoldering, into full fury. Meanwhile, none other than J. Edgar Hoover, angered by attacks on the FBI's inaction in the Till case and other crimes, launched a coordinated media campaign to destroy Howard's credibility.

The catalyst for these events was an article in *Look* magazine, appropriately titled "The Shocking Story of Approved Killing in Mississippi." It hit the newsstands on January 11, 1956. The author, William Bradford Huie, revealed that J. W. Milam and Roy Bryant, now safe from prosecution, had proudly confessed (after Huie paid them more than $3,000) to the murder of Emmett Till. They apparently were Huie's only sources for the actual details of the crime.[1]

Milam and Bryant told Huie that they had intended merely to frighten Till but that he had enraged them with his brazenness. After a long drive with many detours, they took him to a shed in back of Milam's house for a pistol whipping. The beating had no effect. "We were never able to scare him," Milam fumed. "They had just filled him so full of that poison he was hopeless." Till even repeated that he had "had" white women and that his grandmother was white. He was indeed hopeless! Huie then quoted Milam's well-known declaration: "Well, what else could we do? . . . I like niggers—in their place—I know how to work 'em. But I just decided that it was time a few people got put on notice. . . . Niggers ain't gonna vote where I live. . . . They ain't gonna go to school with my kids. And when a nigger even gets close to mentioning sex with a white woman, he's tired o' livin."[2]

Determined to finish the job, the pair said that they picked up an abandoned gin fan near Boyle. Although it weighed seventy-five pounds, they ordered Till to lift it onto the truck. They drove to the Tallahatchie River, where they told him to carry it to the bank and strip naked. Milam asked Till one last time: Did he think he was as good as any white man and had he been with white women? When Till answered "yeah," Milam blasted him in the head with his .45. They wired the fan around his neck and pushed him into the water. Huie concluded that white Mississippians "either approve Big Milam's action" or "don't disapprove enough to risk giving their 'enemies' the satisfaction of a conviction."[3]

Huie's article was such a smashing sensation that few noted just how much it diverged from previous accounts, including those of Howard and Hicks. It left the clear impression that the crime was an exclusively Milam and Bryant affair. Willie Reed, Mary Amanda Bradley, and Add Reed—not to mention Levi "Too Tight" Collins, Henry Lee Loggins, and Willie Hubbard—shared the status of *persona incognita* in the article. Huie had originally shared Howard's view that others had taken part. In October 1955, for example, he had declared matter-of-factly that the "torture-and-murder party" included two other men but also warned that it was essential to "have their releases—or no publisher will touch it. I know who these men are: they are important to the story, but I have to pay them because of their 'risks.'" He never indicated their identity or race. Although Huie considered four more releases as possibly "too heavy a handicap," he suggested that "we can if necessary, omit the names of the other two. We can even avoid all reference to them." He cautioned, however, that he would urge "any publisher to state that they were present."[4]

Huie abruptly shifted gears after first meeting Milam and Bryant on October 23. Without elaboration, he reported to his publisher that he now believed that the two had acted alone. Perhaps not coincidentally, Huie emphasized how this simplified the otherwise laborious and expensive process of getting releases. This was the last time he openly acknowledged, or even hinted, at a broader conspiracy. The closest Huie came to addressing the issue was when he turned to the question of why Till did not try to escape though he was alone in the back of the truck and not tied up. For Huie, this was "the remarkable part of the story." Till did not flee because he "wasn't afraid of them! He was as tough as they were. He didn't think they had the guts to kill him." But these were only conjectures. Possibly, despite Huie's statement that Milam and Bryant were the sole perpetrators, he still had doubts and did not want to give his editors a pretext to veto publication.[5]

Huie's failure to explicitly raise in the article the possibility of coconspirators does not mean that he ignored the issue in other contexts. Almost certainly, he was the anonymous "informant" for an overlooked, but fascinating, story in the *Tri-State Defender* of Memphis on January 14, 1956. Huie's probable intention was to launch a preemptive strike against any counterattack by Howard, Hicks, and other advocates of a conspiracy theory. The informant dismissed claims that others helped Milam and Bryant as "a myth, sheer nonsense" because the two men "would hardly take a Negro along on such a mission." While a pickup truck with four whites and three blacks had indeed pulled into the equipment shed, it was for an innocent fishing trip. Reed did not hear noise from a beating but "the sound of persons playing around as the boat was being loaded."[6]

Huie need not have worried about making a preemptive strike. The shock created by the breathtaking boldness of the confession in *Look* overshadowed nearly all else. This was true even for blacks who had worked the hardest to uncover and publicize possible accomplices. Although he had personally aided Reed when he fled to Chicago, for example, Representative Charles Diggs implied that the *Look* article was the unvarnished truth. As he inserted the article into the *Congressional Record,* he remarked that the "stunning revelations are so detailed [that] there is no doubt in my mind that the information came from the killers themselves." Not even Hicks complained. Like Diggs, he seized upon Milam and Bryant's confession as a pretext for federal action. He wrote a second open letter to Brownell, citing Huie to back up his demand for an investigation. Never once mentioning Loggins, Collins, Hubbard, or Reed, he stressed that "you now have the net result of my charges dumped right into your lap by none other than Milam and Bryant themselves." To be fair to Hicks, Milam and Bryant's confession was so blatant and racially charged that Hicks had good reason to see it as offering the best chance ever to get some traction for the case.[7]

Howard was probably the most prominent black leader to remain fixated on possible black accomplices. He immediately went to work on publishing his own version of events. In February 1956, Howard rushed *Time Bomb: Mississippi Exposed and the Full Story of Emmett Till* through to press. The author was Olive Arnold Adams, the wife of Julius J. Adams, the general manager of the *New York Age,* but Howard was her main source. He also wrote the foreword. Strangely, *Time Bomb* used pseudonyms: Wiggins for Loggins, Herbert for Hubbard, and Fred Yonkers for Frank Young. *Time Bomb* speculated that the "recent boastful confession" in *Look* actually generated sympathy for Milam and Bryant in Mississippi because it "aimed at fitting Emmett Till into the 'sexually depraved' category among the stereotypes into which Negroes are so often cast. It was an obvious attempt to dream up a crime to fit the punishment."[8]

In addition to *Time Bomb,* Howard was probably a key source for a series of articles that appeared in the *California Eagle,* a black newspaper in Los Angeles. The author was a mysterious white Southern reporter who wrote under the pseudonym of Amos Dixon. Dixon put forward essentially the same thesis as *Time Bomb* but offered more details on the possible roles of Loggins, Hubbard, and Collins. He also alleged that Leslie Milam, the brother of Milam and Bryant, took part in the crime. Unlike Huie, Dixon described Till as bewildered and confused during the kidnapping rather than intentionally defiant. He portrayed the killing as more an act of desperation than a conscious political statement. Dixon dismissed Milam's proclamation that he had killed Till to strike a blow for white supremacy. Milam was "trying to picture himself as a man ready to go to any lengths to uphold the things in which he and his neighbors believe" and thus be "transformed from a brutal murderer into a hero." The true basis of the killing was messier. Dixon attributed it to panic as well as to Milam's need to prove himself to his "hero worshipping brothers," and the fear that Till might talk if they released him.[9]

Time Bomb also differed from Dixon's account in certain details. For example, it claimed that Carolyn Bryant and a black man were the only two people with Milam and Roy Bryant in the truck at the time of the abduction. The two other white men (never identified) joined the group later. *Time Bomb* presented a more sympathetic picture of Till as "a strapping youth" who was "shy and sensitive" though "beginning to overcome his reticence, although he still stammered noticeably." But most of the discrepancies were of emphasis and tone rather than substance. The two accounts obviously drew, at least ultimately, on a common source.[10]

While researching this book, we tracked down and questioned two of the principal witnesses, Willie Reed and Henry Lee Loggins, to determine whether Huie or Howard was right. We found Reed to be just as credible as most of the journalists and prosecutors who heard him testify in 1955. When we asked whether the group at the equipment shed could have been a fishing party, he laughed, pointing out that the men did not have any fishing poles. He was emphatic that the noises were from a suffering human rather than the racket associated with a fishing party. Reed identified the two black men on the truck as Hubbard and Collins; the name Loggins (described in nearly all versions) did not ring a bell. At the trial itself, he had said that he did not recognize any of the men on the truck, other than Till. Most of Reed's recollections, however, jibe with his earlier testimony and seemed sincere and compelling.[11]

Loggins, who, like Reed, had apparently not spoken to any researcher in decades, flatly denied any involvement, though he readily admitted that he had worked for Milam and knew Collins and Hubbard. While he was somewhat vague on his whereabouts during the kidnapping, he indicated that he was in bed at home in Glendora. Several of Loggins's statements raised questions about his credibility. More than once, he not only denied that he was in the truck but also that anyone ever claimed otherwise: "No, they didn't say I was on the back of that truck. They say Too Tight was on the back and some other boy, named, we called him Oso." Oso was Otha Johnson Jr., another of Milam's black employees.[12]

In response to new interest in the case, the FBI opened an investigation of the Till case. It found no credible evidence to legally implicate any living possible conspirators. Even so, the final, heavily redacted, FBI report includes much valuable information. It lays out compelling evidence about the identities of those who were present during the beating at the equipment shed. The whites who were there, in addition to J. W. Milam and Bryant, were probably Leslie Milam (who gave a deathbed confession to his minister during the 1970s), Hubert Clark, a friend of Milam, and a brother-in-law, Melvin Campbell. Two of the three blacks were probably Otha Johnson Jr. (who confessed to his son before his death in 2003) and Levi Collins. Despite the media attention given to Loggins, the evidence against him is comparatively weak. It is not surprising that a black prosecutor and predominately black grand jury in Leflore County decided in 2007 not to issue any new indictments. The case appeared to be closed for good.[13]

To those familiar with the case, the unsatisfactory conclusion was expected. It is almost certain that others, besides Milam and Bryant, took part in Till's kidnapping and killing, but proving guilt more than fifty years later, much less identifying coconspirators, was always an uphill battle. Memories had become hazy and unreliable. Key possible witnesses and suspects—including Roy Bryant, J. W. Milam, Leslie Milam, Hubert Clark, Melvin Campbell, and Levi Collins—were dead. Taken together, the evidence was too thin, too circumstantial, and too contradictory for definitive conclusions, especially about living people who could be charged.

Time Bomb appeared just as Howard was winding down his activities in Mississippi. It prominently featured his photo as the president of the RCNL and included an appeal for contributions to the Mound Bayou office. Perhaps Howard was hedging his bets on whether to leave Mississippi permanently. His introduction promised a coauthored book with Adams in 1957, *The Gathering Storm along the Mississippi*, to discuss the entire race problem in the state. It was never published. Dixon's articles and *Time Bomb* had almost no lasting impact. Huie's version of events thoroughly dominated the discourse and pushed aside competing accounts, including the one promoted by Howard. It enshrined the impression of Milam and Bryant as the lone killers and Till as boastful, fearless, and sexually overbearing. Only in the 1990s did scholars begin to seriously challenge this portrait.[14]

Howard had other concerns during this period besides exposing possible conspiracies in the Till case. He was raising money to help his hard-pressed colleagues, such as Robert L. Drew, with loans. By this time, Howard was proposing that the NAACP supplement the Tri-State loan program with cash grants to victims of segregationist pressure. A key obstacle was a Tennessee law that allowed loans on first mortgages only. Wilkins did not show any interest in Howard's proposal. He was understandably reluctant to assume the necessary bureaucratic and fundraising obligations. He considered the idea harmful because of a possible deluge of "applications from any and all people from all sections of the South, most of whom have suffered no special economic pressure on account of the desegregation campaign."[15]

The particular case of financial pressure that preoccupied Howard involved his friend and civil rights associate, Amzie Moore. This affair gradually developed into a major headache and was rife with misunderstanding, bad feelings, and great quantities of ink and paper. Moore's financial difficulties dated back to early 1954, when he borrowed about $10,000 to build an attractive and elaborate business complex in Cleveland, Mississippi, that featured a filling station, a restaurant, and a beauty shop. Moore pursued the same kind of ambitious business strategy that had served Howard so well in Mound Bayou. He recognized that the RCNL's continuing "don't buy gas where you can't use the restroom" campaign had opened up a potential customer base. But almost from the beginning he ran into trouble. Whites told him to put up "Colored Only" signs around his restaurant and allegedly organized a boycott. His business suffered and he was unable to pay his debts when they came due. Many confusing twists and turns followed.[16]

In January 1956 Moore applied to Tri-State Bank for a loan of $7,000. Both the NAACP and bank officials were leery. They acknowledged that Moore was a valuable fighter for civil rights but suspected that he had brought on many of his own financial troubles. Daniel E. Byrd of the NAACP Legal Defense and Educational Fund evaluated Moore as "an excellent person" who "really took on too large an obligation." Tri-State, with Wilkins's support, turned down the loan request, stating that Moore had insufficient collateral. Wilkins finally made a special arrangement for an emergency loan of $1,000 although Moore did not technically qualify. After that, Wilkins lost interest. The loan was not nearly enough to prevent a forced sale of Moore's property in December.[17]

At this point, Howard went to bat for Moore by putting more than $2,000 into an escrow account as a guarantee. He also interested the famous socialist leader Norman Thomas in the case. Howard's brief in favor of Moore so impressed Thomas that he chipped in $1,000. Howard also helped secure pledges of another $1,000 from former Senator Frank Graham of North Carolina, a prominent white racial moderate, and $500 from the National Sharecroppers Fund. Thomas, in turn, solicited additional help from his friend, Jacob M. Kaplan, the dominant investor in the Welch Grape Juice Company. The RCNL deposited an additional $3,000 into the escrow account. The complicated arrangements took time, and apparently not everyone followed through with the pledges. Moore became frustrated at the delays. In late January 1956 he complained to Wilkins that despite Howard's promises, the loan had not been forthcoming. He implied that Howard was cheating him out of his due. This did not prove to be accurate. In February, as Howard had promised, Tri-State loaned $4,000 to Moore but, as before, he quickly fell behind in his payments.[18]

The Amzie Moore case amounted to a minor distraction, however, compared to Howard's renewed clash with Hoover. It started because of a speech in Chicago to the Alpha Phi Alpha fraternity in late December. Howard alleged that "Confidential information usually leaks from the local FBI offices and witnesses in Negro slaying are subjected to pressures as a result." Others, most notably Adam Clayton Powell Jr., had made similar claims, but no one was more relentless than Howard. He followed up the Chicago appearance by leveling two more blasts against the FBI in successive speeches in Baton Rouge and New York. He repeated his charge that the "FBI can pick up pieces of a fallen airplane on the slopes of a Colorado mountain and find the man who caused the crash, but they can't find a white man when he kills a Negro in the South."[19]

This was too much for Louis B. Nichols and his boss, J. Edgar Hoover. After Nichols read an FBI report warning that "Howard's unfounded allegations concerning the FBI received considerable publicity and undoubtedly influences a number of Negroes in their feelings toward the FBI," he persuaded Hoover to write directly to Howard. Nichols's goal was to discredit Howard publicly as a "phony" through a media barrage. The plan was to send the letter through regular mail on the evening of January 16 and release it to the press, whether or not Howard had received it, on the morning of January 18.[20]

Hoover's letter berated Howard for making "intemperate and baseless charges" that were a "disservice to common decency." Much of it was standard FBI boilerplate. He reminded Howard that the FBI was "not a policy-making organization" and acted on orders from the Criminal Division of the Department of Justice. Because of the restraints imposed by "existing legislation," it was doing what it could. The FBI's "fair and prompt" investigations, Hoover boasted, had greatly elevated the "public consciousness of civil rights." Howard had "conveniently forgotten the work of this Bureau which was largely responsible for the virtual elimination of lynching in the South and also was mainly responsible for the breaking up of the Ku Klux Klan in the Carolinas and Georgia." Hoover was indignant about accusations that native agents were guilty of leaks. If Howard had personal knowledge, he was obligated to "submit such evidence as you have to sustain your irresponsible charge or that you issue a public retraction." Hoover's letter caught Howard, then in Los Angeles, by surprise. He first heard about it when reporters called him on January 18; it did not arrive at his Mound Bayou address until the next day.[21]

Nevertheless, Howard immediately fired back a response letter. He pounced on Hoover's declaration that the FBI was responsible for the "virtual elimination of lynching in the South." He pointed out that, if true, this contradicted Hoover's excuse that lack of enabling legislation tied the FBI's hands. Howard found it hard to "understand how the FBI was able to take effective action to 'virtually eliminate' lynching in light of your statement that the Department of Justice can act only when Federal statutes have been violated." Howard suggested that it was not the FBI that brought down the Klan and stemmed lynching but rather "persistent action by the NAACP and by an aroused public opinion." Moreover, if the FBI had successfully quashed lynching, why had it so clearly failed to bring to justice the killers of George W. Lee, Lamar Smith, and Emmett Till? Instead of berating critics, Howard urged Hoover to use the prestige of his office to condemn these murders.[22]

Howard sent a second confidential letter on January 20 that he did not release to the press. This time he laid out specific allegations, including names, about leaks by southern-born FBI agents to local police in civil rights investigations. He charged that FBI agents had pressured a man in Cleveland, Mississippi, who had filed a voting rights grievance, to sign a statement that the FBI had treated him fairly. The most serious claim was that these agents had tipped off the local police who then "upbraided him for making the complaint to the FBI." Howard asked Hoover for a personal meeting so that he could bring along this man and witnesses. He recommended that future investigations be "conducted by agents who are not themselves residents of the area."[23]

Hoover instructed the Memphis FBI office to look into Howard's allegations. After a perfunctory investigation, it sent back its findings. The report concluded that Howard's charges were untrue and that the agents had "categorically denied" asking the complainant in Cleveland to sign a statement praising the FBI. But it was silent on whether agents had tipped off the local police. With somewhat less fervor, and much less evidence, the report brushed aside accusations that biased native-born agents had undermined civil rights investigations. Instead, it narrowed the focus to two agents who were Mississippi natives. Even within these limits, however, the investigation was superficial. Although the report made much of the fact that one agent had died prior to some of the alleged incidents, it failed to discuss the behavior of the other.[24]

White newspapers in the South did not bother to wait for Howard's response before reacting swiftly and favorably to Hoover's first letter. The *Jackson Daily News* was elated that someone had put "Mississippi's radical Negro agitator, Dr. T. R. M. Howard, in his proper place." Two days later, it piled on by labeling Howard "a blatant, loud-mouthed and irresponsible liar." The more moderate southern white press agreed. The *Atlanta Constitution* considered Hoover's defense "entirely proper," while the *Commercial Appeal* of Memphis condemned Howard as "completely reckless" for questioning the "integrity and efficiency" of the FBI.[25]

FBI officials aggressively used the content of Hoover's letter to cultivate white support in the South. Nichols hand-delivered a copy to Senator James O. Eastland, who, echoing the sentiments of his segregationist allies at the *Jackson Daily News,* proclaimed that it was "high time that somebody was putting Howard in his place." Eastland confided that he had reason to believe that unless Howard "mended his ways" he "was going to be taken care of by some of the negroes of Mound Bayou." Eastland cited his source as a black former Republican National Committeeman from Mound Bayou. The FBI blacked out the name, but the profile closely fits Howard's old enemy, Fred H. Miller. Later, Eastland announced his intention to introduce Hoover's letter into *The Congressional Record.* A "confidential source" also said that Howard's "income tax returns would bear looking into."[26]

Mississippi's two leading white racial moderates, Congressman Frank Smith and Hodding Carter, showed no inclination to throw Howard a lifeline. Smith dismissed him as a "'Simon Legree' type" who mistreated his tenants. Addressing the director as "J. Edgar," Carter credited Hoover's letter with "relieving the explosive pressure" between the races, but he cautioned that Howard had good reason to fear attacks from whites and to hire bodyguards: "I wouldn't want to gamble on Howard's life expectancy in the Delta," he remarked.[27]

In contrast to the universally pro-Hoover southern white press, the black newspapers took Howard's side. Their reactions reveal a deeper undercurrent of black distrust of the FBI during the 1950s than historians have previously recognized. The *California Eagle* blamed Hoover for "intemperate" behavior and, like Howard, wondered how "the FBI could 'virtually eliminate' lynching when, according to Mr. Hoover, his bureau has no competence to even investigate where no federal crime is committed." It charged that Hoover's letter had given "aid and comfort" to enemies of civil rights. The *Chicago Defender* suggested that "Mr. Hoover is riding the wrong horse when he castigates Dr. Howard for saying what are the thoughts of decent people all over the country. 'Where is the FBI? Can't they do something about this?'" The *New York Amsterdam News* took the same stance, while the *Baltimore Afro-American* carried a cartoon depicting Howard and Hoover in a wrestling match. The *Tri-State Defender,* often a pro-Howard voice, ran two editorials on a single day on the subject. One asked why Hoover was wasting "time in indulging in personalities and name calling" instead of finding ways to deploy the FBI "to help in the civil rights fight, just as it sought means to apply its force and effectiveness against the rampaging gangsters of another recent era."[28]

Hoover drafted a final letter to Howard on January 27, but it is not clear whether he ever sent it. If he did, the press ignored it. He curtly dismissed the allegation about leaks, noting that agents in the field had assured him that they had not asked the complainant in Cleveland to sign a statement stipulating the fairness of the FBI. While Hoover did not say so in the letter, he privately conceded (as Howard had claimed) that his previous claim that the FBI had "broken up" the Klan was "too sweeping."[29]

Not all blacks took Howard's side. Thurgood Marshall cast his lot with Hoover, but this time he did so secretly. Writing to Hoover in January, he dismissed Howard as a "rugged individualist" who did not represent the views of the NAACP. Marshall's disdain for Howard was almost visceral. Soon after Hoover's letter appeared an agent reported that he had "no use for Howard and nothing would please him more than to see Howard completely crushed." Marshall was well aware that Hoover's attack served to take the heat off the NAACP and provided opportunities for closer collaboration in civil rights.

At least some suspected hidden intrigues. Most revealing was a brief snippet in *Jet* that suggested that Hoover's decision to single out Howard "rather than the NAACP for criticizing his agency is the $64 question. People in the know say Hoover has a special reason."[30]

Although Howard showed no inclination to let up on his jeremiads against FBI inaction on civil rights, he was mindful of potential dangers. He took care to avoid a taint of Communist association. His militant stands on specific issues, such as the proposed march on Washington, had drawn praise from the *Daily Worker,* the publication of the Communist Party, and the *Militant,* the voice of the Trotskyite Socialist Workers Party. In January, the *Militant* had editorialized that Howard had "probably done more investigation of the lynchings in Mississippi than the whole FBI combined." The independent, but generally pro-Marxist, *National Guardian* dubbed him "the leader of Mississippi resistance to racism." But Howard had kept his distance from these publications.[31]

In January Howard left himself open to charges that he was a fellow traveler by accepting a speaking invitation in New York from the Provisional Committee for Justice in Mississippi. The committee had close associations with Communist Party elements, and members included W. E. B. Du Bois and Lyman Beecher Stowe. Howard claimed later (probably with sincerity) that he did not know the nature of the group. After his brother-in-law tipped him off, he immediately pulled out of the speaking engagement. Howard took the opportunity to remind the press that he had consistently refused "to appear before any group that seems red-tinged or red-dominated. I want justice and democracy in Mississippi, but I want it in the American way. . . . I am interested in no other form of government than democracy in America and I feel our only hope is in the Bill of Rights, the Declaration of Independence and the Constitution." He added that it "would be just duck soup for Hoover" if he had not withdrawn.[32]

Howard's decision to withdraw resulted in much goodwill from anti-Communist leftists, including A. Philip Randolph, who praised it as "quite wise." Randolph observed that Howard's "splendid job" as a champion of civil rights "would be greatly impaired, if not destroyed, by any connection with any Communist forces or fronts." Fay Bennett of the National Sharecroppers Fund, a political ally of Randolph and Norman Thomas, agreed. Because of "the need this country has for your kind of leadership, it is most important that you not give the Eastlands of the country the chance they are no doubt looking for to discredit you."[33]

Howard's wariness of Communist associations helped to insulate him when circumstances once again pushed Hoover into the Till case. A meeting on February 28 in the U.S. attorney general's office with a delegation representing the National Council of Negro Women forced Hoover's hand. Hoover had expected a routine affair, but he was in for a nasty shock. Juanita Mitchell, the chair of the council's legal committee, used the occasion to prod him to look into allegations that Sheriff Strider had held Loggins and Collins in the Charleston jail during the trial. During the meeting, Mitchell emphasized that Howard's criticisms of the FBI "voiced the complaints of thousands of citizens around the country." Nichols was outraged.[34]

Hoover was caught flat-footed. As Mitchell burrowed in ever deeper with pointed questions, he admitted that he did not know about the allegation involving Loggins and Collins. Thrown on the defensive, he pledged to look into the matter "immediately." Mitchell was not about to relent. Nichols ranked it as "one of the rudest demonstrations of anyone I have ever seen in a conference." She reminded Hoover of Hicks's first letter to Brownell describing the possible role of Collins and Loggins. Mitchell had offended her hosts, but she had gotten results. Hoover ordered an investigation and scrawled a note instructing his subordinates to interview Hicks and "any other pertinent witness."[35]

Nichols almost immediately threw cold water on the idea. He wondered if by interviewing Hicks, the FBI would create a dilemma because "we can expect to have a story that we are investigating the Till case" and thus contradict the FBI's assertion that it did not have jurisdiction. Furthermore, "Hicks got his information from Dr. Howard and if we interview Hicks we would then have to go to Howard." Giving Howard this kind of credibility was risky because the director had just publicly denounced him in unforgiving terms. After an inquiry to the Memphis office, Nichols decided that Mitchell's charges had no merit. He said that the office had already investigated whether Loggins and Collins were in the Charleston jail during the trial. Agents had questioned special prosecutor Robert B. Smith III (himself a former FBI man) about the matter. Smith reported that he had sent the highway patrol to conduct a physical search and to interview the prisoners: "Officers determined that Collins and Logan [sic] were definitely not in the jail and had not been held there during the trial." On Nichols's recommendation, Hoover decided not to order an official investigation after all.[36]

Throughout this period, Howard continued to agitate for a march on Washington. His best hope for an opening to promote it was the upcoming National Delegate Assembly of the Leadership Conference on Civil Rights beginning in March. The NAACP had established the conference as a clear-inghouse of about fifty civil rights, fraternal, and other organizations. As the date for the meeting approached, Howard took every opportunity to beat the drums for his longtime proposal to send federal troops to Mississippi as a last resort. He reasoned that if the United States could deploy them in "Korea to see that human rights are not trampled upon," it should be able to do so in "the South to see that the rights of American citizens are respected." Although prominent black leaders, such as Randolph, had also endorsed sending in troops, it was far too radical for the NAACP.[37]

As the date approached for the delegate assembly, Thurgood Marshall again stood in Howard's way. Cooperating with the FBI, he led a surreptitious campaign to keep the meeting under firm NAACP control. Speaking to an FBI agent, Marshall expressed concern that Howard "is very outspoken and would undoubtedly bring up some resolution criticizing the Department of Justice." Marshall told another FBI source that Howard might try to secure the necessary credentials to attend from any one of more than a thousand NAACP branches. To block this, Marshall said that NAACP officials planned that "if Howard does show up with credentials, to endeavor to have the credentials revoked by the head of the state delegation, if it is not possible to have the head of the chapter revoke them."[38]

News that something was afoot leaked to the black press. About a week before the conference, Simeon Booker reported in *Jet* that Howard was "barred" from the proceedings, marking "the first open break between the surgeon and other national civil rights leaders. The rift came after behind-the-scenes feuds over the Mound Bayou physician's tactics and actions." Booker's article incited a small but intense outcry. Nat Turner, the chair of the National Association of Negro Trade Unionists, protested to Wilkins that the exclusion was a "grave error and definitely a backward step for civil rights" and insisted that Howard's "militancy and courage on the American scene qualifies him for full participation." Wilkins denied there was any personal exclusion, but he was not convincing. He stated that Howard did not qualify because the rules limited participation to delegates from the fifty participating organizations chosen on the basis of congressional districts. It cannot be determined whether Wilkins was privy to Marshall's clandestine alliance with Hoover against Howard. Still, if Wilkins had wanted to make a place for Howard, either as a delegate or as a guest, he could easily have arranged it.[39]

The pro-Howard protests did little good. He was not present when more than two thousand delegates convened in Washington, D.C., on March 4. The NAACP leadership tightly regulated the agenda and the permitted topics of debate. At the outset, Wilkins prohibited resolutions from getting to the floor. He pointedly reminded the delegates that their role was to discuss strategies on how best to advance an eight-point program for civil rights that had already been prepared for them. Of course, a byproduct was to preclude such proposals as a march on Washington or sending federal troops to Mississippi. Here and there, some discordant notes interrupted the generally choreographed quality of the proceedings. Most notably, delegates heckled a speech by Paul M. Butler, the national chair of the Democratic Party, with cries of "What about Eastland? . . . Eastland! Eastland! What about Eastland?" Only two days before the conference, the U.S. Senate (acting on the unanimous recommendation of the Democratic Steering Committee) had elevated Eastland to be chair of the Judiciary Committee. Compared to Butler's stormy reception, the delegates were more cordial to Hugh Scott, who represented the GOP. Had Howard been there, he might have used these rumblings to mobilize a more serious rebellion.[40]

Howard's exclusion from the conference did not go unnoticed. The *American Negro,* a publication of the rising black political insurgency in Chicago edited and published by Gus Savage, called it the "greatest treachery" and demanded "an answer from Roy Wilkins and the Leadership Conference on Civil Rights. FBI Director Hoover must not be permitted to select leaders for American Negroes." Expressing a common view among black militants, the article blamed the conference for derailing the momentum for a march: "A march is still in order—a march of all who wish to go, with Dr. Howard in front rather than left-out."[41]

This was too much for Howard. Although he continued to extol the NAACP publicly, he wrote a lengthy complaint to Roy Wilkins. He detailed a history of real or perceived slights dating back to the previous year that showed "a growing hostility toward me on your part, and on the part of other NAACP officials, an apparent campaign to discredit me." He cited the story from *Jet* that the NAACP had barred him from the delegate assembly in Washington, D.C. Because he was president-elect of the National Medical Association and vice president of the National Business League, he had "supposed that the NAACP would want and welcome the support of those organizations and would at least tolerate me because of my positions with them."[42]

Howard bitterly reminded Wilkins of his speeches to "numerous branches of the NAACP throughout the nation, particularly since the Till case." After a rundown of some cities where he had appeared, he said that he doubted that "any official of the Association has spoken to as many thousands of people as I have in that period or that any of them has been instrumental in raising as much money for the NAACP." He was particularly miffed by allegations that he had personally benefited from his activism. To the contrary, he had suffered "severe financial losses" and "could have kept silent and continued to enjoy a lucrative practice of medicine in the South."[43]

As for the Amzie Moore matter, Howard chastised Wilkins for not correcting Moore's misimpression that he had pocketed the money. He stressed that "every cent" had gone into an "escrow loan account and that Moore ultimately borrowed the money as was the plan. . . . you have created distrust and doubt where none was necessary. It is my belief that Mr. Moore is now trying to make a 'racket' out of the condition." Howard related several incidents that disturbed him. Wilkins had made light of his habit of hunting deer from an air-conditioned Cadillac, the NAACP youth leader had called him a "phony," and Gloster Current had dismissed the RCNL as a paper organization.[44]

In his response, Wilkins tried to calm the waters. He underscored that Howard had rendered "very valuable aid" to the NAACP and emphasized that he had "reported to our staff and Board your effective speeches for the cause." He pointed out that he was the one who arranged for Howard to speak in Baltimore in September. Although Wilkins did not mention it, this was the same speech that had featured Howard's opening shot against the FBI. Wilkins claimed once again that the organizers of the delegate assembly had not intentionally tried to exclude Howard. He insisted that it "was not a 'speaking' meeting" and that "participation was confined to persons chosen by local units of the 50-odd organizations making up the Leadership Conference on Civil Rights."[45]

Turning to the Amzie Moore affair, Wilkins denied that he had implied anything. He had merely informed Moore that he could not discuss details. Agreeing with Howard's overall assessment, he characterized Moore as "not an *otherwise good* credit risk who was being subjected to special pressures because of his civil rights views," but rather "a poor credit risk (overloaded to the gills)." Wilkins promised at the first opportunity to question the NAACP youth leader. He conceded that Current, while tired and frustrated by other matters, had "perhaps said some things that he ought not have said." Wilkins admitted that he had poked fun at Howard's practice of hunting deer from his Cadillac but did not intend it to be either "vicious or significant." He made it "in a humorous fashion as all of us do at one time or another in our 'in-the-family' comments."[46]

The rest of the letter reflected Wilkins's nuanced relationship with Howard. Along with the praise, he made sure to raise criticism. He called Howard's attention to disturbing secondhand and "garbled" reports about some of his remarks. These had seemed to reflect badly "upon the integrity of the NAACP, its ability to recognize the 'real' problems in the South, and its expenditure of funds. Mind you, this was not in the nature of a concrete, itemized charge, but a passing implication—a far more deadly thing." While Wilkins did not mention Thurgood Marshall (nor, for that matter, did Howard), he promised that no "hostility has been projected from this office toward you."[47]

Howard met Wilkins more than halfway. He phoned to say that their correspondence had cleared the air and vowed to do everything in his power to help the NAACP. He also agreed with Wilkins that *Jet* had tried to stir up a fight. Howard might have been less conciliatory if he had known about Marshall's secret maneuverings with Hoover. Whatever Wilkins's role (if any) in the Marshall intrigues, he seemed eager to pull back from the brink. He assured a local NAACP official that there was no "hostility between us, but some people have tried to create a division. Also, to be frank, some careless statements have been made by some NAACP adherents, including some in the National Office."[48]

By this time, Howard had finally decided to move permanently to Chicago. The choice made sense. Chicago offered a built-in constituency of potential customers and political supporters. For many years, black migrants from Mississippi (usually the Delta) had made it their primary destination. The connection to the black areas of Chicago was so close that some referred to the city as a northern suburb of Mississippi. Many of these migrants had direct knowledge of Howard either as a doctor or as a champion of civil rights. Chicago was going to be Howard's new home, but he was in no hurry to make the full transition. He was determined, at least for the time being, to maintain ties to Mississippi. Helen told journalists that he traveled there "incognito" once a month, riding around not in a car but "in trucks and other inconspicuous conveyances." In the meantime, he showed no inclination to pull his punches in response to white hostility. He regularly condemned "Mississippi, the cotton curtain of the South," which had "laws protecting the rat, the skunk, the hog and cow, but not the Negro."[49]

Helen was a valuable ally to her husband and came forward several times to support his goals publicly. In a statement to the *Pittsburgh Courier* in April, she chimed in that Mississippi's "representation in Congress should be reduced unless Negroes are given their justly due rights to the ballot." She occasionally gave speeches such as one in Los Angeles on "Open Hunting Season on Negroes." Civil rights work may have dominated her husband's time, but the couple still showed up at social and sporting events. A reporter from *Jet* saw them at Churchill Downs with well-known Alabama civil rights attorney Arthur Shores, where T. R. M. bet on a horse named Just Freedom. As a long shot, it "paid $28 for a $2 wager. The good Doc cleaned up."[50]

In April Howard's most immediate concern was the fourth annual conference of the RCNL in Mississippi. He tried to outdo himself with two headliners guaranteed to draw a massive crowd: Congressman Adam Clayton Powell Jr. and Rev. Martin Luther King Jr. Powell's life had many parallels to Howard's. The two were about the same age, had reputations as civil rights mavericks and militants, and were known for their flamboyance and charisma. King, on the other hand, was nearly twenty years Howard's junior. His persona was more intellectual and ethereal than either of the others. Compared to Howard, King's rise as a civil rights leader was meteoric. Less than two months after he had hosted Howard in Montgomery, King outshone him in national prominence.

Circumstances and bad luck conspired against Howard's choice of speakers. It did not help that he was not particularly close to either man. During the 1940s, Powell, largely on Howard's instigation, had gone to bat for locating the Veterans' Hospital in Mound Bayou, but otherwise they had had minimal contact. Probably Howard's best entrée to Powell was through Edward F. Boyd, who knew him in New York. King and Howard expressed mutual respect, but they had rarely crossed paths. Nevertheless, they had continued to work together, at least in a general way, on common projects. In March, for example, Howard was the lead speaker at a rally in Chicago that raised money for the ongoing Montgomery bus boycott. Howard read a message from King asking him to tell "the folks in Chicago we have enlisted in this fight for the duration."[51]

Howard sent a letter of invitation to Powell in January 1956. In making his pitch, he pointed out the history of the RCNL rallies and the past list of speakers including, of course, Marshall and Diggs. Predicting a bigger crowd than had heard Diggs in April, he declared that he knew of "no man in America who is better fitted to do the job that we need done in Mississippi." Powell was not sure how to respond and sent the letter to Clarence Mitchell of the NAACP with the question, "Clarence, What do you think?" Howard did not personally make the invitation to King. J. F. Redmon and G. R. Haughton of the RCNL's Ministers Conference sent it fairly late, on March 14.[52]

In the meantime, RCNL officials went ahead and advertised the event showing King and Powell as the speakers, predicting a turnout of ten thousand. When the RCNL announced a shift in the meeting's location from Mound Bayou to Jackson, Medgar Evers reacted with anger. Writing to Wilkins, he condemned the move as a direct attack on the NAACP's bailiwick. This was the first evidence of his discontent with Howard. Evers, once a stalwart of the RCNL, had become fiercely loyal to the NAACP and his comments reflected this. He accused the RCNL of scheming "to capitalize on the services" of King and Powell. He warned that the "bringing of national figures down here will tend to confuse the people and make them more gullible to the 'hog wash' of the Regional Council. If you see fit to take any possible action of restraint as far as the above mentioned names are concerned, please rest assured that we the N.A.A.C.P. stand 100% with you." Evers was not the only one to anticipate a turf war. "The boys in race relations circles," Booker reported, "are girding for sensational news from Mississippi. Since the forces of Dr. T. R. M. Howard have moved from the Delta to the Jackson area, they'll face stiff opposition from the NAACP."[53]

Ironically, it was Wilkins, often considered the quintessential Washington insider and jealous guardian of the NAACP's predominance, who once again stepped in to keep the peace. Stressing Howard's pledge of support for the NAACP, he discounted Evers' fears: "I do not know who will be speaking for his meeting in Jackson but I don't think our people will be confused." Nevertheless, he instructed Evers to monitor the situation and to send a full report.[54]

It became public knowledge that the headliners would not be King and Powell after Governor James P. Coleman of Mississippi wired them four days before the conference, asking that they "indefinitely postpone" their visits. By showing up, he asserted, they would undermine Mississippi's increasingly "tranquil" race relations. Gratuitously, Coleman publicly stated his "hope the sound thinking Negroes of Mississippi will not lend their approval to the presence of overnight scalawags and carpetbaggers in our midst." In a major embarrassment for Howard and the RCNL, Powell and King stressed that they had never accepted the invitations. Powell insisted that he had repeatedly stated his unavailability because of "two engagements of long standing on the same day. . . . Howard just left my office and admitted that he had not been in Mississippi recently and did not know I was being advertised to appear there. . . . I gave no word to appear there and he so admitted." King, then preoccupied with appealing a conviction for an illegal boycott, pointed out that he had turned down the invitation in a letter on March 27. Howard acknowledged as much when he announced that RCNL members had continued to advertise, "living in hope that Rev. King and Congressman Powell would find it possible to come."[55]

King and Powell did not reconsider their decisions, but each bristled at Coleman's letter. In his response to the governor, Powell stated that if he came to Mississippi in the future, "I will most certainly advise you so that your office can extend to me the courtesies always extended to Representatives of the United States." Similarly, King announced ironically that he would never come to Mississippi to disturb "the so-called peace of the community although I wonder what type of peace he [Coleman] was talking about." The RCNL's board interpreted Coleman's letter as a subtle threat to the safety of the speakers. It found it "unfortunate that conditions in Mississippi are such that Negroes can't invite leaders of their race to the state . . . without being able to turn to anyone to guarantee their protection."[56]

The controversy cast a pall over the conference itself. Fewer than a thousand people turned up on April 27, by far the lowest in the RCNL's history. As a substitute for King, the Montgomery Improvement Association sent Rev. B. D. Lambert, a relatively low-level leader of the bus boycott. In his report to Wilkins, Medgar Evers characterized the conference as a "financial flop," estimating the total take as less than $500.[57]

The low turnout did not dampen Howard's combativeness. He suggested in his speech that if Coleman "wants tranquil race relations in Mississippi, let him: Give the Negro the right to vote. Give him equal job opportunities. Stop violating the 14th and 15th amendments. Accept the U.S. Supreme Court decision on integration." He urged blacks to report every violation of their rights to the Department of Justice by sending sworn notarized statements and to "stop lying to the Mississippi white man. Let's stop lying about you don't want to be free. Tell him you want anything any other free American has." If Howard was trying to undermine the NAACP, as Evers had implied, he did not reveal it in his speech. He expressed pride in his life membership and proclaimed that the hostility of whites had convinced him of its central importance. He proposed that the NAACP "go underground" if whites followed through on threats to ban the organization. Howard and the RCNL repeated the call from 1954 for a biracial conference with the governor to discuss race problems. Naturally, Coleman dismissed the idea.[58]

The nonappearance of King and Powell obviously contributed to the disappointing turnout, but it was not the only reason. The shift from Mound Bayou, where the RCNL had a large following, to Jackson, which was the NAACP's bailiwick, was a major miscalculation. RCNL officials made the decision in March, but it is not clear why. Possibly they were reacting to the hostility of Mound Bayou's officials, or they hoped that the change would broaden the base beyond the Delta. In addition, Howard had so much else on his plate in early 1956 that planning was haphazard. The organizers gambled nearly everything on King and Powell. Compared to past RCNL rallies, they paid little attention to such crowd-pleasing amenities as entertainment and food. Governmental harassment further depressed attendance. Evers, who was otherwise rather pleased by the failure of the conference, counted more than two dozen "highway patrol, local police officers, and detectives, in and around the Masonic Temple Building on the 27th, whose objective, apparently, was to create a psychological fear in the people."[59]

The heavy-handed police presence was consistent with a general pattern of political repression of black aspirations. Segregationist hard-liners were riding high in what one scholar later called "the Closed Society." Mississippi had just established the Sovereignty Commission to spy on civil rights leaders, and NAACP membership was in free fall. A week after Eastland's election as chair of the Senate Judiciary Committee, members of Congress from the South issued the "Southern Manifesto," defending massive resistance to integration. The sustained segregationist offensive intimidated even seasoned civil rights activists. Denouncing the RCNL's militancy as counterproductive, Isaac Daniels, a longtime ally of Howard's, refused election as the RCNL's treasurer. Levye Chapple, another RCNL veteran, also pulled back. Soon, he was serving as an informant for the Sovereignty Commission. Whites preferred to interpret black intimidation as evidence that race relations had improved. In a speech that coincided with the RCNL conference, for example, Senator Eastland boasted that the South had "no racial tension or friction. . . . If agitators were kept out of the South there would be no problem at all."[60]

Howard's last major official hurrah as a Mississippi civil rights leader was his speech for a "Heroes of the South" rally in Madison Square Garden in May. It was part of a stellar lineup that included Eleanor Roosevelt, Adam Clayton Powell Jr., Roy Wilkins, Autherine Lucy Foster, and Rosa Parks. Martin Luther King Jr. was originally billed as the headliner (just ahead of Howard and Lucy in the advertisements), but he had to back out. Boycott leader E. D. Nixon filled in for him. Sammy Davis Jr., Tallulah Bankhead, and Cab Calloway provided the entertainment. The main sponsors of the rally were the Brotherhood of Sleeping Car Porters and the NAACP, and the goal was to raise money for the civil rights fights in Mississippi and Montgomery. Between fifteen and twenty thousand attended, making it one of the largest civil rights rallies in the North up to that time. A. Philip Randolph's introduction saluted Howard for challenging the "racialism and the tribalism of those who would strike down the Constitution and take away the rights of the people of Mississippi merely because of color." Although Howard was now a de facto Chicagoan, Randolph described him as a resident of Mound Bayou.[61]

Howard's speech, captured on tape, shows him in fine form. Much of the content, including his call for sending troops to the South, was familiar. Mixing outrage, righteous passion, and optimism, he characterized the Association of Citizens' Councils as "the worst internal threat that we have to our American way of life." Pointing to the killing of George W. Lee and the disenfranchisement of black voters, he exclaimed "We have grown tired of fighting for something across the sea that we can't vote for in Belzoni, Mississippi." Howard made sure to interject humor. He declared that "my state would have liked to have seceded for a second time from the Union on the afternoon of May 17, 1954, if there would have been any place for Mississippi to have gone on that afternoon. As there was just one place she could have gone, since another infamous Mississippian named Bilbo has been giving them trouble down there for seven years they just wouldn't move over and let Mississippi move in." Howard hinted that he was broadening his focus. After asking for a show of hands of people born in the South, he chastised them for forgetting "about the conditions in the South" and, just as important, for "not doing much about the damnable conditions that exist right here in New York City."[62]

The rally was a financial success, raising $6,000. A recently formed organization, In Friendship, helped to organize it and disburse the funds. Leaders of the group included Randolph, Norman Thomas, and civil rights legend Ella Baker. In Friendship took up where the NAACP/Tri-State Bank program left off, with one major difference. Rather than just loans, it gave direct aid to civil rights activists under pressure. Although Howard had been recommending such a program for more than a year, he apparently did not take part in its organization.[63]

By the time of the Madison Square Garden rally, Howard had stepped down as president of the RCNL, and he returned only periodically to Mississippi in later years. Now a refugee from the state that had defined his public persona, Howard's prominence as a civil rights leader was fading. In April the

Pittsburgh Courier commented on his changing fortunes: "Popularity and the national spotlight are one and the same—a fickle old lady. Just a few months ago the name of Dr. T. R. M. Howard (remember Emmett Till?) was being cried from housetops. Then came Autherine Lucy, the girl with guts enough to enroll at the University of Alabama. And now, the Rev. Martin Luther King, the bus boycott spokesman. And, whatever became of Mamie Bradley?" This was an exaggeration. As the Madison Square Garden rally indicated, Howard still drew crowds and generated headlines. Moreover, he gave no hint of feeling slighted, bitter, or pessimistic about his future prospects. He looked forward to taking over formally as president of the National Medical Association and an exciting career as a doctor in Chicago. He also had ambitious political dreams: he was running for Congress.[64]

8

Taking On the Machine in Chicago
A Republican Campaign for Congress

HOWARD FOLLOWED A well-trodden path for black Mississippians in beginning a new life in Chicago. The Second Great Migration was in full force. During the 1950s, Chicago's black population grew by 65 percent, exceeding 800,000 by 1960. At the time Howard made his move, more than two thousand were arriving in a single week, many from the Delta. They came to escape political oppression and in search of economic improvement. Howard, like many other migrants, found Chicago to be a welcome respite from the confines of white supremacy. In particular, he no longer had to be in constant fear of an early grave. But moving to Chicago was also a step down in some ways. In Mississippi, he was one of the two or three best-known black leaders, but now he had many competitors.[1]

Howard knew that race relations in his new hometown left much to be desired. The situation was undoubtedly better than Mississippi, but Chicago was already developing a reputation as "the most residentially segregated city in America." As middle-class blacks sought improved housing, whites fought them every inch of the way. Ugly incidents occurred at the Trumbull Park Homes on the far South Side. When a few blacks moved into the public housing project in 1953, the existing residents drove them out through violence and intimidation. The cycle of brutality repeated in 1957 when more returned under a limited quota system. In most neighborhoods, whites left en masse, however, rather than strike back violently. Between 1950 and 1960, two nearly all-black strips pushed south and west. One expanded from 71st to 100th Street in the south, while the other stretched all the way to the city's western limits.[2]

For the next twenty years, the shifting fortunes of the South Side shaped the personal, political, social, and professional lives of T. R. M and Helen

Howard. They moved onto the penthouse floor of the fashionable Lake Meadows Apartments on E. 32nd Street. Built with financing from a New York insurance company, the complex, which overlooked Lake Michigan, had opened in 1952 as a bold experiment in racially "integrated living." Located in the middle of the city's oldest black neighborhood, many of the tenants were affluent black professionals and businesspeople.[3]

Simultaneously, Howard opened the Howard Medical Center at 63rd Street and Rhodes in the Woodlawn area. The clinic was nestled in one of Chicago's liveliest and most prosperous business strips. The area had a contentious history. In 1937 Carl Hansberry, a black real estate developer and Republican activist, had purchased and moved into an apartment building in an all-white neighborhood. It was less than two blocks from the future location of the Howard Medical Center. Within a few days, someone threw a brick through the window, almost hitting Hansberry's little girl, Lorraine. Eventually, the family won a favorable court decision against whites who had tried to bar them from the community. Lorraine Hansberry drew on her experiences for a play, *A Raisin in the Sun*, first performed in 1959. Although the Hansberrys had left long before Howard arrived, a hotel they owned was still right down the street.[4]

Howard drew heavily on a clientele who had known him in the Delta but, unlike the old Friendship Clinic, the Howard Medical Center did not operate under the fraternal plan. While most of his income still came from a general practice, something had changed. He and his wife had expensive tastes and had to earn money fast. He increasingly specialized in two quick and profitable sidelines: thyroidectomies and illegal abortions. The police did not greatly trouble him yet, in part, because he had the right connections and did not hesitate to pay bribes. Howard also had staff privileges at the black-owned Ida Mae Scott Hospital on the South Side and became medical director of the Chicago-based S. B. Fuller Products Company.[5]

His duties and salary at Fuller seem to have been nominal, but the prestige value was considerable. The owner of the company, Samuel B. Fuller, had started in the 1920s with an investment of twenty-five dollars. By 1956, he was the richest black man in the United States. His company, which sold primarily cosmetics, had $18 million in sales and a sales force of five thousand (one-third of them white). It gave training to many future entrepreneurs. Fuller had probably met Howard at one of the meetings of the National Business League. Fuller was periodically president of the league during the 1940s and 1950s and Howard was a vice president and chair of the board. From 1956 or earlier, he encouraged Howard's run for Congress.[6]

Their friendship illustrated yet again Howard's capacity for building bridges to a wide array of black leaders. Howard was an independent-thinking Democrat, but Fuller was a rock-ribbed Republican. While Fuller shared Howard's interest in civil rights, few regarded him as a militant. His reputation was that of a black conservative. In 1958 he blasted the federal government for undermining free enterprise and fostering socialism. He feared that it was "doing the same thing today as was done in the days of Caesar—destroying incentive and initiative." In contrast, Howard's political philosophy was more difficult to pin down. Oscar J. Moore Jr., who knew both, characterizes Howard as "to the right of S. B. Fuller" particularly in his disdain for government handouts. Others depict Howard as a political liberal. Perhaps too much can be made of these distinctions. Political ideology as such was secondary to Howard's overriding concern for civil rights.[7]

In many of the basics, Fuller and Howard were alike. Both were energetic, self-confident, driven, largely self-made men who knew how to charm and inspire ordinary people. They were equally adept at forming cordial and profitable relationships with whites. A former employee's recollection of Fuller applied equally to Howard: "Mr. Fuller never had a small thought" and he "could paint a picture that would really blow your mind. He said, 'Reach for the stars,' and he meant *literally* reach for those stars."[8]

Howard's noticeable tilt toward the Republicans in early 1956 must have pleased Fuller. Howard fulsomely praised President Eisenhower's State of the Union address, particularly the passage that "in some localities allegations persist that Negro citizens are being . . . subjected to unwarranted economic pressure." For Howard, the address was "the brightest star that has appeared on the horizon during the past twelve months." He predicted a black switch to the Republicans if the Democrats persisted in appeasing the South. He followed up in April by characterizing Eastland as "a foe of Democracy and a strong aid to Communists" and urged opposition to "any party that supports such a man." The final phase of Howard's political transformation became public knowledge on May 1, 1956, when the *Chicago Daily Defender* carried the front-page headline, "T. R. M. Howard Swings to GOP." Howard promised to campaign hard for Eisenhower's reelection. This announcement marked the *de facto* opening shot of his race for Congress in 1958—though he did not formally throw his hat in the ring until late 1957.[9]

Howard's defection to the GOP was consistent with a nationwide trend. Cracks had begun to appear in black loyalty to the Democratic Party soon after Eisenhower took office. A return to the party of Lincoln was not out of the question. The alignment of blacks to the Democrats, after all, was a recent phenomenon and not unshakable. They had moved into the Democratic column only in 1936. Blacks remained loyal despite FDR's consistent appeasement of the South on the hot-button issues of lynching, segregation, and disenfranchisement. They gave greater support to President Harry Truman because of his civil rights overtures. By 1956, however, black disillusionment was too obvious to ignore. The Democrats had largely brought it on themselves. They had flunked several critical tests for black voters during the campaign. Two days after white mobs drove Autherine Lucy out of the University of Alabama, for example, Adlai Stevenson, the likely Democratic standard-bearer, angered a black audience in Los Angeles by counseling gradualism. Nobody was more upset than Roy Wilkins, who had already warned that blacks might desert the Democratic Party.[10]

By comparison, the Republican record was looking better all the time. Eisenhower had moved resolutely against segregation in public facilities in the District of Columbia and speeded the integration of the military begun by Truman. He made unprecedented appointments including J. Ernest Wilkins as assistant secretary of labor, only the second black man to hold a subcabinet post (the first was in 1911). Although Eisenhower was personally unenthusiastic about the *Brown* decision, many blacks appreciated his naming of Earl Warren as chief justice. The consensus held that the Republican platform in 1956 took a firmer stand on civil rights than its Democratic counterpart.[11]

The inroads of the pro-Eisenhower camp extended to the top ranks of black leadership. The best-known example was Adam Clayton Powell Jr. Although he remained a Democrat, he supported the president in 1956. Others who cast their ballots for Ike were Martin Luther King Jr. and journalist James Hicks. While the *Chicago Defender* and the *California Eagle* endorsed Adlai Stevenson, the *Afro-American* of Baltimore, the *Pittsburgh Courier,* the

Amsterdam News of New York, and the *Tri-State Defender* of Memphis swung over to his opponent. It is important, of course, not to exaggerate the extent of the GOP's civil rights initiatives. The shift in black attitudes stemmed more from Democratic weaknesses than from Republican strengths. Howard never had any illusions on this score. He was often acerbic in his criticism of his new party and, indirectly, of the president. "How can Dulles talk about free elections in Germany or behind the Iron Curtain," he demanded, "when we can't have free elections in Mississippi?"[12]

While Howard faulted GOP shortcomings, he was remorseless in attacking the Democrats. Sometimes he seemed determined to win first prize in a contest for political incorrectness. His answer to an often-asked question about how he "can go along with people like Wisconsin Sen. Joseph McCarthy" was priceless. "I don't like to but I will," he said. "I'd far rather side with McCarthy who thinks there's a Communist under every bed, than with Senator Eastland who thinks there should be a Negro dangling from every rope."[13]

The November results revealed substantial GOP gains. "[O]f all the major groups in the nation's population," the Gallup Poll found, "the one that shifted most to the Eisenhower-Nixon ticket was the Negro voter." About 39 percent of blacks voted for the president, a seven-point loss for the Democrats from 1952. Nowhere else was the swing to Eisenhower so pronounced as in the South. Both blacks and whites joined in. Journalist Ethel L. Payne wrote that blacks "voted Republican in protest to the too-weak Democratic stand on civil rights and white southerners went Republican in protest of what they termed the too-liberal attitude of the Democratic party." For the first time in decades, the GOP won black majorities in cities like Atlanta, Memphis, and Baltimore. From Montgomery, Martin Luther King Jr., who along with Ralph Abernathy voted for Ike, commented that "our people seemed to feel there was no need to change from Eisenhower progress. I talked with many after they voted and I do not recall a single person telling me he voted for Stevenson." Republican gains in the North were less spectacular but still significant. Eisenhower's vote almost doubled in Powell's Harlem district from 17 percent in 1952 to 32 percent. On Chicago's South Side, he was the choice of just under 40 percent of black voters compared to 25 percent in 1952. As a result of the election, an unprecedented three of the ten blacks in the Illinois legislature were Republican.[14]

The Chicago voting trend must have whetted Howard's optimism, but it was a poor guide to the fight that lay ahead. In challenging William L. Dawson, he was taking on a formidable politician. A generation older than Howard, Dawson was originally from Georgia. He graduated magna cum laude from Fisk University and received his law degree from Northwestern University. After seeing action in World War I, he built a lucrative legal practice in Chicago. During the 1920s, he was a protégé of Oscar DePriest, a Republican, who in 1929 became the first black in the U.S. House since the turn of the century. In 1934, when Howard was an assistant chairman of the Democratic Party in California, Dawson was a well-known Republican politician in Chicago. But the GOP was in decline and Dawson was never one to go down with the ship.[15]

Dawson formally switched sides in 1939 when Mayor Edward Kelly offered him a chance to head the heavily black second ward Democratic Party organization. Now assured of machine backing, he gradually accumulated more power. He won election in 1942 to represent the First Congressional District, an area that encompassed the Loop as well as the black majority on the South Side. After an initial close victory, his majorities during the next twelve years typically topped 66 percent. He carefully constructed a black-controlled autonomous "sub-machine" that dominated five of Chicago's six black wards. In 1955 Dawson's power was so great that his decision to support Richard J. Daley's first campaign for mayor was enough to tip the balance.[16]

Dawson and Howard were opposites in their careers and personalities. Howard was passionate, impulsive, outgoing, and a skilled orator. He had excelled in medicine, business, community building, and civil rights through resourcefulness and taking risks. Dawson's much longer career reflected a single-minded preoccupation with politics and a mastery of its arts. Nicknamed "William the Silent," he was methodical, patient, cautious, and so disdainful of publicity that he shunned even favorable press coverage. According to Dawson, "Bragging too much just gives the other fellow a tip-off on what you're planning to do." He much preferred cutting deals in backrooms to giving speeches. "Power was Bill's passion," one of his associates later observed. "It was all he cared about and lived for." By steering advertising revenue and special favors to the publisher of the *Chicago Defender*, for example, he kept the paper snugly in his hip pocket.[17]

Through a combination of scrupulous attention to the needs of his constituents, organizational acumen, and ruthless cunning, he secured the fealty
of black Chicagoans. His network of precinct captains efficiently mobilized
the vote through rewards and punishments. In one ward during the Christmas holidays, they dispensed clothing, food, and other aid to more than a
hundred families. For those struggling on the margin, as many blacks were
in 1956, even small favors counted for a lot. As Barbara A. Reynolds puts it,
"Dawson, shrewd and close-mouthed, redefined patronage as an instrument
for containing the black poor. In white wards committeemen passed out
$10,000 jobs, for example. But Dawson would request three $3,333–a-year
jobs, which spread the 'wealth and multiplied his power.'" Even as Eisenhower
won more black support, Dawson cut the Republicans down to size on his
own turf. In 1955 he engineered the defeat of Alderman Archibald J. Carey
Jr., perhaps the most prestigious Republican black politician. The winning
candidate was Ralph Metcalfe, an Olympic silver medalist in 1936.[18]

Although Dawson was not as famous as his colleague, Powell, he had much
greater influence in national Democratic Party circles. Unlike Powell, he was
a team player and a loyal partisan. In 1949 he became chair of the House
Committee on Government Operations, the first black man to hold a permanent committee chairmanship. President Truman entrusted him to carry
the Democratic message to blacks in the South. In this capacity Dawson had
accepted Howard's offer to be the featured speaker at the first RCNL annual
rally in 1952. The two men remained on friendly terms, at least until 1956.[19]

Dawson's power was so formidable by 1956 that many wondered if Howard truly thought he could beat him. Certainly, Howard was always outwardly
optimistic about his prospects. Writing to Sherman Adams, he opined that
his candidacy gave the Republicans their best chance to win "since the days
of Oscar DePriest." On the other hand, Howard's friend Oscar J. Moore Jr.,
who was then a teenager, speculates that Howard's goal was not to win but "to
establish himself in Chicago. . . . Doc was not a finisher. . . . I think emotion-
ally, he was satisfied just to be in the limelight and running the dynamics of a
campaign." One problem with this explanation is that it was out of character
for Howard to act in this way. While he was well aware that the publicity
might be good for his medical career, he was not about to waste his time on
what he thought was a losing battle. Bennett J. Johnson, who worked on the

1958 campaign, asserts that Howard "thought he could win because he was well known, because he had wealth, because he had done all these things."[20]

Howard was not alone in his thinking. Others sensed that Dawson might be vulnerable. Critics raised questions about his advanced age (seventy-two), high absentee rate, almost unquestioning party loyalty, and controversial compromises on civil rights. Another sore point was his opposition to the Powell amendment barring federal funds to segregated schools. Dawson handed more ammunition to civil rights advocates by his relative silence on the segregationist crackdown after the *Brown* decision and the murder of Emmett Till. "How can you help Negroes in Mississippi or South Carolina," he asked, "by running your mouth in the North?"[21]

Howard's first priority was to mobilize the assorted critics of Dawson behind his campaign. He already had a head start, or so it seemed. Since 1955, Howard had forged ties with Willoughby Abner, the youthful president of the Chicago branch of the NAACP. Abner, the former political action director of the United Auto Workers, was charismatic, aggressive, and ambitious. Membership rose to record highs on his watch, and he seemed on the verge of an even brighter future. He brought Howard to speak in Chicago in the wake of the Till murder. He easily qualified as Dawson's most dangerous adversary.[22]

Abner's declaration of independence came in the form of a combative open letter to Dawson from the Chicago branch of the NAACP in August 1956. The catalyst was the Democratic Party's adoption of a weak civil rights plank at the convention despite Dawson's much-heralded appointment to the platform committee. The letter pointed to this failure as yet another indication that the strategy of "working behind the scenes" had led only to "pretension and evasion." The letter related other examples of Dawson's "compromise and meaningless moderation" such as his votes against the Powell amendment even after the rise of massive resistance to the *Brown* decision and his silence "when the young son of one of your constituents was brutally murdered in Mississippi."[23]

Howard endeavored to pick up recruits from a hotbed of anti-Dawsonism: the Chicago district of the left-wing United Packinghouse Workers of America (UPWA). Blacks had dominated the leadership in the city for several years. The district's newsletter ran several articles about Howard, one with his picture on the cover. Howard was close to the district's director, Charles Hayes, who had fought for integration of lunch counters during the 1940s. Hayes's barbs against Dawson were often sharper than Abner's. He suggested that Dawson "cannot forever play coy, and continue to be re-elected. He cannot ignore the spirit of militancy and sacrifice that has risen in the hearts of freedom loving Americans today. . . . The question is being asked—Where is Dawson? So far the answer is—nowhere!" Howard drew closer to the UPWA in early 1956 when he joined Hayes and Abner at a joint benefit rally for the Montgomery bus boycott that drew a crowd of three thousand. In a statement that could also apply to Dawson's legendary caution, Howard compared the civil rights gradualist to a doctor who prescribed "aspirin for a ruptured appendix."[24]

Howard did his best to win the political affections of black independents. Members of this group (if it can be called such) ran the gamut from conservatives to leftists. They agreed only in their contempt for the Cook County Democratic organization. While the black independents in Dawson's district were few and far between, they were beginning to stir. Their first big victory came in 1955, when Sidney Jones, a black reform candidate, was elected alderman. Publisher Gus Savage was their most visible spokesman. In November 1955, his journal, the *American Negro,* condemned Dawson as "infamous for his conspicuous absences from mass meetings held to protest the lynching of Emmett Till." It often juxtaposed these attacks with favorable articles on Howard, including a cover story. If Howard could unite the disparate elements, he would have the makings of a coalition that spanned from the UPWA on the left to Fuller on the right.[25]

The publicity generated by Howard's one-year term as president of the National Medical Association, which began in August 1956 (one year after his election), indirectly aided the campaign. His inaugural address was an indictment of the white medical establishment, particularly the American Medical Association. To those who dismissed the NMA as an anachronistic Jim Crow holdover, he said its mission was to be in the vanguard of the fight against discrimination in medicine.[26]

Howard's presidency struck a major blow against medical Jim Crow through sponsoring the Imhotep National Conference on Hospital Integration in 1957. The name came from a physician of an Egyptian pharaoh and was a "reminder that a dark skin was associated with distinction in medicine before that of any other color." This was the first conference of its type and showed a new seriousness by black medical professionals to confront the color bar. The meeting allowed for black doctors from around the country to compare notes on hospital discrimination. The NAACP was an equal cosponsor, and Roy Wilkins and Gloster Current were in the lineup of speakers. In his remarks both at Imhotep and the NMA, Howard stressed that hospital segregation was, in some ways, worse in the North. He pointed out that many of the large hospitals in the Mississippi Delta gave black doctors "definite staff appointments" (although only to serve black patients) while just seven out of seventy predominantly white hospitals in Chicago did so.[27]

To fight these practices, Howard worked with the Chicago Committee to End Discrimination in Chicago Medical Institutions. It was an interracial coalition of doctors and civil rights advocates such as Gerald D. Bullock of the NAACP, an ally of Abner's. One of Howard's first appearances after he moved to Chicago was at a banquet in Bullock's honor sponsored by the committee. The other honoree was Howard's former adversary on the issue of where to locate a black veteran's hospital in Mound Bayou, Dr. W. Montague Cobb. Howard's speech was so eloquent that Cobb's first words on stepping to the microphone were, "When the nightingale sings all the other birds are silent lest their feeble efforts disturb the echo."[28]

In his capacity as NMA president, Howard spoke at high-profile functions such as the Chicago NAACP branch's Freedom Fund Campaign dinner in July. Joining him were Abner and the main speaker, Jackie Robinson who, like Howard, was a Republican. Howard described the South as "a snake pit of inflamed passions and infected prejudices which turns a man into an animal and rots his very soul." He also condemned the apathy of professionals who had not shown up for the event but thought "nothing of spending $500 each for an evening of entertainment." Howard's pessimism notwithstanding, the proceeds were a hefty $25,000, making it the "most successful Freedom Fund Dinner to be held by the Chicago branch."[29]

Howard's farewell address to the NMA in August 1957 was a salute to the family doctor and a critique of increased specialization in the profession. In these respects as well, he thought that Chicago compared unfavorably to Mississippi. Mississippi had only fifty black doctors, but these few "will go night or day, Sundays and holidays, to see the sick patient." In Chicago, which had many more black doctors, it was often impossible for a patient to get help. Howard made his usual pitch for the NAACP. He berated black doctors for failing to share their prosperity by donating money. Wilkins was grateful for the free advertisement and did not hesitate to say so. In a private letter to Howard, he emphasized that "you, personally, have greatly aided the NAACP since 1954 by example, by contribution, by inspiring speeches and I, for one, am deeply appreciative."[30]

As Howard gave his farewell to the NMA, Congress was in the middle of one of its perennial debates on civil rights legislation. The prospects for passage had never looked better. A tough bill had won the support of a coalition of such strange bedfellows as conservative GOP minority leader William Knowland (its floor manager) and liberal Democratic Senator Paul Douglas of Illinois. The outcome was to have a direct bearing on Howard's campaign. A meaningful bill signed by Eisenhower, especially if rammed through over southern Democratic opposition, had the makings of an ideal election issue. Howard was not the only member of his party to think so. In 1956 a key Republican depicted the bill as the entering wedge to "break the Roosevelt coalition in the big cities and the South, even without Eisenhower."[31]

It was beginning to look like civil rights–oriented Republicans would get their wish. The House of Representatives overwhelmingly passed a far-reaching bill in June 1957 that empowered the attorney general to seek injunctions for criminal contempt from a federal judge in voting rights cases. But Democratic Majority Leader Lyndon B. Johnson watered down the Senate version by adding an amendment requiring jury trials for defendants accused of violating federal court orders. Ethel Payne spoke for many civil rights advocates: "We all sat watching while Lyndon Johnson, the most astute maneuverer on the hill, cracked his whip and marshaled his forces to cut the guts and the heart out of the bill." Johnson's defenders argued that the changes were necessary to preclude a filibuster by southern Democrats.[32]

Eisenhower called passage of the jury trial amendment one of his "most serious political defeats" and "a denial of a basic principle of the United States." Several black leaders shared his dismay. To A. Philip Randolph, it was "worse than no bill at all" while E. Frederic Morrow saw it as "pitiful" and "emasculated." Agreeing, Jackie Robinson sent a wire to Eisenhower, "Have waited this long for bill with meaning—can wait a little longer." The passage of the Senate version put the president and his party in a no-win political situation. Instead of an Eisenhower accomplishment, it was "Johnson's masterpiece." If it became law under these circumstances, it had limited value for Republican politicians, including Howard, who wanted to attract black voters.[33]

The matter was not so simple, however. The political consequences of delaying legislation for another year might be worse than signing it. If Eisenhower used his veto pen, northern Democrats would attack him for throwing away the best opportunity for legislative progress on civil rights since Reconstruction. An added reason to sign was the surprising endorsement of the watered-down bill by such prominent civil rights advocates as Roy Wilkins, Martin Luther King Jr., Clarence Mitchell, and Eleanor Roosevelt. Each favored it primarily because of its symbolic value. Choosing safety and expediency, Eisenhower grudgingly signed the weakened bill. Robert A. Caro sums up the dilemma for Republicans: "Somehow the civil rights issue, which was *their* issue, had been captured by the Democrats."[34]

As many had predicted, the Civil Rights Act of 1957 was nearly superfluous in the fight against segregation and disenfranchisement. It had no particular import, for example, in the Little Rock drama that followed directly after passage. Dragging on for weeks, television viewers saw daily scenes of mobs taunting black students juxtaposed with futile negotiations between the president and the governor. In late September, Eisenhower deployed units of the 101st Airborne Division. For the first time since Reconstruction, a president had sent federal troops to protect civil rights. While Eisenhower's laggardness frustrated many, the fact that he took action was a net benefit for Republicans, and certainly Howard, in appealing to black voters.[35]

Sometime in 1957, possibly earlier, William L. Dawson had decided to silence his most troublesome critic, Willoughby Abner, and by extension the Chicago NAACP. The conspiracy was already afoot when Howard officially announced his candidacy in November. By this time, Dawson had secretly purchased memberships in the NAACP for six hundred precinct captains. He gave them word either to defeat Abner at the Chicago NAACP's conference in December or forfeit their patronage jobs. With breathtaking and ruthless efficiency, Dawson's minions descended on the gathering. They caught the hapless Abner completely unaware. Charles Hayes, who was at the scene, recalled that the "invaders of the NAACP were elected to make certain that no one in the newly elected NAACP hierarchy or their successors would ever rock Daley's boat, and they didn't." If Howard had thought that Dawson was getting rusty in the Machiavellian arts, Abner's overthrow was stunning evidence to the contrary. NAACP support of any kind for his campaign was now out of the question.[36]

Meanwhile, Howard was negotiating an uneasy and much belated reconciliation with Amzie Moore. In an exchange of letters, he held out an olive branch for the relief of Moore's crushing debt. He promised to endorse an appeal to Tri-State Bank and the board of the Regional Council of Negro Leadership to forgive an outstanding loan of $3,000. Still conscious of past slights, Howard testily reminded Moore that he had "single-handedly fought from the beginning for you to have the loan and then after they would not make the loan to you, I went out and begged up the money to be kept there in Escrow to guarantee the loan." Moore was ready to make peace and gave his good wishes for the campaign, but he had some uncomfortable reminders of his own. He told Howard that he had resisted urgings by his partisans to call a press conference to denounce him. The accommodation with Moore was well timed. The last thing Howard needed was a public feud with one of his best-known Mississippi civil rights allies.[37]

The next major episode in Howard's campaign for Congress was the most bizarre. Appropriately, the main player was Arrington High. After Howard's departure in 1956, High had persisted in his one-man crusade against segregation. He made himself such a nuisance that the governor called for an "eagle eye bill" making it a crime to defame "any state, county, city, community, their inhabitants, their institutions, or their government." The proposal stalled but mainly because of fears that it might be turned against whites. Not about to blink under pressure, on October 12, 1957, High published an exposé of a black brothel catering to white men, which he dubbed the "Massie Hawkins College of Prostitution." In his trademark hyperbole, he blamed it for "89% of the illegitimate children" in the state. "If Gov. Coleman is honest that he loves the Negro race," High wondered, "why don't he send the Guard to close Massie's place of prostitution." Twelve days after this screed, High's stepfather committed him to the state mental hospital in Whitfield. The diagnosis was "paranoid delusions," but it seemed logical to blame white retaliation.[38]

The climax in High's strange odyssey was his escape from the mental hospital in February 1958. Stories in *Jet* and the *Chicago Daily Defender* quoted him as giving credit to a "Negro underground organized by Dr. Howard." High told an incredible tale. Rescuers in five cars had picked him up after a prearranged signal. Then they concealed him in a casket that was put in a hearse for the journey to the railroad station. "Flowers were placed on top of the box," High added, "and air holes were bored at the head end so I could breathe." Pictures in *Jet* showed High being greeted by Howard upon arrival in Chicago and playing dead for reporters in a casket.[39]

An escape had clearly occurred, but the details, including the trip in the casket, were hard to swallow. It did not help that High's credibility had long been suspect. The staged photo in the casket was memorable but did not build confidence in the story. Howard's role is difficult to evaluate. The consequences for his campaign were mixed, but there is no doubt that he had a soft spot in his heart for High. He raised funds to help get him a fresh start in Chicago and, a little over a month after the escape, wrote affectionately to Amzie Moore that the "ole 'Eagle Eye' is right here with me, I see him everyday."[40]

In addition to his continuing association with High, Howard never passed up a chance to remind voters that he had once stood up to Jim Crow in the belly of the beast. In June his old comrades turned out in Chicago to lend support for his campaign. Arrington High, Gus Courts, Edward P. Burton (the new chief surgeon at the Friendship Clinic), Robert L. Drew (the Worthy Grand Master of the United Order of Friendship), and John C. Melchor (the president of the Magnolia Mutual Life Insurance Company) appeared at a pro-Howard testimonial. Their presence served to counter accusations that Howard had alienated his former civil rights and business associates.[41]

Howard was having a little success in recruiting longtime critics of Dawson. Among them were Addie Wyatt, the energetic program director of the United Packinghouse Workers of America, and Richard Durham, the press agent of the union. Durham went on to handle publicity for the congressional campaign. But Samuel B. Fuller was Howard's most valuable backer. He lent his name to the campaign, contributed money, and organized fundraisers. Fred Wall, Fuller's chief adviser, doubled as Howard's campaign manager. Wall had learned at the feet of the master. For several years, he had worked as Dawson's chief assistant. Their relationship had ended abruptly when a jury sent Wall to prison for several months on charges of exchanging bribes for post office jobs. Rumor had it that Wall took the rap for his former boss unwillingly and now wanted revenge.[42]

As Howard toured the district, the large and friendly crowds that turned out must have lifted his spirits. On Sunday afternoons, says Moore, he drew "five or six hundred people for tea or for a ten-minute speech." This was not like Mound Bayou, however. Instead of the masses, his audiences were more likely to be black professionals and from the middle class. A prominent example was Lewis A. H. Caldwell, an official of the Cosmopolitan Chamber of Commerce, the main black business organization. In his column for the *Chicago Daily Defender,* Caldwell praised Howard for "reviving the Republican Party in Chicago and causing voters to realize that they do not have to be content with puppet roles." This attention was a mixed blessing. He was getting the ear of black professionals, but he was not breaking through to the lower-income majority that kept Dawson in power.[43]

Howard made his greatest headway with the churches. He made his break with the Seventh-day Adventist church more or less official when he joined the spacious Pilgrim Baptist Church, which had been headed by Reverend Junius C. Austin since the 1920s. Austin gave Howard an invaluable entrée to the rest of the black clergy. Described as one of the "three or four greatest preachers in the National Baptist Convention," he had upheld such causes as Marcus Garvey's United Negro Improvement Association, the Scottsboro boys, and Oscar DePriest's election campaigns. As co-chair of Southside Ministers for Howard, Austin was instrumental in recruiting about a hundred ministers to the campaign who represented "an aggregate congregation of 125,000." A fellow parishioner of Howard in the Pilgrim Baptist Church was S. B. Fuller.[44]

Three other key ministers who supported Howard were William M. Lambert, Roy L. Miller, and Clay Evans, the co-chair (with Austin) of Southside Ministers for Howard. Austin (age seventy-one) and Lambert (age sixty-two) were the oldest. Because they pastored bigger, established churches, they were better able to withstand the bribes and sanctions of the machine. Miller (age forty-five) and Evans (age thirty-two) were relatively new to Chicago, but both had successful careers ahead of them. During the 1960s, Evans would be one of the first black leaders to put out the welcome mat for King when the Southern Christian Leadership Conference established its first beachhead in Chicago. Lambert slammed Dawson's failure to speak out on the Trumbull Park and Calumet Park riots as part of a general pattern of inaction. By contrast, he declared that "the civil rights record of Dr. Howard, who has actually experienced the struggles for Civil Rights, in the deep South, is one of the best in the Nation." Howard further strengthened his relationship with the local black clergy during this period by becoming an ordained Baptist minister.[45]

The old-line Republicans were solidly in Howard's corner. Long accustomed to defeat, they aspired for leftover scraps and crumbs from local, state, and federal patronage. Some, including Jewel S. Rogers, a bright young lawyer and an assistant U.S. attorney, worked through the pro-Howard Negro Alliance of America. The most prominent of Howard's old-line Republican backers was Carey, himself a former opponent of Dawson. In a telegram, he praised Howard as an "an outstanding warrior for freedom and fair play." Carey, despite his 1955 loss to Metcalfe at the hands of Dawson, remained influential and at the time was chair of Eisenhower's Committee on Government Employment Policy. The old-line Republicans also rallied to Jesse Owens, the Olympic legend, and a candidate for county commissioner in the 1958 election.[46]

When Howard won the Republican primary in April, the *Chicago Defender* had a front-page banner headline, "Dawson, Howard Set for War." Indicating that others also took Howard's candidacy seriously, it foresaw a "knock-down, dragout political battle, unprecedented in the history of the Chicago Negro community." The same issue ran a cartoon depicting the candidates in an equal contest as fighters in a boxing ring. Howard may have preferred the analogy of boxers battling toe to toe, but it did not apply to actual conditions on the ground. Dawson was an elusive, almost invisible, foe. He was not going to dignify Howard's proposal for a debate or, for that matter, acknowledge his existence. Journalist Louis Martin reported that Dawson's workers "take the position that the best way to beat Dr. Howard is to ignore him and promote their own candidate." Howard tried to turn this into an advantage by debating an empty chair that represented his opponent. This clever gimmick had little effect. When a reporter pressed Dawson for an election forecast, he responded demurely: "We'll win by our usual significant majority."[47]

Dawson's blasé demeanor notwithstanding, he took nothing for granted. His workers systematically fanned out to keep voters in line through the traditional repertoire of sanctions and rewards. He used a recent infusion of public housing money to good effect. Construction of fifteen thousand units began in 1956, followed by the opening of the massive ten- and seventeen-story complex of Stateway Gardens two years later. Public housing was not only an abundant source of patronage, but residents believed (not without merit) that loyalty to Dawson influenced their priority on the waiting list for an apartment and whether they would keep one once it was granted.[48]

In the face of this onslaught, Howard struggled to exploit his strengths and Dawson's apparent weaknesses. A slick campaign flyer billed him as the "man Eastland fears most." It highlighted Eisenhower's deployment of troops in Little Rock and "the *1st civil rights* legislation ever passed in eighty years . . . against Democratic opposition." The flyer called for a federal investigation of the Trumbull Park riot. The focus was on civil rights, but it also took positions that were more liberal than many others in the Republican party, including expansion of federal unemployment insurance and more relief for the poor. In an obvious personal dig at Dawson, it declared that "In this age of Sputniks and 'Little Rock,' 'Uncle Tom' leadership had got to go—in the North and in the South."[49]

Another pro-Howard flyer featured a panoramic cartoon that mercilessly attacked Dawson's character and record. On each side were illustrations of recent racial incidents in Trumbull Park, Calumet Park, Little Rock, and Clinton, Tennessee, and the murder of Emmett Till. The caption in the middle was "After all, It's Just between Us Democrats. . . ." Underneath, Dawson was timidly kneeling to an assemblage of smirking white men: Senator Eastland of Mississippi, Senator Richard Russell of Georgia, Governor Herman Talmadge of Georgia, Governor Orval Faubus of Arkansas, ex-Governor James Byrnes of South Carolina, Mayor Richard Daley, and the "Till murderers." He pleaded, "No Suh, I ain't said a mumbling word in sixteen years."[50]

Dawson and his supporters were, of course, seasoned professionals at taking the low road. They set up a front group, Independent Republicans for Honest Government, which circulated a flier, "The 'T. R. I. M.' Howard Story." T. R. I. M. was slang for female genitalia. Howard's detractors had whispered it as a nickname for his role as an abortionist. Despite the title, the text was silent on abortion or sexual improprieties. Instead, it made much of alleged financial misappropriations and claims that blacks, not whites, had driven Howard out of Mound Bayou.[51]

Howard's greatest irritation, however, came from national developments rather than Dawson's dirty politics. Eisenhower had frittered away the small political gains from the Civil Rights Act of 1957 and the Little Rock crisis. Nearly two years after he had promised to have a conference with key civil rights leaders, no conference had occurred. Finally, in February 1958, administration officials seriously pondered whether to invite Howard as well as King, Carey, Marshall, Powell, and Wilkins. Howard's presence, of course, would have been a boon to his campaign. For unexplained reasons, he was not included when the meeting finally took place in June. Against the backdrop of a second crisis in Little Rock, Eisenhower met with King, Randolph, Wilkins, and Lester B. Granger, the executive secretary of the National Urban League. Although the meeting was cordial, the president's comments were generally a disappointment to civil rights supporters. Eisenhower mused at length on whether it was worth the trouble to take action because so few had appreciated his previous "constructive" policies. The reaction of the black press ranged from lukewarm to hostile.[52]

Eisenhower's statements at news conferences in July and August dealt further blows to the aspirations of Howard and his fellow civil rights–oriented Republicans. The president reiterated his call for going slower. Howard phoned Val Washington, the head of the minorities division of the GOP, to complain bitterly and ask for clarification. The normally upbeat Washington carried the complaint to Adams and suggested that the president's latest statements had "pulled the rug out from under us." Adams's reassurance to Howard, via Washington, of Eisenhower's unequivocal belief in the "responsibility of the federal government to uphold law" probably did not provide solace.[53]

The economic recession was the main reason voters of all races were defecting to the Democrats in 1958. While Republican civil rights policies had plenty of black detractors, the Democratic record was no better. For blacks, Eisenhower's shortcomings on civil rights compounded existing weaknesses. Yet Howard persevered. The *Chicago Daily News* reported Howard as "hammering away hard at the civil rights issue in an effort to unseat U.S. Rep. William

L. Dawson, a longtime Democratic power. But, at the moment, interviews with typical voters by the *Daily News* indicate that it isn't taking hold." An unemployed black factory hand complained that he had not "worked in five months. Now do you know why I won't vote Republican?" Howard had hit a roadblock that had stymied Republican challengers for more than a decade. For most black voters, the issue of civil rights was secondary to immediate bread-and-butter concerns, including patronage. But their focus on economic self-interest had a brighter side. Because blacks in Chicago had significantly higher median incomes than those in the South, they had a greater interest in personal upward mobility than in collective grievances. To many, Chicago seemed "near heaven" in this regard compared to the place that they had left behind.[54]

With a few weeks to go before the election, the Howard campaign helped to precipitate a turning point in the history of the black independent movement. His supporters were instrumental in the formation of the Chicago League of Negro Voters in October. The key figures in forming it were Gus Savage and Bennett J. Johnson, a young schoolteacher and former classmate of future Chicago mayor Harold Washington. An "unrepentant leftist," Johnson was a prodigious organizer always ready to do battle against the machine. Howard was a vice president of the League, and the publicity highlighted his photo. Another founding member was the black militant writer Frank London Brown, author of the soon-to-be-published novel *Trumbull Park*.[55]

Despite Howard's prominence in the league's literature, the membership included a judicious mixture of Democrats and Republicans. It embraced a political vision that recalled Howard's own California Economic, Commercial, and Political League. One pamphlet explained that the "Democrats have been called the *party of war,* and Republicans the *party of depression,* but neither can be called the *party of equality.* Negroes must not be divided between parties." Although the league denied that it intended to challenge integration, a tinge of black nationalism was detectable. A pamphlet quoted Howard's declaration: "I am a Negro first, and ten more times, and then a Republican." For Johnson, however, the league was no different from countless other interest groups that had marshaled ethnic solidarity in the service of political advantage.[56]

The campaign ended with a flurry. When Eisenhower visited Chicago a week before the election, he met briefly with local candidates, including Howard. Howard tried to stiffen the resolve of the faithful when he related that the president had confided, "Doctor, I will need you with me in Washington during the difficult days ahead. I know your background and record." The culmination of the campaign was a songfest and mass meeting hosted by Fuller, Evans, and Austin. Howard could take heart from editorial endorsements by the *Chicago Daily News,* the *Chicago Sun-Times,* and the *Chicago Tribune.* The *Chicago American,* complaining that Howard was "absorbed, almost to the point of obsession, in civil rights," stayed neutral while the *Chicago Daily Defender* expectably backed Dawson. The general media consensus was that he was going to lose but was more likely to give Dawson a run for his money than previous candidates. To the *Chicago Tribune,* he was a "gallant campaigner," and the *Chicago Sun-Times* described him as "a man of high principle and capability."[57]

The election results were an unmitigated disaster for Howard. Dawson's 72.2 percent of the vote overwhelmed him. Out of more than 350 precincts in the district, Howard carried only five, two of them in the relatively prosperous Lake Meadows area. "I don't think Dawson even made a speech," Moore remembers. "He smashed him like a fly." Howard had obviously overestimated his prospects, but nothing could have prepared him for such a total rout. He was not alone. Vice President Richard Nixon accurately described Republican losses that year as "the worst defeat in history ever suffered by a party having control of the White House." Several other black Republicans in Chicago, notably Jesse Owens and longtime incumbent J. B. Martin, also lost. Almost immediately, Howard graciously conceded to Dawson, but his ego had taken a terrible beating. He never ran for office again.[58]

Howard lost badly, but his campaign had important long-term consequences for Chicago politics. It was a catalyst for the black independent challenge to the machine that finally bore fruit in the 1960s and 1970s. Veterans of the campaign included such later figures in Chicago black politics and civil rights activism as Gus Savage (a future member of the House of Representatives), William Cousins Jr. (a future alderman), Clay Evans, and Bennett J. Johnson.[59]

Howard never lost his interest in politics, but he began to assume the less visible role of facilitator. He was a stalwart of the Chicago League of Negro Voters, giving it significant financial backing as well as advice. The league made a small breakthrough in early 1959 when it successfully petitioned to get a slate of candidates on the ballot, including Lemuel E. Bentley for city clerk, in the Democratic primary. Bentley was the first black primary candidate for citywide office. Although he garnered only 12 percent of the vote, he and other league-supported candidates outpolled the GOP in most black districts. Howard took care to find a place in the league for his old friend Arrington High, often in the modest task of handing out fliers on a street corner. High continued to publish the *Eagle Eye* in Chicago for the next quarter century, but few noticed. An FBI report described him as a harmless "neighborhood character" who frequented the Lake Meadows Shopping Center near Howard's home.[60]

In 1959 Howard spoke at the league's first major public event, a rally attended by about three thousand to protest the lynching of Mack Charles Parker. A group of whites in Poplarville, Mississippi, had abducted Parker from a jail and then murdered him for the alleged rape of a white woman. Later in 1959, the league took the side of Robert F. Williams, the head of the NAACP in Monroe, North Carolina, over Roy Wilkins when they clashed at the NAACP's national conference. Wilkins had objected to Williams's aggressive promotion of meeting white violence through organized armed self-defense. In some ways, Williams followed the same tradition as Howard, who was armed to the teeth. More ambitiously, in 1960, the league tried to draw together similar organizations in other states. As part of this effort, Howard was a speaker at a Midwest Conference of Negro Voters' Leagues.[61]

Howard's days as a national civil rights figure had ended, but he was apparently not resentful about this fact. In 1959 he spoke, along with his former supporters Austin and Lambert, when Martin Luther King Jr. came to town to raise funds. A few months later he served on the Chicago Committee to Defend Martin Luther King Jr. after his indictment on perjury charges.[62]

Howard continued to be a Republican, apparently for the rest of his life. When the party's 1960 national convention met in Chicago, Howard, S. B. Fuller, and Golden B. Darby (a prominent black businessman in Chicago) cohosted an elaborate cocktail party attended by about seven hundred of the early arrivals. Costing about $12,000, the event was the first of this type ever sponsored by black Republicans.[63]

Howard also testified before the GOP platform committee as part of a coordinated effort for stronger language on civil rights. The pressure was on because the Democratic plank had included assertive language that had even praised the sit-ins that began earlier in the year. The Democratic nominee, John F. Kennedy, neutralized possible southern discontent by selecting Lyndon B. Johnson of Texas as his vice presidential running mate. The choice helped to ensure the active support of hard-line segregationists like Richard Russell and James O. Eastland. Howard told the committee that it was not the job of the Republican platform committee to copy "anybody, it's a matter of doing what is right." If the GOP did not beef up the wording on civil rights, it could "kiss the Negro vote goodbye forever. . . . we can not see how the Party of Lincoln can take a weak, vacillating stand on the most vital issue of our day." Howard added that blacks liked the Democratic platform but were not nearly as enthusiastic about the party's nominees. Many still remembered that Kennedy had voted to support the amendment that watered down the Civil Rights Act of 1957. But it was Johnson's close ties to southern segregationists that alarmed them the most.[64]

Even as Howard testified, Bennett J. Johnson and other officials of the Chicago League of Negro Voters communicated their concerns through back channels to the Republican National Committee and the Nixon campaign. Johnson participated in demonstrations outside staged under the banner of a national March on Conventions Movement. King, Wilkins, and Randolph stopped by briefly to join the picket line. Before the demonstrators had finished, they numbered five thousand. This agitation added urgency to demands by Nixon and Rockefeller to beef up the wording about civil rights. Once approved over southern protests, the plank was the toughest in the party's history. While it did not go quite as far as the Democrats', it made a special point of endorsing the *Brown* decision, something Eisenhower had always avoided. Howard had reason to be satisfied about his small role in the new language.[65]

Unfortunately for the GOP, Nixon fumbled the opportunity to exploit Democratic weaknesses during the general campaign. He frustrated many black allies, such as Jackie Robinson, by downplaying civil rights. Nixon faltered in the difficult balancing act of appealing to blacks while simultaneously making gains among whites in the South. Kennedy played the same game but far more adroitly. He appealed to blacks by symbolic gestures such as his famous phone call to Coretta Scott King when her husband was in jail. At the same time, he held onto the traditional southern white Democratic base, mainly through the adept use of his running mate.[66]

Bennett J. Johnson and the league unofficially supported the Nixon–Lodge ticket. Johnson was a committed leftist, but for him ideological distinctions paled alongside the priority of breaking the stranglehold of the machine. He often compared the Democratic Party's stultifying monopoly of Cook County to that of the Communist Party in the Soviet Union. The Republicans and Democrats had every reason to pursue politics as usual, Johnson contended, if either considered the black vote to be a "sure thing." He added that the "time has come for us to reassert our independence within the parties of our choice. For lack of a better word, let us call this action *Intra-Party Independence.*" When Kennedy carried Illinois by a razor-thin margin, the league cooperated with the Republicans to uncover evidence of voter fraud that might throw the state and thus possibly the national election to Nixon.[67]

For Howard, however, politics was not the major priority in the closing month of the campaign. In October he headed off to Africa in preparation for the American–African Trade Relations conference sponsored by the Cosmopolitan Chamber of Commerce. His compatriots in the enterprise were John H. Johnson, who was the publisher of *Ebony* and *Jet,* several black businessmen, and a former ambassador to Liberia. The trip was the beginning of a love affair with Africa. It seemed to presage a less visible but effective role as a respected and prosperous international power broker. Howard's apparent search for a lower profile came to naught. His name became associated with a scandal that threatened to taint his reputation permanently and possibly send him to prison.[68]

Beginning in February 1961, Howard became mired in ugly publicity when a grand jury charged that he was a conspirator in a vast interstate accident insurance ring. Besides Howard, the participants allegedly included another doctor, six lawyers, an insurance adjuster, an ex-convict, a policeman, and about two dozen people accused of being fake accident victims.

According to prosecutors, a typical practice of the ring was to crowd a group of phony victims into a car, pull in front of another car bearing an automobile insurance sticker, and then slam on the brakes. After causing a rear-end collision, they obtained fraudulent medical reports from a doctor in the ring certifying their "injuries." The conspiring lawyer used these reports to get generous settlements from the insurance companies and split the proceeds with the doctor and the fake victims. The indictment charged that the ring had netted $100,000 since 1959 by causing more than a hundred accidents, fifteen in Chicago.[69]

Howard was in perilous straits, and he knew it. He launched a determined counterattack. To represent him, he hired the best lawyer he could find, Charles A. Bellows. His services were expensive. Bellows typically charged from $30,000 to $50,000 for a trial of five weeks. But he was worth every cent. Bellows was one of the most prestigious criminal defense attorneys in the country. He had come to the United States as a child, the son of Russian-Jewish immigrants. After serving as a prosecutor in Cook County, he became a defense attorney in 1933 and handled more than five hundred murder cases. In 1958 his colleagues elected him as the first president of the National Association of Criminal Defense Lawyers, a group he was instrumental in founding. By 1961 Bellows was at the top of his game. Sherman C. Magidson, a junior partner at the time of Howard's trial, states that Bellows had a knack for finding "the smallest hole" in a case before he would "rip it to pieces. He was a tiger in the courtroom."[70]

Bellows and Howard almost immediately hit it off. They also became friends outside the courtroom. This was a rarity for Bellows. Magidson, who assisted in Howard's defense, remembers that Bellows went "to a client's house, maybe twice in forty years. Dr. Howard was one of those twice." Magidson describes Howard as a man of "enormous personality," who was "gregarious, educated, interesting" and "the kind of guy you'd like to spend the night with just talking about the old days." Like many before him, Magidson noticed that Howard "had an air of somebody that was right and knew he was right, and nothing anybody else said or did could dispute the fact that he was right." But in his case, ego did not translate into braggadocio. "When he was talking about mountain goats in Alaska or safaris in Africa," Magidson concludes, "he wasn't bragging. He was extolling his wonderful experiences. Now, there may be a very thin line distinction but it wasn't hard to listen to that." Howard's self-assurance had a practical advantage for his lawyers. It meant that he would be unflappable under tough questioning by prosecutors.[71]

Bellows and his client went on the offensive by depicting Howard as a victim rather than a participant in any crime. They admitted that a lawyer in the alleged ring had paid Howard a check of about $700 in exchange for regularly receiving accident reports but noted (accurately) that such fees were routine in these cases. Howard defended his diagnoses of the patients mentioned in the indictment as sincere and pointed out that even under the best conditions it was nearly impossible to detect fakes. "When a man comes into my office and complains of head, back and internal injuries," he said, "I defy any doctor to prove that these injuries do not exist. . . . If any person thinks at my age (53) that I would lend myself to a ring of people involved in anything such as this, they're out of their mind." Bellows made much of Howard's past record of black leadership to the all-white jury. He stressed that his client had come "up the hard way, as do all Negroes without money, and is held in great esteem."[72]

Howard did not have great difficulty finding blacks to rally to his support. A delegation of more than a hundred ministers, many of them veterans of the Southside Ministers for Howard, visited the state attorney's office to speak on his behalf. John H. Johnson and Leonidas Berry, a nationally known black doctor, came forward as character witnesses. The *New Crusader,* a weekly black newspaper in Chicago, gave especially spirited backing. The paper, like many of the ministers, had endorsed him for Congress in 1958. It editorialized that it was "inconceivable" that a "man whose whole life has been devoted to combating racial bigotry" would "deliberately stoop to consorting with common criminals to pick up what couldn't be other than 'petty cash.'" The *New Crusader* made sure to play up the race angle, asserting that the insurance companies were looking for a "scapegoat" to hide their mistreatment of poor blacks who "are largely defenseless and the easiest to intimidate."[73]

Howard was not able to persuade all blacks to support him. The *Chicago Defender,* for example, was editorially silent. He had ruffled feathers by his failure to hire a black lawyer and then complaining to the critics: "When your children cough or have the croup or a stomach ache, you'd bring them to me. But, when you had something serious, you took them to whites. I'm in trouble and I'm going to the man who has won the most cases." Meanwhile,

Howard's old segregationist enemies were reveling in his misfortunes. The head of the Mississippi State Board of Health sent clippings of unfavorable news articles on the scandal to the chief investigator of the American Medical Association.[74]

The machinations of a bewildering array of lawyers who represented the multiple defendants delayed the trial until February 1962, a year after the indictment. Once it was underway, however, Bellows almost effortlessly took command of the situation. During questions, several important contradictions in the state's case came to light. One witness revealed that she had lied when she told Howard that her injuries were from an automobile accident. They actually came from blows inflicted by her husband. She said that she had walked into Howard's office at random, thus contradicting allegations of a conspiracy. Howard's former secretary, a witness for the prosecution, admitted that Walter Radford, an ex-convict who was a key player in the ring, had housed her in a "swank" apartment and given her two cars. For his part, Radford testified that the secretary was his girlfriend and that they had filled out fraudulent accident reports on Howard's stationery while he was on a safari in Africa. Bellows's courtroom skills won the day for his client. The jury acquitted Howard after deliberating for only two hours. The victory did not come without cost. The sordid details tainted his reputation. As journalist and radio broadcaster Wesley South observes, the general effect "put him on the outs with many, many people in the African-American community."[75]

While doubts persisted about Howard's innocence, the jury had probably made the right decision. Howard was not the type of person to have participated in a conspiracy so immense and complicated. As Magidson points out, he was "a leader not a follower. I don't know how he could conspire with somebody. Certainly, not conspire with somebody who's going to direct him what to do." Moreover, the conspirators did not necessarily need Howard's conscious help. The nature of soft tissue injuries, such as whiplash, made it relatively easy for a phony victim who was well-schooled in textbook symptoms to fool a doctor. Based on his experiences, Magidson rejects claims that Howard was personally corrupt and concludes that he sincerely believed that the patients were injured and deserved compensation. He argues that there was "absolutely no way that a doctor can sit there and say in those days especially when he's seeing thirty, and forty, and fifty patients a day, that this guy's a phony."[76]

The jury's decision did not mean that Howard was completely blameless. At a minimum, he was sloppy and myopic and failed to ask probing questions. He was so focused on his business, Magidson concludes, "that he didn't pay attention to what was going through his office." Few doctors on the South Side saw so many patients in a day. The character and extent of his practice made him tempting prey for potential schemers and for insurance investigators. "Close your eyes and imagine an hourglass," Magidson suggests. "He's the guy in the center. They can't get anyplace without him. If I were an insurance investigator, I'd focus on him too."[77]

Although Howard's legal troubles dominated his attention, he found time to dabble in various activities. He continued to be a donor and adviser to the Chicago League of Negro Voters and was an official of the newly formed Republican Citizens League of Illinois. James C. Worthy, a veteran Republican activist and a senior executive at Sears, had founded the league after the close Democratic victory in Illinois of 1960. Worthy drew the conclusion that the Daley machine had stolen the election because of a lack of reliable Republican poll watchers and election judges. The GOP, he cautioned, would never have an effective electoral policing infrastructure unless "it reestablishes itself in the Negro community." This was a chief goal of the league.[78]

Howard accepted a position on the league's governing board. His fellow members ran the gamut of Republican leadership (black and white) and included Archibald Carey Jr., Jewel S. Rogers, Senator Everett M. Dirksen, future senator Charles Percy, and Phyllis Schlafly, who was then a relatively unknown conservative activist. Howard attended several meetings but otherwise played a fairly minor role. The league had modest success recruiting Republican election workers but proved unable to turn back the tide of rising black support for the Democrats. The group fell apart after Worthy resigned in 1962.[79]

Howard maintained loose ties with his old civil rights comrades in Mississippi and periodically returned for speeches. In 1962, for example, he accepted an invitation from Aaron Henry to be the main speaker at a salute to Robert L. Drew. But the RCNL was never the same after he left. The slick promotional brochures that advertised the annual conferences of the Howard era had long since given way to poorly reproduced mimeographed fliers. Medgar Evers often mentioned his name at rallies in Mississippi when he reeled off the great pioneers of civil rights. But for many Howard was becoming a distant memory. Quite a few had never heard of him.[80]

The rapid emergence of a new generation of civil rights activists pushed his legacy farther into the background. After 1961 the NAACP and the RCNL had to compete with the Congress of Racial Equality (CORE), the Student Nonviolent Coordinating Committee (SNCC), and the Council of Federated Organizations (COFO). COFO was similar in several ways to the RCNL (which apparently breathed its last in 1962). The founding vision of each was to be an umbrella group. Unlike the RCNL, which also included black business and religious leaders, COFO was more narrowly focused on civil rights. Another common thread was Aaron Henry who, for a brief time, was simultaneously the last secretary of the RCNL and the first president of COFO. Younger activists formed the backbone of CORE, SNCC, and COFO. They included Robert Moses, James Bevel, and Diane Nash. Unlike most RCNL leaders, they often came from the North or had studied there. Their youth, economic background, ideology, and tactics set them apart from their predecessors in the RCNL. Howard's name was more likely to mean something to the Mississippi-born activists such as Colia Clark, an assistant to Medgar Evers. For her, Howard was "a childhood memory of a man whose stature was bigger than life."[81]

Howard's most dramatic Mississippi experience after 1956 was his return visit to Jackson in June 1963 to speak at the memorial service for Medgar Evers, who had just died from an assassin's bullet. Apparently Roy Wilkins, who took charge of organizing the event, had invited him. Howard began apologetically by telling the story of a veteran of Bull Run who visited the graves of his comrades many years after the battle: "A young man challenged him: 'How could you have survived such a battle, did you run?' 'Yes, it is true,' the old man replied, 'the only real veterans of this battle are the ones who are buried here.'" He recounted Evers's participation a decade earlier in the activities of the RCNL. He declared, "Lest ye forget, and it does appear that some people have forgotten, it was right here in Mississippi back in 1952 that the first statewide nonviolent protest was carried out by the Mississippi Regional Council of Negro Leadership." Then, as King listened from the audience, he declared that "Medgar Evers was one of the individuals who participated in this first campaign four years before Dr. King marched at Montgomery."[82]

Aside from this pointed reminder about the RCNL's pioneering role, Howard stressed the importance of the NAACP to the struggle for civil rights. He criticized the "wild chatter about the NAACP having outlived its usefulness." Although "several useful organizations had come into the field" in the last decade, he hated to think of where blacks would "be today had it not been for the NAACP that stood as a watchman on the wall for the last fifty years." His zealous brief acknowledgment for the relatively conservative NAACP notwithstanding, his closing words anticipated the militancy of the next few years. He had "all the faith in the world in our nonviolent movement" but warned that "for one hundred years, we have turned one cheek and the other and they've continued to hit us on both cheeks. The neck is getting tired now of turning from side to side." In response, a chorus of "amen" and "yes, yes" rolled through the audience.[83]

If Howard believed at this time that he was finally out of the legal woods in Chicago, Arthur L. Dunne, the assistant state's attorney in the accident insurance case, had other ideas. Stung by the acquittal, Dunne immediately set out to pursue Howard on charges of income tax evasion. Howard was vulnerable because he had accepted a check for more than $700 in fees from one of the attorneys charged in the accident case. It is likely that he did not bother to declare it. In May 1964, a grand jury charged that he had intentionally and significantly underreported his income. Howard had listed a combined income for 1959 and 1960 of $17,000, whereas he had actually earned more than $74,000. As a result, he had paid $4,000 in taxes when the true amount he owed was more than $27,000.[84]

This indictment constituted just part of Howard's legal troubles. Two months later, he had to answer the far more serious charge of committing an illegal abortion. It marked the beginning of an increasingly controversial phase in Howard's career. In less than ten years, Howard completed the transition from a widely acknowledged national leader in civil rights, business, and medicine to one of Chicago's most notorious abortionists.[85]

9

Triumph and Tragedy
The Friendship Medical Center

IT PROBABLY NEVER occurred to the graduates of the College of Medical Evangelists in 1935 that one of their own might become a prominent abortionist. By all appearances at the time, Howard had a bright, but otherwise conventional, future as a general practitioner and surgeon. The threadbare written and oral record does little to explain how, why, and when he began performing abortions. The transition seems to have been a gradual one. Abortions became his main specialty only after he moved to Chicago, but his experiences in Mississippi had pointed the way. He later said that the apparent link between the dire poverty in the Delta and large families had convinced him that abortion was a "blessing in disguise for Black people."[1]

Howard followed in a long tradition of high-profile abortionists in Chicago. His best-known predecessor was Dr. Josephine Gabler, who retired in 1940. Because she was a competent practitioner, the police generally looked the other way. A sustained crackdown in the 1940s and 1950s forced her successors to go underground. According to historian Leslie Reagan, law enforcement began "to shut down the trusted and skilled abortionists, many of them physicians." Only two years before Howard arrived in Chicago, a local prosecutor had promised to call to the stand dozens of doctors accused of giving referrals to illegal abortionists.[2]

A hostile legal climate had never stopped Howard before. He began performing abortions almost as soon as he set foot in the city. By the early 1960s it was common knowledge that a woman in trouble could go to the Howard Medical Center on East 63rd and Rhodes. Men joked, "I'm going to send my girlfriend to Dr. Howard." Howard did not bother with subterfuges such as blindfolding patients. Apparently, he did not need to, at least at first. He had built up sufficient goodwill with the authorities, fortified by liberal bribes, to avoid trouble. Prosecutors did not even broach the issue (at least not publicly) during his accident insurance trial. By then, he was performing about six abortions a day, many on whites. Some patients were the relatives of police officers. Others attended the nearby University of Chicago. A few had connections to influential politicians.[3]

The recollections of Dr. Ed Keemer, a well-known black abortionist from Detroit, are a rare firsthand assessment of Howard's methods and abilities during this period. A graduate of Meharry, Keemer, a dedicated Marxist, had spent fourteen months in prison after a highly publicized arrest in 1956 for illegal abortions. Like Howard, he was a big-game hunter. During the early 1960s, Keemer visited abortionists in several cities and reported what he found in his autobiography published in 1980. His discussion of Chicago singled out Howard for his "large, clean clinic" that had "modern setups in his labs, examination and treatment rooms, with good equipment." Howard invited Keemer "to don a coat and mask and observe his work. It was excellent. He operated under sterile precautions." Howard said that he had decided to become a "full-time abortionist, law or no law" before he left Mississippi because of the "crying need." But Keemer reported some "bad vibes" from the visit. Quite naturally, Howard's obvious willingness to profit from abortion rubbed this critic of capitalism the wrong way. Keemer commented disapprovingly that Howard charged from $300 in most cases to as high as $700 in others: "His high prices he blamed on the claim that he had to pay off at the local, county and state levels in order to stay in business. This was first-class service, all right, but it was available only to well-to-do women."[4]

Howard had held the law at bay for eight years, but in July 1964 his luck almost ran out. The police arrested him at his Lake Meadows apartment for performing an illegal abortion. A white woman in her twenties had filed charges after she checked into the Cook County Hospital because of postoperative complications. Also arrested was her boyfriend, Arnold Warda, an actor, who said he had paid Howard a fee of $350. The timing was unfortunate for Howard, then awaiting trial for income tax evasion.[5]

As before, Charles Bellows was Howard's legal counsel. A few months earlier, Bellows's friend Earl Ruby had presented him with the case of a lifetime. Ruby wanted him to defend his brother Jack, then in prison for the murder of Lee Harvey Oswald. Bellows was leery, confessing to a friend that he had "a bad feeling" about it. Nevertheless, he agreed but asked for a fee that was too high for the family to afford. He did, however, later provide legal help on the appeal after Ruby's conviction. Howard needed Bellows more than ever. An abortion conviction, unlike one for tax evasion, almost certainly meant revocation of his license. Howard denied everything, saying that he had never met the couple in question. Fortunately for him, the newspapers, both black and white, had a short attention span. They did not even report the case's dismissal in September after the accuser mysteriously failed to show up for the trial.[6]

Howard had less luck on the tax charges. Probably on the advice of Bellows, he changed his plea from guilty to *nolo contendere*. Bellows had good reason to urge his client to cut a deal. The evidence, including Howard's admission of making specific payments to lawyers in accident cases, was too much to overcome. More ominously, prosecutors had started to connect the dots between Howard's undeclared income and his profits from abortion. In particular, Bellows may have wanted to prevent the scheduled testimony of Arnold Warda, the boyfriend in the abortion case. The final deal he negotiated with prosecutors and the judge meted out a relatively light punishment. In exchange for the revised plea, Howard received one year of probation and a fine of $10,000. In announcing the sentence in December 1964, the judge explained that he had shown leniency because Howard had "done good for many people in his life." Howard had barely escaped jail time twice in a year, but he kept performing abortions daily.[7]

Throughout his legal troubles Howard maintained at least a toehold in civil rights and politics. He gave money and advice to Protest at the Polls, a group founded by Bennett J. Johnson and others as an interracial successor to the defunct Chicago League of Negro Voters. It also had a more radical side. As early as 1964, Protest at the Polls came out against the Vietnam War, a view shared by Howard. For more than a decade, he had slammed the United States for hypocrisy because it promoted democracy overseas while failing to protect it at home.[8]

Not everyone had forgotten Howard's civil rights accomplishments in Mississippi. When J. Edgar Hoover famously condemned Martin Luther King Jr. as a "notorious liar," *Jet* characterized it as a "shrill echo" of the director's earlier upbraiding of Howard during the Till case. Throughout his years in Chicago, he kept in touch with older civil rights comrades, such as Aaron Henry and Fannie Lou Hamer. Hamer stopped by to see him during her visits to Chicago. A photo in October 1964 showed them at a benefit in Woodlawn for the Mississippi summer volunteers. This was Hamer's first public speech since her memorable appeal to the Democratic Party national convention to seat an integrated Mississippi delegation. Another speaker was Stokely Carmichael, who had worked with Hamer in the Student Non-Violent Coordinating Committee (SNCC). Carmichael later rose to national prominence after he popularized the phrase "black power."[9]

Howard's name, and just as important his pocketbook, occasionally attracted a more visible civil rights role. In February 1965, shortly after the assassination of Malcolm X, he chaired and helped to organize the Chicago Educational Fund for the Children of Malcolm X Shabazz. Members of the fund's board included historian Sterling Stuckey, comedian Dick Gregory, writer Lerone Bennett Jr., the senior editor of *Ebony,* and many of Howard's colleagues from the Chicago League of Negro Voters and Protest at the Polls. Juanita Poitier, the wife of Sidney Poitier, and actress Ruby Dee headed two similar funds in New York. In March 1965, Howard, Ossie Davis, and novelist John Killens spoke at a Chicago fundraising rally. Howard still knew how to rouse a crowd. An informant for the notorious "red squad" (Human Relations Division) of the Chicago Police Department called his speech the "strongest" of those delivered.[10]

Howard's attraction to this cause was understandable. Malcolm X had come to his apartment not long before his death to ask for money and advice. Most of the details of what happened are unknown. The two men had reasons, however, to feel an affinity. They agreed on such goals as the importance of self-defense, black cooperation, and self-help. Like Malcolm X, Howard had mixed feelings about the benefits of integration. Oscar J. Moore Jr., who knew Howard well, characterizes him as an "equalist" rather than an integrationist. He often asked, "How could you integrate a guy with ten with a guy with one?" Despite these areas of agreement, Howard showed no sympathy for the anti-white racism of many black nationalists, including Malcolm's former mentor, Elijah Muhammad. In all the years they knew Howard, neither Moore nor Charles Evers ever heard him utter a racial slur against whites.[11]

Howard's hope of settling down to a low-profile role of civil rights benefactor was not to be. A second arrest on abortion charges came in September
1965, this time by the Cook County sheriff. Howard had received a phone call
from a female undercover agent who said that she had a "problem." He asked:
how old is the "problem"? She told him, and he quoted a fee of $500 to "solve"
it. The woman and another deputy posing as her boyfriend came to the clinic
and counted out the money in marked bills. The deputy wore a wire; a man in
a nearby surveillance truck recorded the conversation. Howard escorted the
woman to the examining room, and he began to prepare her for the abortion.
After a short wait, the male deputy burst in. Once Howard got over the shock,
he asked if something could be done to avoid an arrest (an implied bribe), but
the deputy said no. In addition, the sheriff's department arrested Howard's
salty-talking nurse and chief assistant, Margaret "Corky" Banks.[12]

More than a few people wondered whether someone in the department (or
political higher-ups) was out to "get" Howard. The nature of the arrest raised
suspicions. Some asked why the sheriff's department had not "punted" the
case to the Chicago police, the standard practice for crimes committed within
city limits. If someone had targeted Howard for political reasons, however,
it is a mystery who and why. Felice Sangirardi, the arresting officer, showed
no apparent animus. More than thirty years after the event, he stated that he
believed Howard performed a legitimate service.[13]

Whatever the explanation, Howard was in for a long and grueling legal
fight. The prosecution's case seemed to be airtight. The evidence included
incriminating statements on tape and extensive patient records. But Bellows
quickly rose to the challenge. He hit back hard by filing a battery of motions
accusing the sheriff's department of entrapment and an illegal search. Bellows met the charges head-on through a novel defense. He said that because
the female deputy was not pregnant no crime of attempted abortion had
occurred. Howard made the same point but chose his words carefully when
speaking to reporters. When asked if he had ever performed an abortion, he
did not deny it but explained that the procedure might be legal in certain
cases such as heart trouble.[14]

Howard did not let his legal headaches interfere with his hobby. Barely
two weeks after the arrest, he took a hunting trip to Alaska where he bagged
a moose, a caribou, and a Kodiak bear. Howard also continued to visit Las

Vegas and the Arlington Race Track. His son, Barrett, observed that specta-tors at the track watched how Howard would bet and did likewise. But How-ard's legendary luck was far from foolproof. He later told Arnold Bickham, a fellow doctor and business associate, that he had gambled away several million dollars and that he had so much money that he "didn't know what to do with it." This may be an exaggeration. Howard's wealth probably never reached that scale, but illegal abortions had certainly yielded a lavish lifestyle. He worked hard but knew how to have fun. Friends say he was a perpetually happy man who rarely let anything get him down.[15]

A significant exception was his despondency in 1966 over the death of his grandson from Detroit, Ronald Taylor, in an automobile accident at the age of seventeen. Howard was devastated by the news. He had grown close to Ronald and often brought him along on hunting trips. Helen shared her husband's fondness for the boy. Ronald had excelled in academics and sports and, like his grandfather, had a dynamic personality and leadership skills. The shock of Ronald's death may have contributed to Howard's subsequent stroke. He gradually recovered but was partially weakened on one side. Thereafter, health problem after health problem followed. He was, as his doctor puts it, "an ex-tremely sick man" during the last decade of his life. Besides the stroke, he had heart trouble and type 2 diabetes, but he remained an active and driven man until the day he died. Through it all, he was invariably cheerful and affable.[16]

Black society remained Helen's main outlet during the 1960s and the 1970s. In this realm, she flourished as an accomplished leader. She served as president of the Chicago chapters of the Moles and the Links, both exclusive clubs. Helen took a special interest in the annual débutante cotillion of the Links, where she worked alongside others in the black elite. A good friend and fellow club-woman praised her as "our number one hostess in Chicago" and "a lady to the core, but always courteous and gentle." Helen was well liked, even beloved, by friends for her kindness, charm, and grace, but she lacked her husband's common touch. Her aristocratic demeanor led some outside her social set to criticize her as a standoffish "Miss Elite."[17]

The middle and late 1960s were not an easy time for Helen, either. She had a stroke about the same time as her husband, making it difficult for her to walk. Her brother considered it a delayed reaction to the pressures of Mis-sissippi. The never-ending scandals about accident scams and abortion added to the psychological toll, as did her husband's philandering. She knew that he cheated, although he always denied it, and jealousy often consumed her. Sometimes she borrowed the car of a friend to follow her husband in the hope of catching him. Many wondered why she did not leave him. Family friend Doris Zollar speculates that she still loved him, took pride in his accomplishments, and hoped he would change: "Then also, she was Mrs. T. R. M. Howard. She wanted to remain that way. She had a very comfortable existence" and was willing to tolerate his behavior "as long as he kept things kind of away from her."[18]

Adding to the stress on Helen was her husband's greater recklessness in his affairs. Howard had yet another out-of-wedlock child, apparently his first since he left Mississippi. He had met the mother, Juanita Gilmore, a well-educated and attractive young woman, at his clinic. The boy was named Teddy after his father. In the past, Howard had avoided long-term relationships with the mothers of his children, but not this time. Although he continued to play the field, he saw Gilmore regularly. She often came along, for example, during visits to his daughter Verda C. Harris (formerly Wilson) and her children in Detroit. Howard spent more time with his new mistress but was still fairly discreet, at least sufficiently so not to drive Helen away.[19]

Barrett, the adopted son, was caught in the middle. He suffered from growing up in a dysfunctional household buffeted by endless litigation, sickness, and marital infidelity. His parents spoiled and indulged him, but he paid the price in emotional neglect. Although he deeply admired his father, the two never really bonded. Family friend Julia Futrell calls Barrett "a child that was kind of left behind. . . . They were always leaving Barrett at my house, always going somewhere." As a teenager, he experimented with drugs, and his life lacked direction for many years. The Howards also sponsored more than a dozen young Africans in the United States. They became especially fond of Ethiopia Alfred-Bekele, the daughter of the assistant minister of the interior of Ethiopia. She later moved in and became a kind of surrogate sister for Barrett. Howard put her through college and was always ready to lend a hand. They became so close that she thought of him as a second father.[20]

Months, then years, dragged on after Howard's arrest in 1965 and the case had still not gone to trial. Several factors contributed to the delay, including Howard's health problems, a long parade of judges, and frequent motions challenging the evidence. Meanwhile, Howard continued to perform abortions at his clinic, often with a full waiting room. As a precaution against undercover police officers, he began to require referrals for patients. A woman seeking an abortion had first to come for a regular doctor's appointment. He then examined her and filled out a chart just as if she were a regular patient. Although she paid for the abortion at this time, she had to come back later to get it. When she finally did, he required that someone come along to escort her home. Howard also performed some abortions by special appointment in hotels and other locations.[21]

Of course, bribes added another layer of protection. Barrett recalls seeing "a big box of money" used for this purpose. Howard once confided that he had shelled out more than $10,000 to the police on two occasions. If need be, he was able to call in favors from people in high places. As Arnold Bickham notes, an illegal abortionist like Howard "knew everybody who was anybody." His most reliable source of protection, however, was his reputation for competence.[22]

Activists in the emerging pro-choice movement sought out Howard from the outset. With his record, it was logical that they would. A case in point was Heather Booth, an eighteen-year-old white student at the University of Chicago who had participated in voter registration campaigns in Mississippi in 1964. A few months after she returned to Chicago, a friend appealed for her help to find an abortionist for his sister. Booth asked around and someone, possibly from the Medical Committee for Civil Rights, told her about Howard. She passed on his phone number to the sister of her friend. After the woman gave a favorable report on the treatment she received, Booth recommended Howard to other friends who were in the same predicament.[23]

The flow of patients soon became so great that Booth and Howard worked out an informal arrangement on price for the referrals sent to him. Under the deal, the profits from those able to pay subsidized those who could not. Howard agreed to charge $500 as his regular price but also to do one of every five abortions for free. As the referrals increased, he lowered his regular price to $300. Booth did not share Ed Keemer's misgivings about Howard. Her experiences were overwhelmingly positive. She did not think that Howard was "in this for the money" and came to admire his sincerity, medical skill, readiness to take hardship cases, and generosity with his time. Although she was only eighteen, he patiently answered her questions about the procedure. He never once asked "Why are you raising this question?" or "Is it your place?" and "was professional, gentle, generous, kind." By 1969 Booth's informal network had evolved into Jane, a feminist-dominated abortion service that arranged and eventually performed illegal abortions prior to *Roe v. Wade.* Howard, who had obtained more than enough patients from other sources, decided to end his involvement in the service.[24]

One of these sources was his arrangement, which had begun around 1967, with Reverend E. Spencer Parsons, the dean of the Rockefeller Chapel of the University of Chicago. He headed an even more extensive abortion network than Jane, the Chicago chapter of the Clergy Consultation Service on Problem Pregnancies, which set out to find qualified doctors for women seeking abortions. Howard and Parsons negotiated an informal and nuanced version of the same cross-subsidization agreement. During the next six years, Parsons sent him hundreds (possibly thousands) of patients. They ranged from the affluent to the very poor. Parsons and Howard sat down and discussed the details of each case and tailored the price accordingly. Some women paid full price (from $400 to $500) whereas others received a discounted or free service.[25]

Parsons, like Booth, regards Howard as a conscientious, honest, and compassionate practitioner. He notes that the Clergy Consultation Service required the women to fill out an evaluation report on how each doctor treated them. Nearly all commented that Howard was "gracious and helpful." Parsons underlines that he did not turn away a patient and that "we never had a single complication from Dr. Howard, not one." Even so, he noticed some rather peculiar methods of conducting business. As a general rule, for example, Howard charged whites double the rates of blacks. His rationale was that many of the white girls were college students who had "a lot of money behind them."[26]

After three years of delay, Howard's abortion case finally went to trial in 1968. Once it started, it did not take long. Bellows's creative defense that no crime had occurred because the woman was not pregnant carried the day. In April the jury returned a verdict of not guilty. Few people noticed. As in the first abortion case, newspaper coverage pretty much ceased soon after the arrest and did not include a story on the verdict.[27]

The acquittal was the first of a series of memorable events for Howard in 1968. In July he began a nine-week safari in Africa. The trip presented a rare opportunity for Barrett to spend time with his father. Helen, who did not share her husband's passion for hunting, stayed home. The cost of the tour, conducted in the typically lavish Howard style, was about $12,000. Accompanying father and son was a complete native entourage, including a cook. Botswana, Mozambique, Tanzania, and Kenya were on the itinerary, but leopard hunting in Ethiopia (arranged courtesy of Ethiopia Alfred-Bekele's father) was the high point. Between them, they bagged forty-one trophies. Barrett confessed to his sister Sandra that he hated killing so many animals.[28]

After the return from Africa, the Howards began preparations for the grand opening of the Safari Room in the basement of their new home. Christened "Safari Manor," the ten-room house was in Chatham, a popular neighborhood on the South Side for black professionals and businesspeople. Helen explained to a reporter that they had moved from Lake Meadows because they had run out of space for all the trophies. This was only partly true. After eight years of nearly continuous scandal, litigation, and health setbacks, they both looked forward to the prospect of entertaining visitors on a grand scale.[29]

The launching of the Safari Room on the lower floor of his house in early 1969 was a two-day gala that brought together an accomplished group of black professionals, businesspeople, and politicians. Among them were Jesse Owens, state senator Verda Welcome of Maryland, Archibald J. Carey Jr., and A. Maceo Walker, the son of the founder of the Tri-State Bank of Memphis. The event revealed just how far Howard had risen from his humble origins. Two of the guests were Judge Robert A. Miller of Murray, Kentucky, the husband of Will Mason's daughter Patricia, and their son Dan Miller. During his many trips to Murray, Howard made sure to visit Mason's widow, Ora Kress Mason, who was proud of his achievements. Several of Howard's other white friends came to the opening. The society page writer for the *Chicago Defender* called it "one of the most integrated social functions" she had ever attended. *Ebony* ran a photo spread that included a description of Howard's hunting exploits and his humble origins. This article was the magazine's first about him since 1955.[30]

The Safari Room itself was quite a spectacle, even by Howard's standards. The cost was $75,000, more than the entire rest of the house. It featured two dozen stuffed animals, including a zebra, a Cape buffalo, a tiger, and a lion. The centerpiece was an eleven-foot polar bear, so tall that a section of the floor had to be lowered to accommodate it. The red-carpeted floor depicted an open plain and the ceiling a gray blue sky, which featured hundreds of small lights to give the appearance of twinkling stars. The room also celebrated Howard's love of guns through a display of twenty-one rifles. Before long, the Safari Room was a neighborhood landmark. Howard made it available for tours of schoolchildren. One was for a class taught by Mamie Till-Mobley, the mother of Emmett Till.[31]

People in a more politically correct, pro–animal-rights age might be inclined to dismiss the Safari Room as an ostentatious, even vulgar, hobby by a civil rights leader who was past his prime and out of touch. Howard did not see it that way. He identified the room and the accomplishments it represented with black pride. He reveled in his reputation as "America's greatest black hunter," pointing out that he was the first of his race to bag the big five regarded as most dangerous by hunters: leopard, lion, Cape buffalo, rhinoceros, and elephant. The Safari Room also reflected Howard's admirable ability to reinvent himself, rather than to dwell in past glories. *Ebony* reported that he showed more interest in reminiscing "about his exploits as a hunter than those as a civil rights leader."[32]

During the next few years, the New Year's Eve party at Safari Manor was a regular stop for the black social set. The story invariably dominated the *Chicago Defender*'s society page on the next day. Howard spared no expense. For a typical party, he bought thousands of dollars worth of liquor and hired a live band for the entire evening. The bar in the Safari Room had "one of the best private stocks in Chicago." These extravaganzas usually attracted hundreds and recalled the gigantic annual rallies of the Regional Council of Negro Leadership in Mound Bayou during the 1950s. The main difference was that they were for the black elite, not the masses. At one New Year's Eve party, Howard hired a special security service to escort guests, who typically wore expensive mink and sable, to and from their cars. A hostess pinned an orchid corsage on all women as they walked in. A photo in the *Chicago Defender* for the 1971 party shows none other than Jesse Owens putting a crown on Howard's head as "King Ted." The black (and occasionally white) elite ate the food, but the menu had a populist flavor. The party in 1969 featured a "soul food dinner" of a whole roast pig, chitterlings, and corn bread. Howard, who was an excellent cook, prepared his own recipe of eggnog, which he mixed in a giant kettle. Peach ice cream was another of his specialties. Frances Matlock says that "he liked living and he was a poor boy but he knew when he got money, he knew what to do with it."[33]

The move to Safari Manor enabled the Howards to carve out increasingly separate lives in a relationship that was already distant and businesslike. Because each had separate quarters in the house, he had greater freedom to indulge his idiosyncrasies. Bickham espied that Howard had closets where "the clothes were coordinated from shoes, to socks, to handkerchiefs in the coat pocket in the lapel. You'd see him in the morning and he'd change clothes in the afternoon." The servants included a maid, cook, and "Cuz" Howard (apparently no relation), a valet, who was available to run errands, day and night. Howard often proclaimed that "a man is not a man unless he has a valet."[34]

Howard's interest in his hobbies and enjoying the good life did not mean that he no longer cared about civil rights and related movements. He increasingly aspired, however, to have his involvement take the form of a behind-the-scenes financial angel. One example was the Afro-American Patrolmen's League. Renault A. Robinson and about a dozen fellow officers had formed the league in 1968 to expose discrimination and publicize complaints of police abuse. Howard's support was not surprising. He had fought police abuse since his days as a columnist for the *California Eagle* in the 1930s and as head of the RCNL. Howard's donations allowed the league's police complaint service to extend legal aid and other help to victims of police mistreatment. It fielded four hundred citizen complaints alone in the first four months of 1972.[35]

A defining moment in the league's history was the suspicious killing of Fred Hampton, the head of the Chicago Black Panthers, in 1969. Hampton had died in a hail of police bullets in an early morning raid. Edward V. Hanrahan, the state's attorney of Cook County, a Daley loyalist often mentioned as a possible successor for mayor, was in charge. Renault A. Robinson joined other blacks in the outcry about the slaughter. He announced that the Patrolman's League was conducting an internal investigation. The Chicago police department and the FBI followed with their own inquiries. According to the FBI report, the police had fired ninety rounds but the Panthers had fired only one. The police were not charged with murder, Gary Rivlin concludes, "but the evidence makes it hard to call the incident anything less." In their first important citywide repudiation of the Daley machine, black voters overwhelming rejected Hanrahan's bid for reelection.[36]

Howard also took part in Operation Breadbasket, led by Jesse Jackson. In 1964 Jackson, then twenty-two, left his native South Carolina to study at the Chicago Theological Seminary. A year later, he participated in Martin Luther King Jr.'s movement in Selma. Although King was suspicious of Jackson's burning personal ambition and hunger for attention, he gradually gave him greater responsibilities. Says Calvin Morris, "King would have seen the energy, the intelligence. He would have seen some of himself." Howard probably felt the same way. When Jackson returned from Selma, he threw himself into King's campaign to establish a beachhead in Chicago.[37]

The circumstances of exactly when, where, and how Howard and Jackson met are not clear. It may have been through Clay Evans, a co-chair of the South Side Ministers for Howard in 1958. Evans had helped King set up shop in Chicago in 1966. Jackson was to become an assistant pastor in Evans's church even though he had dropped out of the seminary. In 1966 King selected Jackson as head of the SCLC's Operation Breadbasket in Chicago. Influenced by the example of Reverend Leon Sullivan of Philadelphia, the division fostered "selective buying" (boycotts) as a means of pressuring white businesses to hire blacks and purchase goods and services from black contractors. Sullivan had many precursors, of course. One was Howard. As head of the RCNL, he had successfully developed the service station boycott. Jackson's application of these methods, however, had a seamier aspect, including cronyism and strong-arming to pressure businesses to donate money to Operation Breadbasket.[38]

From an early stage, Howard gave Jackson an important entrée into the business community. Soon after Jackson came to Chicago, Barrett recalls that Howard "opened up his house to him and started calling in all of these black ministers and all his black business friends, and they raised money for Jesse and did a lot of things trying to push his dream along. . . . I think my father was Jesse's doctor as well." Edward F. Boyd has similar memories. Whenever Jackson "had friends or someone he wanted to cultivate or something, he always brought them by Howard's." Doris Zollar goes even further, comparing the Howard–Jackson relationship to that of "a father and son." As with the Afro-American Patrolman's Association, Howard generally stayed in the background, acting as contributor and personal facilitator.[39]

Howard took a special interest in the Commercial Division of Operation Breadbasket. Noah Robinson Jr., who had just graduated from the Wharton Graduate School of Finance and Commerce of the University of Pennsylvania, came to Chicago in 1969 to become full-time director of the division. Robinson was Jesse Jackson's half-brother and sometime rival. He often observed Howard at meetings and gained considerable respect for him. He notes that Howard was "a senior mentor" who was "always there complimenting what I had to say or encouraging the other guys."[40]

Robinson rejects comparisons between Howard and that most famous of all great persuaders, Lyndon B. Johnson. Howard, unlike Johnson, could not resort to pressure tactics because he did not have a personal stake in the outcome of decisions and often was the only nonbusinessperson who was present at meetings of the Commercial Division. Instead he had to sway people through the power of his ideas and the logic of his arguments. Robinson states that Howard showed no interest in being the center of attention: "He was not the type of guy that would run up and have his picture taken at the press conference standing behind somebody." At the regular Saturday meetings of Operation Breadbasket, "he just sat with the others like he was another person from the community interested in what was going on."[41]

One of Howard's major themes was that Operation Breadbasket needed to do more than just finding jobs for blacks in white businesses. If whites wanted to reap the rewards of the black market, he argued, "why not ask them to allow the blacks to build their stores or to sell products to the stores or to provide services to the stores or to have those stores bank in the black banks." Perhaps, using his experiences in Mississippi as an object lesson, Howard depicted the encouragement of black businesses as complementary to a successful Civil Rights Movement. He said that in a crunch they were less likely to get cut "off for political reasons."[42]

When Jackson had his final showdown with Ralph Abernathy, the president of the SCLC, Howard was in Jackson's corner. Abernathy never trusted the young upstart from Chicago. By December 1971 they had a complete falling out as Abernathy suspended Jackson for "administrative improprieties and repeated acts of violation of organizational policy." Jackson resigned and called together his allies. They met at the Safari Room in Howard's home and Operation PUSH (People United to Save Humanity) was born.[43]

Howard was a member of PUSH's board of directors, chaired the finance committee, and continued to make his home available for meetings. But he was first and foremost a donor. He did not take much interest in matters of governance. As Zollar puts it, whenever Jackson "needed a big sum he would go to Dr. Howard." If Howard was being used, however, he did not seem greatly troubled. He had different priorities on his mind. He was going to build a much larger state-of-the-art medical center to serve blacks on the South Side.[44]

Howard was putting the final touches on what he envisioned as his crown jewel: the Friendship Medical Center (FMC). He had wanted to build it since he came to Chicago, but not until the 1970s did he begin to plan in earnest. He had ruled out the option of renovating or expanding the Howard Medical Center at 63rd and Rhodes. Blight and crime had overtaken the once-vibrant surrounding neighborhood. Blacks were moving farther south in the city, and he would have to follow them. Howard's wife, relatives, and friends overwhelmingly opposed his plan. After all, he was in poor health and approaching an age when most people anticipated retirement. His clinic was still profitable. They asked why he didn't relax now and enjoy life. But when Howard made up his mind, he was unmovable and unstoppable.[45]

Although Howard's goal was to create a comprehensive medical center, abortions were always central to his conception of the bottom line. They had generated the seed money to build the FMC and, in his view, presented the best prospect for future profits. If abortions became legal, Howard had every reason to expect a financial harvest. By the end of the 1960s, the prospects for legalization had never looked better. In 1969 doctors, feminists, and family planning activists formed the National Association for the Repeal of Abortion Law (NARAL). Meanwhile, the American Civil Liberties Union was mounting a court challenge to an Illinois state law that banned abortion unless the life of the mother was in danger. It had the active support of Total Repeal of Illinois Abortion Law (TRIAL).[46]

When New York State legalized abortions in 1970, doctors and other providers invited Howard to the state to teach them how to perform the procedure between the thirteenth and sixteenth week of pregnancy. He had been doing it for years. The trip must have had an impact on his thinking. Only two years earlier, he was in the dock for an illegal abortion; now, New York's best-known doctors and hospitals sought him out for advice. His specialty was suddenly respectable, or at least more respectable than before.[47]

Howard had more than a few close calls ahead of him, however. Being an abortion doctor in Chicago was still a risky business. His opponents had no intention of conceding defeat. In 1971 the judiciary committee of the Illinois House voted twelve to six against a bill to legalize abortion in the state. E. Spencer Parsons of the Clergy Consultation Service had testified in favor. He said that he knew of twelve men and one woman who had illegally performed abortions in Chicago. This immediately caught the ear of Henry Hyde, the Republican majority leader of the Illinois House and the future chair of the U.S. House Judiciary Committee. He publicly demanded that Parsons name names. State's attorney Edward V. Hanrahan convened a grand jury to call Parsons in for questioning. A juror asked if he knew of any doctors who had paid off the police. This put Parsons on the spot, because Howard had once confided to him about giving bribes. Because he had not actually witnessed money changing hands, he answered that he did not. The grand jury did not bring any charges this time, but Hanrahan took it upon himself to launch a crackdown on illegal abortionists.[48]

Through it all, Howard pushed ahead deliberately, but cautiously. Around 1971 he purchased a vacant Jewel grocery store on 103rd Street (which had ample parking) and hired a well-known black architect to redesign it. Financing came from a combination of personal funds and private loans. He did not find it difficult to borrow money for such a project. As Oscar J. Moore Jr. observes, health care was "a boom profession and the possibilities in the black communities in Chicago were just everywhere. . . . The banks were just passing out the checks." But there was a catch. Most of the FMC's loans were on a short-term basis.[49]

Raising money for the physical plant was just half the battle for Howard. To overcome the "abortion mill" stigma attached to his name, he needed to recruit a top-flight medical staff. Pouring on the charm as never before, he wined and dined doctors in fields such as podiatry, pediatrics, optometry, and dentistry. Avoiding the slightest hint of the subject of abortion, he laid out an enticing vision for them: they could be in on the ground floor of the largest privately owned black medical institution in the city. Moore witnessed Howard's methods at many of these meetings. "He could talk your shoes off your feet in a snowstorm," he comments. "His hands were soft as cotton and he'll look you straight in the eye and get a commitment of you then and there. . . . A commitment with a smile. . . . He carried an army of goodwill around him and nobody really could ever say anything bad about him."[50]

Throughout the planning process, the great unmentionable issue of abortions always lurked beneath the surface. For the time being, Howard stopped doing them. He knew that an arrest by the ever-watchful Hanrahan would jeopardize everything. But he needed the money. He had another doctor, Arnold Bickham, do abortions offsite and share the profits. A graduate of Meharry, Bickham had practiced in the South and was relatively unknown to the Chicago police. Howard had the future possibility of legal abortions in mind when he planned the building's design. The layout allowed women to exit discreetly from his office without returning through the reception room. All this greatly alarmed Edward F. Boyd, who had come to Chicago to handle public relations. He feared that a taint of abortion, illegal or legal, would completely undermine the project.[51]

When the Friendship Medical Center opened in June 1972, Howard handled it in his typically exuberant and theatrical style. He recruited Senator Adlai E. Stevenson III, Jesse Jackson, and Representative Ralph H. Metcalfe to speak at the dedication ceremony. As the choir from Operation PUSH sang in the background, nurses dressed in Florence Nightingale garb greeted visitors at the door. The publicity stated that Howard had raised the more than $1 million in construction costs "without any kind of special governmental assistance" but understandably did not mention that most of these funds came directly, or indirectly, from illegal abortions. The medical equipment was worth more than $500,000.[52]

Reviving the "temple of health" slogan once used for the Taborian Hospital in Mound Bayou, the FMC embodied Howard's longstanding belief in patient-friendly care. A story in the *Chicago Tribune* reported that he tried to "impart the sense of friendship and welcome in the center's waiting room. Large, comfortable chairs face a color television set, a waterfall, and a tableau of wild animal trophies he collected on numerous safaris to Africa. Pictures of Angela Davis, Dr. Martin Luther King, and Isaac Hayes and posters emphasizing black pride fill the walls." The inviting and relaxing atmosphere, the article continued, stood apart from the typical "unattractive waiting rooms" and the "indifferent attention from attendants" of most hospitals. The one hundred sixty-five employees included twenty-seven doctors who provided such services as pediatrics, dental care, a pharmacy, ear, nose, and throat, and psychological and drug counseling. The FMC had an emergency room and intensive care unit. Howard portrayed both as potential lifesavers for many people who would otherwise die en route to Cook County Hospital, two miles distant. He promised never to turn anyone away and apparently meant what he said. Moore saw him fire "a lady one night because there was a sick person at the door and the receptionist said, 'The clinic is closed.' That's all she had to do. He said, 'We will see patients in here as long as there is a doctor on the property.'"[53]

This was the FMC's honeymoon period. During its first year, fifty thousand patients passed through the doors. Press coverage was generally favorable. But several storm clouds were on the horizon. The debt was piling up, and loans were already coming due. Only a month after the opening, Howard tried to plug the holes by taking out a first mortgage of nearly $600,000. He raised additional funds by recruiting stockholders, including Bickham. Bickham's double role in performing illegal abortions at another location remained a closely guarded secret. Newspaper references to the FMC never mentioned the subject of abortion.[54]

Howard's most quotable public announcements were on an entirely different topic. In January 1973, he blasted a new state law that required permits for "any hides, heads, rugs and other products" from a list of more than four hundred endangered species. It was vintage Howard. He commented to *Jet* that he thought it "strange that lawmakers in these United States could pass an Endangered Species Protection Act to protect animals and birds but could not pass an anti-lynching bill." Half in jest, he suggested adding Black Panthers to this endangered list. Instead of passing laws, he called for trusting the experts in Africa "whose job it is to control wild life." He cited a study by the Wild Life Association of Kenya that credited efficient game management, rather than bans on hunting, for recent increases in the leopard population.[55]

Hyperbole and self-interest notwithstanding, Howard's arguments had merit. They anticipated those made by later resource economists who concluded that protection of endangered species and hunting might not only coexist but complement each other. Like Howard, these economists emphasized how Zimbabwe and other countries began to boost their elephant populations in the 1990s by partially legalizing the ivory trade. Like Howard, too, they asserted that those nearest to the problem were best able to do the job, especially if given incentives to protect species as economic assets.[56]

On February 26, 1973, Howard's long wait for legal abortions finally ended. In a preliminary decision, the United States Supreme Court upheld the right of women to have the procedure. Even before the final ruling came through, Howard announced the readiness of the FMC to perform sixty to a hundred abortions per day. Most spectacularly, his photo took up half the front page of the *Chicago Daily Defender*. It showed him in the operating room demonstrating a "common abortion technique for an early-term pregnancy." The Supreme Court handed down the final decision at 10:21 a.m. on March 1. An hour later, the FMC became the first clinic in Illinois to perform a legal abortion. Twenty-five women were waiting in line at the time. One of the first on the table was a fourteen-year-old girl.[57]

Howard stayed in the media spotlight during the next few weeks after the implementation of *Roe v. Wade*. Reporters, much like their predecessors in the 1950s, sought him out because he gave them good copy. A Chicago television news crew stopped by to film an abortion. Boyd remembers that Howard "was just delighted" by the publicity, and "went out of his way to cultivate the news media." *Jet* put his picture on the cover, doing an abortion of course. Howard's exuberance was not surprising. After years of suffering the stigma associated with illegal abortions, he was in the same corner as the nation's highest court. It was tempting to react on an emotional level and to shout from the rooftops.[58]

The press had not been so eager to quote him since his run-in with J. Edgar Hoover in 1956. He seized the opportunity to expound at length on his views. Although he defended abortion as a matter of individual rights, he emphasized pragmatic and utilitarian justifications. He said that his experiences in Mississippi had convinced him that "babies are made that aren't always wanted and people end up with large families because abortion wasn't within their reach. So we end up with people who are poorly fed, poorly housed and poorly clothed." Poor blacks on plantations had "so much free time on their hands, and so little enjoyment, that sex becomes a part-time hobby for some." In reference to accusations that abortion was a white racist plot, he said that his critics were "too hung up" on fears of genocide. Howard was as controversially quotable as ever. At this time, he coined the phrase "lunch-hour abortion." In his view, there was "no reason" why a woman during the first three months of pregnancy could not have "an abortion during her lunch break and then go back to work." This was an exaggeration. The entire process actually took about three hours.[59]

This publicity brought in much new business but came at a steep price. It left in the public mind an indelible impression that the FMC was just a place to get abortions. The effect was to undermine the original goal of creating a respected center for comprehensive medical care on the South Side. Although the vast majority of patients came for such routine services as optometry and pediatrics, Howard's association with abortion had become impossible to shake. The FMC took in about $4 million in the first year. During the same period, twenty thousand women had abortions there, nearly half those performed in the entire state. Initially, most were performed on whites, but blacks later predominated.[60]

This association made for a constant struggle to recruit and keep good doctors. Several dropped out at an early stage. The biggest loss was Moore, who initially agreed to be the head of internal medicine. He had formerly held that position at the U.S. Naval Hospital in New London, Connecticut and had won high regard for his medical skills and leadership ability. Howard made even less headway with Louis Boshes, a nationally known neurologist who had treated him for his stroke. Boshes respected and liked Howard, but he turned down an offer to be "specialist consultant." The FMC had several credible practitioners, but the overall record was mixed.[61]

Howard knew that he was challenging deeply held black cultural, moral, religious, and political attitudes. While the *Chicago Defender* and *Jet* and nationally known politicians such as Shirley Chisholm increasingly defended legal abortion, many others linked it with sterilization as twin plots to keep the black population small and powerless. Political activist and comedian Dick Gregory declared, for example, that his "answer to genocide, quite simply, is eight Black kids and another one on the way." Even mainstream civil rights leaders, such as Whitney Young, fretted about the racist implications of abortion. In Chicago, the Nation of Islam, led by Elijah Muhammad, was Howard's most vocal black critic, at least initially. *Muhammad Speaks* circulated cartoons depicting the graves of aborted children under the slogan "Abortion: Killing Black Babies." In the month after *Roe v. Wade,* two articles appeared that condemned the FMC. One compared the patients who sat in the waiting room to "sheep going to slaughter." *Muhammad Speaks* asked ironically, "Friendship for Whom?" and attributed the speedy processing of patients to Howard's hunger to make money "no matter what."[62]

Howard had expected criticism from these quarters, but not from Jesse Jackson. Less than a month after *Roe v. Wade,* a front-page headline in the *Chicago Daily Defender* blared, "Jesse Launches War on Abortion." Jackson promised an "all-out PUSH campaign" and called for the formation of a Right-to-Live Committee. "It's murder no matter what you call it," he pronounced. He said that if abortion had been popular in biblical times, Jesus and Moses might never have been born. Jackson did not mention Howard by name; he hardly needed to, especially with statements like this: "We used to look for death from the man in the blue coat and now it comes in a white coat."[63]

Jackson's jeremiad made Howard hopping mad, and he did not try to hide it. He barred the members of PUSH's finance committee (which he had once chaired) from his house, saying he was "sure that they didn't want to meet in a murderer's home and take a murderer's money." A columnist for the *Chicago Metro News* took Howard's side in the feud. Asking if Jackson had lost "his cotton picking mind," he branded him as an ingrate who had benefited greatly from Howard's donations and hospitality. No individual, the columnist asserted, had been more successful in raising "funds for PUSH than Dr. Howard." Along the same lines, Ethiopia Alfred-Bekele complains that Howard had "bailed Jesse Jackson out of every financial problem he had. . . . So, if he disagreed with him, why . . . didn't he give it back and say that it was bad money?" She regards Jackson as "a very selfish man." Others are more forgiving. Renault A. Robinson asks, "absent having another outlet, what more legitimate way" did Jackson have to get funding?[64]

Realizing his strategic miscalculation, Jackson quickly backtracked. He phoned Howard to mend fences. Whatever he said, it worked. The main mystery is why Jackson was caught off guard in the first place. He had long known that Howard made his living from abortions. Jackson temporarily toned down his rhetoric after the reconciliation. Shortly after Howard's death, however, he published a no-holds-barred anti-abortion article in the *Right to*

Life News. Coincident with his run for president in 1984, he shifted into full reverse and adopted an equally strong pro-choice position.[65]

Howard's dispute with Jackson was a sideshow compared to a run of bad news for the FMC. During March and April, the press highlighted several suspicious deaths and health mishaps. Two women died, allegedly from botched abortions, while four had serious complications. In response to this barrage of negative publicity, Howard countered that the FMC had performed 1,500 legal abortions thus far, more than any other Illinois provider. Given such numbers, he concluded, only six major complications were not unusual. A lack of detailed comparative statistics makes it almost impossible to determine if he was right. What can be said is that the rapid influx of patients put the staff and facilities of the FMC under a tremendous strain. Says Sandra Morgan, the women "would be lined up and the seats would be filled. They would be sitting on the floor."[66]

Fueled by the bad publicity, cries for more regulation grew louder. Using the FMC as an example, Charles Weigel, the president of the Chicago Medical Society, wanted to restrict abortions to hospitals. William J. Scott, the Illinois attorney general, agreed. He said that the Supreme Court had ruled that abortion was between a woman and her doctor, not "between a woman and her plumber." Of course, this was a misleading statement. Doctors, not laymen, performed the abortions at the FMC. To Howard, the hue and cry was a smokescreen by the medical and political establishment to quash their lower-priced competitors. He had a basis for this belief. An abortion at the FMC cost about fifty dollars less than at hospitals. In a sympathetic article for *Jet,* executive editor Robert E. Johnson, Howard's longtime friend, elaborated. He suggested that the complaints from doctors were primarily sour grapes because they "didn't have the foresight to plan ahead like Dr. Howard in order to cash in on the abortion bonanza."[67]

Howard's defenders rejected the claim that the FMC posed an unusual danger for women. A representative from Jane, the feminist pro-abortion provider group, doubted that hospitals were really as safe as they claimed and pointed out that they had yet to publish any statistics on mortality and complications. She predicted that a law banning abortions from freestanding clinics might actually harm the health of women by pushing the already limited capacity of hospitals beyond the breaking point. As it was, Cook County Hospital only managed to perform eighteen abortions per week, far lower than the FMC's daily rate. Others went further by directly questioning the motives of those who advocated legal restrictions. In a sledgehammer attack, columnist Charles B. Armstrong Sr. attributed the campaign against Howard to a "white racist system" that resented the success of a black man. The fact that "rich whites from north shore and elsewhere go to Dr. Howard to receive their abortions . . . blows white males egos."[68]

While a ban on abortions at freestanding clinics, such as the FMC, never became law, the movement for stepped-up regulation did make headway. In May 1973, the Chicago Board of Health implemented several inhibiting regulations, including a twenty-four-hour waiting period, a three-hour post-operative recovery before discharge, regular state inspections, and mandatory reporting. Howard's response to the news was conciliatory. He had grown weary of the controversy and wanted to rebuild the FMC's reputation as a general-purpose clinic. He praised the Board's requirements as "a tremendous step forward" and pledged to enforce them. But he made one exception that showed the continuing importance of abortions as the FMC's bread and butter. He vowed to appeal the twenty-four-hour waiting period. In his view, it was "twenty-four hours of torture" and a violation of "personal and marital privacy." Howard had good reason to gamble on a legal challenge. In the wake of *Roe v. Wade,* the general approach of the courts was to give women seeking abortions and their doctors the benefit of the doubt.[69]

In 1974 the U.S. Court of Appeals for the Seventh Circuit gave Howard more than he asked for. Ruling on the earlier case brought by the FMC, it invalidated *all* the Chicago Board of Health's restrictions. The court held that a woman's right of privacy trumped other considerations. This decision helped establish a precedent that made abortion clinics probably the least regulated medical facilities in the United States. Rather than crow too much about vindication, however, Howard held out an olive branch. Although the court had struck down the board's regulations, he pledged to continue to abide by them with the exception of the twenty-four-hour waiting period. He added triumphantly: "By the time a woman comes to Friendship . . . she doesn't need any more time to think it over." Later, the Friendship Medical Center, along with Planned Parenthood and several other leading providers, organized the Chicago Abortion Services Council. It set out to establish and enforce self-imposed rules to "maintain good quality health care in abortion."[70]

T. R. M. Howard was slaying legal dragons left and right, but Helen Howard had finally had enough of his infidelity. Upon returning from his latest safari, he found to his shock that she had locked him out of the house. The increased public flaunting of his affair with Juanita Gilmore, including the discovery that their son Teddy had accompanied him on the trip, had finally pushed Helen over the edge. She confessed to her brother that she wanted "a little peace" for the rest of her life. In October 1973, a judge awarded her "exclusive, unhindered occupancy" of the house. Howard took up residence in a hotel, and she eventually filed for divorce. In the divorce complaint, her years of pent-up anger and frustration blasted into the open with a vengeance. Her husband had held her "up to public ridicule, embarrassment and shame" by flaunting his adultery in public places where friends could see them. She accused him of paying for Gilmore's apartment and giving her a Cadillac that he replaced annually. The complaint listed the first names of seven of his illegitimate children. Stating somewhat disingenuously that Helen had "just learned" about them, it did not include Verda (his child from before their marriage).[71]

Although she was awarded an annual alimony of $24,000, neither T. R. M. nor Helen showed any inclination to rush into a divorce. Howard wanted to keep seeing Juanita and even toyed with the possibility of building her (or Helen) a condominium, but he expressed no desire for a second marriage. Also, he continued to have sexual relationships on the side. He tried to tempt one woman by offering to put her car on a ship so she could join him on a trip to Africa. Helen was in bad health and ill prepared for such a radical break as divorce. And she still loved her husband. He probably loved her too in his own way. At the same time, she had no reason to believe he would change his philandering ways. They wrangled over the amount of alimony, but neither could make the final move. At the end of the year, they were still legally married. Through it all, they remained civil. He always showed respect when they were together in public and never forgot to send her gifts and flowers on birthdays and his signature long-stemmed roses at Christmas. They even entertained guests together on occasion. Oscar J. Moore Jr. says that "if you didn't know those papers had been filed, you couldn't tell."[72]

Plagued by ill health, divorce, and financial problems, Howard still summoned the energy for one last political crusade. He became treasurer of the Committee for a Black Mayor. Much about Howard had changed in the previous forty years, but one constant was a commitment to black insurgent politics. He always stood ready to confront the Daley machine and support the advancement of blacks in politics.

The prime movers behind the Committee had only nibbled at the edges of the machine for a decade or more, but by late 1974 they sensed that their time had come. Howard had known most of them for years. Charles Hayes, the former head of the Chicago division of the United Packinghouse Workers of America, was the chair. Other key members were Renault A. Robinson, James Montgomery (well known as a lawyer for the Black Panthers), Philip G. Smith, Gus Savage, Clay Evans, and Alderman William Cousins Jr. Savage, Evans, and Cousins were veterans of the Howard campaign in 1958. Howard's close personal friend, William Green, was a major donor. Harold Washington, recently elected to the state legislature, took part behind the scenes. Bennett J. Johnson, the coordinator and sole paid member, describes Howard as one of the three "key players" on the committee. As with the Chicago League of Negro Voters and Operation PUSH, Howard's participation did not generally have a public face. News reports about the committee's activities rarely included his name, much less quoted him.[73]

The members drew inspiration from the recent election of Tom Bradley as mayor of Los Angeles. If Los Angeles, where blacks constituted 16 percent of the population, had elected a black mayor, they asked, why couldn't Chicago, where they were nearly 40 percent? The committee's statement of purpose expressed views that Howard had long held dear: "While we do not necessarily sanction ethnic politics, we believe that the principles of democracy demand that black voters should wield a greater influence than any other single community in the election of our city's next mayor in 1975." The committee announced plans to conduct a survey of more than three thousand prominent blacks, interview potential candidates, and then mobilize around the best choice for mayor. This public openness did not necessarily reflect the private views of key members. Many, but not all, had made up their minds that they wanted Ralph H. Metcalfe to run, regardless of what they said publicly. Metcalfe had partially broken with the machine in the years just after the Fred Hampton killing and similar incidents of police brutality. Although Howard liked Metcalfe, he was open to alternatives. In this respect, he differed from the other members.[74]

The committee soon fell into infighting and confusion. Much of the trouble started after the results of its survey (sent out on FMC stationery) became public. The top choice of respondents was Richard Newhouse, a black state senator. Despite this, Newhouse did not get the committee's endorsement. Understandably, Newhouse did not take it well. He denounced the committee as a "self-serving, shuffling, backside-scratching cadre of worse than Uncle Toms," and "plantation civic leaders compared to whom Judas is a paragon of virtue."[75]

Instead of backing Newhouse, the committee continued to court Metcalfe, who most members thought had the best chance to beat Daley. Although the media increasingly dismissed the whole effort as a farce, members took heart when Harold Washington came out in the open to urge Metcalfe, his friend and mentor, to run. This was Washington's first significant break from the Daley organization. Metcalfe partially relented. He agreed to run if the committee raised $500,000 in ten days and if he were the only black candidate, both unrealistic goals. The members scrambled to raise as much as possible, hoping that Metcalfe would run if they made a credible effort. Ten days later, they had pulled together nearly $200,000, an impressive amount. Apparently, some people who had wanted to contribute held back because they feared Daley's retaliation. After temporizing, Metcalfe decided not to run and Daley won handily.[76]

Howard had contributed an estimated $10,000 in personal funds to the committee, prompting a columnist for the *Chicago Metro News* to conclude that he had been "ripped off." When viewed from another angle, however, the money was well spent. The committee had spurred a momentum. It set a precedent for a later committee that backed Harold Washington's unsuccessful bid for mayor in 1977. When Washington finally won in 1983, several of his key backers were veterans of the Committee for a Black Mayor, including Bennett J. Johnson, Renault A. Robinson, and Dempsey J. Travis. Two supporters of Howard's campaign for Congress in 1958 on the committee, Gus Savage and Charles Hayes, eventually won election to the U.S. House of Representatives.[77]

Shortly after Metcalfe bowed out of the mayor's race, Howard left again for Africa. It would be his last safari. This time he combined hunting, teaching, and medical practice. He taught gynecology and obstetrics to residents of the medical school of the University of Dar es Salaam in Tanzania and treated hundreds of patients. Several of his students became prominent physicians in Tanzania. They included a dean of the faculty of medicine at the university. Howard's abilities as a teacher and a doctor greatly impressed his patients and students. Shortly after he returned, the U.S. Supreme Court handed him another victory in 1975 by refusing to hear a challenge to the Court of Appeal's decision of 1974 striking down abortion regulations affecting the FMC.[78]

Consolation from the news, however, could do little to brighten an otherwise gloomy picture. The FMC's finances were on a rapid downward slide. Howard fought back by admonishing his associates to "beat the bushes" for money. This strategy had served him well in Mississippi and even when he built the FMC. But reliance on the old ways was no longer enough. Howard never came to grips with changes after the 1950s. The Friendship Clinic in Mississippi had depended almost wholly on patient fees or voluntary contributions. This kept it anchored in financial realities.[79]

By contrast, the lifeblood of the new FMC, once it was up and running, was government money (mostly Medicaid), which constituted nine of every ten dollars of revenue. This dependence on taxpayer funding undercut the motivation to use resources efficiently and sparingly. Howard had often founded and maintained his enterprises in Mississippi on a shoestring, but to keep them in the field he had needed more. He had to rely on resourcefulness, community goodwill, down-to-earth financial realities, and alertness to the market. In Chicago, the influx of "free money" led him to be careless and profligate. The most controversial examples of government-funded spending were not altogether under Howard's control. In 1974 the newspapers widely reported that Medicaid had paid Dr. Arnold Bickham, the head of the gynecology and obstetrics department, a whopping $792,266 (primarily in abortion reimbursements), more than any doctor in the United States. The following year he received just over $500,000.[80]

Since the opening of the FMC in 1972, Howard had indulged in the luxury of spreading the money around. While he often had the best of intentions, the consequences for the bottom line were disastrous. Everyone, friend and foe, agrees that he took on too many people and kept them on longer than he should have. "He was a very benevolent man," remembers a doctor at the FMC. "Lots of people who were unemployed and even unemployable, we hired. The clinic suffered. We were overstaffed." Furthermore, Howard failed to keep a watchful eye on finances; the billing and record system was chaotic.[81]

Howard was not completely to blame. The notoriously slow and inefficient government reimbursement system presented more than enough twists and turns to frustrate even the best of administrators. The delays often meant that basic costs, such as payroll, had to be put on hold. Sometimes, payments lagged several months behind. One delay so infuriated Howard that he tore up employee paychecks (which could not be paid on time) and threw them in the trash can. "I'd say to his secretary," Sandra Morgan recalls, "'Do you know what daddy just did?' And she said, 'Yeah, he does that all the time.' I said, 'We gonna get paid?' 'Yeah, maybe tomorrow.'" But, in the end, he always met the payroll.[82]

While nearly all observers blame poor management and delays in government aid, some trace the FMC's troubles back to the original planning stage. Citing the extensive square footage devoted to waterfalls and trophies, Moore describes the design as needlessly extravagant and "completely dysfunctional." He compares the FMC to "a one-story hotel with five elevators. . . . The financing and capitalization of it was unreal from the beginning. It could not work." Not everyone shares this view. Bickham and English contend that these amenities helped the bottom line by attracting patients. The carefully crafted environment in the lobby and elsewhere left behind pleasant memories for many patients.[83]

By the second half of 1975, Howard recognized the urgent need for reforms. He hired as administrator Perry T. English and gave him authority to start economizing. English was able to make the hard choices that Howard could no longer bring himself to carry out. According to English, Howard never had the heart to fire people himself so "he had me do that. . . . I had no problem with it because it was a business move to me."[84]

As he struggled to dig out of the ever-deeper financial hole, Howard suffered a heart attack in September 1975. The doctors installed a pacemaker. In the last decade, he had shrugged off strokes, high blood pressure, and diabetes, but this time the heavy weight of health and debt troubles shook his confidence. He no longer had the energy or means to live a separate life, much less pay alimony. He asked Helen to let him move back to Safari Manor and she accepted. They put their divorce on hold for good. Helen, now under the constant supervision of a nurse, had recently suffered a stroke herself and was probably glad to have him back.[85]

As death drew near, Howard contemplated anew his relationship with God. Religion had never been absent in his life. During the 1950s and 1960s, he had attended the Liberty Baptist Church and had even become an ordained minister. Some friends doubt that it ever went beyond appearances. Moore, for one, concludes that "everything in his life was utilitarian. If he'd go to church, he'd go there to make a speech." Otherwise his behavior shows a quest for deeper meaning, however. Nothing had ever filled the void left behind when he drifted from the Seventh-day Adventist Church. Boyd describes his brother-in-law as "a very mixed-up person" who led a "double life" in his approach to religion: "Every night he'd get on his knees and pray to God. He had the faith, but his practices were different." He also said a prayer prior to each operation.[86]

At this time, Howard showed a renewed interest in the Adventist religious ideals of his youth. He had continued to contribute to the SDA institutions, including Oakwood College and Loma Linda University, but he had never rejoined the church. Now, in meetings with old friends and classmates, he spoke fondly about their shared past and his agreement with many SDA doctrines. Frederick Crowe, an Adventist friend, said that "he talked very affectionately of the church . . . about his younger days and how . . . he preached around the churches." Sometimes he blurted out, "I'm coming back. I'm coming back." But he never did. It was probably too late anyway. Howard's personal behavior was at odds with the conservative religious doctrines of the church. The philandering was a sticking point and so was his role as an abortionist, though the SDA had never taken an official stand on the origins of human life.[87]

As he searched for otherworldly solace, the financial troubles at the FMC bore down harder. The layoffs and various economy measures did not do much good. Howard "beat the bushes" yet again, but he merely added another layer of debt. In January he borrowed $44,000 and in February $100,000. He repeatedly put up his personal assets, including his house, as collateral. An agreement with the Illinois Department of Public Aid in April to infuse $100,000 in cash through loans gave immediate relief. The long-term effect, however, was to worsen the already crushing debt burden. Doris Zollar believes that by this time he was well aware that the FMC was "a doomed thing." This was a time when, as Renault A. Robinson remembers, "Everybody was hounding him . . . so it was an unpleasant situation for him, very unpleasant."[88]

Despite an unrelenting deluge of personal and financial trouble, he continued to lead an active life. He put in many hours at the FMC. It was still a busy place. In the year prior to May 1976, the FMC served more than eighty thousand patients. Howard still took part in a few social activities. In January he and Helen hosted a cocktail party for Charles Rangel and the Congressional Black Caucus. He also kept watch over Helen when she went to the hospital in February because of another bout of bad health, leaving her housebound. Most family and friends expected her to die before he did.[89]

Another looming concern was the fate of his family. While his will named only Helen and Barrett, he had made legal provision for his out-of-wedlock children. All would be rendered meaningless if the debt remained unpaid. There was one hope. Despite his poor health, his friends had arranged for him to purchase a $1 million life insurance policy. The policy had to remain in force for two more years before his beneficiaries would be entitled to collect upon his death. Aware that he was not likely to make it, sometime in late 1975 or early 1976 Howard called in a group of his children. He told them that they might not get a penny unless he lived another two years. He was doing his best to put everything in order. In his last conversation with Sandra Morgan, he apologized for not being a good father.[90]

Howard's friend and chief assistant, Perry T. English, made a last try to save his life. In late April 1976 he arranged a flight for Howard to the Mayo Clinic in Rochester, Minnesota. The doctors kept him ten days for observation, but their prognosis was bleak. The homecoming to Chicago did little to buoy his spirits. Only a few days after he returned, he had to take out another bank loan of $150,000 to keep the FMC afloat. Otherwise, Howard went on as before. He had agreed to meet English at the FMC early to pick horses for the Kentucky Derby later that day. But he failed to show up. About thirty minutes went by. English got a call from a nurse with whom he had arranged to keep an eye on Howard. She said that she found Howard in bed, apparently not breathing. English rushed over, but it was too late. Howard, a native of the Bluegrass State and a lover of horse racing, had died on May 1, 1976, Kentucky Derby day. He was sixty-eight.[91]

Media coverage of Howard's death was highly uneven. The *Chicago Daily Defender* ran a front-page story along with a photo spread. The words of columnist Lewis A. H. Caldwell of the *New Crusader* were especially heartfelt: "Dr. Howard was our friend because he had expressed the thesis by which blacks could free themselves. He had demonstrated that blacks had to do their own thing—and *demonstrating* this in the deep South took courage." The *Chicago Metro News* editorialized that "no matter what minor stigmas were attached to him, his greater contributions in the civil rights struggle, the field of his medicine and his simply overwhelming philanthropy will stand as everlasting monuments. . . . Dr. Howard was always a 'common man,' he always 'had time' for anyone."[92]

Outside of the black press in Chicago, few noted his passing. *Jet* had an article, but the *Chicago Tribune* and the *New York Times* did not mention it, nor did *Ebony*. Newspapers in Mississippi (black or white) were silent, though his old friend, Arrington High, published a salute in the *Eagle Eye*. Renault A. Robinson blames the abortions for wiping away "anything else he was doing. People only looked to the negative." But the neglect also can be traced to another source. Howard's memory was a victim of the overpowering legacy of Martin Luther King Jr. The pre-King entrepreneurial and self-help–oriented generation of civil rights leaders that Howard had embodied was out of fashion.[93]

Controversy marked Howard's funeral just as it had his life. Although many of his old comrades wanted to hold it in a local SDA church, the leadership refused. He had not been a member in good standing in many years. Instead, the service was at the Liberty Baptist Church. Jesse Jackson officiated. He had heard about Howard's death while at a conference of the Caucus of Black Democrats in Charlotte, North Carolina. Ethiopia Alfred-Bekele was also there. She says that Jackson withheld the news from her for three days.

He had entrusted Alfred-Bekele with a high-priority project at the conference and apparently feared that the shock of hearing about the death of the man she called her father would make her too distraught to carry on. She never forgave Jackson for the deception.[94]

These difficulties aside, the service was a fitting memorial. Jackson delivered a well-received eulogy, Clay Evans said the prayer, and Harold A. Lindsey, the pastor at the Shiloh Seventh-day Adventist Church, gave the obituary. Jasper Williams, the president of the National Medical Association, offered a tribute from the medical profession. Williams must have had mixed feelings. At the time, he was a prominent right-to-life crusader in Chicago, who often gave slide presentations of fetuses to show the evils of abortion. The honorary pallbearers represented the cream of black leadership in Chicago, past, present, and future. They included Harold Washington, Ralph Metcalfe, S. B. Fuller, Charles Chew (a state senator and a pioneer in independent black politics), John H. Johnson, Robert E. Johnson, William Cousins Jr., Archibald J. Carey Jr., and Sidney Jones (one of the judges at his abortion trial). Joining them was Edward P. Burton, Howard's successor as chief surgeon at the Friendship Clinic at Mound Bayou.[95]

Soon after the funeral, much of what Howard had struggled to build began to crumble. Creditors descended on the family in droves and the short-term loans came due, but the resources had run out to pay them. With the help of his cousin, Timothy Boyd, Barrett tried to retrieve stray cash and possessions from the house, but his father's belongings had already been picked clean. Barrett and the rest of the children got virtually nothing, though a court order awarded Helen the house. The ruling did not give much consolation. She lived on another eleven years, but she was already losing the ability to care for herself either physically or mentally. Her brother Edward F. Boyd looked after her in New York for most of those years. In 1980 a court declared Howard's estate completely insolvent. Claims against it exceeded $1 million, far more than the assets. If he had lived two more years to qualify for the life insurance, his family might have had just enough to pay the debt. Cash was so tight that Howard's grave did not even have a tombstone until several years after his death, when Lucius Earles and other friends took up a collection. The FMC fared poorly as well. Because of a shortage of medical facilities on the South Side, the Illinois Department of Public Aid infused cash temporarily. Meanwhile, stockholders, top medical staff, and family members dueled in the courts for control. By this time, the FMC was only a shell of what it once had been. The doors closed for good after a fire around 1978.[96]

Howard's legacy, however, was more than bricks and mortar. He was instrumental in inspiring and encouraging many of the top leaders of civil rights during the twentieth century, including Charles and Medgar Evers, Fannie Lou Hamer, Aaron Henry, and Benjamin Hooks. His enterprises and investments in Mississippi provided employment, recreation, insurance, and medical care that contributed to well-being on a mass scale. He had extended much-needed aid and comfort to the struggling black independent movement in Chicago, a movement that later brought Harold Washington to the mayor's office. Howard had stood out as a personal example for young blacks in business, medicine, and politics. He showed them that they could rise through hard work, self-confidence, big dreams, and risk-taking.

His loyalty, thoughtfulness, and generosity were legendary. Just about everyone who knew him well commented on these qualities. To Moore, he was "one of the most generous and kind-hearted people" he had ever met who "would do anything for a patient. . . . He would give you his last dollar. I've seen him do it." Says Futrell, "Howard was always a nice kind man, always nice and kind, very, very compassionate." Alfred-Bekele was only one of many young people who benefited from his financial aid and lodging. He frequently gave free care, and it visibly grieved him when he lost a patient. Frances Matlock remembers that he "had a good soul and he had a soft spot for everything." This was not always a plus. Howard's trusting nature left him vulnerable to people who took advantage of him.[97]

Counterbalancing Howard's generosity were examples of moral recklessness, irresponsibility, and hypocrisy. His philandering led to great emotional distress for his wife. He had a tendency to cut corners in business and not ask needed questions. While he defended abortion as necessary to reduce unwanted pregnancies, he fathered at least eight children from a variety of mothers. He acknowledged and helped them, but assistance was a poor substitute for a full-time father. Deprived of a stable family life and starved for attention, his children, both in wedlock and out, often had a difficult time.

Like many of the great black leaders of the past, Howard is not easily pigeonholed. Champions of both Booker T. Washington and W. E. B. Du Bois can claim him as one of their own. Like Washington, he embraced a vision of hard work, property accumulation, and entrepreneurship. He equaled, in some ways excelled, Washington's skills as a diplomat. Using charm, wit, and grit, he won concessions from even strident segregationists, such as Theodore G. Bilbo. He more closely resembled Du Bois in his willingness to confront the evils of segregation publicly and head-on with plain, blunt speaking. Long before Malcolm X or Robert Williams, Howard promoted the legitimacy of armed self-defense both as a means to keep the peace and as a last resort. As a product of the southern gun culture, he had grown to maturity in an era when some of his black neighbors fought back rather than turn the other cheek.

T. R. M. Howard was a classically American "man on the make." He defies the usual stereotypes of black history (at least as commonly propagated). His formative years were reminiscent of a Horatio Alger novel. Like one of Alger's heroes, he rose from poverty through a combination of luck and pluck. The luck, of course, came from the early patronage of Dr. Will Mason. But this luck meant nothing without the pluck to put it to good use. Few poor boys in Kentucky at the time, black or white, would have had the fortitude or confidence to confess to Will Mason their dream to be a doctor. While luck played a crucial part in Howard's rise and success, action followed only because he knew how to recognize it and, just as often, create it. He had a keen sense of how "to capture the moment," and "he was a man who knew where he was going and paved a way to get there," who would not "let anything stand in his way of getting there."[98]

Howard fit the profile of a man on the make in another sense. Rather than stick to his knitting, he was always in the process of starting a program. His reasons for changing course, and he did it often, varied. Sometimes he had decided that the benefits from the old projects had run dry. Sometimes he was simply restless and wanted to try something new. Moore found it hard to tell whether "doc was a businessman or whether he was a physician or whether he was a politician. . . . He sort of butterflied his life, a dip a little bit here and dab a little bit there." Added to this was a resourcefulness and ability to bounce back. He could "lose five thousand dollars today," Moore observes, and "go out and make ten tomorrow. . . . He was a pitchman. He could sell anything and mostly what he sold was himself." This ability was also a weakness. He started numberless projects that he failed to complete. Perhaps this helps explain why so few Americans remember him. As a man on the make, Howard was in his best element in Mississippi and the early years in Chicago when he had to scramble for resources to support his projects. The FMC's dependence on government money served to dull his creative edge.[99]

T. R. M. Howard was a critically important pioneer and deserves recognition as such. Long before the *Brown* decision, the Montgomery Bus Boycott, and the Freedom Riders, he—along with other local black leaders in the South—fought a lonely struggle against segregation and voting disenfranchisement. This work was instrumental, especially in Mississippi, in making way for the civil rights victories between 1956 and 1965. He built his successes on an earlier foundation of black self-help, mutual aid, and business investment. Without leaders like T. R. M. Howard and organizations and businesses such as the United Order of Friendship of America, the Magnolia Mutual Life Insurance Company, the Regional Council of Negro Leadership, and the Chicago League of Negro Voters, the modern Civil Rights Movement could not have succeeded.

Afterword

MUCH HAS HAPPENED since our original edition of this book appeared in 2009, but one thing is still true: T.R.M. Howard remains largely unknown. Yet, there are signs that this will soon not be the case. Various historians, more or less independently, are beginning to notice him. He figures prominently in two studies of armed self-defense and civil rights: *We Will Shoot Back: Armed Resistance in the Mississippi Freedom Movement* (2014) by Akinyele Omowale Umoja and *This Nonviolent Stuff'll Get You Killed: How Guns Made the Civil Rights Movement Possible* (2015) by Charles E. Cobb.

Of perhaps greater import, interest is building in the most sensational phase of Howard's life: his role in seeking justice for the murder of Emmett Till. Since 2009, more than two dozen books have appeared with Till's name in the title. Among these are two fine historical overviews, *Emmett Till: The Murder That Shocked the World and Propelled the Civil Rights Movement* (2015) by Devery Anderson and *The Blood of Emmett Till* (2017) by Timothy B. Tyson. Both Anderson and Tyson give Howard his due. Howard's role in the Till case is also a focal point of William J. Southerland's insightful "Negotiating the Delta: T.R.M. Howard in Mound Bayou, Mississippi" (M.A. Thesis, University of South Florida, 2016). Hollywood is also starting to pay attention. Several movies and a miniseries centering on the Till murder are in various stages of production.

Though Howard zealously sought to find witnesses and evidence, he never defined his life by the Till case. In August 1955, he already had a secure reputation as a physician, planter, and civil rights leader. He had taken on racists in a campaign against discriminatory service stations (and won), agitated for implementation of the *Brown* decision, and staged rallies featuring such major figures as Thurgood Marshall. His colleagues in both the National Negro Business League and the National Medical Association thought enough of him to give him top leadership positions. It was because of this track record that Howard was probably the only Mississippian who had the ability to get a national hearing (at least in the black press) to publicize the Till case and get some action.

But only six months after an all-white jury acquitted Till's killers, Howard had moved on to other concerns. After arriving in Chicago, running for Congress and building a new medical center topped his agenda. By the 1960s, he was devoting increasing energy to his passion for big game hunting as well as developing a reputation as one of Chicago's premiere party-givers. At the same time, he played a crucial (though, more frequently, behind-the-scenes) part in efforts to support black police officers, lay the groundwork to elect a future black mayor, and to establish Operation PUSH. Despite these forays, he was no longer primarily identified with political issues. This was apparently the way he wanted it. As noted by a writer for *Ebony* in 1969, Howard "would rather talk about his exploits as a hunter than those as a civil rights leader."[1]

By the time of his death, relatively few remembered his illustrious civil rights past. This was understandable given Howard's changed priorities. Less easy to explain was a thirty-three-year drought of interest in him (with some rare exceptions) by historians. The exceptions included two excellent overviews of Mississippi civil rights history, *I've Got the Light of Freedom: The Organizing Tradition and the Mississippi Freedom Struggle* (1995) by Charles Payne and *Local People: The Struggle for Civil Rights in Mississippi* (1995) by John Dittmer, as well as *Death of Innocence: The Story of the Hate Crime That Changed America* (2004) by Mamie Till-Mobley and Christopher Benson.

During this drought, Howard became the great "forgotten man" of civil rights history. His name was (and still is) almost entirely absent from U.S. history survey texts and, even more surprisingly, those in American black history. The best known overview of the Civil Rights Movement published during the drought, *Parting the Waters: America in the King Years, 1954–63* (1988) by Taylor Branch, mentioned Howard just once, and briefly, in the context of his eulogy at Medgar Evers's funeral. In fairness to Branch and others, however, it can be a challenge to "fit" Howard's story into standard historical narratives of civil rights. He not only predated Martin Luther King Jr. as a civil rights leader but was beginning to shed that role as King's star was rising.

Mind you, we are not complaining about the history profession's neglect of Howard. It was our pot of gold and we grabbed it. Once we "discovered" him we put other projects on hold and made telling his story all-consuming. We had to write about this man. In doing so, we conceived it as a "warts and all" biography. The warts included serial philandering and numerous out-of-wedlock children. For some, these also included his love of gambling and big-game hunting as well as, of course, providing abortions. These aspects of Howard's biography did not diminish our interest; in some ways, they whetted our curiosity and made him absolutely fascinating. We knew that any flaws, real or not, paled in insignificance compared to his great accomplishments, his originality, and his genuine heroism.

Also driving us on was the belief that in Howard we had found a rare black civil rights leader who might attract readers from across the political spectrum. His story seems to offer something for everyone. To conservatives and libertarians, it is a case study of a "rugged individualist" who championed self-help, entrepreneurship, and armed self-defense, while for those on the left, it is the story of a civil rights trailblazer who overcame many obstacles.

We faced trouble getting support from conservatives. If it wasn't for Howard's work as an abortion provider conservatives might well tout Howard as a folk hero, not necessarily because he was one of them but because he expressed key values and behaviors they had long voiced.

The response from many of those on the left was equally tepid despite Howard's unquestionable and pioneering civil rights credentials, forthright challenges to police brutality, and leadership in launching a direct attack on Jim Crow in the heart of segregationist Mississippi. We don't know the source of this tepidness. Perhaps some were put off by the same features that conservatives might like: his Republicanism, emphasis on self-help and business success, affinity for guns and material success, and admiration for the ideas of Booker T. Washington.

To some extent, the failure (thus far at least) of T.R.M. Howard's historical reputation to revive is collateral damage of our increasingly polarized society battling between "blue" and "red" teams. Neither side wants to give any benefit of the doubt to unconventional characters who did good things (in Howard's case, doing them in a big way), but also did things they greatly dislike.

Despite this, we are confident that eventually Howard will get some appreciation for his truly great achievements that will span this divide. There is some precedent for this hope. In recent years Americans from widely diverse perspectives have shown a willingness to praise historical figures, including some civil rights icons, despite their possible moral shortcomings and other misdeeds.

On abortion, a few are even coming to regard Howard as a "progressive" pioneer. A case in point is an article for *Dissent* by Cynthia R. Greenlee which lauds not only his pro-choice views but his creativity in forming alliances with feminist groups, such as the Jane Collective in Chicago. "For black communities, often labeled as staunchly anti-choice," writes Greenlee, "Howard's history points to how central African Americans have always been to the fight to maintain reproductive freedom. For a Civil Rights Movement that has focused on 'big men' and still far too few women, Howard's career demonstrates how civil rights and women's rights can and did converge." Many will not agree with Greenlee's perspective and that, of course, is quite understandable. To those who find this part of Howard's life off-putting we might ask, why should one characteristic cancel out any appreciation for other accomplishments?[2]

Even those most critical of Howard's controversial involvement in abortion, (or, for that matter, other aspects of his life) might come to respect his boldness in taking a stand, no matter the consequences. When the U.S. Supreme Court handed down its decision in 1973, Howard could have quietly faded into retirement and enjoyed his favorite pastime of big-game hunting. It seems unlikely that any short-term profits would have compensated for the potential loss of reputation, not to mention the resulting stigma. In making this move, he risked alienation from old friends and allies who were anti-abortion as a matter of moral principle, such as Jesse Jackson and Dick Gregory, not to mention many longtime associates in both the Seventh-day Adventist Church and the medical profession. Much like the early 1970s, those who charge that abortion is genocide, such as Alveda King, the niece of Martin Luther King, Jr., have stressed that African-Americans are far more likely to have abortions than whites. This is indeed the case. Currently, for example, blacks have 35.6 of abortions though they are only 13% of American women. Put another way, the black rate of abortions is three times higher than that of whites, and according to Ms. King, 79 percent of Planned Parenthood abortion clinics are within walking distance of minority neighborhoods.[3]

Most of all, love or hate Howard for certain aspects of this life, it is impossible to deny his bravery and substantial contributions to both civil rights and black social and economic betterment. He combined so much that was remarkable into one exuberant package, good and bad. Most importantly, Howard was not only present at the creation of the Civil Rights Movement but was instrumental in shaping that creation. Had he not lived, it seems unlikely that historical conditions could have produced another person in the Mississippi of his time with the requisite clout, personality, and sheer grit to pull off what he did. One lesson learned from Dr. T.R.M. Howard was that he never wavered when it came to who he was nor on what he believed.

—*David T. Beito and Linda Royster Beito, October 2017*

Notes

Duplicate copies of transcripts of all interviews conducted by authors are either at Charles W. Capps Jr. Archives, Delta State University, Cleveland, Mississippi, or at Archives and Museum, Eva B. Dykes Library, Oakwood College, Huntsville, Alabama. All FBI files are at Record/Information Dissemination Section Records Management Division, Federal Bureau of Investigation Department of Justice, 170 Marcel Drive, Winchester, VA 22602-4843.

Introduction

1. While lately more historians are showing interest in black business history than used to be the case, the subject matter is still extraordinarily neglected. For example, Thomas C. Holt, "African-American History," in Eric Foner, ed., *The New American History* (Philadelphia: Temple University Press, 1997), 330–32; and Jonathan Earle, *The Routledge Atlas of African American History* (New York: Routledge, 2000), 136–38, cite more than one hundred leading books in black history but not a single one focuses on black entrepreneurs.

2. J. Edgar Hoover to Howard, January 16, 1956, Howard FBI file; Myrlie Evers with William Peters, *For Us, the Living* (Garden City, N.Y.: Doubleday, 1996), 72–74, 87–88; and Charles Evers and Andrew Szanton, *Have No Fear: The Charles Evers Story* (New York: Wiley, 1997), 71–73.

3. Philip S. Foner, ed., *Paul Robeson Speaks: Writings, Speeches, Interviews, 1918–1974* (New York: Brunner/Mazel, 1978), 395–96; "Little Man Will Win Fight, Says Miss. Doctor," *California Eagle,* August 11, 1955, 1; "1955 Honor Roll," *Chicago Defender,* January 7, 1956, 1; and Simeon Booker, *Black Man's America* (Englewood Cliffs, N.J., Prentice-Hall, 1964), 166–67.

4. C. Evers and Szanton, *Have No Fear,* 66; Mamie [Bradley] Till-Mobley, telephone interview by authors, September 28, 1999; and civil rights rally featuring Eleanor Roosevelt and Autherine Lucy, May 24, 1956 [sound recording], Schomburg Center for Research in Black Culture, New York Public Library.

5. David T. Beito and Linda Royster Beito, "T. R. M. Howard: Pragmatism over Strict Integrationist Ideology in the Mississippi Delta, 1942–1954," in Glenn Feldman, ed., *Before Brown: Civil Rights and White Backlash in the Modern South* (Tuscaloosa: University of Alabama Press, 2004), 88–90.

6. Beito and Beito, "T. R. M. Howard," 72–81.

7. Beito and Beito, "T. R. M. Howard," 76–77, 86; M. Evers, *For Us, the Living,* 89; "Mississippi Faces Economic War," *Tri-State Defender,* October 9, 1954, 2; "Mississippi Fund Now $100,000," *Chicago Defender,* February 12, 1955, 1; and Gloster Current to Roy Wilkins, December 13, 1954, "Mississippi Pressures, Reports and Statements, 1954–55" folder, Box 424, Group 2, NAACP Papers, Library of Congress, Washington, D.C. [hereafter, NAACP Papers].

8. Frederick Sullens, "Lowdown on the Higher Ups," *Jackson Daily News,* June 8, 1955, 1; "Howard's Poison Tongue," *Jackson Daily News,* October 25, 1955, 8; "And They Get 'Honors,'" *Jackson Daily News,* January 9, 1956, 6; and David T. Beito and Linda Royster Beito, "Blacks, Gun Cultures, and Gun Control: T. R. M. Howard, Armed Self-Defense, and the Struggle for Civil Rights," *Journal on Firearms and Public Policy* 17 (Fall 2005): 137–38.

9. Beito and Beito, "T. R. M. Howard," 90; Juan Williams, *Thurgood Marshall: American Revolutionary* (New York: Random House, 1998), 255; and Louis B. Nichols [assistant director of the FBI] to Clyde Tolson [associate director of the FBI], February 9, 1956, Howard FBI file.

10. *Jet* 8 (August 28, 1955), 24; "The President Elect," *Journal of the National Medical Association* 47 (November 1955): 406; and "Business League's Board Holds Cincinnati Session," *Memphis World,* May 10, 1955, 5.

11. "Famed Dr. Howard, Rights Fighter, Montgomery Speaker," *Alabama Tribune* (Montgomery), November 25, 1955, 1; "Howard Thinking about March on Washington," *Birmingham World,* December 6, 1955, 8; transcript of interview of Rosa Parks by Judith Vecchione for the "Eyes on the Prize" television series, November 14, 1985, Henry Hampton Collection, Film and Media Archive, University Libraries, Washington University, St. Louis; and Christopher Benson to David T. Beito, personal communication, March 12, 2007.

12. Theresa Fambro Hooks, "The T. R. M. Howards Ring in New Year at Gala Holiday Fete," *Chicago Defender,* January 11–17, 1969, 17; Hooks, "Dream Come True for Dr. and Mrs. Howard," *Chicago Defender,* May 3–9, 1969, 19; Dick Gregory, interview by authors, May 31, 2001; and "Dr. Howard's Safari Room," *Ebony* 24 (October 1969), 132–38.

13. E. Spencer Parsons, interview by Pat Relf Hanavan, July 31, 2003, copy in the possession of the authors; Booth, interview, June 7, 2000; Dan Engler, "Ex-Super Market Mushrooms into Major Medical Center," *Chicago Tribune,* June 11, 1972, 3; Faith C. Christmas, "Medical Center Opening Set," *Chicago Daily Defender,* June 8, 1972, 10; and Howard to Eric Oldberg, November 6, 1974, Folder 10, Box 7, National Abortion Rights Action League of Illinois Papers, Department of Special Collections, University of Illinois at Chicago.

14. Timothy B. Tyson, *Radio Free Dixie: Robert F. Williams and the Roots of Black Power* (Chapel Hill: University of North Carolina Press, 1999); Timothy Tyson to David T. Beito, personal communication, August 9, 2006; Charles Payne, *I've Got the Light of Freedom: The Organizing Tradition and the Mississippi Freedom Struggle* (Berkeley: University of California Press, 1995), 203–6; John Dittmer, *Local People: The Struggle for Civil Rights in Mississippi* (Urbana: University of Illinois Press, 1995), 252–57, 306–7; Christopher B. Strain, *Pure Fire: Self-Defense as Activism in the Civil Rights Era* (Athens: University of Georgia Press, 2005); Akinyele O. Umoja, "'We Will Shoot Back': The Natchez Model and Paramilitary Organization in the Mississippi Freedom Movement," *Journal of Black Studies* 32 (January 2002): 271–94; and Simon Wendt, "God, Gandhi, and Guns: The African American Freedom Struggle in Tuscaloosa, Alabama, 1964–1965," *Journal of African American History* 89 (Winter 2004): 36.

Chapter 1: Up from the Black Patch

1. Kenneth B. Crouse, "Howard Outclasses Rivals in Oratory and Length of Name," *Clock Tower* 4, January 2, 1930, Union College Library, Lincoln, Nebraska. On the relatively middle-class backgrounds of Howard's civil rights contemporaries, see Williams, *Thurgood Marshall*, 21–22; Roy Wilkins (with Tom Mathews), *Standing Fast: The Autobiography of Roy Wilkins* (New York: Viking Press, 1982), 14–16; Charles V. Hamilton, *Adam Clayton Powell, Jr.: The Political Biography of an American Dilemma* (New York: Atheneum, 1991), 42–43; and Daniel Levine, *Bayard Rustin and the Civil Rights Movement* (New Brunswick, N.J.: Rutgers University Press, 2000), 7–9; Dennis C. Dickerson, "Ringing the Bell of Freedom: Archibald J. Carey Jr., Martin Luther King Jr., and the Transformation of African American Leadership," *A.M.E. Church Review* 67 (January–March 2001), 97.

2. Christopher Waldrep, *Night Riders: Defending Community in the Black Patch, 1890–1915* (Durham, N.C.: Duke University Press, 1993), 5; Suzanne Marshall, *Violence in the Black Patch of Kentucky and Tennessee* (Columbia: University of Missouri Press, 1994), 3; Dorothy and Kirby Jennings, *The Story of Calloway County, 1822–1976* (Murray, Ky.: Jennings, 1980), 31, 74–76; and Marion Brunson Lucas and George C. Wright, *A History of Blacks in Kentucky,* vol. 2 (Frankfort, Ky.: Kentucky Historical Society, 1992), 94–99.

3. U.S. Census, 1880, Tennessee, Henry County, District 13, 178B, 181C; U.S. Census, 1900, Kentucky, Calloway County, Murray Magisterial District 1, 33: 6A; U.S. Census, 1920, Kentucky, Calloway County, Murray Magisterial District 1, 20A-21B; Andrew Lassiter certificate of death, Kentucky, file no. 14852, July 19, 1922, Office of Vital Statistics, Frankfort, Ky.; and Eugene Gordon, "Dr. Howard Foresees Early End to Reign of Terror in South," *National Guardian,* January 16, 1956, 3.

4. U.S. Department of Commerce, Bureau of the Census, *Thirteenth Census of the United States, 1910,* vol. 2 (Washington, D.C.: GPO, 1913), 753; Mary Chandler and Arthur Howard marriage certificate, April 3, 1907, Marriage Bonds, Colored, 1902–1908, 171, County Court House, Murray, Calloway County, Kentucky; U.S. Census, 1910, Kentucky, Calloway County, Murray Magisterial District 1, 33; Mary Howard Palmer death certificate, Tennessee, State Department of Health, Division of Vital Statistics, Nashville, Davidson County, July 20, 1937, Tennessee State Library and Archives, Nashville, Tenn.; Henry Chandler certificate of death, Kentucky, file no. 12772, June 16, 1922, Office of Vital Statistics, Frankfort, Ky.; Roi Ottley, "Negro Doctor Quits South to Fight On Here," *Chicago Tribune,* August 10, 1957, 8; and Barrett B. Howard, interview by authors, March 27, 2000.

5. Marshall, *Violence in the Black Patch,* 113–14; Bill Cunningham, *On Bended Knees: The Night Rider Story* (Nashville, Tenn.: McClanahan, 1983), 111, 133; James O. Nall, *The Tobacco Night Riders* (Louisville, Ky.: Standard Press, 1939), 52; and Waldrep, *Night Riders,* 79.

6. Waldrep, *Night Riders,* 32; Nall, *Tobacco Night Riders,* 52, 141; and Marshall, *Violence in the Black Patch,* 87, 114–15, 130–52.

7. George C. Wright, *Racial Violence in Kentucky, 1865–1940: Lynchings, Mob Rule, and "Legal Lynching"* (Baton Rouge: Louisiana State University Press, 1990), 123, 137–40.

8. "Night Riders in Christian and Calloway Counties Are Active," *Paducah Evening Sun,* March 3, 1908, 1; Wright, *Racial Violence in Kentucky,* 139; Cunningham, *On Bended Knees,* 136; "Threat of Night Riders Met with Mounted Soldiers," *Paducah Evening Sun,* April 3,

1908, 1; "Situation in Murray Grave," *Paducah Evening Sun,* April 15, 1908, 1–2; and quoted from April 29, 1908, issue of *Calloway Times,* reprinted in undated and untitled newspaper, "Night Riders" folder, Pogue Library, Murray State University.

9. Wright, *Racial Violence in Kentucky,* 105, 125; "Murray Asks for State Troops to Guard Property," *Paducah Evening Sun,* April 2, 1908, 1; "Threat of Night Riders," *Paducah Evening Sun,* April 3, 1908, 1; and "Night Riders Intended Whipping Banker," *Paducah Evening Sun,* August 7, 1908, 1; and Marguerite Wells Ransdell, "Night Riders," *Courier-Journal and Times Magazine,* March 31, 1968, 32–34. "Wells did not act too quickly in calling for troops and it is now almost unanimously conceded by all good citizens that had he delayed a few days more, Murray would have been laid in ashes, lives and property lost and crimes committed that would not have added any laurels to the fame of Kentucky" ("Seven More Night Riders Captured at Murray This Morning," *Paducah Evening Sun,* April 11, 1908, 1).

10. Wright, *Racial Violence in Kentucky,* 160–61.

11. *Mary Howard v. Arthur Howard,* Petition in Equity, Depositions, April 21, 1911, Calloway County, Circuit Court, Kentucky Department for Libraries and Archives, Public Records Division, Frankfort, Kentucky.

12. *Howard v. Howard,* Petition in Equity, April 24, 1912; Mary Chandler Howard and Morris Palmer marriage certificate, October 8, 1913, Marriage Bonds, 1913–14, Calloway County, Calloway County Court House, Murray, Kentucky; U.S. Census, 1930, Kentucky, Calloway County, Murray Magisterial District, District 4; Annie R. Walls, telephone interview by authors, September 30, 2001; Ottley, "Negro Doctor Quits South," *Chicago Tribune;* Verda C. Harris [Wilson], interview by authors, November 6, 2000; and Barbara Anderson, telephone interview by authors, September 10, 2001.

13. Deborah J. Bell, "The Eve of Consolidation: Calloway County, Kentucky, Schools in 1925–26" (MA thesis, Murray State University, Murray, Ky., 1981), 12; B. Howard interview, March 27, 2000; and "Dr. Howard's Safari Room," *Ebony* 24 (October 1969), 138.

14. Jennings, *Story of Calloway County,* 43; U.S. Census, 1910, Kentucky, Calloway County, Murray Magisterial District 1, 12–14; "Doings in Darktown and the Aftermath Thereof," *Murray Ledger,* January 27, 1910, 1; "Another Negro Emancipated," *Murray Ledger,* August 11, 1910, 1; "Paducah Mecca for Negroes," *Murray Ledger,* August 12, 1920, 1; Oscar J. Moore Jr., interview by authors, April 4, 2001; and "Eighty Odd Coaches Bring In Celebrants," *Paducah Evening Sun,* August 8, 1913, 1.

15. Frederick and Dorothy Crowe, interview by authors, April 25, 2000; Walls, telephone interview, September 30, 2001; "Calloway Teachers Convened Monday in Annual Institute," *Murray (Kentucky) Ledger,* September 21, 1916, 1; Bell, "Eve of Consolidation," 76–78; Gary Reed, *Photographic Pot-Pourri of Calloway County* (Paducah, Ky.: Turner, 1987), 115; Wright, *Racial Violence in Kentucky,* 131; and *Murray Ledger,* March 2, 1916, 4.

16. *Howard v. Howard,* Petition in Equity, Depositions, April 21, 1911, Calloway County Circuit Court; Jennings, *Story of Calloway County,* 154; and "Labor Trouble at the Griffin and Pitt Factory," *Murray Ledger,* August 31, 1910, 4.

17. Wright, *Racial Violence in Kentucky,* 71, 80; "Judge Explains about Troubles in Calloway County," *Paducah Evening Sun,* April 25, 1908; "Twenty Years in Penitentiary," *Murray Ledger,* August 24, 1916, 1; "Another Negro Emancipated," 1; and "Another Murray Coon Is Dead," *Murray Ledger,* November 2, 1916, 5.

18. "Burning to Death by Mob," *Paducah Evening News,* October 16, 1916, 1, 4; "Infuriated Mob Sends Rapist to His Doom with Rope and Fire," *Murray Ledger,* October 19, 1916, 1–2; "Special Grand Jury Summoned," *Murray Ledger,* October 26, 1916, 1; and Wright, *Racial Violence in Kentucky,* 112–13.

19. "Infuriated Mob Sends Rapist to His Doom"; Wright, *Racial Violence in Kentucky,* 114; and "Grand Jury Refuses to Indict," *Murray Ledger,* November 9, 1916.

20. "Two Negroes Swung to Death," *Paducah Evening Sun,* October 16, 1916, 4; and Chuck Shuffett, "The Commonwealth vs. Lube Martin," part 1, *Montage* 5 (May 2000), 18–20.

21. Thomas Randolph, "The Governor and the Mob," *Independent* 89 (February 26, 1917), 347–48; "Special Term of Court Ordered," *Murray Ledger,* December 14, 1916; and Waldrep, *Night Riders,* 186.

22. Randolph, "The Governor and the Mob," 347–48; Waldrep, *Night Riders,* 186; "Two Companies of State Troops to Be Here during the Martin Trial," *Murray Ledger,* February 15, 1917, 1; Shuffett, "The Commonwealth vs. Lube Martin," part 11, *Montage* 6 (March 2001), 13–14; and Wright, *Racial Violence in Kentucky,* 193–94.

23. "Law and Order Meeting," *Murray Ledger,* May 17, 1917, 4; and U.S. Census, 1920, Kentucky, Calloway County, Murray Magisterial District 1, 42.

24. Hodding Carter, "He's Doing Something about the Race Problem," *Saturday Evening Post* 218 (February 23, 1946), 64.

25. Carter, "He's Doing Something," 64; and Crouse, "Howard Outclasses Rivals."

26. "Final Rites Held Monday for Dr. W. H. Mason," *Murray Ledger and Times,* November 27, 1941; and *History of Calloway County, Together with Sketches of Its Prominent Citizens, Past and Present* (Murray, Ky.: *Murray Ledger and Times,* 1931), n.p.

27. *History of Calloway County,* n.p.; *Calloway Times* [clipping], October 11, 1922, "William H. Mason" folder, Vanderbilt University, Archives; "The Life Lived by Ora K. Mason Will Long Stand As Inspiration to Others," *Murray Ledger and Times,* March 20, 1969; and *Murray Ledger,* May 20, 1909, 4, June 10, 1920. Mason had treated Diuguid after the shooting and testified at the trial (*Commonwealth of Kentucky v. Lube Martin,* Calloway Circuit Court, February Special Term, 1917, Bill of Evidence, 79–84, Kentucky Department of Libraries and Archives, Frankfort).

28. "Mason and Irvan Stables Attracting Attention," *Murray Ledger,* March 17, 1910, 1; "Mason and Irvan Stock Farm," *Paducah Evening Sun,* June 22, 1910, 2; "Rites Held for Dr. W. H. Mason," *Murray Ledger and Times,* November 27, 1941, 1; "The Life Lived by Dr. Ora K. Mason"; and Jennings, *Story of Calloway County,* 215–17.

29. *Murray Ledger,* June 8, 1916, 5; "Kress-Mason," *Murray Ledger,* June 21, 1917, 1; *History of Calloway County,* n.p.; "Hospital Will Be Rebuilt—Dr. Mason," *Murray Ledger and Times,* February 21, 1935, 1; "The Life Lived by Dr. Ora K. Mason"; Marjorie M. Major, "Mason-Miller Home Full of Stories from the Past," *Murray Ledger and Times,* January 11, 1984, 1B; and Daniel H. Kress, "What a Physician Sees in the Cigarette," *News and Truths* 12 (August 15, 1917), 517–18.

30. "The Life Lived by Dr. Ora K. Mason"; "Hospital Will Be Rebuilt—Dr. Mason"; "Mrs. Mason Is Given Welcome," *Paducah News-Democrat,* October 1, 1926; and "Barkley Wins Majority 21,501 with Jefferson County In," *Paducah News-Democrat,* November 4, 1926, 1.

31. Charles Edward Dudley, "'*Thou Who Hath Brought Us . . .*': *The Story of the Growth of the Seventh-day Adventist Denomination As It Relates to African-Americans* (Brushton, N.Y.: TEACH Services, 1997), 117–21; George E. Peters, "Report of the North American Colored Department," *North American Informant* 1 (August 1, 1946), 5; Charles Edward Dudley, "Moments in Black History: Theodore R. M. Howard, M.D., of Murray, Ky.," *North American Regional Voice* (December 1989), 17–19; and Theodore Howard, Student's Application Blank, Oakwood Junior College, June 30, 1924, Joseph A. Tucker to Howard, January 6, 1931, T. R. M. Howard Papers, Eva B. Dykes Library, Oakwood College, Huntsville, Ala. [hereafter, Howard Papers].

32. Dudley, "Moments in Black History," 18; Will H. Mason to Tucker, July 15, 1914, Mary J. Palmer to Tucker, November 12, 1924, Theodore Howard, Student's Application Blank—all in Howard Papers.

33. Harold D. Singleton, interview by authors, December 5, 2002; C.J. Barnes, "Industrial Education at Oakwood," *Adventist Heritage* 17 (March 1996), 25; Otis B. Edwards, "Origin and Development of the Seventh-day Adventist Work among Negroes in the Alabama-Mississippi Conference" (MA thesis, Seventh-day Adventist Theological Seminary, Tacoma Park, Md., 1942), 142–43, 164; Mervyn A. Warren, *Oakwood: A Vision Splendid, 1896–1996* (Collegedale, Tenn.: College Press, 1996), 121–23; and Mary Josephine Tucker, interview by Carl Anderson, early 1970s, 6, "Joseph A. Tucker" folder, Eva B. Dykes Library, Oakwood College, Huntsville, Alabama.

34. Edwards, "Seventh-day Adventist Work among Negroes," 285; *Oakwood Junior College Bulletin* 9 (May 15, 1924), 15, 18–25; Warren, *Oakwood,* 58–61; and Barnes, "Industrial Education at Oakwood," 15, 18–25.

35. *Oakwood Junior College Bulletin* 9 (June 15, 1924), 8–10, 14–15; and Alice Brantley, Jodie Stennis, and Morna Thompson, "We Remember Oakwood When," *Adventist Heritage* 17 (March 1996), 45.

36. D. J. Dixon, "History of the Y.M.B.S.," *Oakwood Junior College Bulletin* 15 (March 1928), Betterment Society Number, 7–10; Warren, *Oakwood,* 126–27; and Singleton interview, December 5, 2002.

37. T. R. M. Howard, "The Hour Has Come," *Oakwood Junior College Bulletin* 15, (March 1928), Betterment Society Number, 4–6; Howard to Joseph A. Tucker, August 1925, Howard Papers; and Singleton interview, December 5, 2002.

38. Jacob Justiss, "Origin and Development of the Seventh-day Adventist Health Message among Negroes" (MA thesis, Seventh-day Adventist Theological Seminary, Tacoma, Md., 1945), 31–34; Howard to Tucker, August 1925, Howard Papers; and *Oakwood Junior College Bulletin* (Annual Announcement, 1925–26, June 1, 1925), 30–31, Eva B. Dykes Library, Oakwood College, Huntsville, Alabama.

39. Blanche Johnson, interview by authors, March 18, 2001; Howard to Tucker, June 29, 1925, September 1, 1927, September 18, 1928—all in Howard Papers; and Carter, "He's Doing Something," 64. The first known appearance of Howard's new middle name was in Howard, "The Hour Has Come," 4.

40. Anderson, interview by authors, September 10, 2001; and Edna Howard Fleming, personal communication, February 8, 2001.

41. "The Life Lived by Ora K. Mason."

42. Calvin Edwin Moseley Jr., "Practices of Evangelism by Negro Methodists and Baptists compared with those of Negro Seventh-day Adventists" (MA thesis, Seventh-day Adventist Theological Seminary, Tacoma Park, Md., 1943), 29–35; Edwards, "Seventh-day Adventist Work among Negroes," 194–95; and Dudley, "Moments in Black History," 18.

43. Howard to Tucker, July 7, 1926, Howard to Tucker, July 28, 1926, Howard to Tucker, September 18, 1928—all in Howard Papers.

44. Howard to Tucker, March 26, 1929, Howard Papers; "Colporteurs' Report for Southern Union," *Southern Union Worker* 22 (June 6, 1928), 6; "Colporteurs' Report for Southern Union," *Southern Union Worker* 22 (June 13, 1928), 6; "Colporteurs' Report for Southern Union," *Southern Union Worker* 22 (June 20, 1928), 7; "Colporteurs' Report for Southern Union," *Southern Union Worker* 22 (June 27, 1928), 5; "Colporteurs' Report for Southern Union," *Southern Union Worker* 22 (July 11, 1928), 6; "Colporteurs' Report for Southern Union," *Southern Union Worker* 22 (July 18, 1928), 7; "Colporteurs' Report for Southern Union," *Southern Union Worker* 22 (July 25, 1928), 6; "Colporteurs' Report for Southern Union," *Southern Union Worker* 22 (August 1, 1928), 6; "Colporteurs' Report for Southern Union," *Southern Union Worker* 22 (August 8, 1928), 6; "Colporteurs' Report for Southern Union," *Southern Union Worker* 22 (August 15, 1928), 6; "Colporteurs' Report for Southern Union," *Southern Union Worker* 22 (August 29, 1928), 6.

45. Moseley, "Evangelism by Negro Methodists and Baptists," 36–37, 53, 72–73; Edwards, "Seventh-day Adventist Work among Negroes," 194; Howard to Tucker, September 21, 1926, Howard Papers; and Ronald L. Numbers and David R. Larson, "The Adventist Tradition," in Numbers and Darrel W. Amundsen, *Caring and Curing: Health and Medicine in the Western Religious Traditions* (Baltimore: Johns Hopkins University Press, 1998), 454–58.

46. "From Victory to Victory," *Central Union Outlook* 19 (July 22, 1930), 2, Seventh-day Adventist General Conference Archives, Silver Spring, Md. [hereafter, Adventist Archives]; Edwards, "Seventh-day Adventist Work among Negroes," 142–43; Howard to Leo F. Thiel, September 27, 1929, Howard Papers; and Everett Dick, *Union: College of the Golden Cords* (Lincoln, Neb.: Union College Press, 1967), 144.

Chapter 2: The Education of a "Race Man"

1. Howard to Leo F. Thiel, September 27, 1929, Howard Papers; and Dick, *Union,* 309–310, 384, 395.

2. Howard to Thiel, September 27, 1929, Howard Papers; and Katherine Meckling, interview by authors, June 20, 2000.

3. Stanley Hilde, interview by authors, June 20, 2000.

4. Dick, *Union,* 307; and Ellen G. White, *The Ministry of Healing* (Mountain View, Calif.: Pacific Press, 1909), 344–45; and Thiel to Howard, January 7, 1930, Howard Papers.

5. Howard to Thiel, January 30, 1930, Howard Papers; Anti-Saloon League of America, *Proceedings,* January 15–19, 1930, 18; "Orator—T. R. M. Howard," *Chicago Defender,* January 25, 1930, 24; and "From Victory to Victory."

6. Howard to Thiel, January 30, 1930, Thiel to Howard, February 4, 1930—both in Howard Papers.

7. "Increasing Success," *Southern Union Worker* 24, May 21, 1930, 2; and Howard to Tucker, March 14, 1931, Howard Papers.

8. Dick, *Union*, 237–38, 389.

9. T. R. M. Howard, "Negro in the Light of History" [feature column], *California Eagle,* September 8, 1933; and "Posse Abandons Search for Four in Fatal Battle," *Atlanta City Journal,* July 6, 1930, 8; and "Alabamans Kill 2 More Negroes," *New York Times,* July 7, 1930, in Part 7: The Anti-Lynching Campaign, 1912–1935, Series A: Emelle, Alabama, Reel 7, NAACP Papers.

10. Patricia Jean Maxwell-Schurkamp, "Maryville to Mobville: The Lynching of Raymond Gunn" (MA thesis, Northwest Missouri State University, Maryville, 1996), 71, 75–78, 88; "Mob Burns Man Alive As Girl's Killer," *New York Daily News,* January 13, 1931, 1–2; Maryville, Mo., Part 7: The Anti-Lynching Campaign, 1912–1955, Series A, Reel 14, NAACP Papers; and Howard, "Negro in the Light of History," September 8, 1933.

11. Howard to Tucker, March 14, 1931, Howard Papers; Union College, Lincoln, Nebraska, Office of the Registrar, Official Transcript of the Record of Theodore Howard, April 1, 1956, "T. R. M. Howard" folder, Illinois Department of Registration and Education, Springfield, Illinois.

12. Howard to Tucker, March 14, 1931, Tucker to Howard, March 22, 1931, Howard to Tucker, April 21, May 10, 1931—all in Howard Papers.

13. U.S. Census, 1930, Kentucky, Calloway County, Murray City, District 18; and V. Harris [Wilson], interview, November 6, 2000.

14. Ronald L. Numbers, *Prophetess of Health: Ellen G. White and the Origins of the Seventh-day Adventist Health Reform* (Knoxville: University of Tennessee Press, 1992), 189–91, 198–99; Sandra Morgan, interview by authors, March 31, 2000; and Martin L. Neff, *For God and C.M.E.: A Biography of Percy Tilson Magan upon the Historical Background of the Educational and Medical Work of Seventh-day Adventists* (Omaha: Pacific Press Publishing, 1964), 178–82.

15. Hilde, interview by authors, June 20, 2000; Eleanor R. Stewart, April 2000, personal communication; Lloyd Rosenvold, April 26, 2000, personal communication; "Interview with Ruth Janetta Temple," June 12, 1978, Black Women Oral History Project [v. 60], Schlesinger Library, Radcliffe College, iii; Leroy Walter Otto, "An Historical Analysis of the Origin and Development of the College of Medical Evangelists" (PhD diss., University of Southern California, 1962), 200–11; and Arthur E. Coyne to Edward A. Sutherland, April 9, 1934, Coyne to Sutherland, April 23, 1934, L. C. Kellogg Papers, "Arthur E. Coyne" folder, Heritage Room, Loma Linda University, Loma Linda, Calif. [hereafter, Kellogg Papers].

16. "Second Year," College of Medical Evangelists *Bulletin* 25 (July 1933), 91–93; "Lawn Party a Huge Success," *California Eagle,* October 7, 1932, 7; Edward F. Boyd, interview by authors, July 21, 2000; and Coyne to Sutherland, April 9, 1934, Kellogg Papers.

17. Mark Sumner Still, "'Fighting Bob' Shuler: Fundamentalist and Reformer" (PhD diss., Claremont Graduate School, Claremont, California, 1988), 27, 58–61, 136–138.

18. Still, "Fighting Bob," 139–43, 152–56, 201–12, 252; and Kevin Starr, *Material Dreams: Southern California through the 1920s* (New York: Oxford University Press, 1990), 172.

19. Still, "Fighting Bob," 170–72, 191–94.

20. Still, "Fighting Bob," 249–55; and Alan Brinkley, *Voices of Protest: Huey Long, Father Coughlin and the Great Depression* (New York: Vintage House, 1982), 90–93.

21. Still, "Fighting Bob," 345, 354–55, 359–61.

22. Ibid., 361–64, 370–74, 379.

23. David M. Chalmers, *Hooded Americanism: A History of the Ku Klux Klan* (New York: New Viewpoints, 1987), 203–5; and "Bob Shuler and Free Speech," *California Eagle,* November 20, 1931, 8; "Howard Defends Prohibition," *California Eagle,* October 28, 1932, 2.

24. Edward F. Boyd, interview by authors, July 21, 2000; and Mark S. Still, personal communication, August 1, 2007.

25. Crowes interview, April 25, 2000; "My Catholic and Jewish Neighbors," *Bob Shuler's Magazine* 11 (April 1932), 347; and "Howard Defends Prohibition."

26. Still, "Fighting Bob," 382–83; "Shuler's Guest," *California Eagle,* February 10, 1933, 1; and T. R. M. Howard, "Our Fight" [feature column], *California Eagle,* April 20, 1934, 14.

27. "Dr. Marmillion Is Convicted of Manslaughter," *California News,* June 22, 1933, 1, 3; Thomas Fleming, "Return to L.A.," *Columbus Free Press,* September 16, 1998; and *California v. Mathew J. Marmillion,* Court of Appeal, Second Appellate District, State of California, Clerk's Transcript, filed on August 15, 1933, California Archives Foundation, Sacramento.

28. "Free Dr. Marmillion," *Los Angeles Sentinel,* September 20, 1934, 1; "Birth Control Information Needed, Local Doctor Claims," *Los Angeles Sentinel,* October 18, 1934, 1; "Dr. Marmillion Gets Five Years in Penitentiary," *California News,* June 29, 1933, 1, 3; and Edward F. Boyd, interviews by authors, October 14, 2001, and September 20, 2003.

29. "Lawn Party Huge Success"; and Edward F. Boyd, interview by authors, July 21, 2000.

30. U.S. Census, 1920, California, Riverside County, Riverside City, District 124, 4B; Edward Boyd, interviews by authors, October 27, 1995, and July 21, 2000; and Stephanie Capparell, *The Real Pepsi Challenge: The Inspirational Story of Breaking the Color Barrier in American Business* (New York: Wall Street Journal Books, 2007), 83–85.

31. E. Boyd interview, July 21, 2000; Charlotta A. Bass, *Forty Years: Memoirs from the Pages of a Newspaper* (Los Angeles: Charlotta A. Bass, 1960), 27, 32–33, 53–61, 76–78; and Howard, "Negro in the Light of History," July 7, 1933. For more on Bass, see Rodger Streitmatter, *Raising Her Voice: African-American Women Journalists Who Changed History* (Lexington: University Press of Kentucky, 1994), 95–106.

32. "California Economic Council at Riverside," *California Eagle,* July 14, 1933; Howard, "Our Fight," May 4, 1934; and E. Boyd interview, July 21, 2000.

33. Howard, "Negro in the Light of History," July 7 and August 4, 1933.

34. Howard, "Negro in the Light of History," August 18, August 25, and September 1, 1933.

35. Howard, "Negro in the Light of History," August 18, 1933.

36. Howard, "Negro in the Light of History," February 9 and February 16, 1934.

37. Howard, "Negro in the Light of History," July 7, 1933.

38. Howard, "Negro in the Light of History," July 14, 1933. For more on how some New Deal legislation fostered discrimination, see David E. Bernstein, *Only One Place of Redress: African Americans, Labor Regulations, and the Courts from Reconstruction to the New Deal* (Durham: Duke University Press, 2001), 85–110; and Paul D. Moreno, *Black Americans and Organized Labor: A New History* (Baton Rouge: Louisiana State University Press, 2006), 163–98; and Richard Rothstein, *The Color of Law: A Forgotten History of How Our Government Segregated America* (New York: W.W. Norton, 2017) 155-67.

39. Howard, "Negro in the Light of History," July 7, 1933, August 25, 1933, and January 12, 1934.

40. Rosenvold, personal communication, April 26, 2000; and Howard, "Negro in the Light of History," August 4, 1933; Howard, "Our Fight," June 22, 1934 and June 29, 1934.

41. Howard, "Negro in the Light of History," September 8, 1933; Howard, "Our Fight," April 13, 1934, and April 20, 1934; and "Supervisor McDonough Denies He Gave Order to Segregate Colored Nurses at L. A. County Hospital," *California Eagle,* April 20, 1934, 12.

42. Howard, "Negro in the Light of History," September 8, 1933; Howard, "Negro in the Light of History," October 6, 1933; Howard, "Our Fight," May 18, 1934, 10; Starr, *Material Dreams,* 172; and Still, "Fighting Bob," 399.

43. Loren Miller, "One Way Out—Communism," *Opportunity* 12 (July 1934), 214; and E. Boyd, interview, September 20, 2003. On the appeal of Communism among the intellectuals in the 1930s, see John Patrick Diggins, *The Rise and Fall of the American Left* (New York: W.W. Norton, 1992), 148–53.

44. Ellen G. White, *The Story of Patriarchs and Prophets* (Washington, D.C.: Review and Herald Publishing, 1923), 55–57, 87; White, *Ministry of Healing,* 346, 380; and Moseley, "Evangelism by Negro Methodists and Baptists," 73.

45. Howard, "Negro in the Light of History," December 1, 1933, and February 2, 1934. Sonia reasoned that Howard was "unable to grasp the fact that it is these horrible conditions forced upon the masses by profit-seeking, exploiting monopolists which is responsible for most of the disease, insanity, prostitution and crime." (Sonia, "As I See It," *California Eagle,* February 9, 1934, 10).

46. Howard, "Negro in the Light of History," January 12, January 26, and February 2, 1934.

47. Howard, "Negro in the Light of History," January 19, January 26, and February 2, 1934; and Numbers, *Prophetess of Health,* 205–6. Black interest in eugenics during this period is briefly discussed in Dorothy Roberts, *Killing the Black Body: Race, Reproduction, and the Meaning of Liberty* (New York: Pantheon, 1997), 85–86.

48. Howard, "Negro in the Light of History," October 27, 1933. For more on the prevalence of prostitution in the Central Avenue area, see J. Max Bond, "The Negro in Los Angeles" (PhD diss., University of Southern California, 1936), 264–67.

49. Howard, "Negro in the Light of History," October 27 and November 10, 1933.

50. Howard, "Negro in the Light of History," October 27 and November 17, 1933. For more on redlight districts in U.S. history, see Barbara Meil Hobson, *Uneasy Virtue: The Politics of Prostitution and the American Reform Tradition* (New York: Basic Books, 1987), 143, 157–58.

51. College of Medical Evangelists, Theodore R. M. Howard Official Transcript of Record, "T. R. M. Howard" folder, Illinois, Department of Education and Registration. Classmate Stanley Hilde's assessment was about right: "He wasn't any brilliant genius or anything. But he didn't flunk. He passed his tests all right" (Hilde, telephone interview, June 20, 2000).

52. Ira Gish and Harry Christman, *Madison, God's Beautiful Farm: The E. A. Sutherland Story* (Nampa, Ida.: Upward Way, 1989), 104–5, 130–34; Emmett K. Vande Vere, *The Wisdom Seekers: The Intriguing Story of the Men and Women Who Made the First Institution for Higher*

Learning among Seventh-day Adventists (Nashville, Tenn.: Southern Publishing, 1972), 104–5; Dick, *Union,* 309; and Justiss, "Seventh-day Adventist Health Message among Negroes," 41–44.

53. Justiss, "Seventh-day Adventist Health Message among Negroes," 42–43.

54. Sutherland to John J. Mullowney, March 30, 1934, Kellogg Papers.

55. Carol S. Small, *Diamond Memories: Celebrating the Seventy-Fifth Anniversary of the School of Medicine of the College of Medical Evangelists/Loma Linda University* (Loma Linda: Alumni Association, School of Medicine of Loma Linda University, 1984), 66; and Coyne to Sutherland, April 9, 1934, Coyne to Mullowney, September 20, 1934, Sutherland to Coyne, March 30, 1934, Sutherland to Coyne, August 28, 1934, Coyne to Sutherland, September 13, 1934, Kellogg Papers.

56. Howard, "Our Fight," May 4 and May 25, 1934; "League Planning Lavish Program on Memorial Day, San Bernardino," *California Eagle,* May 11, 1934, 1; "Greatest Meet in History of State Planned," *California Eagle,* May 25, 1934, 1.

57. "League Planning Lavish Program"; Howard, "Our Fight," May 4, 1934; "Greatest Meet in History of State Planned"; Howard, "Our Fight," May 25 and June 8, 1934.

58. Greg Mitchell, *The Campaign of the Century: Upton Sinclair's Race for Governor of California and the Birth of Media Politics* (New York: Random House, 1992), ixx–xx, 9–11, 118; and E. Boyd, interview, October 14, 2001.

59. Upton Sinclair, *The Jungle* (Boston: Bedford St. Martin's, 2005), 290, 295; and Upton Sinclair, *The Profits of Religion: An Essay in Economic Interpretation* (New York: AMS, 1970, reprint of 1918 edition), 195.

60. Mitchell, *Campaign of the Century,* 22–23, 97.

61. Howard, "Our Fight," June 8, 1934; "Upton Sinclair Will Speak at Church," *Los Angeles Sentinel,* June 28, 1934, 13; "Negro Leader," *Upton Sinclair's EPIC News 1* (July 16, 1934), 2; and "EPIC Radio Log," *Upton Sinclair's EPIC News 1* (October 15, 1934), 2.

62. Mitchell, *Campaign of the Century,* 20–23.

63. E. Boyd interview, July 21, 2000; and *California Eagle,* September 1, 1933. On the back-to-the-land movement, see T. H. Watkins, *The Hungry Years: A Narrative History of the Great Depression in America* (New York: Henry Holt, 1999), 447–48.

64. "Howard Named to Party Post," *Los Angeles Sentinel,* October 25, 1934, 6.

65. Sinclair, *Profits of Religion,* 237–39; and United for California League, "Upton Sinclair Publishes His Own Opinion of the Seventh-day Adventists" (Los Angeles: United League for California, 1934), n.p., Upton Sinclair Papers, Manuscripts Department, Lilly Library, Indiana University, Bloomington.

66. Coyne to Sutherland, October 2, 1934, Kellogg Papers; Sinclair, *Profits of Religion,* 286–94; and Mitchell, *Campaign of the Century,* 361–63.

67. Coyne to Sutherland, October 2, 1934, and October 28, 1934, Kellogg Papers; and Carol S. Small, ed., *Diamond Memories,* 66.

68. Mitchell, *Campaign of the Century,* 21–22, 55, 211, 404, 469–70.

69. Sutherland to Coyne, October 10, 1934, Kellogg Papers.

70. Coyne to Sutherland, December 2, December 13, December 24, 1934, and January 28, 1935, Sutherland to Coyne, February 3, 1935, Kellogg Papers.

71. Coyne to O. R. Staines, April 15, 1935, Kellogg Papers; and "Hospital Will Be Re-built—Dr. Mason," *Murray Ledger and Times,* February 21, 1935, 1; "$10,000 Is Needed to Complete Hospital," *Murray Ledger and Times,* July 23, 1936, 2–3.

72. *California Eagle,* June 21, 1935; E. Boyd, interviews by authors, July 19, 1999, July 21, 2000; and Kathryn L. Jensen, "The Report of a Study of Conditions at the Riverside Sanitarium and Oakwood Junior College," 3, January 15–17, 1939, Adventist Archives.

73. Priscilla A. Dowden, "Over This Point We Are Determined to Fight: African-American Public Education and Health Care in St. Louis, Missouri, 1910–1949" (PhD diss., Indiana University, 1997), 260–63, 271; and Frank O. Richards, "The St. Louis Story: The Training of Black Surgeons in St. Louis, Missouri," in Claude H. Organ Jr. and Margaret M. Kosiba, eds., *A Century of Black Surgeons: The U.S.A. Experience,* vol. 1 (Norman, Okla.: Transcript Press, 1987), 202–5, 211–13.

74. "New Appointments City Hospital, No. 2," *St. Louis Argus,* July 5, 1935; Richards, "St. Louis Story," 253–56; James M. Whittico, interview by Doris A. Wesley, in Ann Morris, ed., *Lift Every Voice and Sing: St. Louis African Americans in the Twentieth Century* (Columbia: University of Missouri Press, 1999), 91; William H. Sinkler to Illinois State Board of Medical Examiners, May 2, 1956, Illinois, Department of Registration and Education; Leslie F. Bond, interview by Doris A. Wesley, in Morris, *Lift Every Voice and Sing,* 135; and John M. Gladney, interview by Doris A. Wesley, in Morris, *Lift Every Voice and Sing,* 99.

75. "Friendship Fetes Third Anniversary," *New Crusader* (Chicago), June 21, 1975, 2.

76. Seventh-day Adventists, General Conference Committee, Minutes of Meetings, August 24, September 24, 1936, Riverside Sanitarium and Hospital, General Board, Minutes, March 2, 1936, Record Group 270, Riverside Sanitarium and Hospital Records, Adventist Archives; Carter, "He's Doing Something," 64; and "Commercial-Appeal Notes Flood Aid Given by Mason Memorial Hospital," *Murray Ledger and Times,* February 25, 1937, 6.

77. E. Boyd, interviews, July 19, 1999, September 20, 2003; Arzalia Wilson death certificate, August 17, 1936, file no. 21003, Kentucky Registrar of Vital Statistics; and V. Harris interview.

78. Frank Loris Peterson, "New Training for Nurses," *Message Magazine* 2 (Second Quarter, 1936), 2; Norwida A. Marshall, *A Star Gives Light: Seventh-day Adventist African-American Heritage* (Silver Spring, Md.: Southern Union Conference of Seventh-day Adventists, 1989), 251; Justiss, "Seventh-day Adventist Health Message among Negroes," 47; and Sutherland to Harry E. Ford, December 18, 1935, Kellogg Papers.

79. "The Riverside Sanitarium, Nashville, Tennessee," *Advent Review and Advent Herald* 114 (July 15, 1937), 17; J. Mark Cox, "History of Riverside Sanitarium and Hospital, Nashville, Tennessee, 1935–1947," 6, Historical Reports of Riverside Sanitarium & Hospital, Riverside Hospital File, Special Collections, Eva B. Dykes Library, Oakwood College, Huntsville, Alabama; Harry E. Ford, "The Riverside Sanitarium and Hospital," *Message Magazine* 2 (2nd Quarter, 1936), 10; and "Mecca of Health," *Message Magazine* 3 (January–February 1937), 14.

80. T. R. M. Howard, "Replies to Health Queries," *Message Magazine* 3 (July–August 1937), 15, and Howard, "A Sick World," *Message Magazine* 3 (September–October 1937), 10–11, 15.

81. Crowes, interview, April 25, 2000; and Justiss, "Seventh-day Adventist Health Message among Negroes," 53–54.

82. Annabelle Simons, interview by authors, April 20, 2000; Ruth Frazier Stafford, interview by authors, January 18, 2002; and "Mecca of Health."

83. Mary Howard Palmer certificate of death, July 20, 1937, Tennessee State Department of Health, Division of Vital Statistics, Davidson County, at Tennessee Library and Archives, Archives Division, Nashville; Walls interview, September 30, 2001; and V. Harris interview.

84. Cox, "History of Riverside Sanitarium and Hospital," 7; W. E. Phillips to J. L. McElhany, November 9, 1939, Riverside Sanitarium, 1936, 1937, 1939 folder, Record Group NA-11, Files of the North American Division President, M. N. Campbell, Adventist Archives; Oakwood Junior College Board of Trustees Meeting, Irwin Hall, March 8–9, 1938; and "Survey of Riverside Sanitarium and Hospital," December 19–20, 1939, 1, 4–5, Riverside Sanitarium, 1936, 1937, 1939 folder, Record Group NA-11, Files of the North American Division President, M. N. Campbell, Adventist Archives.

85. W. E. Phillips to J. L. McElhany and W. E. Nelson, November 9, 1939, Riverside, 1940–41 folder, Record Group NA-11, Files of the North American Division President, M. N. Campbell, Adventist Archives; and Crowes interview, April 25, 2000.

86. "Flying to K.C. for Wedding," *Nashville Globe,* May 24, 1940, 1; "News of Colored People," *Nashville Tennessean,* March 6 and April 3, 1938; and Executive Committee of the National Association for the Advancement of Colored People [Nashville Branch] to Thomas L. Cummings, October 12, 1939, folder 9, box 90, Charles S. Johnson Papers, Archives, Fisk University, Nashville, Tenn.

87. Stafford interview, January 18, 2002; and Jensen, "Report of a Study of Conditions."

88. Phillips to McElhany, November 9, 1939, in "Survey of Riverside Sanitarium and Hospital," December 19–20, 1939, 7, Riverside Sanitarium, 1936, 1937, 1939 folder, Record Group NA-11, Files of the North American Division President, M. N. Campbell, Adventist Archives; *Message Magazine* 13 (Ingathering Issue, February 15, 1938), 12; and Cox, "History of Riverside Sanitarium and Hospital," 7. In his lengthy historical account of Riverside Sanitarium, Jacob Justiss, an Oakwood alumnus, describes Howard as "progressive in professional methods and an orator of national fame" (Justiss, "Seventh-day Adventist Health Message among Negroes," 53).

89. Ottley, "Negro Doctor Quits South," *Chicago Tribune;* Dudley, "Moments in Black History," 18; and Simons interview, April 20, 2000.

90. Stafford interview, January 18, 2002.

91. Simons interview, April 20, 2000; E. Boyd, interviews, July 19, 1999, September 20, 2003; Ivanetta Davis, interview by authors, June 13, 2000; and Carter, "He's Doing Something," 64.

Chapter 3: Fraternalist, Entrepreneur, Planter, and Segregation-Era Pragmatist

1. Payne, *I've Got the Light of Freedom,* 16, 25; James C. Cobb, *The Most Southern Place on Earth: The Mississippi Delta and the Roots of Regional Identity* (New York: Oxford University Press, 1992), 197–98; Neil R. McMillen, *Dark Journey: Black Mississippians in the Age of Jim Crow* (Urbana: University of Illinois Press, 1990), 36; and Earl M. Lewis, "Negro Voter in Mississippi," *Journal of Negro Education* 26 (Summer 1957), 333. David L. Cohn wrote that

the "Mississippi Delta begins in the lobby of the Peabody Hotel in Memphis and ends on Catfish Row in Vicksburg" (David L. Cohn, *Where I Was Born and Raised*, 12).

2. Janet Sharp Hermann, *The Pursuit of a Dream* (New York: Vintage Books, 1983), 17–20, 159, 221–45; McMillen, *Dark Journey*, 189; Anonymous, *Jewel of the Delta: Mound Bayou, Mississippi, 75th Anniversary* (n.p. 1962), 13–14; and Enoc P. Waters, "Post-War Building Boom Seen in Mound Bayou by Founders," *Chicago Defender,* March 20, 1943, 8.

3. David T. Beito, *From Mutual Aid to the Welfare State: Fraternal Societies and Social Services, 1890–1967* (Chapel Hill: University of North Carolina Press, 2000), 182; and *Chicago Defender* (Magazine Section), May 14, 1949, 19.

4. Beito, *From Mutual Aid to the Welfare State,* 182–85.

5. Louis J. Bernard, "The Meharry Story: Boyd, McMillan, Hale, and Walker," in Organ and Kosiba, *Century of Black Surgeons,* vol. 1, 124; Carter, "He's Doing Something," 31, 64; and untitled account by pro–P. M. Smith faction, ca. 1947, Kelly Miller Smith Papers, Jean and Alexander Heard Library, Vanderbilt University, Nashville, Tenn. [hereafter, K. Smith Papers].

6. "Final Rites Held for Dr. W. H. Mason," *Murray Ledger and Times,* November 27, 1941, 1; "Dr. Will H. Mason Jr. Dies Sunday," *Murray Democrat,* November 27, 1941, 1; and Carter, "He's Doing Something," 64.

7. Beito, *From Mutual Aid to the Welfare State,* 181, 185; David H. Jackson Jr., *A Chief Lieutenant of the Tuskegee Machine: Charles Banks of Mississippi* (Gainesville: University Press of Florida, 2002), 171–72; *Taborian Star,* February 1942, n.p.; Waters, "Post-War Building Boom," *Chicago Defender;* and "Dr. Theodore M. Howard to Open Good Will Park for Race at Md. Bayou, Miss.," *Memphis World,* June 15, 1945, 1.

8. E. Boyd interviews, October 27, 1995, and July 19, 1999; Hermann, *Pursuit of a Dream,* 242; *Jet* 8 (June 2, 1955), 28; and *Los Angeles Tribune,* January 20 [1950?], "T. R. M. Howard" folder, Alumni Files, Loma Linda University.

9. Beito, *From Mutual Aid to the Welfare State,* 185–86; Carter, "He's Doing Something," 30; and *Philadelphia Afro-American,* March 30, 1946, Folder 1, Box 372, Claude A. Barnett Papers, Chicago Historical Society [hereafter, Barnett Papers].

10. "Taborian Hospital Fills Long Felt Need for Colored Hospital," *Bolivar Commercial,* June 4, 1943, "T. R. M. Howard" folder, Mississippi State Board of Medical Examiners, Archives and Library Division, Mississippi Department of Archives and History, Jackson; "Dr. Theodore M. Howard to Open Good Will Park," *Memphis World;* "Dr. T. R. M. Howard Speaks at Lane," *Memphis World,* April 2, 1946, 1; M. Evers, *For Us, the Living,* 89–90; Dr. T. R. M. Howard et al., February 27, 1947, Deed of Trust, Land Trust Deed Record, Book N-33, Second District, Bolivar County, Bolivar County Court House, Cleveland, Mississippi; Howard to Jere B. Nash, April 12, 1950, Correspondence 1950 folder: N, Hodding and Betty Werlein Carter Papers, Special Collections, Mitchell Memorial Library, Mississippi State University, Mississippi State, Miss. [hereafter, Carter Papers]; George F. David, "Deep in the Delta," *Journal of Human Relations* 2 (Spring 1954), 73–74; and Carter, "He's Doing Something," 30.

11. V. Harris [Wilson], interview by authors, November 6, 2000.

12. "Dr. T. R. M. Howard Speaks at Lane," *Memphis World;* and E. Boyd, interviews, October 27, 1995, and July 19, 2002.

13. "Highlights of the 52nd Annual Grand Session," *Taborian Star,* November 1941, n.p.

14. "Post-War Building Boom," *Chicago Defender.*

15. "Editorial," *Taborian Star*, November–December 1943, n.p.; and "Tabor Grand Lodge Meet Is Great Success," *Taborian Star,* November–December 1943, n.p.

16. "Dr. Theodore M. Howard to Open Good Will Park," *Memphis World*; "Good Will Park," *Taborian Star*, May–June 1945, n.p; and "Great Crowd Attends Mound Bayou Celebration," *Jackson Advocate*, June 20, 1945.

17. "Dr. Theodore M. Howard to Open Good Will Park," *Memphis World*; "Great Crowd Attends Mound Bayou Celebration," *Jackson Advocate*; "Park Spurs 'Home' Interest for Negroes in Mississippi," *Christian Science Monitor*, September 17, 1945; Morgan interview, March 31, 2000; and Carter, "He's Doing Something," 64, 66.

18. The emphasis is in the original. Carter, "He's Doing Something," 30; and Dittmer, *Local People*, 67. For more on Carter, see Anna Waldron, *Hodding Carter: The Reconstruction of a Racist* (Chapel Hill: Algonquin Books, 1993).

19. "Park Spurs 'Home' Interest,*" Christian Science Monitor*; and Carter, "He's Doing Something," 69.

20. Carter, "He's Doing Something," 30, 64, 66, 69; and *Christian Science Monitor*, September 10, 1945.

21. David M. Tucker, *Lieutenant Lee of Beale Street* (Nashville, Tenn.: Vanderbilt University Press, 1971), 120–21; George A. Sewell and Margaret L. Dwight, *Mississippi Black History Makers* (Jackson: University Press of Mississippi, 1984), 170–74; Nat D. Williams, "New Bank Makes History Here; Doctor Walker Elected President," *Memphis World,* November 12, 1946, 1; Williams, "Universal Life Capital Stock Raised Million Dollars at Annual Meet," *Memphis World*, February 11, 1947, 1; "Dr. Martin Attends Institute for Hospital Administrators," *Memphis World*, March 22, 1949, 1; "Tri-State Bank Carries On in Tradition of Negro Business," *Our World* 2 (June 1947), 11; and Homer Wheaton, interview by authors, June 14, 2000.

22. Howard to Claude A. Barnett, April 29, 1946, Folder 7, Box 371, Barnett Papers; and Lawrence D. Hogan, *A Black National News Service: The Associated Negro Press and Claude Barnett, 1919–1945* (Toronto: Associated University Presses, 1984), 234–38.

23. Julius E. Thompson, *Percy Greene and the Jackson Advocate: The Life and Times of a Radical Conservative Black Newspaperman, 1897–1977* (Jefferson, N.C.: McFarland, 1994), 36–47; "Chicago Defender Honor Roll of 1946," *Chicago Defender,* January 4, 1947, 1; "State Doctors Endorse Mound Bayou for Negro Veterans Hospital," *Jackson Advocate*, May 4, 1946, 1; and Petition to Theodore G. Bilbo, Thomas L. Bailey, et al., May 22, 1945, Folder 18, Box 865, Theodore G. Bilbo Papers, McCain Library and Archives, University of Southern Mississippi, Hattiesburg, Miss. [hereafter, Bilbo Papers]. Greene asserted that the hospital "will hasten, rather than delay the removal of Jim Crow from the American scene" ("Something about President Truman and the Hospital for Negro Veterans at Mound Bayou, Mississippi," *Jackson Advocate*, March 29, 1947, 4.)

24. Dittmer, *Local People*, 15–18.

25. "Local and Personals," *Taborian Star,* July–August, 1945, 5; Will Whittington to Howard, September 27, 1945, Correspondence, Folder 2, Box 188, William L. Dawson Papers, Moorland-Springarn Collection, Howard University, Washington, D.C. [hereafter, Dawson Papers]; and Walter Sillers Jr. to John E. Rankin, June 8, 1945, Folder 18, Box 50, Walter Sillers

Jr. Papers, Charles W. Capps Jr. Archives and Museum, Delta State University, Cleveland, Miss. [hereafter, Sillers Papers].

26. Howard to Rankin, March 30, 1946, Folder 8, Box 50, Sillers Papers; and Kenneth W. Vickers, "John Rankin: Democrat and Demagogue" (MA thesis, Mississippi State University, 1993), 25–30, 42, 86, 104.

27. A. Wigfall Green, *The Man Bilbo* (Baton Rouge: Louisiana State University Press, 1963), 100–102; "Drive to Send Bilbo Back to Dixie," *Chicago Defender,* August 11, 1945, 5; "Bilbo Blames Defender for Foes in Home State," *Chicago Defender,* September 1, 1945, 1; and Gerald Horne, *Communist Front? The Civil Rights Congress, 1946–1956* (London: Associated University Presses, 1988), 56.

28. "The All-Negro Veterans Hospital," *Jackson Advocate,* March 23, 1946, 8; Rankin to Sillers, June 7, 1945, Sillers to Rankin, June 8, 1945—both in Folder 18, Box 50, Sillers Papers; and Howard to Bilbo, June 6, 1945, Bilbo to Howard, June 7, 1945—both in Folder 2, Box 1129, Bilbo Papers.

29. Jesse O. Dedmon Jr. to William L. Dawson, October 12, 1945, Folder 2, Box 188, Dawson Papers; *Jackson Advocate,* April 12, 1947, 1; "Is Jim Crow the Only Way?" *Chicago Defender,* December 22, 1945, 12; and "Protest Vets' Mound Bayou Hospital," *Chicago Defender,* March 29, 1947, 1, 4.

30. Dedmon to Dawson, October 12, 1945; "General Says He'll Follow 'Social Customs,'" *Chicago Defender,* December 15, 1945, 1; and "Bradley Admits Vet Agency Respects Dixie States' Rights," *Chicago Defender,* January 12, 1946, 1.

31. Whittington to Howard, September 29, 1945, Bilbo to Howard, September 9, 1945—both in Folder 2, Box 1129, Bilbo Papers; and Sillers to Rankin, June 18, 1945, Folder 18, Box 50, Sillers Papers.

32. Jimmie Pierce to Bilbo, February 22, 1946, Folder 1, Box 912, Bilbo Papers; "The All-Negro Veterans Hospital," 8; J. H. Brent to Bilbo, February 26, 1946, Folder 12, Box 912, Bilbo Papers; and Bilbo to J. H. Brent, March 2, 1946, Folder 12, Box 913, Bilbo Papers. Howard complained that local whites "didn't mind having German prisoners working almost in their front yards, but would be afraid of American Negro soldiers—invalid soldiers" (Carter, "He's Doing Something," 69).

33. Charles Pope Smith, "Theodore G. Bilbo's Senatorial Career: The Final Years, 1941–1947" (PhD diss., University of Southern Mississippi, 1983), 175–76.

34. Howard to Bilbo, August 11, 1945, Folder 2, Box 1129, Bilbo Papers.

35. Bilbo to Omar Bradley, March 15, 1946, Folder 3, Box 916, Bilbo to Bradley, March 21, 1946, Folder 2, Box 1129, Bilbo to Howard, March 21, 1946, Folder 2, Box 1129—all in Bilbo Papers.

36. "Medics Rap Jim Crow in Vet Hospitals," *Chicago Defender,* March 20, 1946, 9. The John E. Rankin papers (at the Modern Political Archives, Archives and Special Collections, University of Mississippi, Jackson) are closed for the foreseeable future at the request of the family.

37. Howard to Dawson, March 20, 1946, Benjamin A. Green to Dawson, March 20, 1946—both in Folder 2, Box, 188, Dawson Papers; and M. A. Jones to Louis B. Nichols, memorandum, September 26, 1955, Howard FBI file, Washington, D.C.

38. Howard to Barnett, November 10, 1945, March 20, 1946, Folder 7, Box 371, Barnett Papers.

39. Barnett to Howard, March 23, 1946, Barnett to Howard, April 20, 1946, Howard to Barnett, April 29, 1946, Folder 7, Box 371, Barnett Papers; "National Medical Association against Policy," *Memphis World*, October 5, 1945, 5; and "NMA Items of Interest," *Journal of the National Medical Association* 38 (July 1946), 148–49.

40. "Mound Bayou Gets Veterans Hospital," *Jackson Advocate*, March 22, 1947, 1; "Something about President Truman," *Jackson Advocate*; "Protest Jim Crow Vets Hospital in Mound Bayou," 4; and "Vet Hospital for Md. Bayou," *Memphis World*, March 25, 1947, 6.

41. "We Your Committee, James Dobbins, Walter Wright, etc.," January 1, 1947, Folder 16, Box 64, K. Smith Papers; "Knights and Daughters of Tabor Face Serious Division over Ouster of Famed Surgeon," *Jackson Advocate*, February 1, 1947, 1; and E. Boyd interview, July 19, 1999; and James Dobbins, Joe Turner, Walter Wright, W. H. Johnigan, W. M. Carter, and Joseph Jude, "Notice: P. M. Smith Must Go," October 1947, January 1, 1947, Folder 16, Box 64, Kelly Smith Papers.

42. "Some Hospital Roles, Rules and Regulations," *Taborian Star*, February 1943, 1; untitled written account of Taborian Hospital by pro–P. M. Smith faction, ca. 1947, Folder 6, Box 65, Kelly Smith Papers.

43. "Knights and Daughters of Tabor Face Serious Division," 1; "The Taborian Hospital Operating to Fullest Capacity," *Jackson Advocate*, February 8, 1947, 1.

44. "Sir Robert L. Drew Writes," *Taborian Star*, November 1941, n.p.; and address by Sir Walter H. Fisher, March 23, 1947, Walter H. Fisher, et al. to Presider, January 14, 1947, Folder 16, Box 64, Kelly Smith Papers.

45. Untitled written account of Taborian Hospital by pro–P. M. Smith faction, ca. 1947, Folder, 6, Box 65, Kelly Smith Papers; "Taborian Hospital Operating to Fullest Capacity," *Jackson Advocate*; and W. H. Faulkner to Mississippi Board of Health, January 13, 1942, Edward L. Turner to Felix J. Underwood, January 13, 1942, J. E. Sutherland M.D. to Underwood, January 14, 1942, "Dr. T. R. M. Howard" folder, Mississippi State Board of Medical Examiners, Archives and Library Division, Mississippi Department of Archives and History, Jackson.

46. "A Warning to the Knights and Daughters of Tabor," *Jackson Advocate*, February 8, 1947, 4.

47. "Dr. Howard Heading New Organization," *Jackson Advocate*, November 15, 1947, 1.

48. "Swift Transition Period," *Jackson Advocate*; "Dr. Howard Heading New Organization," *Jackson Advocate*; "Elks State Convention to Open in Greenwood Sunday," *Jackson Advocate*, June 5, 1948, 1.

49. Walter H. Fisher to Dear Friend, November 20, 1947, Constitution of United Order of Friendship of America Incorporated, 1947, "Magnolia Mutual Life Insurance Company" folder, Mississippi Department of Insurance, Jackson; "Dr. Howard Heading New Organization," *Jackson Advocate*; and "Predict Hot Time at State Baptist Convention," *Jackson Advocate*, July 1, 1950, 1–2.

50. "Dr. Howard Heading New Organization," *Jackson Advocate*; J. W. Wright and Walter H. Fisher to Friendship Leader, April 23, 1948, "Magnolia Mutual Life Insurance Company"

folder, Mississippi Department of Insurance, Jackson; and Annyce Campbell, interview by authors, October 17, 1995.

51. Asa Yancey, interview by authors, December 14, 1995; Charles S. Snow to J. L. White, January 9, 1948, Mississippi Department of Insurance, Jackson; Sillers to White, April 23, 1948, "The Knights and Daughters of Tabor" folder, Mississippi Department of Insurance, Jackson; Campbell interview, October 17, 1995; and W. B. Alexander to Bilbo, March 6, 1946, Folder 7, Box 914, Bilbo Papers.

52. T. R. M. Howard, Radio Message, Sunday, September 26, 1948, "Magnolia Mutual Life Insurance Company" folder, Mississippi Department of Insurance, Jackson.

53. J. W. Wright and Walter H. Fisher to Friendship Leader, April 23, 1948, T. R. M. Howard, Radio Message, Sunday, September 26, 1948, Constitution of United Order of Friendship Incorporated, 1947, "Magnolia Mutual Life Insurance Company" folder, Mississippi Department of Insurance, Jackson; "Former Californian Reviews Life in All-Negro Mississippi Town, Mound Bayou," *Los Angeles Tribune*, January 20 [1951?], T. R. M. Howard, Alumni Files, Loma Linda University; Beito, *From Mutual Aid to the Welfare State*, 188, 192–95; and Campbell interview, October 17, 1995.

54. E. Boyd interview, October 27, 1995.

55. "State Hospital among 24 Proposed Units Canceled by Vet Administration," *Jackson Advocate*, January 29, 1949, 1. Senator John Stennis (who succeeded Bilbo when he died in 1947) and Senator James Eastland tried to get the cancellation reversed but to no avail (U.S. Congress, U.S. Senate, Subcommittee of the Committee on Labor and Public Welfare, *Curtailment of the Veterans' Hospital Construction Program*, Part 1, March 10–19, 1949 [Washington, D.C. GPO, 1949], 430–33).

56. "Leader in His Field," *Chicago Defender*, October 11, 1947, August 28, 1948, 8; Capparell, *Real Pepsi Challenge*, 113–16; and Cohn, *Where I Was Born and Raised*, 270–71, 324–25.

57. E. Boyd interviews, October 27, 1995, and September 20, 2003; Maurice L. Sisson, interview by authors, October 22, 1999; and Ed Kossman Jr., personal communication.

58. E. Boyd interview, July 19, 1999.

59. Jere B. Nash to Jim Hand, April 10, 1950, Correspondence 1950 folder: M, Carter Papers.

60. Howard to Nash, April 12, 1950, Correspondence 1950 folder: M, Carter Papers.

61. Howard to Nash, April 12, 1950, Nash to Howard, April 19, 1950, Correspondence 1950 folder: N, Carter Papers.

62. *Helen Howard v. Theodore R. M. Howard*, Complaint for Divorce, October 5, 1973, Circuit Court of Cook County, Illinois, Divorce Division, Clerk of the Circuit Court of Cook County, Archives Department, Chicago, Ill.; Crowes interview, April 25, 2000; and Singleton interview, December 5, 2002.

63. E. Boyd interview, July 21, 2000; and Morgan interview, March 31, 2000.

64. Doris L. Zollar, interview by authors, April 17, 2001; and Jewel Gentry, "Bluff City Society," *Memphis World*, December 24, 1948, 3.

65. V. Harris [Wilson] interview, November 6, 2000; and Morgan interview, March 31, 2000.

66. Gentry, "Memphis Bluff Society," *Memphis World*, December 20, 1946, 4; Gentry, "Memphis Society," *Memphis World*, October 17, 1947, 3; Gentry, "Bluff City Society," *Mem-*

phis World, December 10, 1948, 3; "Annual Scout Meeting Tonight," *Memphis World,* December 17, 1948, 2; E. Boyd interview, July 19, 1999; and Matthew Havard, interview by authors, June 10, 2000.

67. Gentry, "Memphis Society," *Memphis World,* December 20, 1946, 4; Gentry, "Memphis Society," *Memphis World,* October 17, 1947, 3; Gentry, "Bluff City Society," *Memphis World,* December 10, 1948, 3; "Annual Scout Meeting Tonight, Dr. Theodore Howard Is Speaker," *Memphis World,* December 17, 1948, 2; "Adds Charm and New Social Life to All-Colored Town," *Memphis World,* April 8, 1942, 2; Gentry, "Bluff City Society," *Memphis World,* November 3, 1951, 3; and Tucker, *Lieutenant Lee of Beale Street,* 134.

68. "Medic Gives $40,000 for Hospital in Mound Bayou," March 22, 1950, Folder 1, Box 372, Barnett Papers; and Howard to Carter, March 12, 1950, Correspondence 1950 folder: H (January–March), Box 5, Carter Papers.

69. S. M. Harvey, "Son Born to Mrs. H. H. Humes during Funeral Services for Noted Husband," *Mississippi Enterprise,* January 11, 1958, 1–2.

70. Harvey, "Son Born to Mrs. H. H. Humes," *Mississippi Enterprise;* "Howard Sues Delta Leader for $50,000," *Jackson Advocate,* February 8, 1947, 1; "Predict Hot Time at State Baptist Convention at Clarksdale," *Jackson Advocate,* July 1, 1950, 1; and Julius E. Thompson, *The Black Press in Mississippi, 1865–1985* (Gainesville: University Press of Florida, 1993), 18–19.

71. "Leland Negro Citizens Invite Whites to Join in Organizing Better Citizenship Group," *Jackson Advocate,* June 4, 1949; and Payne, *I've Got the Light of Freedom,* 21–23.

72. "Predict Hot Time at State Baptist Convention at Clarksdale," *Jackson Advocate,* July 22, 1950, 1; "State Baptist Convention Ends on a Note of Harmony and Cooperation As Hume Is Re-elected President," *Jackson Advocate,* July 22, 1950, 1; and Yancey, telephone interview, December 14, 1995. Howard brought Dorothy B. Ferebee, the president of the National Council of Negro Women, to be the UOFA's featured speaker for 1950. Ferebee had headed the Alpha Kappa Alpha Health Project until it was disbanded in 1942. The two praised each other in their speeches. In a much later interview, however, Ida L. Jackson, the president of Alpha Kappa Alpha, complained that in 1942 Howard had not cooperated with the Health Project because he feared it would undermine his private practice (Gentry, "Bluff City Society," *Memphis World,* December 1, 1950, 3; "United Order of Friendship in 3rd Annual Convention," *Jackson Advocate,* December 9, 1950, 1; and Susan L. Smith, *Sick and Tired of Being Sick and Tired: Black Women's Health Activism in America, 1890–1950* [Philadelphia: University of Pennsylvania Press, 1995], 160).

Chapter 4: A "Modern 'Moses'" for Civil Rights in Mississippi

1. Payne, *I've Got the Light of Freedom,* 17; Cobb, *Most Southern Place,* 204–5; and Cohn, *Where I Was Born and Raised,* 324–25.

2. Payne, *I've Got the Light of Freedom,* 13–17, 20, 27.

3. Dittmer, *Local People,* 34.

4. Adam Nossiter, *Of Long Memory: Mississippi and the Murder of Medgar Evers* (Reading, Mass.: Addison-Wesley, 1994), 40; Lewis, "Negro Voter in Mississippi," 334–35; Dittmer, *Local People,* 28; Payne, *I've Got the Light of Freedom,* 24–25; and Mississippi Regional Council of

Negro Leadership, *Prospectus of the First Annual Meeting of the Mississippi Regional Council of Negro Leadership* (Mound Bayou, Miss.: n.p., 1952), 11, copy in author's possession.

5. Aaron Henry with Constance Curry, *Aaron Henry: The Fire Ever Burning* (Jackson: University Press of Mississippi, 2000), 80; "Howard Stresses Pattern of Partnership for Races," *Memphis World,* November 23, 1951, 3; "Mississippi Civic Leader Urges Better Deal . . .," *Tri-State Defender* (Memphis), December 1, 1951, 1–2; and "United Friendship Order Holds Conclave," *Tri-State Defender,* December 8, 1951, 3.

6. "Mississippi Civic Leader Urges Better Deal . . .," *Tri-State Defender;* "Dr. Howard Calls for 'Equal Partnership' for Negroes in Solving Racial Problems," *Mississippi Enterprise* (Jackson), November 24, 1951, 1; and Mississippi Regional Council of Negro Leadership, *Prospectus,* 7.

7. "Dr. Howard Proposes a Delta Negro Council," *Tri-State Defender,* December 15, 1951, 6; and "Fresh Reassurance," *Memphis Commercial Appeal,* December 19, 1951, 6.

8. Howard to Maury S. Knowlton, December 17, 1951, Howard et al. to leader, December 12, 1951, December 17, 1951—all in Folder 1, Box 30, Sillers Papers; and Mississippi Regional Council of Negro Leadership, *Prospectus,* 7–8. On the Delta Council, see Cobb, *Most Southern Place,* 201–6.

9. "Dr. Howard Calls for 'Equal Partnership,'" *Mississippi Enterprise;* Knowlton to Howard, December 17, 1951, and Howard to Knowlton, December 19, 1951—both in Folder 1, Box 30, Sillers Papers.

10. Howard to Knowlton, December 19, 1951, Folder 1, Box 30, Sillers Papers; Statement of Delta Council with Reference to the Proposed Negro Organization, Cleveland, Mississippi, December 28, 1951, Folder 1, Box 30, Sillers Papers; and "Delta Council Denies Affiliation with New Negro Organization," *Clarksdale (Mississippi) Press Register,* January 3, 1952, 1.

11. Henry, *Aaron Henry,* 80; and Mississippi Regional Council of Negro Leadership, *Prospectus,* 8, 16. Henry had first heard of Howard in 1946 after reading Hodding Carter's article in the *Saturday Evening Post:* "When we did meet, I told Dr. Howard how much I admired him, that we were fortunate to have a man like him in our community, and that I would like to help promote his ideas. A close friendship developed from our meeting" (Henry, *Aaron Henry,* 79).

12. Mississippi Regional Council of Negro Leadership, *Prospectus,* 10, 16–17; Henry, *Aaron Henry,* 81; and "Equalization Plan Outlined," *Clarksdale Press Register,* October 14, 1953, 1, 6.

13. Mississippi Regional Council of Negro Leadership, *Prospectus,* 13–14.

14. Mississippi Regional Council of Negro Leadership, *Prospectus,* 15; and T. R. M. Howard, "Dignity of Equality," *Jackson Advocate,* February 7, 1953, 6.

15. "Welcome to Mound Bayou," *Jackson Advocate,* February 7, 1953, 5.

16. Mississippi Regional Council of Negro Leadership, *Prospectus,* 12, 14; and *Tri-State Defender,* December 1, 1951. For more on this argumentative approach, see Mary L. Dudziak, *Cold War Civil Rights: Race and Image of American Democracy* (Princeton: Princeton University Press, 2000).

17. Mississippi Regional Council of Negro Leadership, *Prospectus,* 15.

18. "Dr. Howard Calls for 'Equal Partnership,'" *Mississippi Enterprise;* "Mississippi Civic Leader Urges Better Deal . . .," *Tri-State Defender;* and *Jet* 1 (December 6, 1951), 9.

19. "United Order of Friendship Holds Confab," *Tri-State Defender,* November 17, 1951, 1–2; Mississippi Council of Negro Leadership, *Prospectus,* 4–6; and Jerry Thornbery, "Amzie Moore and His Civil Rights Allies, 1951–1961," paper presented at the Annual Meeting of the Southern Historical Association, November 12, 1993 (copy in the author's possession).

20. "Magnolia Mutual Life Insurance Company," *Jackson Advocate,* May 17, 1952, 7; Mississippi, Insurance Department, *Biennial Report,* March 1, 1951, to February 29, 1952, 154, 245; Mississippi, Insurance Department, *Annual Report,* March 1, 1953, to February 29, 1954, 168; Mississippi Regional Council of Negro Leadership, *Prospectus,* 4–6; Howard to Claude Barnett, April 26, 1954, Folder 7, Box 371, Barnett Papers; Maurice L. Sisson to Board Member, February 12, 1952, Correspondence, 1955–56, Folder 2, Box 1, Moore Papers, Wisconsin Historical Society, Madison; Thornbery, "Amzie Moore," 4; Henry, *Aaron Henry,* 79; and Nossiter, *Of Long Memory,* 38.

21. M. Evers, *For Us, the Living,* 72–77; Nossiter, *Of Long Memory,* 38; Henry, *Aaron Henry,* 80; and C. Evers and Szanton, *Have No Fear,* 71.

22. Mississippi Regional Council of Negro Leadership, *Prospectus,* 4–6, 16; and Henry, *Aaron Henry,* 80–82.

23. Mississippi Regional Council of Negro Leadership, *Prospectus,* 4–6; "Elks State Convention to Open in Greenwood Sunday," *Jackson Advocate,* June 5, 1948, 1; Sewell and Dwight, *Mississippi Black History Makers,* 245; and Beito, *From Mutual Aid to the Welfare State,* 181–82.

24. Mississippi Regional Council of Negro Leadership, *Prospectus,* 4–6; and Dudley, interview by authors.

25. Payne, *I've Got the Light of Freedom,* 191–92.

26. Charles Evers, interview by authors, September 2, 1999; and Dittmer, *Local People,* 30.

27. Dittmer, *Local People,* 32–33; Lewis, "Negro Voter in Mississippi," 348; and "Mississippi Faces Economic War," *Tri-State Defender.*

28. Henry, *Aaron Henry,* 80.

29. Dittmer, *Local People,* 25–26, 28; Payne, *I've Got the Light of Freedom,* 57; "State Negro Democrats Set Labor Day Meeting Here," *Jackson Advocate,* August 16, 1952, 1; Lewis, "Negro Voter in Mississippi," 348; and "Ask Negro Policemen Be Appointed," *Clarksdale Press Register,* January 7, 1955, 1.

30. Mississippi Regional Council of Negro Leadership, *Prospectus,* 4–6; Henry, *Aaron Henry,* 73; Clarice T. Campbell and Oscar Allan Rogers Jr., *Mississippi: The View from Tougaloo* (Jackson: University Press of Mississippi, 1979), 185–87; Dittmer, *Local People,* 26, 29–32, 39–42, 48, 53; and Thornbery, "Amzie Moore," 6.

31. Thompson, *Percy Greene and the Jackson Advocate,* 32–59; Dittmer, *Local People,* 28; "Chicago Defender Honor Roll of 1946," *Chicago Defender;* "Organize State Democratic Body," *Memphis World,* March 15, 1949, 1; and Henry, *Aaron Henry,* 83.

32. "Warning to the Knights and Daughters of Tabor," *Jackson Advocate;* "Meet of State Regional Council of Negro Leadership Praised," *Jackson Advocate,* May 10, 1952, 1; and "Set Record for 'Y' Observance Here Sunday," *Jackson Advocate,* January 24, 1953, 1.

33. "Mound Bayou Speaker Set," *Clarksdale Press Register,* April 8, 1952, 6; "Mound Bayou Sees Largest Crowd in Its History, Honors Negro Congressman," *Jackson Advocate,* May 3, 1952, 1; and "Vote for Lawmakers Who Defend Rights," *Tri-State Defender,* May 10, 1952, 1–2, 9. Dawson had campaigned extensively in the South for the Truman campaign in 1948 (William

J. Grimshaw, *Bitter Fruit: Black Politics and the Chicago Machine, 1931–1991* [Chicago: University of Chicago Press, 1992], 81).

34. "1st Annual Meeting Council of Negro Leaders," *Memphis World,* May 6, 1952, 1; Gentry, "Bluff City Society," *Memphis World,* May 6, 1952, 3; "Vote for Lawmakers Who Defend Rights," *Tri-State Defender;* and "Don't Get Mad . . . Get Smart," *Tri-State Defender,* May 17, 1952, 4.

35. M. Evers, *For Us, the Living,* 88; Kay Mills, *This Little Light of Mine: The Life of Fannie Lou Hamer* (New York: Dutton, 1993), 40–41; Payne, *I've Got the Light of Freedom,* 154; and C. Evers, interview by authors, September 2, 1999.

36. "State Negro Democrats," *Jackson Advocate;* "Four Miss. Demo Delegates Give Views at Confab," *Tri-State Defender,* August 2, 1952, 1, 2; and Gentry, "Bluff City Society," *Memphis World,* October 7, 1952, 3.

37. M. Evers, *For Us, the Living,* 76, 88–90, 94; "Dr. Howard Addresses Evers Memorial," *Chicago Defender,* June 14, 1965, 4; Irnez Applin, interview by authors, July 20, 2005; and Henry, *Aaron Henry,* 80.

38. M. Evers, *For Us, the Living,* 76–79, 85–88; and Henry, *Aaron Henry,* 80–81, 85–86. According to Charles Evers, his brother Medgar first proposed the boycott of service stations; Henry credits Howard (C. Evers interview, September 2, 1999; and Henry, *Aaron Henry,* 81). Whatever the truth, long before Howard had met Evers, he had highlighted the lack of restrooms as illustrative of "separate but never equal." Mississippi Regional Council of Negro Leadership, *Prospectus,* 13.

39. Mississippi Regional Council of Negro Leadership, *Prospectus,* 13; Henry, *Aaron Henry,* 81; Wheaton interview, June 14, 2000; and C. Evers interview, September 2, 1999.

40. "Four Miss. Demo Delegates Give Views at Confab," *Tri-State Defender;* "State Leadership Council Starts Campaign for Rest Rooms at Service Stations," *Jackson Advocate,* October 4, 1952, 1; Sisson interview, October 22, 1999; Charles Tisdale, interview by authors, January 2, 2001; Henry, *Aaron Henry,* 80–82; C. Evers interview, September 2, 1999; Annyce Campbell interview, March 3, 2000; E. Boyd interview, July 19, 1999; and Taylor Branch, *Parting the Waters: America in the King Years, 1954–63* (New York: Simon and Schuster, 1988), 144–47.

41. "Negro Leadership Council Protests Brutality of Highway Patrolmen in Conference with T. B. Birdsong," *Jackson Advocate,* October 4, 1952, 1; "Vows End of Miss. Police Brutality," *Chicago Defender,* October 11, 1952, 1; and Press Release: Brutality by Highway Patrolmen of Negroes in Mississippi to Cease, ca. October 1952, "Mississippi Pressures, Howard, T. R. M." folder, Box 422, Group 2, NAACP Papers.

42. Payne, *I've Got the Light of Freedom,* 59; "Four Miss. Demo Delegates," *Tri-State Defender;* Dittmer, *Local People,* 28, 70; and Henry, *Aaron Henry,* 81.

43. Civil rights rally featuring Eleanor Roosevelt and Autherine Lucy, May 24, 1956 [sound recording], Schomburg Center for Research in Black Culture, New York Public Library; and C. Evers and Szanton, *Have No Fear,* 65.

44. Sisson interview, October 22, 1999; Tisdale interview, January 2, 2001; and Wheaton interview, June 14, 2000.

45. Sisson interview, October 22, 1999; Tisdale interview, January 2, 2001; and Wheaton interview, June 14, 2000.

46. Dittmer, *Local People,* 32–33; and memorandum, Gloster Current to Walter White, September 30, 1952, Group II, Box 381, NAACP Papers; memorandum, Ruby Hurley to Walter White, October 8, 1952, Group II, Box 381, NAACP Papers; "The Accomplishments and Objectives of the Regional Council of Negro Leadership," ca. 1954, "Mississippi Pressures, Reports and Statements 1954–55" folder, Box 422, Group 2, NAACP Papers; Mississippi Regional Council of Negro Leadership, *Prospectus,* 6; and Payne, *I've Got the Light of Freedom,* 41–42.

47. Dittmer, *Local People,* 32–34, 49; and Payne, *I've Got the Light of Freedom,* 61. "That Moore and other NAACP leaders felt a need for the RCNL suggests they found the program of the NAACP wanting in some respects" (Payne, *I've Got the Light of Freedom,* 32).

48. Dittmer, *Local People,* 32–33.

49. Juliet E. K. Walker, *The History of Black Business in America: Capitalism, Race, Entrepreneurship* (New York: Macmillan Library Reference, 1998), 184, 240–41; "53rd Annual Meet Opens at Waluhaje," *Memphis World,* November 6, 1953, 1; "Business League's Board Holds Cincinnati Session," *Memphis World,* May 10, 1955, 5; "Business League Meets in Atlanta, T. R. M. Howard in Keynote Address," *Chicago Defender,* November 7, 1953, 2; and "Blasts False Limits of 'Negro Business,'" *Chicago Defender,* November 21, 1953, 2.

50. "People Are Talking About," *Jet* 7 (March 24, 1955), 46; Wheaton interview, June 14, 2000; Gentry, "Bluff City Society," *Memphis World,* May 8, 1953, 3; and M. Evers, *For Us, the Living,* 90.

51. Gentry, "Bluff City Society," *Memphis World,* November 21, 1952; Gentry, "Bluff City Society," *Memphis World,* June 4, 1954, 3; "Links Honor Miss Daisy Lampkins," *Memphis World,* February 25, 1955, 1; and Marjorie H. Parker, *A History of the Links Incorporated* (Washington, D.C.: The Links, 1992), 7, 173.

52. Moore interview, April 4, 2001; Morgan interview, March 31, 2000; Wheaton interview, June 14, 2000; and Hugh Pearson, *Under the Knife: How a Wealthy Negro Surgeon Wielded Power in the Jim Crow South* (New York: Free Press, 2000), 190, 211; *Mississippi State Board of Health v. Johnson,* November 27, 1944, 197 Mississippi, 417; and *Lackey v. State of Mississippi,* June 11, 1951, 211 Mississippi 892.

53. Dittmer, *Local People,* 36; "White Sees Boosted Sales Tax As State Starts Equalization Plan," *Clarksdale Press Register,* November 21, 1952, 1; "Miss. Governor to Equalize Schools," *Tri-State Defender,* February 21, 1953, 1–2; and "Welcome to Mound Bayou Taborian Hospital Celebration," *Jackson Advocate,* February 7, 1953, 2.

54. Howard, "Dignity of Equality," *Jackson Advocate.*

55. "State Regional Council of Negro Leadership Holds Successful 2nd Annual Meeting," *Jackson Advocate,* May 9, 1953, 1, 8; Archibald J. Carey Jr. to T. R. M. and Helen Howard, May 4, 1953, Folder 103, Box 15, Archibald J. Carey Jr. Papers, Chicago Historical Society [hereafter, Carey Papers]. Carey had declared in this speech, for example, "From every mountain side, let freedom ring. Not only from the Green Mountains and the White Mountains of Vermont and New Hampshire; not only from the Catskills of New York; but from the Ozarks of Arkansas, from the Stone Mountain in Georgia, from the Great Smokies of Tennessee and from the Blue Ridge Mountains of Virginia—Not only for the minorities of the United States, but for the persecuted of Europe, for the rejected of Asia, for the disfranchised of South Africa and for the disinherited of all the earth—may the Republican Party, under God, from every

mountain side, *let freedom ring.*" "Address of Honorable Archibald J. Carey Jr., Member of the Chicago City Council, to the Republican National Convention, Chicago, Illinois, Tuesday morning, July 8, 1952," Folder 81, Box 81, Carey Papers. Also see Dickerson, "Ringing the Bell of Freedom," 93–96.

56. Charles M. Hills, "Revenue Major Problem in School Equalization," *Clarkdale Press Register,* November 12, 1953, 10; "White Sees Boosted Sales Tax," *Clarksdale Press Register; Jackson Clarion-Ledger,* December 24, 1953, 1; and *Jackson Clarion-Ledger,* December 25, 1953, 1.

57. "Negroes Reveal Opposition to School Bonds," *Clarksdale Press Register,* November 3, 1953, 1–2; "Negroes to Follow Lead of U. S. Supreme Court," *Clarksdale Press Register,* November 4, 1953, 1; Dittmer, *Local People,* 53; "Dr. Howard Lashes Out at 'Spineless' Leaders," *Memphis World,* November 20, 1953, 1; and "Dr. Howard Rejects Equalization Plan As Too Expensive," *Delta Democrat Times* (Greenville), November 16, 1953.

58. "Dr. Howard Rejects Equalization Plan," *Delta Democrat Times;* Charles M. Hills, "Legislative News Digest," *Clarksdale Press Register,* November 6, 1953, 4; "Miss. Editor Takes Stand in Favor of Bias," *Tri-State Defender,* December 27, 1952, 1; "NAACP Conference Opens at Indianola," *Jackson Clarion-Ledger,* November 7, 1953, 1; "Negro Citizens Praise Governor's Stand," *Jackson Advocate,* November 7, 1953, 1; and "The Regional Council of Negro Leadership and the Mississippi Negro," *Jackson Advocate,* May 15, 1954, 4.

59. Henry, *Aaron Henry,* 83; and "Regional Council of Negro Leadership," *Jackson Advocate.*

60. Payne, *I've Got the Light of Freedom,* 50–51, 56; M. Evers, *For Us, the Living,* 98, 102; "Negro Hopes to Enroll at Ole Miss," *Clarksdale Press Register,* January 22, 1954, 1; "Officers of the Mississippi State Conference of NAACP Branches, January 1, 1954," NAACP 1940–1955, Branch File, Geographical File, Mississippi State Conference of Branches, 1954–55, Group II, C98, NAACP Papers.

61. Mississippi Regional Council of Negro Leadership, *Program of the Third Annual Meeting,* Friday, May 7, 1954, Moore Papers; "NAACP Council Tells Mound Bayou, Bias Is on Way Out," *Memphis World,* May 11, 1954, 1; "Thurgood Marshall Says U.S. Has Already Lost World Leadership Because of Segregation Laws," *Jackson Advocate,* May 15, 1954, 8; "People, Places and Things," *Tri-State Defender,* May 15, 1954, 6; and "Two State Bands to Play at Regional Meet, May 7th in Mound Bayou, Miss.," *Mississippi Enterprise,* April 17, 1954.

62. "Regional Council of Negro Leadership," *Jackson Advocate.*

63. "Predict Record Crowd for Mound Bayou," *Jackson Advocate,* May 1, 1954, 1; *Jackson Advocate,* May 15, 1954, 8; "Negro Group Plans Fund to Increase Registered Voters," *Delta Democrat Times,* April 27, 1954, 1; "Mississippians Might Sue Sheriffs, Clerks," *Tri-State Defender,* May 8, 1954; "'We'll Fight to Finish Line'—Marshall," *Tri-State Defender,* May 15, 1954, 1; and "Charges Officers Refused to Accept Poll Tax Payments," *Memphis World,* April 20, 1954, 1.

64. Raymond F. Tisby, "NAACP Counsel Tells Mound Bayou Bias Is on Way Out," *Memphis World,* May 11, 1954, 1; "'We'll Fight Bias to Finish Line'—Marshall," *Tri-State Defender;* and Nat D. Williams, "Six Making Political History," *Tri-State Defender,* July 17, 1954, 1; and Benjamin L. Hooks, telephone interview, June 15, 2000.

Chapter 5: "The Most Hated, and the Best Loved, Man in Mississippi"

1. "Jackson Parents Take News of Segregation Very Calmly," *Jackson Clarion-Ledger,* May 18, 1954, 16; Henry, *Aaron Henry,* 86–87; and "Continued Segregation Expected in This Area," *Clarksdale Press Register,* May 18, 1954, 1.

2. "The Court's Decision," *Delta Democrat Times,* May 18, 1954, 4; and "Mississippi Editors Differ on Court Decision," *Clarksdale Press Register,* May 20, 1954, 11; and Susan Weill, *In a Madhouse's Din: Civil Rights Coverage by Mississippi's Daily Press* (Westport, Conn.: Praeger, 2002), 63.

3. Weill, *In a Madhouse's Din,* 6–7; and Fred Sullens, "Bloodstains on the Marble Steps," *Jackson Daily News,* May 18, 1954, 1.

4. "White Delays Statement," *Clarksdale Press Register,* May 17, 1954, 1; "Mississippi," *Southern School News* 1 (September 3, 1954), 8; "State Stunned," *Jackson Clarion-Ledger,* May 18, 1954, 1; "Mississippi and School Segregation Decision," *Jackson Advocate,* May 22, 1954, 4; and A. Maurice Mackel to Roy Wilkins, July 17, 1955, "Mississippi Pressures, Howard, T. R. M., 1954–55" folder, General Office File, Box 422, Group 2, NAACP Papers.

5. Henry, *Aaron Henry,* 87.

6. Sam Johnson, "Committee Is Seeking Support of Negroes in Maintaining Segregation," *Jackson Advocate,* July 10, 1954, 1; Dittmer, *Local People,* 38; "White Says Negro Group to Cooperate," *Clarksdale Press Register,* July 1, 1954, 1; "Governor Confers with Negro Leaders," *Jackson Clarion-Ledger,* July 1, 1954, 20; "Widespread Comment on Meeting with Governor," *Jackson Advocate,* July 10, 1954, 1, 6.

7. Dittmer, *Local People,* 38–39; Charles C. Bolton, *The Hardest Deal of All: The Battle over School Integration in Mississippi, 1870–1980* (Jackson: University of Mississippi, 2005), 62–65; Henry, *Aaron Henry,* 88–89; "Dr. T. R. M. Howard Lambasted in Attack by Rev. H. H. Humes," *Jackson Advocate,* January 22, 1955, 1, 6; "State Negro Group Says Gov. White Lies, Calls for Integration Now," *Delta Democrat Times,* July 26, 1954, 1; "Bi-Racial Board Urged by Negroes," *Jackson Clarion-Ledger,* July 26, 1954, 5; James H. White to Emmett J. Stringer, August 25, 1954, "Desegregation, Schools" folder, Branch Action—Mississippi, 1950–54, NAACP, 1940–54, General Office File, Box A227, Group 2, NAACP Papers; and "The NAACP Seeks Social Equality," *Jackson Daily News,* July 29, 1954, 1.

8. Henry, *Aaron Henry,* 89; Dittmer, *Local People,* 39; Bolton, *Hardest Deal of All,* 63; and "White Talks Schools with Negroes; To Relax 'Curtain,'" *Jackson Clarion-Ledger,* July 18, 1954, 4.

9. Bolton, *Hardest Deal of All,* 63–64; "Negroes Insist on Integration," *Jackson Clarion-Ledger,* July 31, 1954, 1, 3; Henry, *Aaron Henry,* 90; Statement Issued by Negro Leaders from Every Area of the State of Mississippi, July 30, 1954, Folder 3, Box 83, Sillers Papers; and Henry, *Aaron Henry,* 90.

10. T. R. M. Howard, speech at governor's conference, July 30, 1954, Folder 3, Box 83, Sillers Papers.

11. Howard, speech at governor's conference, July 30, 1954, Folder 3, Box 83, Sillers Papers; and Bolton, *Hardest Deal of All,* 66.

12. J. H. White, J. W. Jones, Percy Greene, speeches at governor's conference, July 30, 1954, Folder 3, Box 83, Sillers Papers.

13. H. H. Humes, speech at governor's conference, July 20, 1954, Folder 3, Box 83, Sillers Papers; and Henry, *Aaron Henry*, 90–91. Although the context was different, this was not the first time that Humes had used the same colorful imagery to describe the unequal conditions of black schools ("Rap Miss. Governor's 'Wait and See' Policy," *Chicago Defender*, February 23, 1952, 4).

14. "May Ask Authority to Abolish Public System of Schools," *Jackson Clarion-Ledger*, July 31, 1954, 1, 3; "Mississippi," *Southern School News;* and "Governor Stunned by Blount Refusal," *Memphis Commercial Appeal*, July 31, 1954.

15. Henry, *Aaron Henry*, 9; "Leaders Say 'No Retreat on Schools,'" *Tri-State Defender*, August 7, 1954, 1; "Jackson Negroes Share Desire for Public School Integration," *Jackson Clarion-Ledger*, August 2, 1954, 5; and "Mississippians Show Courage," *Memphis World*, August 6, 1954, 8.

16. Hodding Carter III, *The South Strikes Back* (Garden City, N.Y.: Doubleday, 1959), 26, 29; M. Evers, *For Us, the Living*, 109–11; Neil R. McMillen, *The Citizens' Councils: Organized Resistance to the Second Reconstruction, 1954–64* (Urbana: University of Illinois Press, 1971), 17–19; and Tom P. Brady, *Black Monday* (Winona, Miss.: Association of Citizens Councils, 1955), 63–65.

17. McMillen, *Citizens' Councils*, 16–19; Carter, *South Strikes Back*, 30–31; and Payne, *I've Got the Light of Freedom*, 56.

18. McMillen, *Citizens' Councils*, 28; "Mound Bayouans Applaude [*sic.*] Dr. Howard's Departure," *Jackson Advocate*, December 24, 1955, 2; Carter, *South Strikes Back*, 32–33; and "Citizens' Councils Enforce Segregation but Hope to Avoid Outbreaks of Violence," *Jackson Clarion-Ledger*, September 13, 1954, 1.

19. Percy Green, "Negroes Will Prefer Negro Schools," *Jackson Advocate*, August 7, 1954, 8.

20. White to Stringer, August 25, 1954, "Desegregation, Schools" folder, NAACP Papers.

21. "Dr. T. R. M. Howard Lambasted," *Jackson Advocate;* Bolton, *Hardest Deal of All*, 65–66; "Voluntary Segregation Hopes Fade As Negro Leaders Emphatically Reject Whole Idea," *Clarksdale Press Register*, July 31, 1954, 1, 5; and Dittmer, *Local People*, 44. Fred H. Miller of Mound Bayou was another prominent (though less publicly vocal) ally of Humes, White, and Greene (Mackel to Walter White, August 11, 1954, "Desegregation, Schools" folder, Branch Action—Mississippi, 1950–54, NAACP 1940–55, General Office File, Box A227, Group 2, NAACP Papers).

22. Dittmer, *Local People*, 44–46; Bolton, *Hardest Deal of All*, 73–75; and Payne, *I've Got the Light of Freedom*, 114.

23. "'Citizens Councils' to Use 'Persuasion, Pressure, Force' to Retain Segregation," *Clarksdale Press Register*, September 10, 1954, 1; "Citizens' Councils Enforce Segregation," *Jackson Clarion-Ledger;* "Citizens' Councils Opens State Office," *Jackson Clarion-Ledger*, October 21, 1954, 1; and "All Counties of State Asked to Form Citizens' Councils," *Jackson Clarion-Ledger*, October 24, 1954, 4.

24. "The Fight in Mississippi Will Be of Long Duration," *Jackson Clarion-Ledger*, October 31, 1954, 8.

25. Dittmer, *Local People,* 48; and Current to Wilkins, December 13, 1954, "Mississippi Pressures, Reports and Statements, 1954–55" folder, Box 424, Group 2, NAACP Papers.

26. David Brown, "There's a List in Belzoni," *Delta Democrat Times,* March 27, 1955, 1; "Miss. Whites Force Negro Grocer from Store," *Jet* 7 (March 24, 1955), 6; "How the South Is Organizing to Silence Negroes," *Jet* 7 (March 24, 1955), 11–12; Current to Wilkins, December 13, 1954, "Mississippi Pressures, Reports and Statements, 1954–55" folder, Box 424, Group 2, NAACP Papers; and Dittmer, *Local People,* 47. By 1956 T. V. Johnson had become active in the RCNL again (J. F. Redmon and G. R. Haughton to Martin Luther King Jr., March 14, 1956, Martin Luther King Jr. Papers Project, Cypress Hall, D-Wing, Stanford University, Stanford, Calif.).

27. Henry, *Aaron Henry,* 82; Lewis, "Negro Voter in Mississippi," 339–42; Payne, *I've Got the Light of Freedom,* 35; and Carter, *South Strikes Back,* 41–42, 45.

28. "Negro Leaders Don't Want to Integrate Now," *Delta Democrat Times,* September 27, 1954, 1; A. Maurice Mackel to Wilkins, September 27, 1954, and Stringer to Thurgood Marshall, October 7, 1954, both in "Desegregation, Schools" folder, Branch Action—Mississippi, 1950–54, NAACP 1940–55, General Office File, Box A227, Group 2, NAACP Papers; and "Dr. Howard Halts Drive for Integration," *Jackson Advocate,* September 18, 1954, 6.

29. Current to Wilkins, December 13, 1954, "Mississippi Pressures, Reports and Statements, 1954–55" folder, Box 424, Group 2, NAACP Papers; "Mississippi Faces Economic War," *Tri-State Defender,* October 9, 1954, 2; Bolton, *Hardest Deal of All,* 67–68; "Negro Leaders Don't Want to Integrate Now," *Delta Democrat Times;* and "Dr. Howard a Leader of His People," *Jackson Advocate,* October 2, 1954, 4.

30. "Negro Leaders Don't Want to Integrate Now," *Delta Democrat Times;* "Mississippi Faces Economic War," *Tri-State Defender;* and Current to Wilkins, December 13, 1954, "Mississippi Pressures, Reports and Statements 1954–55" folder, Box 424, Group 2, NAACP Papers.

31. Current to Wilkins, December 13, 1954, "Mississippi Pressures, Reports and Statements 1954–55" folder, Box 424, Group 2, NAACP Papers.

32. Ibid.

33. Ibid.; Wilkins to Howard, December 16, 1954, "Mississippi Pressures, Howard, T. R. M., 1954–55" folder, General Office File, Box 422, Group 2, NAACP Papers; "May Pull Million from Miss. Banks," *Chicago Defender,* January 15, 1955, 1–2; "Porters Add $10,000 to Freeze Fund," *Chicago Defender,* 1–2; "Mississippi Fund Now $100,000," *Chicago Defender,* February 12, 1955, 1–2; "Freeze Fund Hits $13,000," *Chicago Defender,* February 26, 1955, 12; "Mississippi Fund Now $100,000," *New York Age Defender,* February 12, 1955, 9; and M. Evers, *For Us, the Living,* 169. The increase coincided with a healthy spurt in Tri-State's assets from $2.0 million to $2.8 million from February to May 1955 ("Ticker Tape U.S.A.," *Jet* 8 [June 2, 1955], 9).

34. L. Alex Wilson, "May Pull Million from Miss. Banks," *Chicago Defender,* January 15, 1955; "More Anti-Freeze Boys," *Tri-State Defender,* February 19, 1955, 7; "NAACP Dixie 'War Chest' Swells past $100,000," *Jet* 7 (February 10, 1955), 7; "Despite Terror, Miss. Negroes Vow to Stay and Fight Racists," *Jet* 7 (April 21, 1951), 11.

35. Wilkins to Howard, January 19, February 11, 1955, "Mississippi Pressures, Howard, T. R. M., General Office File, 1954–55" folder, Box 422, Group 2, NAACP Papers; and Wilkins

to Richard J. Henry, December 23, 1955, "Mississippi Pressures, Financial Pressures, General Office File, Amzie Moore, Case of, 1955" folder, Box 422, Group 2, NAACP Papers.

36. Howard to Wilkins, April 15, 1955, "Mississippi Pressures, Howard, T. R. M., 1954–55, General Office File" folder, Box 422, Group 2, NAACP Papers; "Despite Terror, Miss. Negroes Vow to Stay and Fight Racists," *Jet.*

37. Current to Clarence Mitchell, February 9, 1955, "Mississippi Pressures, Howard, T. R. M., 1954–55, General Office File" folder, Box 422, Group 2, NAACP Papers; L. Alex Wilson, "Mississippi Reverses Its Stands," *Tri-State Defender,* April 16, 1955, 1–2; and "Southern Deep Freeze," *Say* 2 (May 12, 1955), 51, Mississippi Pressures, Howard, T. R. M., folder, 1954–55, General Office File, Box 422, Group 2, NAACP Papers.

38. Ruby Hurley to Roy Wilkins, April 8, 1955, "Mississippi Pressures, Reports and Statements, 1954–55" folder, Box 424, Group 2, NAACP Papers. For George S. Schuyler, a columnist for the *Pittsburgh Courier,* the inability to raise $500,000 testified to the failure of blacks to pull together, not to "any lack of Negro bank deposits in financial institutions across the county because the total must certainly be far in excess of a billion dollars. . . . We have overstressed abstract rights and underestimated basic economic realities. . . . the million Negroes in Mississippi by organizing the economic power they have, and the political power they could use, if they would, should have nothing to fear from any credit boycott" (*Pittsburgh Courier,* April 30, 1955, 6).

39. Current to Clarence Mitchell [enclosed transcript], February 9, 1955, "Mississippi Pressures, Howard, T. R. M., 1954–55, General Office File, 1940–55" folder, Box 422, Group 2, NAACP Papers.

40. Press Release: "Probe Mississippi Bias, Selective Service Urged," January 20, 1955, "Mississippi Pressures, Howard, T. R. M., 1954–55, General Office File" folder, Box 422, Group 2, NAACP Papers; "Probe Plan to Banish Dr. Howard," *Chicago Defender,* January 29, 1955, 1; Mitchell to Howard, January 26, 1955, "Branch File, Geographical File, Mississippi State Conference, 1954–55" folder, Box C98, Group 2, NAACP Papers; and Wilkins to Howard, February 11, 1955, "Mississippi Pressures, Howard, T. R. M., General Office File, 1954–55" folder, Box 422, Group 2, NAACP Papers.

41. "Selective Service Deny Spite Effort to Put Dr. T. R. M. Howard in Army," *Jackson Advocate,* January 29, 1955, 1, 5; and Wilkins to Howard, February 11, 1955, "Mississippi Pressures, Howard, T. R. M., General Office File, 1954–55" folder, Box 422, Group 2, NAACP Papers.

42. Howard to Wilkins, April 15, 1955, "Mississippi Pressures, Howard, T. R. M., 1954–55, General Office File" folder, Box 422, Group 2, NAACP Papers.

43. "Huge Los Angeles Crowd Protests Lynching of Till," *Labor Daily,* October 14, 1955, Program Department, Subject and Correspondence Files, 1955, South-Till Lynching, Folder 7, Box 369, United Packinghouse Workers of America Papers, Wisconsin Historical Society, Madison [hereafter, UPW Papers]; "He Rode Highways with Hidden Gun . . . Always Cocked," *Pittsburgh Courier,* September 1, 1956, NAACP Administration, 1959–1965, General Office File, Crime, Mississippi, 1956–1965, Box A91, Group 3; and C. Evers interview, September 2, 1999.

44. G. B. Swafford to J. P. Coleman, April 24, 1958, "T. R. M. Howard, Mississippi" folder, Sovereignty Commission Files, Mississippi Department of Archives and History, Jack-

son; Wheaton interview, June 14, 2000; E. Boyd interview, October 27, 1995; and C. Evers interview, September 2, 1999.

45. Robert J. Cottrol and Raymond T. Diamond, "The Second Amendment: Toward an Afro-Americanist Reconsideration," *Georgetown Law Journal* 80 (1990), 309; Clayton E. Cramer, "The Racist Roots of Gun Control," *Kansas Journal of Law and Public Policy* 4 (Winter 1995), 20–21; B. Bruce-Briggs, "The Great American Gun Control," *Public Interest* 45 (1976), 37, 50; and "The .22 Is Becoming a Criminals' Weapon," *Jackson Clarion-Ledger*, January 16, 1954, 6.

46. "Mississippi," *Southern School News.*

47. *Helen Boyd Howard v. Theodore R. M. Howard,* Complaint for Divorce, October 5, 1973, Divorce Division, Circuit Court of Cook County, Cook County Archives, Chicago; V. Harris [Wilson] interview, November 6, 2000; Barrett Boyd Howard, Certification of Birth Record, October 11, 1954, New Jersey State Department of Health, Estate of Theodore R. M. Howard, Deceased, August 9, 1976, No. 76 P 3743, Circuit Court of Cook County, Illinois, Probate Division, Chicago; "Mississippi's Most Controversial Negro," *Our World* 10 (June 1955), 31; and Howard, "Dignity of Equality," *Jackson Advocate;* Certification of Birth Record, October 11, 1954.

48. Wheaton interview, June 14, 2000; and Havard, telephone interview, June 10, 2000. Ammon Hennacy, a Christian anarchist and pacifist during the 1950s, used the term "one-man revolution" to characterize High's style of personal protest (Hennacy, *The One-Man Revolution in America [Salt Lake City, Utah: Ammon Hennacy, 1970]).*

49. Arrington W. High, Application for Social Security Account Number, July 1, 1943; "Arrington W. High Is No Longer with the Enterprise," *Mississippi Enterprise,* September 11, 1943, 1; Willie J. Miller, "Arrington High Does Not Represent the Mississippi Enterprise," *Mississippi Enterprise,* January 12, 1946, 2; and "Ticker Tape U.S.A.," *Jet* 8 (May 19, 1955), 9.

50. Arrington W. High, "Cast Down Your Bucket Where You Are," *Mississippi Enterprise,* January 23, 1943, 1; "Arrington W. High Is No Longer with the Enterprise," *Mississippi Enterprise;* "Arrington W. High Taken into Custody," *Mississippi Enterprise,* April 29, 1944, 1; Miller, "Arrington High Does Not Represent," *Mississippi Enterprise;* and "Blames NAACP for attempt on His Life," *Jackson Advocate,* August 21, 1943, 1.

51. Miller, "Arrington High Does Not Represent," *Mississippi Enterprise;* Havard interview, June 10, 2000; and "Eagle Eye Editor Dies in Chicago," *Jackson Advocate,* April 28–May 4, 1988.

52. "Legal Voters League Hold Annual Election," *Mississippi Enterprise,* January 29, 1954, 2; and "Rev. H. H. Humes Stands Watching," *Eagle Eye,* March 5, 1955, 1, Subject Files, Newspaper, Eagle Eye, Mississippi Department of Archives and History, Jackson.

53. "Jackson Commie-Like Citizens Council Stinks," *Eagle Eye,* May 14, 1955, 1, "Eagle Eye" folder, Mississippi Department of Archives and History, Jackson; and "Dr. Howard Shows Up Fake Leadership," *Eagle Eye,* January 29, 1955, 2, Branch File, Geographical File, Mississippi State Conference of Branches, 1954–55, Box C98, Group 2, NAACP Papers.

54. A. M. Rivera and Robert M. Ratcliffe, "Jacksonians High off Old 'Eagle Eye,'" *Pittsburgh Courier,* December 11, 1954, 1; Jordana Y. Shakoor, *Civil Rights Childhood* (Jackson: University Press of Mississippi, 1999), 73; and Wheaton interview, June 14, 2000.

55. Rivera and Ratcliffe, "Jacksonians High off Old 'Eagle Eye,'" *Pittsburgh Courier;* and "Arrington High Arrested for Distributing Literature," *Jackson Advocate,* September 4, 1954, 6; "Mutt High in New Brush with Police," *Jackson Advocate,* December 18, 1954, 1, 6; "Eagle Eye Editors Arrest Called Violation of Press Freedom," *Jackson Advocate,* January 1, 1955, 1.

56. Rivera and Ratcliffe, "Jacksonians High off Old 'Eagle Eye,'" *Pittsburgh Courier;* "Say High Should Be in Prison or the Insane Asylum," *Jackson Advocate,* April 3, 1954, 1; C. Evers interview, September 2, 1999; and Wheaton interview, June 14, 2000.

57. E. Boyd interview, September 20, 2003; Carolyn P. DuBose, *The Untold Story of Charles Diggs: The Public Figure, the Private Man* (Arlington, Va.: Barton, 1998), 6–9; Wilkins to Howard, January 19, 1955; and "Rep. Diggs Rouses Miss. Rally," *Chicago Defender,* May 14, 1955, 2.

58. "13,000 Hear Diggs Hit in Miss. Speech," *Jet* 8 (May 12, 1955), 3–4; and "Segregation Time 'Running Out,' Negroes Told," *Jackson Daily News,* April 30, 1955, 1.

59. "12,000 Jam 'Rights' Confab in Mississippi's All Negro Town," *Louisiana Weekly,* May 7, 1955, 2.

60. "Full Fight Promised by Diggs," *Pittsburgh Courier,* May 7, 1955, 1; "Hear U.S. Statesman C. C. Diggs," *Tri-State Defender,* May 7, 1955, 1, 2; "Start Fund to Prosecute Whites Abusing Negroes at RCNL Meet," *Delta Democrat Times,* May 1, 1955, 2; and "Regional Council of Negro Leadership Holds Meeting," *Jackson Advocate,* May 7, 1955, 8.

61. Jack Mendelson, *The Martyrs: Sixteen Who Gave Their Lives for Racial Justice* (New York: Harper and Row, 1966), 2–3, 6–7; "Lynching in Mississippi, Minister Shotgunned to Death Gang Style," *Chicago Defender,* May 21, 1955, 2; civil rights rally featuring Eleanor Roosevelt and Autherine Lucy, May 24, 1956 [sound recording], Schomburg Center for Research in Black Culture, New York Public Library; Payne, *I've Got the Light of Freedom,* 36–37; and Booker, *Black Man's America,* 161–62.

62. Mendelson, *Martyrs,* 3–6; Booker, *Black Man's America,* 162–65; "Vote Drive to Avenge Lynching," *Chicago Defender,* May 28, 1955, 1–2; and "Negro Leader Dies in Odd Accident," *Jackson Clarion-Ledger,* May 9, 1955, 16.

63. Booker, *Black Man's America,* 162–63; "White Ignores NAACP's Plea in Death Case," *Jackson Clarion-Ledger,* May 12, 1955, 1; "Justice Department Asks FBI to Probe Delta Negro Death," *Jackson Clarion-Ledger,* May 22, 1955, 1; and Wilkins to Medgar Evers, May 26, 1955, Mississippi Pressures, Lee, George, Slaying of, 1955, General Office File, Box 422, Group 2, NAACP Papers.

64. E. H. Winterrowd to Alex Rosen, May 9, 1955, Howard FBI file; and J. Edgar Hoover to Herbert Brownell Jr., May 11, 1955, Howard FBI file.

65. Winterrowd to Rosen; Hoover to Brownell, May 11, 1955, Howard FBI file; and Report, Unknown Subjects, Belzoni, Mississippi; Reverend George Wesley Lee, June 15, 1955, 44–8949, Howard FBI file.

66. "Exclusive Pictures of Lynch Victim's Funeral," *Chicago Defender,* May 28, 1955, 2; "A Murderous Belzoni," *Eagle Eye,* May 21, 1955, Howard FBI File; "Plan Rally to Protest Lynching," *Tri-State Defender,* May 21, 1955, 1–2; "Contribute $1,236 to Campaign," *Tri-State Defender,* May 28, 1955, 1; Booker, *Black Man's America,* 164; and Mendelson, *Martyrs,* 11.

67. Payne, *I've Got the Light of Freedom,* 37; "Retraction Defined," *Delta Democrat Times,* May 15, 1955, 4; Report, Unknown Subject; Rev. Willie George Lee—Victim; Dr. T. R. M. Howard, May 27, 1955, Howard FBI file; and Price to Alex Rosen, June 4, 1955, Howard FBI file.

68. McMillen, *Citizens' Councils,* 28.

69. "Hit Bias in Cotton Picking," *Tri-State Defender,* June 18, 1955, 1; Howard to A. H. McCoy, June 13, 1955, copy in author's possession, courtesy of Jerry Thornbery; "Mississippi LEAC Reaffirms Stand against Desegregation 'In Any Form,'" *Southern School News* 2 (July 6, 1955), 4; "Ticker Tape U.S.A.," *Jet* 8 (May 19, 1955), 9; and "Miss. Group Launches Drive to Fight Registration Clause," *Memphis World,* June 10, 1955, 1.

70. "Greene Says His Candidate for Gov. the Winner," *Jackson Advocate,* June 4, 1955, 8; and Tom Ethridge, "Low Down on the Higher Ups," *Jackson Daily News,* June 8, 1955, 1.

71. Mackel to Wilkins, July 17, 1955, Wilkins to Mackel, "Mississippi Pressures, Howard, T. R. M., 1954–55, General Office File" folder, Box 422, Group 2, NAACP Papers.

72. Hurley to Wilkins, April 8, 1955, "Mississippi Pressures, Reports and Statements, 1954–55" folder, Box 424, Group 2, NAACP Papers.

73. David Halberstam, "A County Divided against Itself," *Reporter* 13 (December 15, 1955), 30–32; M. Evers, *For Us, the Living,* 166–67; "Editorials Unanimously Deplore NAACP Action in Vicksburg," *Clarksdale Press Register,* July 21, 1955, 6; "Miss. Whites Fail to Halt Plans for New $650,000 Negro Project," *Jet* 8 (August 11, 1955), 6; and "Flaming Cross Burns at Negro Leader's Home," *Jackson Daily News,* August 19, 1955, 1.

74. "342 Names on NAACP Petitions," *Clarksdale Press Register,* August 2, 1955, 1; "School Board Files Petition from Local NAACP Unit," *Clarksdale Press Register,* August 12, 1955, 1, 6.

75. "County to Organize Citizens' Council, 60 Residents Decide at Preliminary Meeting," *Clarksdale Press Register,* August 5, 1955, 1; "School Board Files Petition," *Clarksdale Press Register;* "Judge Brady to 'Kick Off' Local Citizens' Council," *Clarksdale Press Register,* August 13, 1955, 1; "Citizens' Council Organized after Appeal from Brady," *Clarksdale Press Register,* August 17, 1955, 1, 8; "Local Citizens' Council Completes Organization," *Clarksdale Press Register,* September 2, 1955, 1; and Payne, *I've Got the Light of Freedom,* 55.

76. Tom Ethridge, "Mississippi Notebook," *Jackson Clarion-Ledger,* May 26, 1955, 2; John Herbers, "No Negro Vote Stigma Possible in Governor's Race This Time," *Delta Democrat Times,* July 24, 1955, 1; "Challenging of Negro Vote Is Widespread," *Delta Democrat Times,* August 23, 1955, 1; McMillen, *Citizens' Councils,* 219; "Congressman Demands Probe of Miss. Voting," *Jet* 8 (August 18, 1955), 3; Lewis, "Negro Voter in Mississippi," 336, 342; "Mound Bayou Voters Disfranchised," *Jackson Advocate,* August 6, 1955, 6; and Carter, *South Strikes Back,* 42, 45.

77. "Mound Bayou Voters Disfranchised," *Jackson Advocate;* "Candidates Say Delta Negroes Aren't Democrats," *Jackson Daily News,* August 2, 1955, 1; and "Mound Bayou Went for Johnson 80 to 8; Not Counted," *Delta Democrat Times,* August 24, 1955, 1. Perhaps Mound Bayou's votes were thrown out for county candidates, but they were counted and tallied in the primary for governor ("Mound Bayou Went for Johnson 80 to 8," *Delta Democrat Times).*

78. Payne, *I've Got the Light of Freedom,* 39; Jay Milner, "Lincoln Killing Has No Race or Citizens Council Angles," *Jackson Clarion-Ledger,* August 19, 1955, 1; civil rights rally featuring Eleanor Roosevelt and Autherine Lucy, May 24, 1956 [sound recording], Schomburg Center for Research in Black Culture, New York Public Library; and "Say U.S. Government Has No Authority to Investigate Election Held in Mississippi," *Jackson Advocate,* August 20, 1955, 1–2.

79. "Little Man Will Win Fight, Says Miss. Doctor," *California Eagle,* August 11, 1955, 1, 4; Foner, *Paul Robeson Speaks,* 395–96; *Ebony* 10 (August 1955), 68–74; and Booker, *Black Man's America,* 166–67. *Ebony* did not identify the person or persons who issued the "death list" while *Jet* only went so far as to say it came from "white supremacists" ("Seven Miss. Negroes Marked for Death by Whites," *Jet* 8 [June 9, 1955], 4).

80. "Little Man Will Win Fight," *California Eagle;* "Dr. Howard Heads National Medical Assn.," *Jet* 8 (August 28, 1955), 24; and "The President Elect," *Journal of the National Medical Association* 47 (November 1955), 406.

Chapter 6: "Hell to Pay in Mississippi": The Murder of Emmett Till

1. Gentry, "Bluff City Society," *Memphis World,* August 16, 1955, 3; Gentry, "Bluff City Society," *Memphis World,* September 16, 1953; and Robert L. Birchman, "Howard Raps Apathy of Urban Negro," *Chicago Defender,* September 10, 1955, 3.

2. Mamie Till-Mobley and Christopher Benson, *Death of Innocence: The Story of the Hate Crime That Changed America* (New York: Random House, 2003), 98–102.

3. Payne, *I've Got the Light of Freedom,* 133; and Till-Mobley and Benson, *Death of Innocence,* 107–9.

4. Till-Mobley and Benson, *Death of Innocence,* 122; Juan Williams, *Eyes on the Prize: America's Civil Rights Years, 1954–1955* (New York: Viking Penguin, 1987), 43; and Olive Arnold Adams, *Time Bomb: Mississippi Exposed and the Full Story of Emmett Till* (Mound Bayou: Mississippi Regional Council of Negro Leadership, 1956), 17.

5. "Charge 2 Men in Kidnapping," *Jackson Clarion-Ledger,* August 30, 1955, 1; "Officers Hunting Third Man," *Memphis Press Scimitar,* September 1, 1955, 1, 4; Clark Porteous, "Mississippi Hunt for Clews Goes On," *Memphis Press Scimitar,* September 2, 1955, 5; "White Storekeeper Held in Abduction of Negro Youth," *Jackson Daily News,* August 29, 1955, 1; and "Two White Men Charged with Kidnapping Negro," *Delta Democrat Times,* August 30, 1955.

6. See Timothy Tyson, *The Blood of Emmett Till* (New York: Simon & Schuster, 2017).

7. Till-Mobley and Benson, *Death of Innocence,* 122–23; and Mattie S. Colin and Robert Elliott, "Mother Waits in Vain for Her 'Bo,'" *New York Age Defender,* September 10, 1955, 10.

8. Charles R. Ealy, "The Emmett Till Case: A Comparative Analysis of Newspaper Coverage" (MA thesis, University of Texas at Dallas, 1996), 24; Whitaker, 108; and Till-Mobley and Benson, *Death of Innocence,* 123.

9. "Charge 2 Men in Kidnapping," *Jackson Clarion-Ledger;* "Negro Describes Boy's Abduction," *Jackson Clarion-Ledger,* September 2, 1955, 1; "Officers Hunt Third Man," *Memphis Press Scimitar,* September 1, 1955, 4; "Two White Men Charged with Kidnapping Negro," *Memphis Press Scimitar,* September 3, 1955, 1; *State of Mississippi v. J. W. Milam and Roy Bryant,* Proceedings of Trial, In the Circuit Court, Second District of Tallahatchie County, Seventh Judicial District, State of Mississippi, September Term 1955, Sumner, Mississippi, 15–20; and Christopher Metress, ed., *The Lynching of Emmett Till: A Documentary Narrative* (Charlottesville: University of Virginia Press, 2002), 69, 72.

10. Williams, *Eyes on the Prize,* 43; David A. Shostak, "Crosby Smith: Forgotten Witness to a Missouri Nightmare," *Negro History Bulletin* 38 (December 1974–January 1975), 322; "Boy Disappears: White Men Held in Greenwood," *Memphis Press Scimitar,* August 30, 1955,

11; "Officers Hunting Third Man," *Memphis Press Scimitar;* "Negro Describes Boy's Abduction," *Jackson Clarion-Ledger; Jackson Clarion-Ledger,* September 4, 1955, 1; "Two White Men Charged with 'Kidnapping Negro,'" *Delta Democrat Times,* August 30, 1955, 1; and *Mississippi v. Milam and Bryant,* 94.

11. "Chicago Boy, 14, Kidnapped by Miss. Whites," *Jet* 8 (September 8, 1955), 4; Mattie Colin Smith, "Mother's Tears Greet Son Who Died a Martyr," *Chicago Defender,* September 10, 1955, 1–2; and Till-Mobley and Benson, *Death of Innocence,* 120; F. L. Price to Alex Rosen, Unknown Subjects, Emmett Lewis [sic] Till, Age 15 [sic]—Victim Kidnapping, August 29, 1955, Addendum August 30, 1955, J. Edgar Hoover to John Sengstacke, September 2, 1955, Emmett Louis Till FBI file; "Body of Negro Found in River," *Jackson Clarion-Ledger,* September 1, 1955, 1, 5; and *Mississippi v. Milam and Bryant,* 104–5.

12. "Mississippi Shame," *New York Age Defender,* September 10, 1955, 1; "Mother's Tears Greet Son," *Chicago Defender;* "Mississippi's Reaction to Death," *Memphis Press Scimitar,* September 3, 1955, 11; Till-Mobley and Benson, *Death of Innocence,* 141–42; Ealy, "Emmett Till Case," 34–35; and Federal Bureau of Investigation, Prosecutive Report of Investigative Concerning . . . Emmett Till, Deceased, Victim, February 9, 2006, 107–9, Emmett Louis Till FBI file.

13. "A Brutal Murder," *Clarksdale Press Register,* September 1, 1955, 4; "Lynching Post-Facto," *Delta Democrat Times,* September 6, 1955, 4; Whitaker, 196; and "White Orders Full Probe of Delta's Kidnap-Murder," *Jackson Clarion-Ledger,* September 2, 1955, 1.

14. "A Just Appraisal," *Clarksdale Press Register,* September 5, 1955, 4; "State Papers Hit Slaying of Negro," *Jackson Clarion-Ledger,* September 3, 1955, 1; Tom Ethridge, "Mississippi Notebook," *Jackson Clarion-Ledger,* September 4, 1955, 7; Ruby Hurley, transcript, recorded interview by John H. Britton, Atlanta, Georgia, January 26, 1968, Civil Rights Documentation Project, Howard University, Washington, D.C.; and "Dr. Howard: Situation in Mississippi Extremely Serious, Tension Is Continuing to Mount," *Pittsburgh Courier,* October 8, 1955, 4.

15. "Sheriff Believes Body Not Till's, Family Disagrees," *Jackson Clarion-Ledger,* September 4, 1955, 1; Jay Milner, "Doctor's Testimony May Alter Inquiry," *Jackson Clarion-Ledger,* September 6, 1955, 1, 13; Hugh Stephen Whitaker, "A Case Study in Southern Justice: The Murder of Emmett Till," *Rhetoric & Public Affairs* 8, no. 2 (2005), 199–202, 210–11; and William M. Simpson, "Reflections on a Murder: The Emmett Till Case," in Frank Allen Dennis, ed., *Southern Miscellany: Essays in History in Honor of Glover Moore* (Jackson: University of Mississippi Press, 1981), 183–86.

16. Simpson, "Reflections on a Murder," 184–85; "On Mississippi's Conscience: Emmett Louis Till, Age 14," *National Guardian,* October 3, 1955, 1, 4; "Two White Men Go On Trial for Slaying of Negro," *Jackson Clarion-Ledger,* September 18, 1955, 4; and Whitaker, "Case Study in Southern Justice," 198–200.

17. Whitaker, "Case Study in Southern Justice," 200–201; and "Picking of Jury Delays Opening," *Tri-State Defender,* September 24, 1955, 1–2.

18. Till-Mobley and Benson, *Death of Innocence,* 152–56; Till-Mobley interview, September 28, 1999; DuBose, *Untold Story of Charles Diggs,* 51; Booker, *Black Man's America,* 166; and Wheaton interview, June 14, 2000.

19. Clark Porteous, "Instead of Lunch, the 'Surprises,'" *Memphis Press Scimitar,* September 21, 1955, 1–2; Porteous, "Officers Work All Night on Searches," *Memphis Press Scimitar,* September 21, 1955, 1, 7; and "Dr. Howard: Situation in Mississippi Extremely Serious," *Pittsburgh Courier.*

20. "Mother of Dead Negro Says Body Was Her Son," *Greenwood (Mississippi) Morning Star,* September 22, 1955, 1, Program Department, Subject and Correspondence Files, 1955, South–Till Lynching, Folder 7, Box 369, UPW Papers, Wisconsin Historical Society, Madison; and Metress, *Lynching of Emmett Till,* 165–66.

21. *Jackson Daily News,* September 9, 1955; "Newsmen from All Over, Daily Worker's Reporter at Trial Is Mississippian," *Jackson Daily News,* September 20, 1955, 6; "Newspapers and Photographers Are Frisked for Weapons," *Memphis Commercial Appeal,* September 21, 1955, 1; Whitaker, "Case Study in Southern Justice," 208; Oral History Interview with John Herbers, http://civilrightsandthepress.syr.edu/pdfs/John%20Herbers.pdf, accessed September 2, 2007; Metress, *Lynching of Emmett Till,* 138–43; Harry Marsh, "Communist Writer at Trial Lauds Citizens," *Delta Democrat Times,* September 22, 1955, 1; and Stephen J. Whitfield, *A Death in the Delta: The Story of Emmett Till* (Baltimore: Johns Hopkins University Press, 1988), 36.

22. John H. Telfer to Richard Durham, September 21, 1955, Program Department, Subject and Correspondence Files, 1955, South–Till Lynching, Folder 7, Box 369, UPW Papers; "Jim Crow Press Table," *Chicago Defender,* October 1, 1955, 3; Metress, *Lynching of Emmett Till,* 48, 50; Tom Yarbrough, "Odds 10 to 1 for Acquittal, 'Intrusion' Resented in Mississippi Murder Trial," *St. Louis Post-Dispatch,* September 22, 1955, Emmett Louis Till, Clippings File, Southern Educational Reporting Service Library, Fisk University; Whitfield, *Death in the Delta,* 37; and Till-Mobley and Benson, *Death of Innocence,* 162.

23. Jimmy L. Hicks, "Unbelievable!" *Baltimore Afro-American,* October 15, 1955, 1, 2; Robert M. Ratcliffe, "Headlines," *Pittsburgh Courier,* October 1, 1955, 9; and Simeon Booker, "A Negro Reporter at the Till Trial," *Nieman Reports* (Special Double Issue) 53–54 (Winter 1999–Spring 2000) [originally published in January 1956], 136.

24. Hicks, "Unbelievable!" *Baltimore Afro-American;* Booker, "Negro Reporter," 136–37; and "Popular White Newsman Reports for Induction in Army amidst Many Regrets," *Memphis World,* February 11, 1944, 1.

25. Hicks, "Unbelievable!" *Baltimore Afro-American;* and Booker, "Negro Reporter," 136–37; Porteous, "Officers Work All Night," *Memphis Press Scimitar;* and Ruby Hurley interview.

26. Metress, *Lynching of Emmett Till,* 55–57; and Till-Mobley interview, September 28, 1999.

27. Till-Mobley interview, September 28, 1999; Metress, *Lynching of Emmett Till,* 57; and Till-Mobley and Benson, *Death of Innocence,* 163–64.

28. "Sheriff Takes Precautions to Keep Trial Orderly," *Memphis Press Scimitar,* September 20, 1955, 4; Porteous, "Officers Work All Night," *Memphis Press Scimitar;* Porteous, "Mrs. Bryant on Stand," *Memphis Press Scimitar,* September 22, 1955, 4; and Ralph Hutto, "NAACP Leader Says Two Witnesses Disappeared," *Mississippi State Times,* September 23, 1955; and *Mississippi State Times,* September 23, 1955, Emmett Till folder, Mississippi Department of Archives and History, Jackson. We contacted Gwin Cole, an identification officer for the Mississippi Highway Patrol appointed by the governor to help with the investiga-

tion. Although directly involved in the search at the equipment shed, he said that he had no memory of the case.

29. M. Evers, *For Us, the Living,* 172; Hicks, "Unbelievable," *Baltimore Afro-American,* October 22, 1955, 2; Ruby Hurley to Gloster Current, Report for the October Meeting of the Board, September 30, 1955, Southeast Regional Office Reports 1955, Box C325, Group 2, NAACP Papers; Booker, "Negro Reporter," 137; and Porteous, "Officers Work All Night," *Memphis Press Scimitar.* Smith's statements on this issue were somewhat inconsistent. Not long after recovery of the body, he said that he had concluded that only Bryant and Milam were at the kidnapping scene (*Memphis World,* September 9, 1955).

30. Booker, "Negro Reporter," 137; Metress, *Lynching of Emmett Till,* 169–70; Porteous, "Mrs. Bryant on Stand," *Memphis Press Scimitar,* September 22, 1955, 4; [Louis] Willie Reed, interview by authors, May 18, 2001; and Till-Mobley and Benson, *Death of Innocence,* 176–77.

31. Metress, *Lynching of Emmett Till,* 65–69, 72, 87; Till-Mobley and Benson, *Death of Innocence,* 173, 175; Porteous, "Instead of Lunch, the 'Surprises,'" *Memphis Press Scimitar; Mississippi v. Milam and Bryant,* 21, 38. Nearly all the newspaper stories at the time, including those in the *Greenwood Commonwealth,* the *Memphis Press Scimitar,* and the *New York Post,* reported that Wright said "There he is" when asked to identify who kidnapped his great nephew. More definitively, a copy of the trial transcript discovered in 2005 reports it as "There he is." As far as can be determined, the earliest recorded claim that Wright said "Thar he" was by James Hicks, who attended the trial, in an interview for Williams, *Eyes on the Prize* (50–51; Metress, *Lynching of Emmett Till,* 65, 68; Porteous, "Instead of Lunch, the 'Surprises,'" *Memphis Press Scimitar; Mississippi v. Milam and Bryant,* 9, 22, 35). While the truth will never be known, the regionalism is not consistent with Wright's local reputation as well-spoken or his statements in a filmed interview in 1955, in which he shows considerable care in pronunciation and choice of words. Moreover, it should be noted that Hicks's original news stories in 1955 stated that it was "There he is" and that his interview for *Eyes on the Prize* was more than thirty years after the fact (Till-Mobley and Benson, *Death of Innocence,* 107–9; and Herb Boyd, "The Real Deal on Emmett Till," *Black World Today,* May 18, 2004).

32. Metress, *Lynching of Emmett Till,* 85; and *Mississippi v. Milam and Bryant,* 183, 185–87, 193–94.

33. Hutto, "NAACP Leader Says Two Witnesses Disappeared," *Mississippi State Times;* "Whistling Killing May Go to Jury Today, 2nd Negro Accuses Two Defendants," *New York Post,* September 23, 1955, 3; Porteous, "Mrs. Bryant on Stand," *Memphis Press Scimitar; Mississippi v. Milam and Bryant,* 213–48; John Herberg, "Witness Says He Saw Milam Take Lad into Barn; Heard Screaming," *Delta Democrat Times,* September 22, 1955, 1; Till-Mobley and Benson, *Death of Innocence,* 183–84; and Jimmy L. Hicks, "Lynch Prosecutor's Plea Convicts Miss.," *Baltimore Afro-American,* October 1, 1955, 1.

34. *Mississippi v. Milam and Bryant,* 248–58; Porteous, "Mrs. Bryant on Stand," *Memphis Press Scimitar;* "Whistling Killing May Go to Jury Today," 3; Hutto, "NAACP Leader Says Two Witnesses Disappeared," *Mississippi State Times;* and "Till Trial," *Jackson Daily News,* September 21, 1955, 2.

35. Clark Porteous, "Kidnap Trial Delays Sure," *Memphis Press Scimitar,* September 23, 1955, 1; and "Whistling Killing May Go to Jury Today," 3.

36. James Featherstone and W. C. Shoemaker, "State Demands Conviction; Defense Says No Proof Presented, Asks Acquittal," *Jackson Daily News,* September 23, 1955, 2; *Mississippi v. Milam and Bryant,* 266, 269, 272–75, 278–79; and Metress, *Lynching of Emmett Till,* 90–92.

37. *Mississippi v. Milam and Bryant,* 290–91, 300–301.

38. Alex Wilson, "Reveal Two Key Witnesses Jailed," *Tri-State Defender,* October 1, 1955, 1–2.

39. Metress, *Lynching of Emmett Till,* 102–4, 108–9; Dan Wakefield, "Justice in Sumner: Land of the Free," *Nation* 181 (October 1, 1955), 285; Whitaker, 210; and Rob F. Hall, "Sheriff Showed Jury How to Acquit," *Daily Worker,* September 26, 1955, 1–2.

40. DuBose, *Untold Story of Charles Diggs,* 55; Clark Porteous, "Next: 2 Face Till Kidnap Charges," *Memphis Press Scimitar,* September 24, 1955, 3; Whitfield, *Death in the Delta,* 42; Wilson, "Reveal Two Key Witnesses Jailed," *Tri-State Defender;* and Till-Mobley and Benson, *Death of Innocence,* 189.

41. Porteous, "Next: 2 Face Till Kidnap Charges," *Memphis Press Scimitar;* Till-Mobley and Benson, *Death of Innocence,* 196; "Audience Donates to Till Witnesses," *Chicago Defender,* March 17, 1956, 10; Reed interview, May 18, 2001; and Till-Mobley interview, September 28, 1999.

42. Whitaker, 205–7.

43. Ibid., 207, 210–11.

44. L. Alex Wilson, "Sidelights of the Till Trial," *Tri-State Defender,* October 1, 1955, 5; "Kept from Talking," *Chicago Defender,* October 1, 1955, 1–2; "Mary Bradley, Reed Boy Leave with Congressman after Testifying at Trial," *Jackson Daily News,* September 24, 1955, 1; Ruby Hurley to Gloster Current, September 30, 1955, Branch File, Southeast Regional Office Reports, 1955, Group 2, Box C225, NAACP Papers; Wakefield, "Justice in Sumner," 284; and Booker, "Negro Reporter," 136. In part, some blacks may have praised the conduct of the trial out of fear that criticism of Mississippi's criminal justice system could jeopardize a conviction on kidnapping charges.

45. "Howard Sees Light Sentence," *Chicago Defender,* September 17, 1955, 5; Jimmy L. Hicks, "Lynch Trial Begins," *Baltimore Afro-American,* September 24, 1955, 1–2; "Dr. Howard: Situation in Mississippi Extremely Serious," *Pittsburgh Courier;* "Tension Is Continuing to Mount," 1–4; "Miss. Negroes Not Running; Prepared to Stand and Fight," *California Eagle,* October 13, 1955, 3; and Eugene Gordon, "Dr. Howard Asks to See Brownell; Tells of Daily Threats of Death," *National Guardian,* October 31, 1955, 5.

46. "Dr. Howard: Situation in Mississippi Extremely Serious," *Pittsburgh Courier.*

47. Whitaker, "Case Study in Southern Justice," 212–13; Telfer to Durham, September 21, 1955; "Miss. Negroes Not Running," *California Eagle;* and Gordon, "Dr. Howard Asks to See Brownell," *National Guardian.* Porteous explained that the new evidence perturbed prosecutors because they feared it might undermine their trial in Tallahatchie County and shift it to Sunflower County. If true, one wonders why they were so upset; they should have welcomed an opportunity to get rid of the case (Porteous, "Officers Work All Night," *Memphis Press Scimitar).*

48. Till-Mobley and Benson, *Death of Innocence,* 161–62, 182–83; Till-Mobley interview, September 28, 1999; and Reed interview, May 18, 2001.

49. "Shame of Mississippi," *Chicago Defender,* September 10, 1955, 9.

50. Henry J. Davis to Jesse J. Breland, September 23, 1955, folder on Emmett Till, William Bradford Huie Papers, Rare Books and Manuscript Special Collections Library, Ohio State University; Telfer to Durham, September 21, 1955; "The Verdict at Sumner," *Jackson Daily News,* September 25, 1955; and "The Verdict at Sumner," *Jackson Clarion-Ledger,* September 25, 1955, 8.

51. "Verdict at Sumner," *Jackson Clarion-Ledger.*

52. Whitaker, "Case Study in Southern Justice," 219; Louis E. Lomax, *The Negro Revolt* (New York: New American Library, 1963), 87–93; and Clenora Hudson-Weems, *Emmett Till: The Sacrificial Lamb of the Civil Rights Movement* (Troy, Mich.: Bedford, 1994), 21, 95.

53. Curt Gentry, *J. Edgar Hoover: The Man and the Secrets* (New York: Norton, 1991), 407.

54. "Probe of FBI Agents Asked," *Baltimore Morning Sun,* September 26, 1955, Howard FBI file; and "Dr. Howard: Situation in Mississippi Extremely Serious," *Pittsburgh Courier.*

55. Gentry, *J. Edgar Hoover,* 450; Kenneth O'Reilly, *"Racial Matters:" The FBI's Secret File on Black America, 1960–1972* (New York: Free Press, 1989), 209; Louis B. Nichols to Clyde Tolson, September 26, 1955, Howard FBI file; Williams, *Thurgood Marshall,* 254; M. A. Jones to Nichols, September 26, 1955, F. L. Price to Alex Rosen, September 26, 1955—both in Howard FBI file; and "Correlation Summary," February 28, 1958, Roy Wilkins FBI file.

56. Williams, *Thurgood Marshall,* 254–55.

57. Ibid., 255; and "Hoover, FBI Head, Hits Charges of Negligence," *Baltimore Afro-American,* October 15, 1955, 1; and Howard Ball, *A Defiant Life: Thurgood Marshall and the Persistence of American Racism* (New York: Crown, 1998), 65–67.

58. Jones to Nichols, September 26, 1955, Howard FBI file; and "1st Annual Meeting of Negro Council Leaders," *Memphis World,* May 6, 1952, 1. In the same speech that had led to his row with Marshall and Hoover, Howard had called on the crowd to assure that the Baltimore NAACP would be able to "telephone Thurgood Marshall in the morning and tell him that the citizens of Baltimore placed on the table $5,000 in cash to help carry into court one of these school cases in Mississippi" (T. R. M. Howard, "Terror Reigns in Mississippi," *Baltimore Afro-American,* October 8, 1955, 6).

59. Williams, *Thurgood Marshall,* 253, 255.

60. Tisdale interview, January 2, 2001; C. Evers interview, September 2, 1999; "Riddle of Missing Witnesses Clears; Body to Be Exhumed," *Clarksdale Press Register,* October 1, 1955, 1; "Wilson 'Steals' Levy Collins," *New York Age Defender,* October 8, 1955, 1; and "What the Public Didn't Know about the Till Trial," *Jet* 8 (October 13, 1955), 14.

61. "Collins Denies Any Link to Till," *New York Age Defender,* October 8, 1955, 1–2.

62. Ibid.

63. Howard, "Terror Reigns in Mississippi," *Baltimore Afro-American.*

64. "Grand Jury Decision on Bryant and Milam Seen Today, Thursday," *Jackson Clarion-Ledger,* November 9, 1955, 1; "NAACP Asks Who Did It As Bryant, Milam Freed," *Jackson Clarion-Ledger,* November 10, 1955, 4; and John Herbers, "Fails to Indict Pair for Till Kidnapping," *Delta Democrat Times,* October 10, 1955, 1.

65. Wilkins to Mrs. C. V. Adair, October 20, 1955, Madison S. Jones to Wilkins, December 5, 1955, Jones to Wilkins, November 14, 1955, "Mississippi Pressures, Howard, T. R. M., 1954–55, General Office File" folder, Group 2, Box 422, NAACP Papers; Wilkins to Joseph A.

Pitts, October 24, 1955, "Mississippi Pressures, Rallies and Meetings, Branches, General Office File" folder, Group 2, Box A424, NAACP Papers; and "Boost for Till Fund," *Pittsburgh Courier,* October 22, 1955, 11.

66. Wilkins to Adair, Wilkins to Pitts, Wilkins to Audley Maurice Mackel, November 21, 1955—all in "Mississippi Pressures, Howard, T. R. M., 1954–55, General Office File" folder, Group 2, Box 422, NAACP Papers; and Howard, "Terror Reigns in Mississippi," *Baltimore Afro-American.* Gloster Current, often a critic of Howard, joined in the praise. In a letter to a member in Baton Rouge, he wrote that Howard's "speeches are accurate and factual in content. . . . we would endorse any meeting sponsored by one of our Branches at which Dr. Howard is the principal speaker." Gloster Current to Noland P. Robertson, November 10, 1955, General Office File, "Mississippi Pressures, Rallies and Meetings, Branches, 1955, November–December 1955" folder, Group 2, Box A424, NAACP Papers.

67. Howard, "Terror Reigns in Mississippi," *Baltimore Afro-American;* and "Dr. Howard: Situation in Mississippi Extremely Serious," *Pittsburgh Courier.*

68. Howard to Richard M. Nixon, October 20, 1955, T. R. M. Howard folder, Series 320, General Correspondence, Box 358, Pre-Presidential Papers of Richard M. Nixon, National Archives and Records Administration, Pacific Region, Laguna Niguel, Calif.; "Dr. Howard Wants to Discuss Till Case with Brownell," *Delta Democrat Times,* October 21, 1955, 1; and Louis E. Martin, "Dope and Data," *Tri-State Defender,* November 12, 1955, 7.

69. Jimmy L. Hicks, "New Till Evidence Disclosed in Letter," *Baltimore Afro-American,* November 26, 1955, 2.

70. Howard, "Terror Reigns in Mississippi," *Baltimore Afro-American;* and "Donate $10,000 at Till Rally in Los Angeles," *Chicago Defender,* October 22, 1955, 3.

71. Howard, "Terror Reigns in Mississippi," *Baltimore Afro-American.*

72. "An Enemy of His Race," *Jackson Daily News,* October 15, 1955, 6; Sullens, "Low Down on the Higher Ups," *Jackson Daily News;* "Howard's Poison Tongue," *Jackson Daily News,* October 25, 1955, 8.

73. "Dr. Howard Wants Action," *Pittsburgh Courier,* October 29, 1955, 2; Toki Schalk Johnson, "Toki Types," *Pittsburgh Courier,* October 29, 1955, 18; Robert M. Ratcliffe, "Behind the Headlines," *Pittsburgh Courier,* November 5, 1955, 9; William A. Fowlkes, "Greenwood Tense but Willie and Mose Are There," *Pittsburgh Courier,* November 12, 1955, 2; and "Dr. Howard to Get AVE Award," *Jackson Clarion-Ledger,* November 1, 1955, 2.

74. "New Belzoni Incident Keeps Spotlight on Mississippi," *Jackson Advocate,* December 3, 1955, 6; and L. Alex Wilson, "Accuse White Council Head," *Tri-State Defender,* December 3, 1955, 1.

75. "Officers Have No Suspects in Shooting," *Jackson Clarion-Ledger,* November 27, 1955, 1, 5; Payne, *I've Got the Light of Freedom,* 38; and Hurley to Current, Report for the January Meeting of the Board, December 28, 1955, NAACP, 1940–55, Southeast Regional Office Reports 1955, Box C225, Group 2, NAACP Papers.

76. "Dr. Howard Sees No Arrests Likely in Miss. Shooting," *California Eagle,* December 1, 1955, 1, 12; and "Howard Urges March on Washington," *Pittsburgh Courier,* December 3, 1955, 2.

77. Paula F. Pfeffer, *A. Philip Randolph, Pioneer of the Civil Rights Movement* (Baton Rouge: Louisiana State University Press, 1990), 47–55, 82–83; Roosevelt H. Ward Jr., "Har-

lemites Applaud Plan for March on Washington," *Daily Worker,* October 13, 1955, 1; "Plan Follow-up on March on Washington," *Daily Worker,* November 11, 1955, 4; and *Militant,* January 23, 1956, 1.

78. "Famed Dr. Howard, Rights Fighter, Montgomery Speaker," *Alabama Tribune* (Montgomery), November 25, 1955, 1; and Emory O. Jackson, "Howard Thinking about 'March on Washington,'" *Birmingham World,* December 2, 1955, 1.

79. Jackson, "Howard Thinking about 'March on Washington,'" *Birmingham World;* and E. Culpepper Clark, *The Schoolhouse Door: Segregation's Last Stand at the University of Alabama* (New York: Oxford University Press, 1993), 48–50, 71–80.

80. Jackson, "Howard Thinking about 'March on Washington,'" *Birmingham World;* Don Whitehead, *The FBI Story: A Report to the People* (New York: Random House, 1956), 3–11. *The FBI Story* was at the top of *The New York Times's* bestseller list in 1957 (see http://www.hawes.com/no1_nf_d.htm, accessed September 2, 2007).

81. Transcript of interview of Rosa Parks by Judith Vecchione, for the *Eyes on the Prize* Television Series, November 14, 1985, Henry Hampton Collection, Film and Media Archive, University Libraries, Washington University in St. Louis; Branch, *Parting the Waters,* 128–37; and Christopher Benson to David T. Beito, personal communication, March 12, 2007.

82. Clenora Hudson-Weems, "Emmett Till: The Impetus for the Modern Civil Rights Movement" (PhD diss., University of Iowa, 1988), 86.

83. E. Frederic Morrow, *Forty Years a Guinea Pig* (New York: Pilgrim Press, 1980), 102–3. Undaunted, Morrow wrote directly to Sherman Adams on December 16 with a similar suggestion. As before, it was "vetoed" by "higher authorities in the White House" (Morrow, *Forty Years a Guinea Pig,* 104).

84. "Attention Focused on Till Case Defendant in Aftermath of Shooting in Glendora," *Clarksdale Press Register,* December 8, 1955, 1, 8; "Seeks Bond for Kimbell," *Clarksdale Press Register,* December 29, 1955, 1, 8; "Elmer Kimbell Pleads Not Guilty in Murder of Glendora Man," *Clarksdale Press Register,* March 1, 1956, 1; and "White Man Accused in Slaying of Negro Says He's Not Talking," *Delta Democrat Times,* December 9, 1955, 1; and "Glendora Scene of New Outrage," *Chicago Defender,* December 17, 1955, 1–2.

85. Wilkins to Curtis McClain, December 12, 1955, Courts, Gus, Shooting of, 1955, General Office File, Box A227, Group 2, NAACP Papers; "Link with Till in Glendora Case," *Tri-State Defender,* December 17, 1955, 1–2; "Attention Focused on Till Case Defendant in Aftermath of Shooting in Glendora," *Clarksdale Press Register,* December 7, 1955, 1, 8; "Seeks Bond for Kimbell," *Clarksdale Press Register;* "Elmer Kimbell Pleads Not Guilty in Murder of Glendora Man," *Clarksdale Press Register;* "Tallahatchie County Jury Accepts Claim of Kimbell Killed Negro in Self Defense," *Clarksdale Press Register,* March 14, 1955; and "Widow Drowns As Trial of Mate's Slayer Opens," *Chicago Defender,* March 17, 1956, 1; and Carter to Charles Burton, December 14, 1955, Correspondence 1955 folder: B, Carter Papers.

86. V. Harris [Wilson] interview, November 6, 2000; "Miss. Delegation to Bare 'All' to Justice Dept.," *Louisiana Weekly,* November 26, 1955, 3; and "Dr. Howard on Council Death List," *Tri-State Defender,* December 10, 1955, 1.

87. "Mound Bayou Leader Raps Hodding Carter," *Jackson Clarion-Ledger,* July 13, 1955, 4; "Little Man Will Win Says Miss. Doctor," *California Eagle;* E. Boyd interviews, October

27, 1995, September 23, 2003; Tisdale interview, January 2, 2001; and Central Bolivar Citizens' Council, Report, ca. September 30, 1955, Folder 3, Box 2, Medgar Evers Papers, Special Collections, Mississippi Department of Archives and History, Jackson.

88. "Files Lawsuit against NAACP Leader," *Jackson Daily News,* October 6, 1955, 13; "Ex-Farmhand Sues Dr. Howard for $25,000," *Jet* 8 (October 27, 1955), 9; and "Howard vs. Winters," *Newark (New Jersey) Telegram,* January 22, 1956, 4–5, Howard FBI file.

89. "Huge Los Angeles Crowd Protests Lynching of Till," *Labor Daily;* "The One Man Mississippi Can't Scare," *Hue* 3 (January 1956), 22; and "Dr. Howard on Council Death List," *Tri-State Defender.*

90. "Wealthy Negro Is Selling Delta Property but Denies He Is Fleeing State," *Jackson Daily News,* December 14, 1955; "Negro's Work Taking Him Away from State," *Jackson Clarion-Ledger,* December 15, 1955, 4; and "Dr. Howard's Wife, Tots Leave Miss.," *Chicago Defender,* December 17, 1955, 1–2.

91. "Dr. Howard's Wife, Tots Leave Miss.," *Chicago Defender;* "Is He Leaving State? Dr. Howard Denies Rumors," *Delta Democrat Times,* December 14, 1955, 1; "Wealthy Negro Is Selling Delta Property," *Jackson Daily News;* Irnez Applin, telephone interview, July 20, 2005; "The Other Side of Mississippi," *National Guardian,* December 26, 1955; "Negro's Work Taking Him Away," *Jackson Clarion-Ledger;* "Dr. Howard to Leave? Today He Says Not Quite," *Delta Democrat Times,* December 15, 1955, 2; and E. Boyd interview, October 27, 1995.

92. "2 Top Negro Leaders Plan to Leave Miss.," *Jet* 9 (December 22, 1955), 3–4.

93. Perry T. English, interview by authors, November 6, 1999; B. Howard interview, March 27, 2000; Moore interview, April 4, 2001; and Morgan interview, March 31, 2000.

94. B. Howard interview, March 27, 2000; Henry Hampton and Steve Fayer, *Voices of Freedom: An Oral History of the Civil Rights Movement from the 1950s through the 1980s* (New York: Bantam, 1990), 8; and Wheaton interview, June 14, 2000.

95. Homer Wheaton, personal communication, January 24, 2004.

96. Audley M. Mackel Jr., interview by authors, November 14, 2003. Mackel said that Howard was not literally in the casket but in the wooden box used to hold the casket.

97. "Dr. Howard on Council Death List," *Tri-State Defender;* "Dr. Howard Sells Property, Sends Family to California," *Tri-State Defender,* December 10, 1955; "Dr. Howard's Wife, Tots Leave Miss.," *Chicago Defender;* and "Huge Los Angeles Crowd Protests Lynching," *Labor Daily.*

98. Havard interview, June 10, 2000; C. Evers interview, September 2, 1999; "Dr. Howard Sells Property," *Tri-State Defender;* "2 Top Negro Leaders to Leave Miss.," *Jet;* "Seven Miss. Negro Leaders Marked for Death," *Jet;* "Death List," *Ebony* 10 (August 1955), 7–11; "How the South Is Organizing," *Jet;* Payne, *I've Got the Light of Freedom,* 40–41; Dittmer, *Local People,* 46–47; and "Jackson Doctor's Home Is Fired On," *Baltimore Afro-American,* September 24, 1955, 1.

99. C. Evers interview, September 2, 1999; "Terror Victims," *Daily Worker,* December 27, 1955, 5; Payne, *I've Got the Light of Freedom,* 40–41; and "12,000 Jam 'Rights' Confab in Mississippi's All-Negro Town," *Louisiana Weekly,* May 7, 1955, 2.

100. Undated interview, Aaron Henry, Series I, Subseries C, Folder 9, Box 1, Aaron Henry Papers, Archives, Tougaloo College, Miss.; and "Mound Bayouans Applaud Dr. Howard's Departure," *Jackson Advocate,* December 24, 1955, 1–2.

101. Mississippi Insurance Department, *Biennial Report*, March 1, 1949, to March 1, 1951, 154; Mississippi Insurance Department, *Biennial Report,* March 1, 1955, to February 28, 1957, 186; Examination Report of Magnolia Mutual Life Insurance Company as of December 31, 1958, Magnolia Mutual Life Insurance Company, Mississippi Insurance Department; Mississippi Insurance Department, *Biennial Report,* March 1, 1957 to February 28, 1959, 271, 665; "Negro Physician Says Howard's Fortune Not Acquired at Expense of Insurance Firm," *Tupelo Daily Journal,* January 20, 1956, 14, Howard FBI file; and Beito, *From Mutual Aid to the Welfare State,* 198, 202–3.

102. C. Evers interview, September 2, 1999.

103. "Ticker Tape U.S.A.," *Jet* 8 (May 19, 1955), 9.

104. "His Spirit Still Lives," *Jackson Clarion-Ledger,* January 1, 1956, 6; and "Good Riddance," *Jackson Daily News,* December 17, 1955, 6.

105. "Other Side of Mississippi," *National Guardian;* "Dr. Howard Will Speak at Benefit Show," *California Eagle,* December 15, 1955, 1–2; "Truckloads of Gifts Speeding to Mississippi," *California Eagle,* December 22, 1955, 1; "Ticker Tape U.S.A.," *Jet* 9 (December 15, 1955), 10; "Dr. Howard Sells Miss. Home, Farm," *Pittsburgh Courier,* December 24, 1955, 3; "Four Truckloads of 'Relief' Food, Toys Reach Mound Bayou," *Delta Democrat Times,* December 28, 1955, 1; Medgar W. Evers, Field Secretary—Miss. 1954–55, Monthly Report, December 30, 1955, Mississippi, Box C341, Group 2, NAACP Papers; and "Loads of Merchandise for Victims of 'Squeeze' in Mississippi," *Tri-State Defender,* January 7, 1956, 1.

106. "Mound Bayou Would Stop Race Agitators," *Jackson Clarion-Ledger,* December 22, 1955, 8; L. Alex Wilson, "Denies Ban on NAACP Meetings," *Tri-State Defender,* December 13, 1955, 1–2; and "Dr. Howard Vows to Continue Meetings in Mound Bayou," *Jackson Advocate,* December 31, 1955, 1, 8.

107. "1955 Honor Roll," *Chicago Defender,* January 7, 1956, 1; and "And They Got 'Honors,'" *Jackson Daily News,* January 9, 1956, 6.

108. "Negro Who Sued Dr. Howard Reported Missing from Home," *Jackson Clarion-Ledger,* December 24, 1955, 1; *Newark Telegram* 12, January 22, 1956, 4–5, Howard FBI file; "Dr. Howard Reveals Affidavit of Withdrawal of $25,000 Damage Suit against Him," *Jackson Advocate,* January 14, 1956, 1, 4; and "'Marked' Man Flees Miss. Plot to Frame Dr. T. R. M. Howard," *Jet* 9 (January 26, 1956), 8–9.

Chapter 7: "Time Bomb": Howard, J. Edgar Hoover, and the Emmett Till Mystery

1. William Bradford Huie, "The Shocking Story of Approved Killing in Mississippi," *Look* 20 (January 24, 1956), 46–48; and Whitfield, *Death in the Delta,* 52–53.

2. Huie, "Shocking Story," 48, 50.

3. Ibid., 50.

4. Ibid., 46–48; and Huie to Wilkins, October 12, 1955, Huie to Dan Mich, October 17, 1955, Huie to Walters, October 18, 1955—all in CMS 84, Folder 3536, Huie Papers.

5. Huie to Mich, October 23, 1955, CMS 84, Folder 3536, Huie Papers; and Huie, "Shocking Story," 50.

6. "Look Magazine Names Milam, Bryant in Confession Story," *Tri-State Defender,* January 14, 1956, 2. Huie's correspondence strongly suggests that he was the informant for the *Tri-State Defender.* In his notes, Huie states: "Note on the 'red barn' story. Aubrey Moody and Carver Haney got a boat that sunday morning out of that shed. One of them has a green and white truck—like Milam's." Otherwise, his correspondence is silent on Reed's story. The *Tri-State Defender* article is apparently the only published source for the "fishing party" explanation. Undated note beginning "(Audrey Moody . . .," CMS 84, Folder 3539, Huie Papers); undated typed compilation beginning "Here are the excerpts from letters:" (CMS 84, Folder 3536, Huie Papers).

7. Simpson, "Reflections on a Murder," 198; and "Writer Challenges Brownell to Action in Till Kidnap-Murder Case," *Baltimore Afro-American,* January 21, 1956, 2; "Ask New Till Probe," *Baltimore Afro-American,* January 21, 1956, 2.

8. Adams, *Time Bomb,* 10, 16–21; and Olive Arnold Adams, interview by authors, May 25, 2000. Julius J. Adams had helped to sponsor one of Howard's Till-related speeches in November. Jones to Wilkins, November 14, 1955, "Mississippi Pressures, General Office File" folder, Box A424, Group 2, NAACP Papers.

9. Amos Dixon, "Mrs. Bryant Didn't Even Hear Emmett Till Whistle," *California Eagle,* January 26, 1956; Dixon, "Milam Master-Minded Emmett Till Killing," *California Eagle,* February 2, 1956; Dixon, "True Story of Emmett Till's Torture-Filled Last Hours," *California Eagle,* February 9, 1956; Dixon, "Torture and Murder," *California Eagle,* February 16, 1956; Dixon, "South Wins Out in Lynching Trial," *California Eagle,* February 23, 1956, 2; E. Boyd interview, September 20, 2003; and Loren Miller Jr., interview by authors, January 2, 2004.

10. Adams, *Time Bomb,* 15.

11. Reed, telephone interview, May 18, 2001; and *Mississippi v. Milam and Bryant,* 234. On March 20, 2001, we had a brief conversation with Aubrey Moody, who, in Huie's notes, helped to retrieve the boat for the fishing party. He refused to be taped or interviewed, but he vigorously asserted that he had never been in the equipment shed.

12. Henry Lee Loggins, interview by authors, July 21, 2001; Henry Lee Loggins, interview by Keith Beauchamp, February 12, 2002 (copy in possession of the authors); and Federal Bureau of Investigation, Prosecutive Report of Investigative Concerning . . . Emmett Till, Deceased, Victim, February 9, 2006, 30–31.

13. Federal Bureau of Investigation, Prosecutive Report of Investigation, 26–30, 49; Jerry Mitchell, "Fact, Fiction of Till's Murder," *Jackson Clarion-Ledger,* February 18, 2007, 00; and Mitchell, "Grand Jury Issues No Indictments in Till Killing," *Jackson Clarion-Ledger,* February 27, 2007.

14. Collins died in 1992. Federal Bureau of Investigation, Prosecutive Report of Investigation, 29. Adams, *Time Bomb,* 6.

15. "Undertaker Denies Foreclosure Threat," *Jackson Clarion-Ledger,* February 14, 1956; "Sent Gifts, Others Weep 2,000 in Miss. 'Squeeze,'" *Chicago Defender,* January 7, 1956, 3; and Wilkins to George Kaufman, January 27, 1956, NAACP Administration, General Office File, "Mississippi Pressures, Howard, T. R. M." folder, Group 3, Box A230, NAACP papers.

16. Jerry Thornbery, "Amzie Moore," 4–5; and Amzie Moore, Affidavit, December 29, 1954, General Office File, Mississippi Pressures, Amzie Moore, Case of 1955, Box 422, Group 2, NAACP Papers.

17. Daniel E. Byrd to Wilkins, January 18, 1955, Wilkins to Amzie Moore, January 27, 1955, Wilkins to Moore, November 18, 1955—all in "Mississippi Pressures, General Office File" folder, Box 422, Group 2, NAACP Papers; Moore to Charles Diggs Jr., July 28, 1955, Folder 2, Box 1, Amzie Moore Papers, Wisconsin Historical Society, Madison, Wisc.; and Thornbery, "Amzie Moore," 8.

18. Thornbery, "Amzie Moore," 9–10; Curtis F. McClane to Norman Thomas, November 25, 1955, Thomas to Jesse Turner, November 28, 1955, Thomas to J. M. Kaplan, December 2, 1955, Thomas to Raymond S. Rubinow, November 28, 1955—all in Series I, General Correspondence 1904–1967, Norman Thomas Papers, Manuscripts Division, New York Public Library; unsigned memorandum to unidentified recipient, November 28, 1955, Bennett to Turner, February 16, 1956—both in Tri-State Bank folder, National Sharecroppers Fund Papers, Wayne State University, Detroit, Mich.; W. A. Swanberg, *Norman Thomas: the Last Idealist* (New York: Charles Scribner's Sons, 1976), 429–30; Moore to Wilkins, January 30, 1956, Folder 2, Box 1, Moore Papers; and From the Minutes of the Executive Board of the Regional Council of Negro Leadership, January 5, 1956, Jesse H. Turner to Moore, January 16 and January 24, 1956—all in NAACP Administration, Cases, Amzie Moore, 1956, Reprisals, Mississippi, Box A229, Group 3, NAACP Papers.

19. M. A. Jones to Nichols, January 9, 1956, Howard FBI file; Hamilton, *Adam Clayton Powell,* 221; "Dr. Howard Assails Plot to Drive Negroes from Mississippi," *Daily Worker,* January 3, 1956, 3; and Gordon, "Dr. Howard Foresees Early End," *National Guardian.*

20. Jones to Nichols, January 9, 1956; Nichols to Tolson, January 16, 1956, Hoover to Brownell, January 16, 1956—all in Howard FBI file.

21. Hoover to Howard, January 16, 1956, Howard FBI file; and Dixon, "Hoover and Dr. Howard Row Over Killings in Mississippi," *California Eagle,* January 26, 1956, 1.

22. Howard to Hoover, January 19, 1956, Howard FBI file.

23. Howard to Hoover, January 20, 1956, Howard FBI file. The letter is heavily redacted.

24. Price to Rosen, January 23, 1956, Nichols to Tolson, January 25, 1956, Nichols to Tolson, January 26, 1956—all in Howard FBI file. Much of the content is redacted.

25. "Properly Rebuked," *Jackson Daily News,* January 20, 1956, "A Loud-Mouthed Liar," *Jackson Daily News,* January 22, 1956, 2; "Hoover Defends FBI against Unjust Charges," *Atlanta Constitution,* January 20, 1956; and "Qualifies As Reckless," *Memphis Commercial Appeal,* January 20, 1956.

26. Nichols to Tolson, January 18 and January 19, 1956, FBI Memphis to Hoover, January 24, 1956, and SAC, Memphis to Hoover, FBI, January 20, 1956—all in Howard FBI file.

27. [Redacted] to Hoover, January 26, 1956, [redacted: identified as Ed Brewer] to [redacted: identified as Hodding Carter], January 25, 1956—both in Howard FBI file; Brewer to Carter, January 25, 1956, Correspondence 1956 folder: B, Hodding and Betty Werlein Carter Papers; and [redacted: identified as Hodding Carter] to Hoover, January 27, 1956, Howard FBI file.

28. "Mr. Hoover Is Wrong," *California Eagle,* January 26, 1956, 4; "Conscience Hurting?" *Chicago Defender,* January 28, 1956, 9; "Mr. Hoover vs. Dr. Howard," *New York Amsterdam News,* February 4, 1956, 8; "Wrong Foe, Wrong Place, Wrong Time," *Baltimore Afro-American,* February 4, 1956, 4; and "Dr. Howard Is Right," *Tri-State Defender,* January 28, 1956, 1; "Conscience Hurting?" *Tri-State Defender,* January 28, 1956, 7.

29. Price to Rosen, January 23, 1956, Hoover to Howard, January 27, 1956—both in Howard FBI file. The letter is heavily redacted.

30. Williams, *Thurgood Marshall,* 255; Nichols to Tolson, February 9, 1956, Howard FBI file; and "Ticker Tape U.S.A.," *Jet* 9 (February 9, 1956), 11.

31. Roosevelt Ward Jr., "Rally Lauds Dr. Howard's Courage," *Daily Worker,* November 14, 1955, 2; "The FBI Attacks Dr. Howard," *Militant,* January 30, 1956, 3; and "The Hoover-Howard Exchange, 'The Kind of Justice That Permits Murderers to Go Free and Boast,'" *National Guardian,* February 6, 1956, 7.

32. "Howard to Speak at Feb. 8 Rally," *National Guardian,* January 30, 1956, 4; James Booker, "Dr. Howard Says He Wants to Speak at Rally Wednesday," *New York Amsterdam News,* February 4, 1956, 6; and "Howard Quits 'Mississippi Justice' Rally," *New York Post,* February 1, 1956, 25, T. R. M. Howard folder, National Sharecroppers Papers.

33. "Labor Leader Praises Dr. Howard's Stand," *Tri-State Defender,* February 25, 1956, 5; and Fay Bennett to Howard, January 31, 1956, T. R. M. Howard folder, National Sharecroppers Papers.

34. Nichols to Tolson, February 29, 1956, Till FBI file.

35. Ibid.

36. Nichols to Hoover, February 29, 1955, Price to Rosen, February 29, 1956, Warren Olney III to Hoover, March 2, 1956—all in Till FBI file.

37. *Louisiana Weekly,* February 18, 1956, 6; George Daniels, "Dr. Howard Gives 3–Point Program to Alpha Confab," *Chicago Defender,* January 14, 1956, 3; "NAACP Takes Steps to Organize Civil Rights Rally," *Militant,* January 30, 1956, 1, 4; and "Negro Advocates Use of Troops to Put Down Southern 'Rebellion,'" *Rocky Mountain News,* February 21, 1956, Howard FBI file.

38. Price to Rosen, February 9, 1956, Thurgood Marshall FBI file; and Nichols to Tolson, February 9, 1956, Howard FBI file.

39. "Dr. Howard Barred from Civil Rights Meet," *Jet* 9 (March 1, 1956), 3; Nat Turner to Wilkins, February 27, 1956, Wilkins to Turner, February 28, 1956, Wilkins to Simeon Booker, February 28, 1956, Wilkins to John Johnson, February 28, 1956—all in Correspondence, 1956, NAACP Administration, 1956, General Office File, Civil Rights Mobilization, National Delegate Assembly, Box A74, Group 3, NAACP Papers.

40. "Along the Battlefront," *Crisis* 63 (April 1956), 229–30; George Lavan, "Both Parties Exposed at Civil Rights Confab," *Militant,* March 12, 1956, 1, 4; Robert A. Caro, *Master of the Senate: The Years of Lyndon Johnson* (New York: Alfred A. Knopf, 2002), 784; and "On the Washington Record," March 19, 1956, Program Department, Subject and Correspondence Files, 1955–56, Folder: Civil Rights, Box 370, UPW Papers, Wisconsin Historical Society; and *Militant,* March 13, 1956.

41. "News and Views," *American Negro* 1 (April 1956), 10–13.

42. Howard to Wilkins, March 15, 1956, NAACP Administration, General Office File, "Mississippi Pressures, Howard, T. R. M., 1956" folder, Box A230, Group 3, NAACP Papers.

43. Ibid.

44. Ibid.

45. Wilkins to Howard, March 29, 1956, NAACP Administration, General Office File, "Mississippi Pressures, Howard, T. R. M., 1956" folder, Box A230, Group 3, NAACP Papers.

46. Ibid.

47. Ibid.

48. Wilkins to Evers, April 16, 1956, Wilkins to Willard Brown, April 3, 1956—both in NAACP Administration, General Office File, "Mississippi Pressures, Howard, T. R. M., 1956" folder, Box A230, Group 3, NAACP Papers.

49. "Will Probably Locate in Chicago, Mrs. Howard Says," March 1956 [clipping; newspaper name and exact date not shown], Folder 1, Box 372, Barnett Papers; E. Boyd interview, October 27, 1995; Nicholas Lemann, *The Promised Land: The Great Black Migration and How It Changed America* (New York: Vintage Books, 1991), 70, 83–84, 95; and "People, Places, and Things," *Tri-State Defender,* February 4, 1956, 6.

50. "Mrs. Helen Boyd Howard," *Pittsburgh Courier,* April 7, 1956, 6; "One of 'Ours' Gave Tips to Killers, Says Mrs. Howard," *California Eagle,* February 2, 1956, 2; "Ky. Derby Still Draws Top Society to Louisville," *Jet* 10 (May 17, 1956), 40; and "People Are Talking About," *Jet* 10 (May 17, 1956), 44.

51. "Audience Donates to Till Witness," *Chicago Defender,* March 17, 1956, 10; and E. Boyd interview, September 20, 2003.

52. Howard to Adam Clayton Powell Jr., January 21, 1956, NAACP Washington Bureau, General Office File, "Adam Clayton Powell Jr., 1956" folder, Box IX: 191, NAACP Papers; J. F. Redmon and G. R. Haughton to Martin Luther King Jr., March 14, 1956, King Papers Project.

53. "Rep. Powell, Dr. King, Dr. Howard to Talk," *Pittsburgh Courier,* April 28, 1956, 1; "Change Meeting Site of Regional Council," *Chicago Defender,* March 24, 1956, 2; Medgar Evers to Wilkins, April 10, 1956, NAACP Administration, General Office File, "Mississippi Pressures, Howard, T. R. M., 1956" folder, Box A230, Group 3, NAACP Papers; and "Ticker Tape U.S.A.," *Jet* 19, April 26, 1956, 15.

54. Wilkins to Medgar Evers, April 16, 1956, NAACP Administration, General Office File, "Mississippi Pressures, Howard, T. R. M." folder, Box A230, Group 3, NAACP Papers.

55. "Powell Telegram Hit Dr. T. R. M. Howard," *Jackson Advocate,* May 5, 1956, 1; "Score Governor at Miss. Confab.," *Chicago Daily Defender,* April 30, 1956, 2; James P. Coleman to King, April 23, 1956, in Clayborne Carson, Stewart Burns, Susan Carson, Peter Holloran, and Dana L. H. Powell, eds., *The Papers of Martin Luther King Jr., vol. 3, Birth of a New Age, December 1955–December 1956* (Berkeley: University of California Press, 1997), 220–21; King to Redmon, March 27, 1956, King Papers Project; and Branch, *Parting the Waters,* 184–86.

56. "Speakers Absent from Miss. Meet," *Chicago Defender,* May 5, 1956, 1; "Miss. Gov. 'Asks' Powell, King Not to Attend Meet," *Louisiana Weekly,* April 28, 1956, 1; King to Coleman, April 24, 1956, in Carson, et al., *Papers of Martin Luther King Jr.,* 221; and "Negroes Rap Governor's Action," *Clarksdale Press Register,* April 25, 1956, 8.

57. Evers to Wilkins, April 30, 1956, NAACP Administration, General Office File, "Mississippi Pressures, Howard, T. R. M., 1956" folder, Box A230, Group 3, NAACP Papers.

58. "Both Sides of Race Issue Aired Last Night," *Clarksdale Press Register,* April 28, 1956, 1; and *Arkansas Gazette,* April 28, 1956, T. R. M. Howard, Clippings File, Southern Educational Reporting Service Library, Fisk University, Nashville, Tenn.

59. "Miss. Council Blames Pressure for Slim Turnout," *Jet* 9 May 10, 1956, 6; "Change Meeting Site of Regional Council," *Chicago Defender;* and Evers to Wilkins, April 30, 1956.

60. Howard's invitation to Powell described Mound Bayou as the site for the rally. (Howard to Powell, January 21, 1956, General Office File, "Adam Clayton Powell Jr., 1956" folder, Box 9: 191, NAACP Papers). Dittmer, *Local People,* 58–59, 72–73, 78–79; and Branch, *Parting the Waters,* 183; Yasuhiro Katagiri, *The Mississippi State Sovereignty Commission: Civil Rights and States' Rights* (Jackson: University Press of Mississippi, 2001), 18; "Say Regional Council Negro Leadership to Abandon Civil Rights Fights," *Jackson Advocate,* January 21, 1956, 6; "Wealthy Farmer Declines Treasury Regional Council Negro Leadership," *Jackson Advocate,* May 12, 1956, 8; and "Both Sides of Race Issue Aired Last Night," *Clarksdale Press Register.*

61. "Salute and Support the Heroes of the South," *New York Amsterdam News,* May 26, 1956, 2–6; Earl Brown, "Garden Rally," *New York Amsterdam News,* May 28, 1956, 12; "Civil Rights Crusade Rally at Madison Square Garden," *Daily Worker,* May 24, 1956, 1; Roosevelt Ward, "Ovation to Heroes Rocks Civil Rights Rally," *Daily Worker,* May 28, 1956, 3; Martin Luther King Jr. to Benjamin F. McLaurin, May 6, 1956, King to A. Philip Randolph, May 10, 1956 in Carson, et al., *Papers of Martin Luther King Jr.,* 246–47, 252–53; civil rights rally featuring Eleanor Roosevelt and Autherine Lucy, May 24, 1956 [sound recording], Schomburg Center for Research in Black Culture, New York Public Library.

62. Civil rights rally recording, May 24, 1956.

63. Barbara Ransby, *Ella Baker and the Black Freedom Movement: A Radical Democratic Vision* (Chapel Hill: University of North Carolina Press, 2003), 161–68; Joanne Grant, *Ella Baker: Freedom Bound* (New York: Wiley, 1998), 100; and Randolph to Ella Baker, March 7, 1956, Series I, General Correspondence, December 1955–May 1956, Norman Thomas Papers.

64. Robert M. Ratcliffe, "Behind the Headlines," *Pittsburgh Courier,* April 7, 1956, 13.

Chapter 8: Taking On the Machine in Chicago: A Republican Campaign for Congress

1. Lemann, *Promised Land,* 70.

2. Lemann, *Promised Land,* 74; Arnold R. Hirsch, *Making the Second Ghetto: Race and Housing in Chicago, 1940–1960* (Cambridge, U.K.: Cambridge University Press, 1983), 7–8, 186–87, 232–34; Christopher Robert Reed, *The Chicago NAACP and the Rise of Black Professional Leadership, 1910–1966* (Bloomington: Indiana University Press, 1997), 168–74; and Dempsey J. Travis, *An Autobiography of Black Politics* (Chicago: Urban Research Institute, 1981) 268.

3. Theresa Fambro Hooks, "A Busy Month for a Busy Helen Howard," *Chicago Daily Defender,* March 4, 1968, 17; Stan West and Jennifer Juarez Robles, "Lake Meadow Residents Unnerved by Rash of Crimes," *Chicago Reporter* (November 1990) (http://www.chicago reporter.com/1990/11–90/1190%2012%20New%20Incidents.htm, accessed August 29, 2007); Gladys M. Johnson, "Gaddings," *Chicago Defender,* April 10–16, 1965, 13; Hirsch, *Making the Second Ghetto,* 206–7, 259–61; and James Q. Wilson, *Negro Politics: The Search for Leadership* (Glencoe, Ill.: Free Press of Glencoe, 1960), 66.

4. Robert Squires, interview by authors, May 11, 2004; Patricia C. McKissack and Fredrick L. McKissack, *Young, Black, and Determined: A Biography of Lorraine Hansberry* (New York: Holiday House, 1998), 23–27, 76; and Wendy Plotkin, "Deeds of Mistrust: Race, Hous-

ing, and Restrictive Covenants in Chicago, 1900–1953" (PhD diss., University of Illinois at Chicago, 1999), 147–48.

5. "Medicine," *Jet* 10 (August 16, 1956), 56 (August 23, 1956), 14–15; Albert G. Barnett, "Famous Surgeon Sets Up Clinic," *Chicago Defender,* January 19, 1957, 7; B. Herbert Martin, telephone interview, May 3, 2004; and Moore interview, April 4, 2001.

6. Alfred Duckett, "We're Drifting to Socialism, Fuller Says," *New York Age,* August 16, 1958, 3; Mary Fuller Casey, *S. B. Fuller: Pioneer in Black Development* (Jamestown, N.C.: Bridgemaster Press, 2003), 65–76; Rachel Kranz, *African-American Business Leaders and Entrepreneurs* (New York: Facts on File, 2004), 97–98; and Robert D. Hobday to Maxwell Rabb, October 11, 1956, Box 343, White House Central Files, Dwight D. Eisenhower Papers, Dwight D. Eisenhower Library, Abilene, Kan.

7. Alfred Duckett, "We're Drifting to Socialism, Fuller Says," *New York Age,* August 23, 1958, 3; Moore interview, April 4, 2001; and Zollar interview, April 17, 2001.

8. The emphasis is in the original. Timuel D. Black Jr., *Bridges of Memory: Chicago's First Wave of Black Migration* (Evanston, Ill.: Northwestern University Press, 2003), 354; and Duckett, "We're Drifting to Socialism, Fuller Says," *New York Age,* August 16, 1958, 3.

9. McMillen, *Citizens' Council,* 213; "Howard Lauds Ike's Statement," *Pittsburgh Courier,* January 14, 1956, 3; "Negro Advocates Use of Troops to Put Down Southern 'Rebellion,'" *Rocky Mountain News,* February 21, 1956, Howard FBI file; "Fight Bigots with Votes, Urges Rights Crusader" (ANP), April 18, 1956, Folder 2, Box 303, Barnett Papers; "T. R. M. Howard Announces Switch to Republicans," *Chicago Daily Defender,* May 1, 1956, 1; "Dr. Howard Switches, to Campaign for GOP," *Jet* 9 (May 10, 1956), 4; and "Ticker Tape U.S.A.," *Jet* 10 (May 24, 1956), 17.

10. Edward G. Carmines and James A Stimson, *Issue Evolution: Race and the Transformation of American Politics* (Princeton, N.J.: Princeton University Press, 1989), 31–32; Wilkins, *Standing Fast,* 231; "Democrats Blasted by Wilkins," *Pittsburgh Courier,* April 30, 1955, 1, 4; and "Mrs. FDR Quits Bethune, Stays on NAACP Board," *Chicago Daily Defender,* May 2, 1956, 3.

11. Robert Frederick Burk, *The Eisenhower Administration and Black Civil Rights* (Knoxville: University of Tennessee Press, 1984), 5, 69–70; Carl M. Brauer, *John F. Kennedy and the Second Reconstruction* (New York: Columbia University Press, 1977), 8; and Wilkins, *Standing Fast,* 241.

12. Hamilton, *Adam Clayton Powell,* 266–74; "Southern Opinion on Ike's Speech," *Jet* 11 (November 22, 1956), 16; *National Guardian,* October 15, 1956, 10, November 12, 1956, 4; Tucker, *Lieutenant Lee of Beale Street,* 166; and "Howard Assails Sen. Eastland," *Chicago Defender,* June 30, 1956, 5.

13. Dale Wright, "Why Dr. Howard Left Mississippi," *Jet* 10 (August 23, 1956), 15.

14. Caro, *Master of the Senate,* 842; Morrow, *Forty Years a Guinea Pig,* 107; Denton L. Watson, *Lion in the Lobby: Clarence Mitchell Jr.'s Struggle for the Passage of Civil Rights Laws,* (New York: William Morrow, 1990), 354–55; Wilkins, *Standing Fast,* 242; *Chicago Daily Defender,* November 8, 1956, 3; Tucker, *Lieutenant Lee of Beale Street,* 167–68; "Southern Opinion on Ike's Speech," *Jet* 11 (November 22, 1956), 16; Branch, *Parting the Waters,* 220; "10 Now in Ill. State Assembly," *Chicago Daily Defender,* November 7, 1956, 5; Ethel L. Payne, "How Ike

Broke Back of South," *Chicago Daily Defender,* November 8, 1956, 1; Hamilton, *Adam Clayton Powell,* 275; and Grimshaw, *Bitter Fruit,* 42, 103.

15. Lemann, *Promised Land,* 74–75; and William L. Clay, *Just Permanent Interests: Black Americans in Congress, 1870–1992* (New York: Amistad, 1993), 76.

16. Christopher E. Manning, "The Ties That Bind: The Congressional Career of William L. Dawson and the Limits of Black Electoral Leadership in the Post-War Period" (PhD diss., Northwestern University, 2003), 164–68; Wilson, 50; and Lemann, *Promised Land,* 76–77.

17. Duckett, "'We're Drifting to Socialism,' Fuller Says," *New York Age,* June 14, 1958; Wilson, 61, 70; Manning, "Ties That Bind," 230–33, 253–55; and Simeon Booker, "Why Congressman Dawson Won't Get Angry about Civil Rights," *Jet* 10 (July 19, 1956), 14.

18. Wilson, *Negro Politics,* 54–56; Barbara A. Reynolds, *Jesse Jackson: The Man, the Movement, the Myth* (Chicago: Nelson-Hall, 1975), 207; *Pittsburgh Courier,* March 5, 1955, 1; and Grimshaw, *Bitter Fruit,* 42.

19. Grimshaw, *Bitter Fruit,* 81; Manning, "Ties That Bind," 230–33, 253–55; and Percy Ward, "G.O.P. Eyes 3 of 5 Seats in Congress Race," *Chicago Tribune,* October 5, 1958, sec. 3, 3.

20. Howard to Adams, May 8, 1957, Box 343, White House Central Files, Eisenhower Papers; Moore interview, April 4, 2001; E. Boyd interview, July 19, 1999; and Bennett J. Johnson, interview by authors, May 26, 2004.

21. "Why Congressman Dawson Won't Get Angry about Civil Rights," *Jet* 10 (July 19, 1956), 14; Ethel L. Payne, "Negro Masses Revolting against Democratic Rule," *New York Age,* June 14, 1958, 4; and Manning, "Ties That Bind," 272–76.

22. Reed, *Chicago NAACP,* 162–67; and United Packinghouse Workers of America-CIO, "Dr. Howard to Speak at Negro History Rally on February 29th," *District One Champion* 9 (February 1956), 3–4, Civil Rights folder, Box 370, Program Department, UPW Papers.

23. Open Letter to Congressman William L. Dawson, By Order of the Executive Committee, Chicago Branch, NAACP, August 29, 1956, UPW Papers, Program Department, Folder: NAACP, Box 373, Wisconsin Historical Society, Madison.

24. Rick Halpern, *Down on the Killing Floor: Black and White Workers in Chicago's Packinghouses, 1904–54* (Urbana: University of Illinois Press, 1997), 241–44; Roger Horowitz, *"Negro and White, Unite and Fight!" A Social History of Industrial Unionism in Meatpacking, 1930–90* (Urbana: University of Illinois Press, 1997), 220–25; James R. Ralph Jr., *Northern Protest: Martin Luther King, Jr., Chicago and the Civil Rights Movement* (Cambridge, Mass.: Harvard University Press, 1993), 71; "Dr. Howard to Speak at . . . Negro History Rally on February 29th," 3; Charles Hayes, "Where Is Dawson?" United Packinghouse Workers of America-CIO, *District One Champion* 9, March 1956, 8; Hayes, "Rally Crowd Vows to Fight Jim Crow," United Packinghouse Workers of America-CIO, *District One Champion* 9, March 1956, 2—Hayes articles in Program Department, Subject and Correspondence Files, Conventions, Folder 6, District #1, Wisconsin Historical Society, Madison—"Chicago Unions, NAACP to Rally," *Militant,* March 12, 1956, 4; and "Howard Assails Sen. Eastland," *Chicago Defender.*

25. Dempsey J. Travis, *"Harold": The People's Mayor* (Chicago: Urban Research Press, 1989), 122; Gary Rivlin, *Fire on the Prairie: Chicago's Harold Washington and the Politics of Race* (New York: Henry Holt, 1992), 57–58; Augustus Savage, "Defend Your Rights," *American Negro* 1 (November 1955), 11, "American Negro of the Year," *American Negro* (February

1956), 3, "T. R. M. Howard: News and Views," *American Negro* (April 1956), 10–13; and Travis, *Autobiography of Black Politics*, 254.

26. T. R. M. Howard, "The Role of the National Medical Association in a Changing Social Order," *Journal of the National Medical Association* 48 (September 1956), 353–54.

27. Imhotep National Conference on Hospital Integration, *Proceedings*, March 8–9, 1957, 1–2, 10–11, 16–19, 52, Leonidas H. Berry Papers, Box 4, Vivian G. Harsh Collection, Woodson Regional Library, Chicago Public Library.

28. "CEO Honors Drs. Howard and Cobb; Points Need for Integration," *Chicago Daily Defender*, June 14, 1956, 18; "Quotes of the Week," *Chicago Daily Defender*, June 30, 1956, 2; and Reed, *Chicago NAACP*, 178.

29. "Howard Backs Freedom Dinner," *Chicago Defender*, July 8, 1957, 7; Theodore C. Stone, "Raise $20G at NAACP Dinner," *Chicago Daily Defender*, July 16, 1957, 2; and Travis, *Autobiography of Black Politics*, 261.

30. T. R. M. Howard, "President's Farewell Address," *Journal of the National Medical Association* 49 (September 1957), 329–31; Wilkins to Howard, August 20, 1957, NAACP Administration 1956–65, General Office File, National, "General Leagues and Organizations" folder, Box A209, Group 3, NAACP Papers.

31. Branch, *Parting the Waters*, 220–21; Caro, *Master of the Senate*, 843–44, 873–74; and Gayle B. Montgomery with James W. Johnson, *One Step from the White House: The Rise and Fall of Senator William F. Knowland* (Berkeley: University of California Press, 1998), 216–19.

32. Caro, *Master of the Senate*, 991; and Brauer, *John F. Kennedy and the Second Reconstruction*, 10.

33. Morrow, *Forty Years a Guinea Pig*, 136; and Caro, *Master of the Senate*, 961–62, 990–91, 1005.

34. Caro, *Master of the Senate*, 961–62, 992–98, 1008; and Branch, *Parting the Waters*, 221–22.

35. Caro, *Master of the Senate*, 1001–1002; and Branch, *Parting the Waters*, 222–24.

36. "T. R. M. Howard to Speak for 24th Young GOP," *Chicago Daily Defender*, November 18, 1957, 4; "T. R. M. Howard," *Chicago Defender*, December 7, 1957, 1; Reed, *Chicago NAACP*, 187–89; and Travis, *Autobiography of Black Politics*, 261–64.

37. Thornbery, "Amzie Moore," 10; Fay Bennett to Percy Dean, February 27, 1958, Howard to Moore, March 27, May 24, 1958, Folder 3, Box 1, Moore Papers; and Moore to Howard, ca. mid-April 1958, Folder 2, Box 2, Moore Papers.

38. Douglas Starr, "State's Segregation Laws May Prove Two-Edged Sword," *Clarksdale Press Register*, February 20, 1956, 8; "Most Clarksdalians Opposed to Controversial Libel Bill," *Clarksdale Press Register*, March 10, 1956, 3; Booker, "Mississippians Wonder Why Bold Racist Was Ruled 'Insane,'" *Jet* 13 (December 12, 1957), 10–12; "Massie Hawkins Bedroom Integration Here between White Men and Negro Women," *Eagle Eye*, October 5, 1957, 1; and "Massie Hawkins College of Prostitution," *Eagle Eye*, October 12, 1957, 1; and Arrington High, Identification Record, SAC, Jackson to SAC, Chicago, December 1, 1965, High FBI file.

39. "Arrington High As Told to Marc Crawford, Jet Exclusive: I Escaped Mississippi in a Casket," *Jet* 13 (February 27, 1958), 11–13; and Dan Burley, "Mississippi Escapee Yearns to Return," *Chicago Daily Defender*, February 24, 1958, 4.

40. Booker, "Mississippians Wonder Why Bold Racist Was Ruled 'Insane,'" *Jet* 13 (December 12, 1957), 10–12; SAC, Chicago to Director, FBI, October 4, 1965, High FBI file; and Howard to Amzie Moore, March 27, 1958.

41. "Testimonial Dinner," *Chicago Defender,* June 7, 1958, 2.

42. United Packinghouse Workers of America, *District One Champion* 9 (February 1958), 6, *The Champion* folder, District 1, Box 389, United Packinghouse Workers of America Papers; Bennett J. Johnson, telephone interviews, February 16, 2002, May 26, 2004; Addie Wyatt, telephone interview, April 21, 2001; "The Greg Harris Notebook," *Chicago Daily Defender,* October 21, 1958, 8; "Hold Rites for Courier Publisher," *New Crusader* (Chicago), June 23, 1973, 1; and Duckett, "We're Drifting to Socialism, Fuller Says" *New York Age,* June 14, 1958.

43. Lewis A. H. Caldwell, "Commentary," *Chicago Daily Defender,* June 14, 1958, 4; Caldwell, "Commentary," *Chicago Daily Defender,* October 15, 1958, 8; Bennett J. Johnson, interview by authors, February 16, 2002; and Moore interview, April 4, 2001.

44. Julia Futrell, interview by authors, May 3, 2001; flier, "Voters Dropping Dawson . . . Want Howard in Congress," Folder 4, Box 3, Lucy Collier Papers, Vivian G. Harsh Collection, Woodson Regional Library, Chicago Public Library; and Randall K. Burkett, "The Baptist Church in Years of Crisis, J. C. Austin and Pilgrim Baptist Church, 1926–1950," in Timothy E. Fulop and Albert J. Raboteau, eds., *African American Religion: Interpretative Essays in History and Culture* (New York: Routledge, 1997), 315–30.

45. Percy Wood, "Byrne Scoffs at 'Stacked' Rating," *Chicago Tribune,* October 26, 1958, 2; Roi Ottley, "Pastor Helps with Babies, Homes, Jobs," *Chicago Tribune,* January 16, 1960; Roy L. Miller Sr. and Eunice L. Lawyer, *From Kibler's Bridge to Miller Road: 65 Years of Christian Service in the African Methodist Episcopal Church* (Cincinnati, Ohio: Stay-in-Touch Publishing, 2000), 35, 44–45, 70–81; "Interdenominational Clergy Praises Howard, Rips Dawson," news release, undated, Junius C. Austin and Clay Evans to City Editor, Associated Negro Press, October 8, 1958, Folder 1, Box 372, Barnett Papers; Reynolds, *Jesse Jackson,* 56–57; Ralph, *Northern Protest,* 67; and "Our Opinion, the Dr. Howard Case," *New Crusader,* January 6, 1962, 1.

46. B. J. Johnson, telephone interview, May 26, 2004; B. C. Coleman to Eisenhower, February 11, 1958, Box 343, White House Central Files, Eisenhower Papers; "Shame of Mississippi," *Chicago Defender; Chicago Defender,* October 27, 1958; Archibald J. Carey Jr. to Howard, May 26, 1958, Folder 237, Box 35, Carey Papers, Chicago Historical Society; and Dickerson, "Ringing the Bell of Freedom," 93–96.

47. "Ex-Demo Aide in Key Role for GOP," *Chicago Defender,* April 19, 1958, 1; Louis Martin, "Off the Cuff," *Chicago Daily Defender,* October 9, 1958, 8; and unidentified newspaper clipping, ca. October 1958, NAACP Administration 1956–65, General Office File, Folder: Hop-How, 1956–65, Group III, A150, NAACP Papers.

48. Lemann, *Promised Land,* 92; Rivlin, *Fire on the Prairie,* 13–14; Reynolds, *Jesse Jackson,* 50; and Wilson, *Negro Politics,* 54.

49. "Choose a Champion of Human Rights, Elect Howard for Congress," Folder 2, Box 3, Collier Papers.

50. "Voters Dropping Dawson."

51. "The Dr. 'T.R.I.M.' Howard Story," [1958], Folder 2, Box 3, Collier Papers; and Wesley South, interview by authors, November 19, 2001.

52. Morrow, *Forty Years a Guinea Pig,* 135, 169–72; and B. C. Coleman to Eisenhower, February 11, 1958, Coleman to Eisenhower, February 23, 1958, Maxwell Rabb to Tom Stephens, March 25, 1958—all in White House Central Files, Box 343, Eisenhower Papers; and "The White House Conference," *Chicago Daily Defender,* June 26, 1958, 11.

53. Val J. Washington to Sherman Adams, September 3, 1958, Adams to Washington, September 5, 1958—both in White House Central Files, Box 343, Eisenhower Papers.

54. "Which Way the Negro Vote?" *Chicago Daily Defender,* June 4, 1958, 11; Ben Holman, "Find Negro Votes Shifting to Dems," *Chicago Daily News,* October 4, 1958, 5; Wilson, 54; and Ralph, *Northern Protest,* 12–13.

55. Rivlin, *Fire on the Prairie,* 51; and Chicago League of Negro Voters, "You Are Invited to a Non-Partisan Conference of Negro Voters," October 1958, Albert Janney to Fellow Citizen, Chicago League of Negro Voters, ca. October 1958, courtesy of Bennett J. Johnson, Evanston, Illinois.

56. Janney to Fellow Citizen; Chicago League of Negro Voters, "You Are Invited to a Non-Partisan Conference"; Chicago League of Negro Voters, *To Increase the Power of Negro Voters—The Chicago Plan, July 1959*—all courtesy of Johnson.

57. Written note [November 1958], Citizens Committee to Elect Dr. T. R. M. Howard to Friend, October 20, 1958, Folder 4, Box 3, Collier Papers; "These Are Our Choices in Congressional Races," *Chicago Daily News,* October 27, 1958, 12; "Three Choices for Congress," *Chicago Sun-Times,* October 29, 1958, 29; "Gallant Campaigner," *Chicago Tribune,* October 31, 1958, 10; "The American's Indorsements," *Chicago American,* October 26, 1958, 1; and Caldwell, "Commentary," *Chicago Daily Defender,* October 15, 1958, 8; Caldwell, "Commentary," *Chicago Daily Defender,* October 22, 1958, 8; Caldwell, "Commentary," *Chicago Daily Defender,* October 29, 1958, 8; and Raymond R. Coffey, "Voter Turnout Key in Election," *Chicago Daily Defender,* November 3, 1958, 1.

58. Congressional Quarterly, *Guide to U.S. Elections* (Washington, D.C.: Congressional Quarterly, 1975), 836; Wilson, *Negro Politics,* 66; Moore interview, April 4, 2001; Caro, *Master of the Senate,* 1015; Morrow, *Forty Years a Guinea Pig,* 195; Greg Harris, "GOP Blasted in Crucial Election," *Chicago Daily Defender,* November 5, 1958, 3; "Dawson Wins; Demo Landslide," *Chicago Daily Defender,* November 6, 1958, 3; and Lee Edwards, *Goldwater: The Man Who Made a Revolution* (Washington, D.C.: Regnery, 1995), 105.

59. Williams Cousins Jr., interview by authors, November 27, 2001; Rivlin, *Fire on the Prairie,* 51–57; and Evans, interview by authors.

60. *Worker,* January 25, 1959, 12; Jim West, "GOP Handed Its Worst Defeat in Chicago History," *Worker,* March 8, 1959, 13; B. J. Johnson interview, February 16, 2002; Robert P. Winbush, interview by authors, August 18, 2001; and Chicago Office of the FBI, Report, Subject: "The Eagle Eye," Arrington High, December 13, 1965, High FBI file.

61. "Map Plan for Race Justice Raise $580 for Mob Victim," *Chicago Daily Defender,* May 7, 1959, 4; "Insists Fair Jury Would Have Freed Lynch Victim," *Chicago Daily Defender,* May 7, 1959, 4; "Mack Parker Must Be Found," *Chicago Daily Defender,* May 16, 1959, 12; Dittmer, *Local People,* 83–84; "Call Midwest Conference of Negro Voters," *Worker,* February 21, 1960, 12; "Speakers and Guests," *Worker,* March 27, 1960, 12; B. J. Johnson interview, February 16, 2002; Chicago League of Negro Voters, Call to a Conference, March 11–13, 1960, courtesy of Bennett J. Johnson; and Tyson, *Radio Free Dixie,* 150–64.

62. Moore interview, April 4, 2001; Evans, interview by authors; Zollar interview, April 17, 2001; Brenetta Howell Barrett, August 14, 2001; and "3,000 Pledge Aid, Give Funds for Freedom Fight," *Chicago Daily Defender,* December 16, 1959, 3; "Chicago Group to Back King, Sit-in," *Chicago Daily Defender,* March 30, 1960, 6.

63. "GOP'ers Temporarily Put Party Activities above the Party," *Jet* 18 (August 11, 1960), 40.

64. "Urges GOP 'Do What Is Right,'" *Chicago Daily Defender,* July 25, 1960, 3; Brauer, *John F. Kennedy and the Second Reconstruction,* 36–38, 74; and typed speaking notes on T. R. M. Howard's stationery, filed under Republican Platform Committee, NAACP Washington Bureau, General Office File, Republican Party, 1960, 1 of 2; Part I: 203, NAACP Papers.

65. B. J. Johnson interview, February 16, 2002; Gerald D. Bullock, "Back Convention March for Civil Rights Here," *Chicago Daily Defender,* July 4, 1960, 7; "Rally Demands Strong Plank on Civil Rights," *Chicago Daily Defender,* July 25, 1960, 3; Travis, *Autobiography of Black Politics,* 275–80; Thomas Powers, "5,000 Demonstrate for Civil Rights Plank," *Chicago Tribune,* July 26, 1960, 1, 10; Karl A. Lamb, "Kennedy and Nixon Leadership on Party Platform," in Paul Tillett, ed., *Inside Politics: The National Conventions, 1960* (Dobbs Ferry, N.Y.: Eagleton Institute of Politics at Rutgers, 1962), 67–82; and "Republican Platform, 1960," Donald Bruce Johnson and Kirk H. Porter, eds., *National Party Platforms, 1840–1972* (Urbana: University of Illinois Press, 1973), 618–19; and Brauer, *John F. Kennedy and the Second Reconstruction,* 39.

66. Brauer, *John F. Kennedy and the Second Reconstruction,* 41–50, 56–58.

67. Lemuel E. Bentley and Bennett J. Johnson, *Freedom Now, A Plan to Increase the Power of Negro Citizens* (Chicago: Chicago League of Negro Voters, 1960), 6; B. J. Johnson interview, February 16, 2002; and "Deny Pamphlet Backing Nixon," *Chicago Daily Defender,* October 31, 1960, 7.

68. The emphasis is in the original. "Words of the Week," *Jet* 18 (October 6, 1960), 30; and Caldwell, "Commentary," *Chicago Defender,* November 19–25, 1960, 4.

69. "Testifies Doctor Ordered Phony Reports Prepared," *Chicago Tribune,* February 10, 1962; "M.D. on Trial Vows He Knew No Fraud," *Chicago Tribune,* February 16, 1962, sec. 1, 18; "$51 Million Fake Accident Plot Charged; 39 Indicted," *Chicago Sun-Times,* November 28, 1961, folder on T. R. M. Howard, Box 14, 155139, Health Care Fraud Collection, American Medical Association Archives, Chicago; "State Negro Faces Conspiracy Charge," undated newspaper article, Folder 2, Box 303, Barnett Papers; "Link Dr. Howard with $100,000 Accident Ring," *Chicago Daily Defender,* February 14, 1961, 5; and Bill of Particulars, *People of Illinois v. Kenneth J. Brundage,* et al., Criminal Court of Cook County, Illinois, March Term, 1961, 4A-38–R-40.g, Records and Archives, Circuit Court of Cook County, Richard J. Daley Building, Chicago.

70. "Tuesday Services Slated for Attorney Bellows," *Chicago Tribune,* September 29, 1979, sec. 1B, 43; and Sherman C. Magidson, interview by authors, May 7, 2002.

71. Magidson interview, May 7, 2002.

72. Ron Chizever, "Fake Injury Trial Testimony Begins," *Chicago Daily News,* February 7, 1962, folder on T. R. M. Howard, Box 14, 155139, Health Care Fraud Collection, American Medical Association Archives, Chicago; and "2 Medics, 2 Cops among 44 to Be Arraigned," *Chicago Defender,* December 2–8, 1961, 3.

73. "Our Opinion, the Dr. Howard Case" *New Crusader;* Dan Burley, "Crowds Await Trial of Dr. Howard Monday," *New Crusader,* February 3, 1962, 10; "State Setback by Ace Witness in Howard Case," *New Crusader,* February 17, 1962, 13.

74. South interview, November 19, 2001; and A. L. Gray to Oliver Field, February 2, 1962, folder on T. R. M. Howard, Box 14, 155139, Health Care Fraud Collection, American Medical Association Archives, Chicago.

75. Dan Burley, "Admits: I Lied to Dr. Howard," *New Crusader,* January 20, 1962, 17; "State Setback by Ace Witness," *New Crusader;* Louis Robinson, "West Coast Scene," *Jet* 21 (March 1, 1962), 47; and South interview, November 19, 2001.

76. South interview, November 19, 2001; Zollar interview, April 17, 2001; and Magidson interview, May 7, 2002.

77. Magidson interview, May 7, 2002.

78. B. J. Johnson interview, February 16, 2002; James C. Worthy, *Brushes with History: Recollections of a Many-Favored Life* (n.p.: James C. Worthy, 1998), 222–25, 255–56; and "Seek New Date for Howard's Other Trial," *Chicago Daily Defender,* March 8, 1961, 10.

79. B. J. Johnson interview, February 16, 2002; Republican Citizens League of Illinois, Governing Board, August 31, 1961 and Republican Citizens League of Illinois, Minutes of the Board of Governors, June 26, 1962 Folder 307, Box 45, Carey Papers; and Worthy, *Brushes with History,* 224, 231–233, 236–37.

80. Eighth Annual Program: Regional Council of Negro Leadership, April 24, 1959, Folder 2, Box 7, Moore Papers; Aaron Henry to Friend of Freedom, July 12, 1962, Folder 1, Box 6, Moore Papers; and Hunter Gray [formerly John Salter] to David T. Beito, personal communication, September 22, 2001.

81. Dittmer, *Local People,* 102–19; James L. Bevel, interview by authors, November 21, 2001; Vera Pigee, interview by authors, December 18, 2001; and Colia Clark, interview by authors, November 21, 2001. A letter to RCNL board members shows that the group was still in existence in May 1962 (E. P. Burton and Aaron E. Henry to Board Member, May 9, 1962, Folder 2, Box 7, Moore Papers).

82. M. Evers, *For Us, the Living,* 316; Clark interview, November 21, 2001; James E. Jackson, *At the Funeral of Medgar Evers in Jackson, Mississippi: A Tribute in Tears and a Thrust for Freedom* (New York: Publisher's New Press, 1963), n.p.; and T. R. M. Howard, eulogy for Medgar Evers, June 15, 1963, "Where Do We Go from Here?" PRA BB4817ab, Pacifica Radio Archives, North Hollywood, California.

83. Howard, eulogy for Medgar Evers; and Relman Morin, "27 Arrested Before Riot Is Stopped," *Shreveport Times,* June 16, 1963, Folder 19, Box 20, Medgar Evers Papers.

84. *United States of America vs. Theodore R. M. Howard,* Indictment, United States District Court, Northern District of Illinois, Eastern Division, May 14, 1964, National Archives, Great Lakes Region, Record Group 21; "Dr. T. R. M. Howard Hit with Tax Indictments," *Chicago Daily Defender,* May 18, 1964, 13; and "Indict Doctor As Tax Evader," *Chicago Tribune,* May 15, 1964.

85. "Dr. T. R. M. Howard Denies Pair's Abortion Charge," *Chicago Daily Defender,* July 16, 1964, 4.

Chapter 9: Triumph and Tragedy: The Friendship Medical Center

1. Moore interview, April 4, 2001; and Robert E. Johnson, "Legal Abortion: Is It genocide or Blessing in Disguise?" *Jet* 43 (March 22, 1973), 18.

2. Leslie J. Reagan, *When Abortion Was a Crime: Women, Medicine, and Law in the United States, 1867–1973* (Berkeley: University of California Press, 1997), 149–64, 171–72.

3. South interview, November 19, 2001; Felice Sangirardi, telephone interview, May 30, 2001; Renault A. Robinson, interview by authors, May 15, 2003; "T. R. M. Howard Says Woman Abortion Charge Is Lie, Smear," *New Crusader,* October 2, 1965, 1–2; Laura Kaplan, *The Story of Jane: The Legendary Underground Feminist Abortion Service* (New York: Pantheon Books, 1995), 11–12; and E. Spencer Parsons, interview by Pat Relf Hanavan, July 31, 2003, copy in the possession of the authors.

4. Ed Keemer, *Confessions of a Pro-Life Abortionist* (Detroit: Vinco Press, 1980), 73–74, 136–37, 153; and David J. Garrow, *Liberty and Sexuality: The Right to Privacy and the Making of Roe v. Wade* (New York: Macmillan, 1994), 361–62.

5. "Delay Hearing for Doctor in Abortion Case," *Chicago Tribune,* July 15, 1964, folder on T. R. M. Howard, Box 14, 155139, Health Care Fraud Collection, American Medical Association Archives; and "Dr. T. R. M. Howard Denies Pair's Abortion Charge," *Chicago Daily Defender,* July 16, 1964, 4.

6. Robert McDonnell, interview by authors, April 2, 2002; Magidson interview, May 7, 2002; Elmer Gertz, *Moment of Madness: The People vs. Jack Ruby* (Chicago: Follett, 1968), 4, 146, 150–52; "Dr. T. R. M. Howard Denies Pair's Abortion Charge," *Chicago Daily Defender;* and "Accepts $500 for Abortion, Police Charge," *Chicago Tribune,* September 24, 1965, sec. 2, 19.

7. Magidson interview, May 7, 2002; Arnold Warda subpoena, December 18, 1964, *United States of America v. Theodore Roosevelt Mason Howard,* Min. Order, United States District Court, Northern District of Illinois, Eastern Division, National Archives, Great Lakes Region, Record Group 21; and "Dr. Howard Draws $10,000 Fine in Tax Evasion Case Here," *Chicago Daily Defender,* December 23, 1964, 3.

8. Rivlin, *Fire on the Prairie,* 51; Reed, *Chicago NAACP,* 199; and Bennett J. Johnson to members of Protest at the Polls, August 6, 1964, courtesy of Bennett J. Johnson.

9. "Fuss with Hoover Goes Way Back in Civil Rights History," *Jet* 27 (December 10, 1964), 6; Ethiopia Alfred-Bekele, interview by authors, September 19, 2001; English interview, November 6, 1999; "Prominent S. Side Medic Nailed for $73,000 U.S. Income Tax," *National Crusader,* October 3, 1964, 3; and "We Shall Overcome," *Woodlawn Booster* 31, October 7, 1964, 1, folder on T. R. M. Howard, DuSable Museum of African American History, Chicago.

10. "Minutes of the III Meeting for the Committee to form an 'Educational Fund for the Children of Malcolm (X) Shabazz,'" March 14, 1965, courtesy of Bennett J. Johnson; "Ossie Davis Leads Area Drive for Malcolm's Kids," *Chicago Defender,* April 3–9, 1965, 2; and "4 April 65 Memorial Service for Malcolm (X) Shabazz, The Educational Fund for Children of Malcolm X," Howard to Freedom Fighter, March 20, 1965, folder on the Organization of Afro-American Unity, Chicago Police Department, Human Relations Division, Chicago Historical Society Research Center.

11. B. Howard interview, March 27, 2000; Moore interview, April 4, 2001; and C. Evers interview, September 2, 1999.

12. "Accepts $500 for Abortion," *Chicago Tribune; Illinois v. T. R. M. Howard and Margaret Banks,* Grand Jury Indictment, October 1965, Case Number 65–2937, Criminal Division, Circuit Court of Cook County, Cook County Archives, Chicago; and Sangirardi interview, May 30, 2001.

13. R. Robinson interview, May 15, 2003; and Sangirardi interview, May 30, 2001.

14. *Illinois v. Howard and Banks,* Memorandum of Orders, Petition to Suppress Evidence, December 3, 1965; Sangirardi interview, May 30, 2001; and "Dr. T. R. M. Howard Says Woman Abortion Charge Is Lie, Smear," *National Crusader.*

15. Certified Appraisal, January 11, 1978, Estate of Theodore R. M. Howard, Probate Division, Circuit Court of Cook County, Cook County Archives, Chicago; B. Howard interview, March 27, 2000; and Arnold Bickham, telephone interview, June 4, 2003.

16. "Detroit Youth, 3 Others Killed in Car Accidents," *Detroit News,* July 1, 1966, 6; Ernest C. Harris, interview by authors, July 15, 2004; V. Harris [Wilson] interview, November 6, 2000; Moore interview, April 4, 2001; Barrett Howard, interview by authors, June 21, 2000; and Louis D. Boshes to defense counsel Charles A. Bellows, April 21, 1967, *Illinois v. Theodore R. M. Howard and Margaret Banks,* Grand Jury Indictment, October 1965, Case Number 65–2937, Criminal Division, Circuit Court of Cook County, Cook County Archives, Chicago.

17. Parker, *History of the Links,* 78; untitled article, *Chicago Daily Defender,* March 11, 1970, 19; Hooks, "Busy Month for a Busy Helen Howard," *Chicago Daily Defender;* "Medic Hosts Lavish Buffet for Cotillion Guests," *Chicago Defender,* July 17–23, 1965, 22; "Links' Cotillion Marked by Elegance, Philanthropy," *Chicago Defender,* July 22–28, 1967, 17; and "Thirty Debs Selected for Links' Eighth Annual Cotillion Ball," *New Crusader,* January 27, 1968, 14; Frances T. Matlock, interview by authors, June 26, 2000; Walls interview, September 30, 2001; and Futrell interview, May 3, 2001.

18. B. Howard interview, March 27, 2000; Edward F. Boyd interview, June 21, 2000; Futrell interview, May 3, 2001; Moore interview, April 4, 2001; and Zollar interview, April 17, 2001.

19. Zollar interview, April 17, 2001; Morgan interview, March 31, 2000; Morgan, personal communication, July 24, 2004; and E. Harris interview, July 15, 2004.

20. B. Howard interview, March 27, 2000; Futrell interview, May 3, 2001; and Alfred Bekele interview, September 19, 2001.

21. *Illinois v. Howard and Banks,* Memorandum of Orders, November 4, 1965–April 22, 1968; and R. Robinson interview, May 15, 2003.

22. B. Howard interview, March 27, 2000; English interview, November 6, 1999; R. Robinson interview, May 15, 2003; E. Spencer Parsons, interview by Pat Relf Hanavan, July 31, 2003, copy in possession of the authors; and Bickham interview, June 4, 2003.

23. Booth interview, June 7, 2000; and Reagan, *When Abortion Was a Crime,* 224, 231, 240. Kaplan clearly identifies but does not name Howard as "a black doctor on Sixty-Third Street in Woodlawn" (Kaplan, *Story of Jane,* 7–11, 39).

24. Booth interview, June 7, 2000; Reagan, *When Abortion Was a Crime,* 224–25; and Kaplan, *Story of Jane,* 7, 9–11, 39.

25. E. Spencer Parsons, interview by authors, May 7, 2000; and Reagan, *When Abortion Was a Crime,* 241.

26. Parsons interview by authors, May 7, 2000; Parsons interview by Pat Relf Hanavan, July 31, 2003; and Kaplan, *Story of Jane,* 62–63.

27. *Illinois v. Howard and Banks,* Memorandum of Orders, April 22, 1968; and Sangirardi interview, May 30, 2001.

28. Theresa Fambro Hooks, "Dr. T. R. M. Howard and Son, Barry, Home from 9–Week African Safari," *Chicago Defender,* September 7–13, 1968, 17; "Dr. Howard's Safari Room," *Ebony* 24 (October 1969), 138, 133; Matlock interview, June 26, 2000; *Jet* 34 (October 3, 1968), 38; and Morgan interview, March 31, 2000.

29. Hooks, "Dr. T. R. M. Howard and Son" *Chicago Defender;* and Hooks, "Two-Day Gala Will Open the Howards' 'Safari Room,'" *Chicago Defender,* April 19–25, 1969, 19.

30. Theresa Fambro Hooks, "'Dream Come True' Weekend for Dr. and Mrs. Howard," *Chicago Defender,* May 3–19, 1969, 19; Lewis Drake, interview by authors, August 23, 2000; Doris E. Saunders, "Two-Day Fete Opens Howards' Safari Manor," *Chicago Daily Defender,* May 6, 1969, 17; and "Dr. Howard's Safari Room," *Ebony* 24 (October 1969), 132–38.

31. "Dr. Howard's Safari Room," *Ebony* 24 (October 1969), 132–33, 138; "Philander Smith Alumni Will Gather at Maywood Park," *Chicago Defender,* November 20, 1971, 22; and Till-Mobley interview, September 28, 1999.

32. "Dr. Howard's Safari Room," *Ebony* 24 (October 1969), 133, 138.

33. B. Howard interview, March 27, 2000; Theresa Fambro Hooks, "The T. R. M. Howards Ring In New Year at Gala Holiday Fete," *Chicago Defender,* January 11–17, 1969, 17; Hooks, "Howards' New Year's Eve Party Tops Glittering Social Season," *Chicago Defender,* January 17–23, 1970, 17; Marion P. Campfield, "Gaiety, Glamor . . . Dazzle, Dash . . . Mean, Happy Times," *Chicago Defender,* January 8–14, 1972, 12; Anne Tyson, "The Social Whirl," *South Side Bulletin,* January 15, 1969, 2; "Dr. Howard's Safari Room," *Ebony* 24 (October 1969), 132; Walls interview, September 30, 2001; and Matlock interview, June 26, 2000.

34. Bickham interview, June 4, 2003; and Alfred-Bekele interview, September 19, 2001.

35. Rivlin, *Fire on the Prairie,* 49–50; Travis, *Autobiography of Black Politics,* 443–44; Robert McClory, *The Man Who Beat Clout City* (Chicago: Swallow Press, 1977), 12–19, 70–71, 122–23, 209–11; and R. Robinson interview, May 15, 2003.

36. Travis, *Autobiography of Black Politics,* 441–43; Rivlin, *Fire on the Prairie,* 19; and R. Robinson interview, May 15, 2003.

37. Ralph, *Northern Protest,* 66–67; and Marshall Frady, *Jesse: The Life and Pilgrimage of Jesse Jackson* (New York: Random House, 1996) 189–90, 198–200, 217. The authors made repeated efforts over more than a three-year period to arrange an interview with Jesse Jackson. Despite several promises from members of his staff to schedule one, they never did.

38. Ralph, *Northern Protest,* 67–68; Reynolds, *Jesse Jackson,* 56–57; and Kenneth R. Timmerman, *Shakedown: Exposing the Real Jesse Jackson* (Washington, D.C.: Regnery, 2002), 27–30.

39. B. Howard interview, March 27, 2000; E. Boyd interview, July 19, 1999; Zollar interview, April 17, 2001; and Noah Robinson Jr., interview by authors, August 22, 2002.

40. Gary Massoni, "Perspectives on Operation Breadbasket" (MDiv thesis, Chicago Theological Seminary, 1971), 45; "Breadbasket Gets Commerce Director Here," *Chicago Daily Defender,* January 8, 1970, 3; and N. Robinson interview, August 22, 2002.

41. N. Robinson interview, August 22, 2002.

42. N. Robinson interview, August 22, 2002.

43. N. Robinson interview, August 22, 2002; Timmerman, *Shakedown,* 41; Rivlin, *Fire on the Prairie,* 89; Angela Parker, "SCLC Asks Jackson for Full Accounting," *Chicago Tribune,* December 16, 1971, 3; and Zollar interview, April 17, 2001.

44. "Charlie Cherokee Says," *Chicago Daily Defender,* May 11, 1971, 5; Operation PUSH, "Convening Board of Directors," January 1972, Folder B-229, Box 80-102, Chicago Urban League Papers, Special Collections, University of Illinois at Chicago; N. Robinson, telephone interview, August 22, 2002; and Zollar interview, April 17, 2001.

45. E. Boyd interview, October 14, 2001; and Zollar interview, April 17, 2001.

46. Reagan, *When Abortion Was a Crime,* 232–39; and "Abortion Meet Set for U. of I.," *Chicago Daily Defender,* October 12, 1970, 2.

47. Parsons, interview by authors, May 7, 2000.

48. "Abortion Measure Is Killed," *Chicago Tribune,* March 17, 1971; Kaplan, *Story of Jane,* 205–6; Parsons; and Reagan, *When Abortion Was a Crime,* 242–43.

49. Parsons; and Moore interview, April 4, 2001.

50. Moore interview, April 4, 2001; and T. R. M. Howard to Eric Oldberg, November 6, 1974, Folder 10, Box 7, National Abortion Rights Action League of Illinois Papers.

51. "Friendship Medical Opens June," *South Side Bulletin,* June 8, 1972, 3; R. Robinson interview, May 15, 2003; Reagan, *When Abortion Was a* Crime, 242–43; Parsons, interview by Pat Relf Hanavan, July 31, 2003, copy in possession of the authors; E. Boyd interview, October 14, 2000; Moore interview, April 4, 2001; and Zollar interview, April 17, 2001.

52. Frances Matlock, "Medical Facility Opens June 11," *Chicago Daily Defender,* May 25, 1972, 12; Faith C. Christmas, "Medical Center Opening Set," *Chicago Daily Defender,* June 8, 1972, 10; and "Chicago Doctor $1. 5 Million Medical Center," *Jet* (June 22, 1972), 9.

53. Dan Egler, "Ex-Supermarket Mushrooms into Major Medical Center," *Chicago Tribune,* June 11, 1972; sec. 10, 3; English interview, November 6, 1999; Christmas, "Medical Center Opening," *Chicago Daily Defender;* and "Dr. T. R. M. Howard's Friendship Medical Center Marks Grand Opening," *Chicago Daily Defender,* June 13, 1972, 14–15.; Hurley Jones, "Dr. T. R. M. Howard Life Giver," *Chicago Independent Bulletin,* December 20, 1973, 4; Lois Willie, "City Lacks the Authority to Inspect Abortion Clinics," *Chicago Daily News,* March 3–4, 1973, 4, Folder 3, Box 5, Clergy Consultation Service Papers, Special Collections, Richard J. Daley Library, University of Illinois at Chicago [hereafter, Clergy Consultation Papers]; Quality of Friendship Built into New Million Dollar Medical Center, Facility Mirrors Dr. Howard's Philosophy, courtesy of Sandra Morgan; and Moore interview, April 4, 2001.

54. Jones, "Dr. T. R. M. Howard Life Giver," *Chicago Independent Bulletin;* Limited Partnership Agreement of T. R. M. Building Company, August 1, 1974, Estate of Theodore R. M. Howard, Probate Division, Circuit Court of Cook County, Cook County Archives, Chicago; and Moore interview, April 4, 2001.

55. *Jet* 43 (January 25, 1973), 25.

56. Terry L. Anderson and Donald R. Leal, *Free Market Environmentalism* (San Francisco: Westview, 1991), 66–67; and Naftali Mungai, "Overrun with Elephants, Zimbabwe Demands Legal Ivory Sales," Environment News Service, January 17, 2001, (http://forests.org/archive/africa/ovelezim.htm, accessed September 1, 2007).

57. Ronald Kotulak and James Elsener, "1st Abortions Here within Hours of OK," *Chicago Tribune,* March 2, 1973, 1, 5; Ronald Kotulak and Marcia Opp, "Lunch Hour Abortions Expected," *Chicago Tribune,* March 3, 1973, 1, 8; Johnson, "Legal Abortion," *Jet* (March 22, 1973), 12; Parsons interview, May 7, 2000; undated article from unidentified newspaper, folder on Howard, Human Relations Section, Chicago Police Department; and Willie, "City Lacks the Authority," *Chicago Daily News,* March 3–4, 1973, Folder 3, Box 5, Clergy Consultation Papers.

58. E. Boyd interview, October 14, 2001; Nancy Day, "City Aide Says Woman's Death Shows Need for Abortion Rules," *Chicago Daily News,* April 30, 1973, Folder 3, Box 5, Clergy Consultation Papers; and *Jet* 43 (March 22, 1973), cover.

59. Johnson, "Legal Abortion," *Jet* 43 (March 22, 1973), 18, 38; *Chicago Daily Defender,* February 28, 1973; Kotulack and Opp, "Lunch Hour Abortions Expected," *Chicago Tribune;* and Flora Johnson, "Buying Protection at the Abortion Mill," *Chicago* (January 1975), 16. Joseph M. Scheidler, an anti-abortion activist, did not have a high opinion of Howard's debating ability. He asserts that Howard "had made his decision to do abortions and now he was going to make the arguments fit his decision" (Joseph M. Scheidler, interview by authors, July 9, 2002).

60. E. Boyd interview, October 14, 2001; Johnson, "Buying Protection," *Chicago* (January 1975), 15; Jean Pierre Guilmant, "Friendship Fetes Third Anniversary," *New Crusader,* June 21, 1975, 1–2; Sheila Wolfe, "Abortions Only Part of Service at Friendship Clinic," *Chicago Tribune,* June 10, 1973, 52; Pam Zekman and Paul Galloway, "Doctor's Legacy: $500,000 I.O.U.," *Chicago Sun-Times,* January 22, 1977, 56, 58; and "Doctor Finds Abortion Rise among Younger Blacks," *Jet* 47 (December 12, 1974), 48.

61. "Friendship Medical Center, Providing Comprehensive Medical and Dental Care for Your Entire Family, Opening June 11, 1972," courtesy of Sandra Morgan; E. Boyd interview, October 14, 2001; Louis Boshes, interview by authors, July 27, 2002; Zollar interview, April 17, 2001; and Moore interview, April 4, 2001.

62. Simeon B. Osby, "Sen. Chew Asks Liberal Abortion, Divorce Laws," *Chicago Daily Defender,* April 19, 1971, 4; "The Black Family," *Chicago Daily Defender,* March 8, 1973, 17; Shirley Chisholm, *Unbought and Unbossed* (Boston: Houghton Mifflin, 1970), 114; Loretta J. Ross, "African-American Women and Abortion," in Rickie Solinger, ed., *Abortion Wars: A Half Century of Struggle, 1950–2000* (Berkeley: University of California Press, 1998), 180; "More Black Women Are Getting Abortions," *Jet* 42 (June 29, 1972), 15; and Samuel 17X, "(Friendship) Center in Chicago," *Muhammad Speaks* 12 (March 23, 1973), 3, Geraldine 10X, "Abortion: 'Friendship' for Whom?," *Muhammad Speaks* 12 (March 30, 1973), 11, "Abortion: Killing Black Babies," *Muhammad Speaks* 12 (April 20, 1973), 52.

63. Robert McClory, "Rev. Jesse Jackson . . . Opens Abortion War," *Chicago Daily Defender,* March 21, 1973, 3, 12.

64. "The Hot Skillet," *Chicago Metro News,* March 31, 1973, 4; "The Hot Skillet," *Chicago Metro News,* May 26, 1973, 8; Alfred-Bekele interview, September 19, 2001; and R. Robinson interview, May 15, 2003.

65. English interview, November 6, 1999; Zollar interview, April 17, 2001; B. Howard interview, March 27, 2000; and *Right to Life News* (January 1977), (http://www-swiss.ai.mit .edu/~rauch/nvp/consistent/jackson.html, accessed September 2, 2007). Alfred-Bekele states that Jackson needed money from Dr. Howard because "he was fooling around with some woman and he spent thousands of dollars, maybe sixty to eighty thousand dollars, on that woman" (Alfred-Bekele interview, September 19, 2001).

66. Diane Monk, "Woman Dies after Illegal Abortion," *Chicago Daily News,* March 22, 1973; "'Inadequate' Number of Abortion Facilities Criticized," *Chicago Sun-Times,* March 23, 1973, 30; Michael Miner, "Two More Reports of Hysterectomies after Abortions at the Friendship Center," *Chicago Sun-Times,* March 24, 1973, 32; and Ellen Warren, "Abortion Death Spurs Call for State Control," *Chicago Daily News,* April 30, 1973—all in Folder 3, Box 5, Clergy Consultation Papers; and Clara Hemphill, "Local Abortion Clinics Face Problems with Cost, Facilities, and Safety," *Chicago Maroon* 81 (May 8, 1973), 1, Folder 1, Box 5, Clergy Consultation Papers; and Morgan interview, March 31, 2000.

67. "Have Abortions in Hospital, Women Urged," *Chicago Tribune,* March 21, 1973, sec. 1C, 1; and Johnson, "Legal Abortion," *Jet* 43 (March 22, 1973), 12–13.

68. Jane, "The Most Remarkable Abortion Story Ever Told," *Voices* (June 1973, http:// www.cwluherstory.com/CWLUFeature/Remarkable1.html, accessed August 30, 2007); and Charles B. Armstrong, "State Harasses Black Clinic," *Chicago Metro News,* June 30, 1973. Howard had this response to critics who stressed his profit motivations, including Eric Oldberg, who headed the Chicago Board of Health: "Sure, this is a money-making business. I haven't been a beggar. But Dr. Oldberg was a brain surgeon. You think he didn't make money?" Johnson, "Buying Protection," *Chicago,* 14.

69. Brenda Stone, "Birth-Control Agency Blasts Abortion Rule," *Chicago Tribune,* May 18, 1973, 3; Johnson, "Buying Protection," *Chicago,* 14, 16; *Friendship Medical Center, Ltd. v. Chicago Board of Health,* November 16, 1973, 367 F. Supp. 597; Howard to Oldberg, November 6, 1974; and Garrow, *Liberty and Sexuality,* 626–29.

70. *Friendship Medical Center, Ltd. v. Chicago Board of Health,* October 30, 1974, 505 F. 2nd 1141; Johnson, "Buying Protection," *Chicago,* 14; and "Abortions Clinics Form Standards Council," *Chicago Tribune,* February 20, 1975, sec. A, 3.

71. Zollar interview, April 17, 2001; Complaint for Divorce, October 5, 1973, *Helen B. Howard v. T. R. M. Howard,* Divorce Division, Circuit Court of Cook County, Cook County Archives; and E. Boyd interview, October 14, 2001.

72. Report of Proceedings, January 23, 1974, Petition, October 15, 1974, *Howard v. Howard;* Lucius Earles, interview by authors, May 12, 2001; Alfred-Bekele interview, September 19, 2001; Moore interview, April 4, 2001; Arnold Bickham, interview by authors, June 4, 2003; and Matlock interview, June 26, 2000.

73. Joseph Langmeyer, "Bertrand in Mayoralty?" *Chicago Daily Defender,* July 10, 1974, 3; "Newhouse Name Polls Widest Recognition," *Chicago Daily Defender,* September 23, 1974, 2; Travis, *Autobiography of Black Politics,* 414; B. J. Johnson interview, February 16, 2002; Travis,

Harold, 88; "Statement of the Committee for a Black Mayor," *Chicago Metro News,* October 5, 1974, 4; and Charles B. Armstrong, "Mayor's Committee: A 'Farce,' As We Said," *Chicago Metro News,* November 30, 1974, 1.

74. "Committee for Black Mayor," *Chicago Daily Defender,* August 28, 1974, 13; *Chicago Metro News,* September 7, 1974, 14; and Grimshaw, *Bitter Fruit,* 136–37.

75. Al Johnson, "The Johnson View," *New Crusader,* July 27, 1974, 10; Charles B. Armstrong Sr., "Newhouse, McNeil, Lead Mayor's Poll," *Chicago Metro News,* September 7, 1974, 1; and "Mayor Group Called 'Toms,'" *Chicago Daily Defender,* November 12, 1974, 3.

76. Travis, *Autobiography of Black Politics,* 500–503; Robert McClory, "Metcalfe to Keep Fighting," *Chicago Daily Defender,* December 4, 1974, 2; "Blacks Pick Candidates," *Chicago Daily Defender,* February 13, 1975, 2; "The Hot Skillet," *Chicago Metro News,* November 11, 1974, 4; "Endorsements from Black Mayors Committee," *Chicago Metro News,* February 22, 1975, 9; and Al Johnson, "The Johnson View," *New Crusader,* November, 16, 1974, 12.

77. "Committee Endorses Congressman Metcalfe for Mayor," *Chicago Metro News,* November 16, 1974, 3; and Travis, *Harold,* 101–3.

78. Jacob P. Mtabaji, personal communication, February 14, 2002; "Deaths," *Journal of the National Medical Association* 68 (November 1976), 544; Bickham interview, June 4, 2003; untitled article by Lewis A. H. Caldwell, *New Crusader,* April 12, 1975, 10; and "Challenged by Dr. Howard: Ban Harsh Abortion Rules," *Chicago Daily Defender,* March 25, 1975, 4.

79. English interview, November 6, 1999; and Morgan interview, March 31, 2000.

80. Morgan interview, March 31, 2000; English, telephone interview, November 6, 1999; Proposal to Continental Bank for the Purchase of Friendship Medical Center in Chicago, Illinois, Prepared by Edward F. Boyd, Samuel E. Morck, and Lawrence Klainer, February 16, 1977, Estate of T. R. M. Howard; and Zekman and Galloway, "Doctor's Legacy," *Chicago Sun-Times.*

81. English interview, November 6, 1999; Morgan interview, March 31, 2000; Bickham interview, June 4, 2003; Earles interview, May 12, 2001; and Zekman and Galloway, "Doctor's Legacy," *Chicago Sun-Times.*

82. English interview, November 6, 1999; Zekman and Galloway, "Doctor's Legacy," *Chicago Sun-Times;* and Moore interview, April 4, 2001.

83. Bickham interview, June 4, 2003; English interview, November 6, 1999; and Moore interview, April 4, 2001.

84. English interview, November 6, 1999.

85. "T. R. M. Howard Recuperating," *Chicago Daily Defender,* September 8, 1975, 3; Moore interview, April 4, 2001; V. Harris [Wilson] interview, November 6, 2000; E. Boyd interview, October 14, 2001; Reconciliation Stipulation, December 2, 1975, *Howard v. Howard;* and Zollar interview, April 17, 2001.

86. E. Boyd interview, September 20, 2003; Morgan interview, March 31, 2000; Moore interview, April 4, 2001; and Alfred-Bekele interview, September 19, 2001.

87. Doris Saunders, "Confetti," *Chicago Daily Defender,* January 11, 1968, 16; 1969 Dues, January 20, 1969, T. R. M. Howard, Alumni Files, Loma Linda University; Crowes inter-

view, April 25, 2000; Earl Calloway, interview by authors, October 9, 1999; Dudley, "Moments in Black History," 19; and Numbers and Larson, "Adventist Tradition," 462–64.

88. English interview, November 6, 1999; Promissory note to the South Side Bank, January 30, 1976, Petition in the Matter of the Estate of T. R. M. Howard, August 1976, Loan from the Continental Bank of Illinois, February 13, 1976, Agreement between the Illinois Department of Public Aid and the Friendship Medical Center, February 27, 1976, Estate of T. R. M. Howard; Zollar interview, April 17, 2001; and R. Robinson interview, May 15, 2003.

89. Proposal to Continental Bank; Hooks, "Teesee's Town," *Chicago Defender,* February 14, 1976, 12; Hooks, "Teesee's Town," *Chicago Defender,* February 28, 1976, 10; "Celebrating 40 Good News," *Chicago Defender,* March 27, 1976, 12; and Mrs. William S. White (George) (Guest Columnist), "Teesee's Town," *Chicago Defender,* April 10, 1976, 10; and B. Howard interview, March 27, 2000.

90. V. Harris [Wilson] interview, November 6, 2000; English interview, November 6, 1999; and Morgan interview, March 31, 2000.

91. English interview, November 6, 1999; "Dr. T. R. M. Howard, Noted Physician, Dies at 68," *Chicago Daily Defender,* May 3, 1976, 3; Charles Harris, "Pay Last Respects to Dr. Howard," *Chicago Metro News,* May 8, 1976, 1; and Loan from South Side Bank, April 30, 1976, Estate of T. R. M. Howard.

92. "Dr. T. R. M. Howard, Noted Physician," *Chicago Daily Defender;* untitled article by Lewis A. H. Caldwell, *New Crusader;* and Harris, "Pay Last Respects," *Chicago Metro News.*

93. "Dr. T. R. M. Howard, Noted Physician, Dies at 68," *Jet* 50 (May 5, 1976), 14; "Mound Bayou Monument to Howard's Constructive Leadership," *Eagle Eye,* May 21, 1976, 1, courtesy of Sandra Morgan; and R. Robinson interview, May 15, 2003.

94. Dudley, "Moments in Black History," 19; Calloway interview, October 9, 1999; "Last Rites for Dr. Howard," *Chicago Daily Defender,* May 8, 1976, 1; and Alfred-Bekele interview, September 19, 2001.

95. "Dr. Howard Best Judged by His Legacy to Mankind," *New Crusader,* May 8, 1976, 1; V. Harris [Wilson] interview, November 6, 2000; "Obsequies for Theodore Roosevelt Howard, 1908–1976, Thursday, May 6, 1976, Liberty Baptist Church," courtesy of Sandra Morgan; "Celebration of Praise and Thanking for Jasper Fleming Williams, Sr., M.D.," April 20, 1985, Leonidas Berry Papers; and Scheidler interview, July 9, 2002.

96. Timothy Boyd, interview by authors, February 3, 2002; Petition for Executor's and Attorneys' Fees for Extraordinary Services Rendered, November 17, 1980, 10, Estate of T. R. M. Howard; Earles interview, May 12, 2001; Robert McClory, "Friendship Slashes Staff," *Chicago Daily Defender,* June 5, 1976, 1; English interview, November 6, 1999; and Zollar interview, April 17, 2001.

97. Moore interview, April 4, 2001; Morgan interview, March 31, 2000; E. Marie Johnson, interview by authors, August 30, 2000; Futrell interview, May 3, 2001; Zollar interview, April 17, 2001; Bickham interview, June 4, 2003; and Matlock interview, June 26, 2000.

98. Zollar interview, April 17, 2001.

99. Moore interview, April 4, 2001.

Afterword

1. "Dr. Howard's Safari Room," *Ebony* 24, no. 12 (October 1969), 133.

2. Cynthia R. Greenlee, "T.R.M. Howard: Civil Rights Rabble-Rouser, Abortion Provider," *Dissent Magazine*, May 16, 2013, https://www.dissentmagazine.org/blog/t-r-m-howard-civil-rights-rabble-rouser-abortion-provider, accessed September 6, 2017.

3. Studnicki, James, Sharon J. MacKinnon and John W. Fisher, "Induced Abortion, Mortality, and the Conduct of Science," *Open Journal of Preventive Medicine* 6 (2016): 170-177. http://file.scirp.org/pdf/OJPM_2016061708580294.pdfx; Willis L. Krumholz. "Yes, Planned Parenthood Targets and Hurts Poor Black Women," *The Federalist* (February 18, 2016), http://thefederalist.com/2016/02/18/yes-planned-parenthood-targets-and-hurts-poor-black-women/; and Barbara Hollingsworth, "Alveda King on Disproportionate Abortion of Black Babies: 'That's Certainly Black Genocide," CNSNews.com (December 5, 2016). https://www.cnsnews.com/news/article.

Acknowledgments

AT THE END of this exciting and often enriching journey of discovery, we appreciate the individuals who held the lantern at every turn. Over nearly a decade, we have strived to uncover and understand the varied life of a remarkable man. We learned from an early stage that the lives of few individuals provide a better illustration of the full panorama of black history during the twentieth century than T. R. M. Howard. We apologize in advance for omitting the name of any of those who helped us along the way.

We want to especially thank the Independent Institute for sponsoring the book, including President David Theroux, Acquisitions Director Roy M. Carlisle, and former Production Editor Cecilia Santini.

For help in funding this research, we are especially grateful to the Earhart Foundation that allowed us to begin the process of digging into Howard's background. The archivists at Charles W. Capps Center at Delta State University and the Eva B. Dykes Library at Oakwood College both took on the Herculean task of transcribing our taped interviews of individuals who knew Howard. No person was more enthusiastic about getting this book finished, with the possible exception of the authors, than Michael Flug, the archivist of the Vivian G. Harsh Collection at the Chicago Public Library.

Ellen and Forrest McDonald played key roles in editing the book down to a manageable length. Others who commented on drafts, gave research leads, and made other valuable suggestions included Daniel Akst, Michael Allen, Kristen C. Ankeny, Nigel Ashford, Bruce Bartlett, William Beach, Jonathan Bean, Ethiopia Bekele, Michael Les Benedict, Christopher D. Benson, David E. Bernstein, Alan Blum, David Boaz, Charles Bolton, Julian Bond, Heather

Booth, Don Boudreaux, Taylor Branch, Alan Brinkley, Luther Brown, Stephanie Capparell, Norma Chase, Colia Clark, Stephen Cox, Donald Critchlow, Bill Cunningham, Constance Curry, Dennis C. Dickerson, John Dittmer, Minneola Dixon, Charles E. Dudley Sr., Charles Evers, Paul Feine, Annazette Fields, Thomas Fleming, Chloe Foutz, Kari Frederickson, Tony Freyer, David J. Garrow, Irv Gellman, Hunter Gray, Adam Green, Chris Greenberg, Ingrid A. Gregg, Anthony Gregory, Dick Gregory, Keith Halderman, Ernest C. Harris, Paul Hendrickson, Matthew Holden Jr., David Holmberg, Benjamin Hooks, Davis Houck, Bennett Johnson, Hermon Johnson, Howard Jones, Carla Kaplan, Gregory P. Kane, David B. Kennedy, Peter Kirsanow, Hank Klibanoff, Elisabeth Lasch-Quinn, Ralph E. Luker, Manning Marable, Bill Maxwell, Colm McAindriu, Reid McKee, Christopher Metress, Jerry Mitchell, K.C. Morrison, Louise Newman, Don Noble, Robert J. Norrell, Charles W. Nuckolls, Ronald Numbers, Todd J. Olson, Clarence Page, Tom G. Palmer, Charles M. Payne, Alan Petigny, Adam Clayton Powell III, Robert D. Putnam, Jim Ralph, Noah Robinson Jr., Plater Robinson, Joseph M. Scheidler, Jane Shaw, Chuck Shuffett, Theda Skocpol, Mark Smith, Bob Sutherland, Jerry Thornbery, Timothy Tyson, Maarten Ultee, Bill Utterback, Nicholas Von Hoffman, Jesse Walker, Juan Williams, Robert Woodson, and the faculty and administration of Stillman College.

Index

About the Authors

DAVID T. BEITO is a Research Fellow at the Independent Institute and Professor of History at the University of Alabama. He received his Ph.D. in history at the University of Wisconsin, and he is the recipient of the Ellis Hawley Prize. Professor Beito is the author of *Taxpayers in Revolt: Tax Resistance during the Great Depression* and *From Mutual Aid to the Welfare State: Fraternal Societies and Social Services, 1890-1967*, and he is editor of the Independent Institute book, *The Voluntary City: Choice Community and Civil Society* (with Peter Gordon and Alexander Tabarrok).

Former President of the Alabama Scholars Association and Chair of the Alabama State Advisory Committee of the United States Commission on Civil Rights, Professor Beito is the Founder of the "Liberty and Power" blog at the History News Network.

An urban and social historian, he has published in the *Journal of Southern History*, *Journal of Policy History*, *Journal of Interdisciplinary History*, *Journal of Urban History*, *The Independent Review*, *Nevada Historical Society Quarterly*, *Journal of Firearms and Public Policy*, and other scholarly journals. And, his popular articles have appeared in the *Wall Street Journal*, *Los Angeles Times*, *Washington Times*, *Atlanta-Journal Constitution*, *Perspectives*, History News Network, *National Review*, *Reason* and elsewhere.

LINDA ROYSTER BEITO is a Research Fellow at the Independent Institute and Professor and Dean of Arts and Science at Stillman College. She received her M.S. in criminal justice and Ph.D. in political science from the University of Alabama, and she has been Assistant Professor of Political Science and Criminal Justice at the University of South Alabama.

Professor Beito is the author of the book, *Leadership Effectiveness in Community Policing*, and her scholarly articles have appeared in *Social Science History*, *Journal of Firearms and Public Policy*, *The Independent Review*, *Nevada Historical Society Quarterly*, History News Network, and *International Journal of Comparative and Applied Criminal Justice*.

Independent Institute Studies in Political Economy

Independent Institute Studies in Political Economy

INDEPENDENT
I N S T I T U T E

100 SWAN WAY, OAKLAND, CA 94621-1428

For further information:
510-632-1366 • orders@independent.org • http://www.independent.org/publications/books/